OTHER BOOKS BY TRAILER LIFE

The RV Handbook
Bill Estes

This new encyclopedia of information on the mechanical aspects of using a recreational vehicle contains chapters on improving engine performance, how to make an engine last longer, troubleshooting gasoline and diesel engines, RV handling, safety and weight ratings, how to choose a tow vehicle, understanding propane, electrical systems, and living without hookups.
7⅜ × 9¼, 352 pages
$29.95 ISBN: 0-934798-28-1

Trailer Life's RV Repair & Maintenance Manual
Edited by Bob Livingston

All-new, updated edition presents recreational vehicle owners with all the practical knowledge needed for diagnosing problems, making repairs, and communicating with mechanics. Detailed troubleshooting guides for all RV systems, hundreds of comprehensive illustrations and photographs, step-by-step instructions for repairing, replacing, and maintaining systems.
8½ × 11, 336 pages
$29.95 ISBN 0-934798-12-5

RVing America's Backroads: California (Longsdorf)
RVing America's Backroads: Florida (Gleasners)

Information-packed, four-color travel guidebooks designed *specifically* for recreational vehicle owners! Each book takes you on spectacular backroads tours, lavishly illustrated with gorgeous color photography by award-winning photojournalists. Clear, accurate maps of suggested backroads tours show easy access from the major interstates.
8½ × 11, 128 pages
$15.95 each

The Good Sam RV Cookbook
Edited by Beverly Edwards and the editors of *Trailer Life*

Over 250 easy and delicious recipes, including 78 prize-winning recipes from the Good Sam Samboree cook-offs held around the country. Contains tips, ideas, and suggestions to help you get the most from your RV galley.
7⅜ × 9¼, 252 pages
$14.95 ISBN: 0-93478-17-6

Continued overleaf

The RVer's Money Book
Bob Howells

Packed with practical, money-saving advice on how RVer's can save money, this book covers information on buying, selling, financing, and insuring your RV; budgeting your money; cutting expenses; earning income on the road, and more. Also includes hundreds of dollars worth of valuable coupons on RV accessories and services.
8½ × 11, 272 pages
$29.95 ISBN: 0-934798-32-X

These books are available at fine bookstores everywhere. Or, you may order directly from Trailer Life Books. For each book ordered, simply send us the name of the book, the price, plus $2 per book for shipping and handling (California residents please add 7¼% sales tax, Colorado 3.8%, and Indiana 5%).

Mail to:

Trailer Life Books, 64 Inverness Drive East, Englewood, CO 80112

You may call our customer-service representatives if you wish to charge your order or if you want more information. Phone, toll-free, Monday through Friday, 6:30 A.M. to 6:30 P.M.; Saturday, 7:30 A.M. to 1:30 P.M., Mountain Time, **1 (800) 234-3450**.

Full-time RVing

*A Complete Guide to
Life on the Open Road*

REVISED EDITION

▼

Bill and Jan Moeller

TRAILER LIFE BOOKS

To Bob and Mildred—
because of their love of books and their love of RVing

Trailer Life Book Division

President/CEO: Joe McAdams
Executive Vice President/Publisher, Book Division: Michael Schneider
Associate Publisher, Book Division: Joe Daquino
General Manager, Book Division: Rena Copperman
Bulk Sales/Distribution Manager, Book Division: Judy Klein

Editor/Production manager: Rena Copperman
Production coordinator: Robert S. Tinnon
Senior editor: Martha Weiler
Cover design: Mike Sincavage
Interior design: Robert S. Tinnon
Illustrations: Robert Lamarche
Indexer: Barbara Wurf
Cover separations: Western Laser Graphics
Background cover photo: ©David Noble 1988
Inset cover photos (top to bottom): Donna Carroll, Rich Johnson,
       Brian Robertson, Brian Robertson

ISBN: 0-934798-34-6

Library of Congress Cataloging-in-Publication Data

Moeller, Bill, 1930—
 Full-time RVing: a complete guide to life on the open road/Bill and
Jan Moeller.
  P. cm.
 Includes index.
 ISBN 0-934798-34-6: $29.95
 1. Mobile home living—United States. I. Moeller, Jan, 1930–
II. Title.
[TX1107.M64 1993]
796.7'9'0973–dc20
            93-3006
            CIP

Contents

▼ ▼ ▼ ▼ ▼ ▼ ▼ ▼ ▼

Preface

I n this new edition of *Full-time RVing: A Complete Guide to Life on the Open Road,* every chapter has been expanded, some considerably, and each contains the latest information that fulltimers, or potential fulltimers, need to know so the lifestyle will be as enjoyable and as trouble-free as possible.

During the years that have passed since we wrote this book, our own fulltiming, along with the recreational vehicle industry, has undergone changes. To provide readers with the latest information about the lifestyle, the RVs that are fulltimers' homes, and the accessories and equipment needed for pursuing the lifestyle called for not only a revision of the first edition, but the addition of much new material. This greatly expanded second edition will answer even more questions along with providing data on the very latest innovations that relate to fulltiming.

This revised edition, thirty-percent larger than the previous one, has more details on how to determine if fulltiming is for you, and if it is, how to handle receiving mail, paying bills, medical matters, and establishing legal residency while living a mobile lifestyle. The costs of fulltiming are covered along with ways fulltimers can earn money if they need to. Readers are advised about how to shop for a suitable RV and how to make it more livable. Lots of new storage tips have been added. In their RVs, fulltimers can have all the comforts and conveniences found in any home, so the chapters covering the electrical system, climate control, and entertainment systems, with much new updated material, explain how to go about this. Satellite television, cellular telephones, and computers are now covered. For those who want many of the conveniences when primitive camping, a new section on solar power and inverters is included.

There are chapters on campground selections, rig maintenance, driving and handling procedures, safety practices on the road or in campgrounds, fulltiming with children and pets, and a new chapter devoted to seniors who are fulltimers.

As we write this, we are still fulltimers, with a 29-foot fifth-wheel trailer as our only home, and we are just as satisfied with this delightful lifestyle now as we were in the early years of our fulltiming.

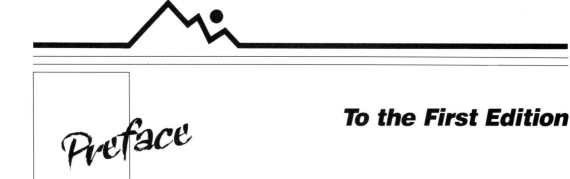

Preface

Fulltiming—having an RV for a home—is different than living in a fixed dwelling. As with any lifestyle it has its own idiosyncracies. However, with fulltiming the problems are few, the pleasures are many, and it is lots of fun. It is one of the few life-styles that offers the freedom to live where you want, when you want, and how you want.

We have been fulltimers for many years. In our travels we constantly meet people who want to become fulltimers but don't quite know how to go about changing their lifestyle, or what living in such a way will entail. We are always happy to answer questions, but in a brief or even lengthy conversation it is impossible to cover everything the potential fulltimer wants to know. This was the main reason for writing this book. We hope it will dispel doubts, answer questions, give you ideas, and be otherwise helpful. For those who want to fulltime we hope it will provide the incentive needed to get you started. Those who are already fulltimers also will find it contains a wealth of useful information for them.

In compiling this book we have drawn upon many of our own experiences, but because everyone's fulltiming is different, we have included the experiences of many others engaged in the lifestyle. Whether your fulltiming includes traveling all the time or just seasonally, whether you do it in a motorhome or trailer, whether you have an income or need to earn money as you go, you will find information that applies to your own individualistic way of fulltiming.

Acknowledgments

▼ ▼ ▼ ▼ ▼ ▼ ▼ ▼

To all the fulltimers and RVers who contributed to this revision we gratefully acknowledge your help. You gave us much valuable information and many useful ideas. Some of you knew we intended to use what you supplied in this book. Others had no inkling that that information would be used in a book. Indeed, when we received much of the information *we* had no idea that it would appear in a book.

Thanks to Mike Schneider for having faith in our abilities to translate his concept into words.

We were fortunate to have the skills of Martha Weiler, not only for her editing, but also for her excellent fact-checking.

Bob Tinnon handled the complicated job of both designing and producing the book, Gale Urtel, the typesetting, Mike Sincavage, the cover, and Robert Lamarche and Mary Andert, the technical art.

Our special thanks to Rena Copperman who coordinated the project and shepherded it through all its various stages, as well as counseling us whenever problems arose. Because of her capable, untiring management the problems were few.

Bill Estes, Jerry Lyle, and Bob Howells, and the staff at Trace Engineering were helpful and generous with their time whenever we needed information and had points to clarify.

We also would like to thank the folks at Foretravel, Fleetwood, Newmar, Western RV, Winegard, and Porta-Bote for their assistance in obtaining photographs.

Our thanks too, to the U.S. Postal Service, often maligned but which never failed to deliver on schedule all the many mailings involved with this book.

The Full-timing Lifestyle: What Is It? Is It for You?

▼ ▼ ▼ ▼ ▼ ▼ ▼ ▼ ▼

We are writing this as we are looking out on the deep-blue waters of Lake Superior from the windows of our RV home. Today, in a brisk, early fall breeze, the lake's surface is ruffled with sparkling, whitecapped wavelets. On shore, the hardwood trees are in a riot of brilliant autumn hues, their colorful mass punctuated now and then by the dark-green spires of evergreens. We are experiencing again one of the many rewards of fulltiming—enjoying our moveable home in a beautiful setting.

Just this spring we were looking out upon another body of water, the Pacific Ocean. Our campsite was on the edge of a rocky cliff high above the crashing waves. When we later moved inland, our living-room window framed the serene majesty of Mount Rainier.

The early summer found us in the Wallowa Mountains of eastern Oregon. Here the mountains towered above us, and we were camped so close to their bases that we could not see their crests without going outside and craning our necks. We had to be content with viewing from our windows the huge evergreens, each tree with its own complement of birds. While escaping the

▼ ▼ ▼

▼ ▼ ▼ ▼ ▼ ▼ ▼ ▼ ▼ ▼ ▼ ▼

heat of summer in the mountains of Idaho, Montana, and Wyoming, we saw many more memorable sights from our windows: dense, fern-filled forests; deer browsing in flowery meadows; a clear-running stream making its pleasantly noisy way among the boulders in its bed; a mountain lake; numerous panoramas of snowcapped peaks; and once, an unconcerned moose wandering through the campground.

Now, it is only mid-September, but fall comes early to this northern part of the United States. We are enjoying this beautiful view from a campground a few miles east of Duluth, Minnesota. Why Duluth, you might wonder? It is because Duluth and Lake Superior are spots we have not seen before, and, as far as we are concerned, that is as good a reason as any to visit a place. We chose to come to this area in the fall because we had heard of the spectacular displays of autumn foliage and wanted to see it. We also chose this time of the year because we prefer to miss the crowds in popular tourist areas and visit them in the off-season. That way, we need no advance reservations at campgrounds, we often have our pick of the campsite we want, we avoid lines at attractions and restaurants, and the highways are uncrowded.

Of course we run the risk of encountering inclement weather, but that causes us no concern because we have no fixed schedule; we don't have to be at a certain place at a specified time. If bad weather interferes with our plans—which are always loose and flexible—we can wait until it improves, all the while ensconced in the comfort of our snug home on wheels. Rainy days will not ruin our vacation because, as fulltimers, we are on vacation all year long.

▼ ▼ ▼

The way we live full time is the way *we* most enjoy it, but other fulltimers have their own ways of pursuing the lifestyle. Some travel most of the time, as we do. Others spend much of their time staying put in a favorite place, or use the mix of traveling and staying put that suits them.

This is what fulltiming is all about: Being able to go where you want, when you want, see new places, revisit old ones, and make friends wherever your fulltiming takes you.

PHOTO: ROBERT J. SMITH

Figure 1.1
Fly-fishing in one of the many beautiful rivers in the northwest brings
special satisfaction and time to refect.

We have been fulltiming, one way or another, for close to
twenty years now. After years of being employed at hectic, high-
pressure jobs, we decided — one cold, snowy, January day — that
there must be more to life than working at jobs that allowed us
to spend only occasional weekends and too-brief vacations doing what we really wanted — travel.

When we did manage to get away, we never had enough time
to spend at our destination. There were so many places we
wanted to see and explore in depth, but there was no way we
ever would be able to visit even a small percentage of them as
long as we were tied down to our jobs.

We wanted to change our lifestyle for other reasons as well:
Neither of us liked the chores that are involved in maintaining a

WHY WE BECAME FULLTIMERS

▼ ▼ ▼ ▼ ▼ ▼ ▼ ▼ ▼ ▼ ▼ ▼ ▼

There is a third dimension to traveling, the longing for what is beyond.

JAN MYRDAL

▼ ▼ ▼ ▼ ▼ ▼ ▼ ▼ ▼ ▼ ▼ ▼ ▼

house and yard. And, even though we enjoyed traveling and living in the various RVs we owned, we did not like the packing, unpacking, loading, and unloading that went with it. The time spent readying our rig was often out of proportion to the leisure time spent in it. More than once we decided it was not worth the effort and stayed home. This was usually a bad trade-off; as long as we were at home, we felt compelled to take care of the lawn or tackle the many other projects that needed doing.

One of the most important reasons for our needing a lifestyle change was that the stresses of our work were beginning to have adverse effects on our health. If we continued on as we were, we figured we would eventually have some serious problems.

We believe in these axioms:

"Don't put off until tomorrow what you can do today."
"Do it now; tomorrow may never come."

Being aware that the best-laid plans may never come to fruition, we did not want to wait for retirement, which at that time was more than twenty years away. So, on that January day, we decided to become fulltimers just as quickly as we could.

Our stressful jobs had one positive factor: We received from them a better-than-average income. Even though most of our extra money was spent on travel or vehicles to travel in (at different times we had a van, a pickup camper, and a seventeen-foot travel trailer), we had managed to save some.

We knew that selling the house, the furniture, and the maintenance equipment we had accumulated would give us a decent nest egg. It would not, however, generate enough income so that we could live on the interest. We calculated that we had enough money to live on for about four years without skimping too much. Four years of living exactly the way we wanted now, we decided, was much better than waiting for the uncertainty of what our retirement years would bring. There was plenty of time to worry about what we would do when we ran out of money four years hence. We decided to go for it. Having the full-timing lifestyle, for however long it lasted, was worth some risk-taking.

If our stress-related health problems didn't clear up (they did), we reasoned, at least we would have spent some time doing what we wanted to do. No matter what happened, we would never have to join the countless others who preface many of their statements with:

"If only I had . . ."
"I wish I could have . . ."
"If things had been different . . ."
"If I had it to do over again . . ."
"I've always been sorry I didn't . . ."

We have extended our fulltiming for many more years than four, and we intend to keep on fulltiming for many more years. We have never once regretted our decision to become fulltimers. In fact, we believe it was one of the best moves we ever made.

FULL-TIMING ATTRACTIONS
▾ ▾ ▾ ▾ ▾ ▾ ▾ ▾ ▾ ▾ ▾ ▾

The opportunity to travel is what attracts most people to the full-timing lifestyle, and this way of life offers it in abundance. You can visit relaxing, romantic places or take off to out-of-the-way areas in search of rugged adventure. You can do it at your own pace and in your own style, spending as much or as little as you choose. Fulltiming can be as individualistic as you want to make it.

▾ ▾ ▾ It's More than Just Traveling

The full-timing lifestyle has many more advantages than just traveling. Living in an RV is a less complicated way of life than living in a fixed dwelling. Not as much maintenance has to be done because RVs are smaller than houses or apartments, they are constructed of materials that require little care, and there is no yard to take care of. Because the lifestyle is not so complex, fulltimers have more time to do the things they *want* to do, not what they think they *should* do.

Fulltiming is not rigidly structured. Most nonfulltimers' lives are dominated by schedules. Work days are generally fairly inflexible. Nonfulltimers arise at a certain hour, go through a prescribed personal routine, arrive at work—going over the same route day after day, month after month, year after year—and carry out virtually the same duties on the job every day. At the

PHOTO: MILLIE EVANS

Figure 1.2
Horsedrawn carts carry visitors past one of the many restored homes at Acadian Historical Village in northern New Brunswick, just a sample of the many spots fulltimers can plan to visit.

end of the day they go home over the same route they traveled earlier. Evenings are filled with other scheduled events, activities that must be participated in, and tasks that must be done. Weekends are often just as structured as days spent on the job; most of this "free" time is taken up with specified chores and duties.

Even nonfulltimers' sleep is controlled by schedules. If you don't fulltime, you need a good night's sleep in order to be alert and ready for the next day's scheduled events.

When a vacation is in the offing, it too is precisely defined by when it begins and when it ends. The activities during a vacation are also preplanned with little or no leeway allowed for variations. Fulltimers have the freedom to set their own schedules and generally can do what they please, when they please.

Fulltiming can be a very economical way to live, although many don't find out about this aspect of living in an RV until they have done it for a while. (We have never encountered anyone who became a fulltimer for this reason alone.) When we started fulltiming we were totally unaware of how inexpensive it could be.

Many believe that to have the freedom fulltiming offers they will have to make certain compromises and sacrifices. This isn't so. Today's RVs are designed so they have all the necessities and conveniences anyone needs for comfortable living. When fulltiming in a modern RV home you never need to "camp out" in spartan living accommodations or do without creature comforts. In fact, your RV home might be more luxurious than the one you are now living in. Fulltiming can be, and should be, comfortable, convenient, safe, easy, and fun.

The lifestyle can be a relatively carefree existence, but none of us can drive off into the sunset without a care in the world. No one should expect fulltiming to be an escape from reality or a panacea for all problems. If you are realistic about what it can offer, you are not likely to be disappointed or disillusioned.

Most fulltimers are retirees, since these are the people who are no longer tied down to a job. Others engaged in this lifestyle, however, are a long way from retirement. Fulltiming is open to anyone who wants to undertake it, young or old. Still, many people do not seize the opportunity at hand and choose instead to plan ahead for fulltiming sometime in the future.

Most of us are acquainted with people who had their future all planned, eagerly anticipating the day when this "future" would begin, but a death, illness, or other unfortunate circumstance occurred, and they found themselves having to either alter their plans or forget about them altogether.

This might not happen to you, but then again, it could. The longer you put off anything, the greater the risk of something interfering with your plans. Even if nothing so drastic as a death or a serious illness occurs, long-range plans have a way of being

CAN YOU BE A FULLTIMER?
▼ ▼ ▼ ▼ ▼ ▼ ▼ ▼ ▼ ▼ ▼ ▼

continually superseded by other events. Eventually, they may be pushed out of the schedule entirely. What's more, if plans are made for well into the future, when the time comes to act, you may find you are too set in your ways. Perhaps, by then, you may decide it is too difficult or inconvenient to change, so your life will continue on in the same old way.

▼ ▼ ▼ Don't Let Excuses Get in the Way

Many people seem to go out of their way to find excuses for not enjoying their lives and doing what they want with them. Don't be one of those who would like to be a fulltimer but who says, "I can't until I retire," or, "I can't until the mortgage is paid off," or, "I can't until the kids are through school."

None of these "I can'ts" is reason enough by itself to keep anyone from fulltiming. To be sure, legitimate "I can'ts" exist that might prevent someone from pursuing the full-timing life-style, but many "I can'ts" are invalid. They are set up by those who really don't want to be fulltimers, those who like to talk about it, but when it comes right down to it, wouldn't change lifestyles even if the opportunity for doing so presented itself without any obstacles. We know from our own and others' experiences if the desire for fulltiming is really there, a way can be found to do it.

▼ ▼ ▼ Fulltiming for the Disabled

A physical disability is often used as an "I can't," but many determined people participate in fulltiming even though they have serious types of physical challenges. On more than one occasion we have been in campgrounds and seen an RV that had a removable ramp or a lifting device at the doorway for use by a person confined to a wheelchair (See Figure 1.3).

One such woman started fulltiming in a conventional trailer. While she and her husband were towing their trailer she was not comfortable when sitting in the truck seat of their tow vehicle, and it was painful for her to shift from the wheelchair to the

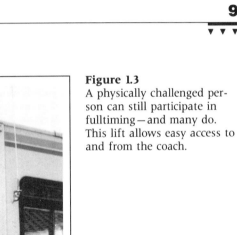

Figure 1.3
A physically challenged person can still participate in fulltiming—and many do. This lift allows easy access to and from the coach.

PHOTO: KEITH PROBERT AND BONNIE MARLEWSKI-PROBERT

seat. They replaced the trailer with a motorhome and now have an arrangement by which her wheelchair can be locked securely in place while they are under way.

Yet another woman's husband is the one who must be in a wheelchair. She does all the driving and parking of their rig. Her husband cooperates by doing certain chores he can handle from the wheelchair, such as cooking.

Women have always yearned for faraway places. It was no accident that a woman financed the first package tour of the New World, and you can bet Isabella would have taken the trip herself, only Ferdinand wouldn't let her go.

ROSLYN FRIEDMAN

▼ ▼ ▼ ▼ ▼ ▼ ▼ ▼ ▼ ▼ ▼ ▼ ▼

Then there are Vera and Cecil: They had been active RVers for years, but when Vera developed kidney problems they gave up RVing because of the daily treatments she needed at a dialysis center.

After some months of this, Cecil, who is more of an "I can" than an "I can't" person, set out to find a way he could give Vera the treatments at home. He did extensive research on his own and consulted with medical professionals and Vera's understanding, cooperative doctor. He found that, with proper training, he could perform the dialysis himself. Cecil took the necessary courses, and soon Vera was able to have the three daily treatments she needed at home. Since the equipment used for Vera's treatment—continuous ambulatory peritoneal dialysis (CAPD)—is portable and relatively simple, and the necessary supplies are readily obtainable throughout the country, Cecil reasoned that the dialysis could be performed in an RV. He proposed to Vera that they buy a motorhome and take it to Yuma, Arizona, to visit their niece. Vera was apprehensive but agreed to try it; she hated being tied down. At the beginning of the trip they stopped each time the dialysis was needed, but it wasn't long before Cecil figured out a method for doing the dialysis while they were under way.

They have just returned from Yuma after a six-week stay there. The trip was such a success that they are planning another trip to a different destination where they will rendezvous with longtime RVing friends.

Because she can travel again, Vera's morale and physical well-being have improved enormously. Oh, we forgot to mention the ages of this intrepid couple: Vera is seventy-six, and Cecil is eighty-two.

In the strictest sense of the word Vera and Cecil are not fulltimers—"Not yet, anyway," says Cecil—but they could be. They should be an inspiration to those who think they can't be fulltimers because of a restrictive medical condition.

We know of fulltimers who have varying degrees of paralysis, others who need a constant supply of oxygen, and many who have crippling or debilitating diseases, but these afflictions don't stop them from pursuing their chosen lifestyle. They take advantage of the numerous devices, both portable and those incorporated into their RVs, that allow them to be mobile and functional. Many such impaired individuals find RVing takes their minds off their troubles, but best of all, it releases them from being housebound and gives them a newfound sense of freedom.

If you have a physical disability and have been living in a house or apartment without any major problems, chances are a recreational vehicle could be found that would be suitable for you to live in. In fact, an RV might even be a better dwelling for you than any other. Being smaller than a fixed dwelling, it takes less time and effort to go from one room to another, and there are easily reachable, sturdy handholds throughout. Consider this if you are disabled: When traveling in your own RV home, you always have a washroom with you and don't have to be concerned with using public facilities that might present some problems.

▼▼▼ Can You Adjust to Fulltiming?

Even though many sincerely believe they want to be fulltimers, they may not be able to give up the security that conventional living represents to them. Some cannot imagine living solely in a movable dwelling. For such people, security means having a permanent, fixed place anchored securely to its foundation to come home to. Those who have such ideas can never experience the total freedom that fulltiming offers.

Is having a telephone part of your security package? Many people become so attached to, and dependent on, a telephone they cannot think of doing without it. In all our full-timing life, we have never been in one place long enough to warrant installing a phone, and if we had been, we probably wouldn't have done so. As a matter of fact, we think this is one of the advantages of fulltiming. We are never bothered by hucksters who want to sell us insurance, real estate, or other things we don't want. We are never disturbed by well-meaning individuals who call to chat at inconvenient times, it is one less item to have repaired when it malfunctions, and best of all, we don't have the monthly bill to pay.

Above all, remember that the most important thing you can take anywhere is not a Gucci bag or French-cut jeans; it's an open mind.

GAIL RUBIN BERENY

As a fulltimer, will you be able to do without the personal attention of your regular doctor or dentist if a medical or dental problem arises when you are on the road? Can you adjust to not having a known and trusted mechanic to call on for your rig repairs?

When living the life of a traveling fulltimer and an emergency arises, you may be far from your regular service and professional people. It is easier than might be expected to find the professionals and service people you need on the road (see Chapter 4, "Special Full-timing Situations and What to Do"), but will you be at ease with strangers doing the work?

You may also have to give up the security that comes from having friends and relatives nearby. You are bound to make more friends wherever you go, but will you feel as comfortable and secure with the new friends as with the old?

All these points must be considered before making the decision to be a fulltimer.

Perhaps simply not knowing what fulltiming is all about or having misconceptions about the lifestyle holds back many from pursuing their dream. We have had people who were contemplating fulltiming anxiously ask us such questions as: *How do you find a place to stay? How do you store everything you need? How do you arrange to get your mail? How do you keep enough ready cash on hand?* These questions and more are answered in the ensuing chapters, but we mention them here to illustrate the concerns of some about real and imagined bugaboos that might be lurking in the full-timing lifestyle.

Good company in a journey makes the way seem shorter.

IZAAK WALTON

▼ ▼ ▼ ▼ ▼ ▼ ▼ ▼ ▼ ▼ ▼ ▼ ▼ ▼

It is always wise to find out as much as you can about any new venture before embarking on it. But remember, thousands of us are out here fulltiming who once were in the same unenlightened state as you may be. We have found the answers to the questions, solved the problems, overcome the obstacles, and found that fulltiming is easy to do.

▼ ▼ ▼ Fulltiming with a Partner

Ideally, if you are planning to fulltime with a spouse or a partner, he or she should be as enthusiastic about the lifestyle as you are. In our case, each of us wanted to be a fulltimer as much as the

PHOTO: BARBARA LEONARD

Figure 1.4
Outdoor Resorts of America, with 14 locations across the country, attracts fulltimers with its luxurious parks and extensive amenities.

other; that is one of the reasons we have been so satisfied with our chosen way of life.

Many people make plans blissfully unaware that what they want to do is not necessarily what their partner wants. If you talk about what you are planning and receive little or no input from your partner, if he or she is evasive when discussing it, or lukewarm about the idea in general, you may be in for some unpleasantness.

Fred and Sylvia, a couple in their early sixties, met and married after their respective spouses had died. When we met them, they had been married for about five years. They were outgoing, fun to be with, and seemed to have a good relationship. One day when Sylvia was away, Fred told us how he had looked forward to becoming a fulltimer and, now that he was, what a great time he was having. His eyes danced as he said, "At last I feel as if I'm really living."

What counts in making a happy marriage is not so much how compatible you are, but how you deal with incompatibility.

GEORGE LEVINGER

Unfortunately, Sylvia harbored other feelings. She told Jan she had agreed to become a fulltimer "so Fred could get it out of his system." She went on to say that she certainly didn't want to spend the rest of her life living in a trailer, and she was sure Fred would see it her way eventually. They had been traveling for only four months, but Sylvia was already anxious to get back to her house and garden.

Over the years we have lost touch with Fred and Sylvia, so we don't know how (or if) they worked out their differences. We hope they reached some sort of a compromise.

The time to find out about your partner's wishes and feelings is not *after* you have moved into your RV home. Talk it over beforehand and be honest. Many people never think to come right out and ask their partner if he or she wants to become a fulltimer. Ask. It can be very illuminating.

Mutual desire alone may not be enough for satisfying fulltiming if you and your partner are not compatible. Some couples, to put it bluntly, simply don't like each other. Sometimes these couples have stayed together for the sake of the children or some other family or monetary reason, but often they remain together because it is easier to go on in the same old way than to change.

Such couples usually have areas in their home or on its grounds where each can get away from the other. This option may not be available once they become fulltimers. By the very nature of the lifestyle, couples must spend more time together in closer quarters since RV homes are a good deal smaller than any fixed dwelling. Disagreements have no room to "spread out" in the relatively confined quarters of the average RV. What's more, in a small environment, little annoyances have a way of festering into major irritations.

Compatibility is the basis for a good relationship anywhere, but it is especially important for fulltimers. The odds are against the lifestyle being a curative for any domestic problems; if they exist, there is a good chance they will become worse with full-timing — a sad but true fact.

Living harmoniously with each other is only one facet of an ideal full-timing partnership. Many partners get along well, but their likes and dislikes vary widely. Your full-timing life will be richer and more rewarding if you and your partner have similar interests.

At the outset of your new lifestyle it will be much easier to choose the size and type of rig if you both have the same point of view. Consider how you would work it out if you want a large motorhome and your partner prefers a compact fifth-wheel. If you reach a happy compromise on the type of full-timing rig, how satisfying will your fulltiming be if one of you likes a wilderness environment and fishing, and the other prefers instead a campsite in an urban park with full hookups and easy accessibility to shopping? What if one likes a change of seasons and the other wants to follow the sun? Does one want to travel most of the time and the other prefer to stay put for long periods?

Before committing yourselves wholeheartedly to fulltiming, differences should be discussed and compromises worked out. Do this *before* you sell the house or buy the RV. If you and your partner have any doubts at all about each of you enjoying fulltiming, don't cut off the avenues of escape entirely. Leave some options open just in case you can't make it work for you.

A LIFE WITHOUT SCHEDULES

You and your partner may have an ideal relationship and similar desires, but can you adjust to being unfettered and free to come and go as you want? Many cannot. They have been tied down by jobs, family responsibilities, and other circumstances for such a long period they find it very difficult to break loose. If they do, they feel as if they are adrift. Not being able to adjust to their new-found freedom, they put themselves back on schedules that are just as restrictive as the ones in the life they have left behind. As a consequence, some turn fulltiming into a job.

Jim was one of these people. He and his wife, Susan, had taken an early retirement and set off in a brand-new rig. When we met them in a campground in North Carolina, they were giving up fulltiming after less than a year and were on their way "home" because Jim hadn't found the lifestyle to be as he expected. We were rather new at fulltiming then and enjoying every minute of it, so we were interested to find out if Jim had discovered something about the lifestyle that we were not aware of. We asked him what the problem was. "Too much traveling," he said disgustedly. He elaborated: "You get up early every day, do three or four hundred miles, and pull into a campground all

Travelling and freedom are perfect partners and offer an opportunity to grow in new dimensions.

DONNA GOLDFEIN

▾ ▾ ▾ ▾ ▾ ▾ ▾ ▾ ▾ ▾ ▾ ▾ ▾

tired out late in the day. You do the same routine seven days a week, week after week. At least when I had a job I got the weekends off." Yes, those were his exact words.

Admittedly, Jim is an extreme example of someone who was not able to adjust to the full-timing way of life, but we have met others who had the same problem to a lesser extent.

Art and Verna lived part of the year in a house and the rest of the year in their trailer, which they took to Arizona each winter. We encountered them in New Mexico when they were on their way to a family reunion in Massachusetts. They wanted to do some sightseeing along the way and had allowed themselves a month for this purpose. They proudly showed us their neatly typed itinerary which listed the number of miles to be covered each day—not small distances, we noted. With few exceptions, nearly every night was to be spent in a different campground. They had allowed no leeway for bad weather or staying over if repairs of some kind were needed.

It was a very tight schedule that involved lots of driving. Such a schedule was necessary, they explained, so they would arrive in time for the reunion. We didn't ask, but wondered why they simply hadn't left earlier and allowed more time for the trip. Since they were retired, they could have taken all year to do it if they wanted to.

▾ ▾ ▾

In Montana we became acquainted with Shirley and Harry, who were having a similar problem. Shirley needed someone to talk to and Jan happened to be available. Her husband, Harry, could not slow down. His doctor had suggested he take an early retirement because he was pushing himself too hard in his work. They planned to tour all the western states in their 29-foot trailer. Shirley complained that she couldn't get Harry to slow his pace. They, or rather Harry, drove all day, every day. He rarely let Shirley drive, even though she was willing to do her share. Harry didn't enjoy driving especially; it was just that he always had to be doing something. He could not relax.

On vacations it is necessary to plan carefully for the optimum use of your time, but none of these couples was on a time-limited vacation. They were all free as birds but did not realize it, and they certainly did not take advantage of their situations.

Some people cannot slow down or break away from set routines. When there is nothing they must do, they invent things to do. If they can't come up with concrete projects, they often create schedules. Then, adhering to the schedule becomes a suitable project. Once it is formulated, the schedule is followed religiously, and the schedule's creator usually becomes upset when anything interferes with what he or she has laid out. People like this set up their own restrictions against the free and easy life they might have if only they could cut loose.

Every land has its own special rhythm, and unless the traveler takes the time to learn the rhythm, he or she will remain an outsider there always.

JULIETTE DE BAIRCLI LEVY

▼ ▼ ▼ Free Yourself from Structure

You will not get the most out of fulltiming unless you can free yourself from a rigidly structured life. Learn to allow plenty of time to travel to events that are held on specific dates. Also realize that you don't have to be in a hurry to get to any place. The Grand Canyon and the Blue Ridge Mountains will be there tomorrow, next week, next year, or ten years from now. Take your time; relax and enjoy.

Our full-timing life is so flexible that some days when we set out we don't know for sure where we will be spending the night. We select a spot once we are on the road. After camp is set up in such a place, we come to the realization that absolutely no one in the whole world knows where we are. It is an interesting feeling to experience. We don't consciously plan these short-lived disappearances; we don't want to drop out of society altogether, but because we have such an unstructured, unscheduled way of traveling, we often find ourselves in this situation.

▼ ▼ ▼

One year, in February, we were heading to Panama City, Florida, after a month's stay in Mobile, Alabama. The traffic on the interstate was heavy, and we had to wait in line to eat and at filling stations to refuel. We figured that the crowds and traffic would only increase the farther we went into Florida. We prefer an uncrowded, quieter, hassle-free type of travel, so we quickly reached a mutual decision. We exited the interstate, turned in the opposite direction, and ended up spending the remainder of the winter along the Gulf Coast in Mississippi, Louisiana, and Texas.

We are not advocating that others fulltime the way we do — it is probably too unstructured for many. We use the preceding examples to illustrate how the lifestyle can be adapted to what suits you as long as you don't allow yourself to be restrained by inflexible schedules.

FULLTIMING VERSUS VACATIONS

▼ ▼ ▼ ▼ ▼ ▼ ▼ ▼ ▼ ▼ ▼ ▼ ▼

No one should judge fulltiming by unpleasant experiences they might have had when vacationing in an RV, expecially on shorter trips. But remember, not all vacation RVs are suitable for fulltiming, and an occasional trip in such a rig can't replicate the lifestyle one lives full time. First of all, on a vacation, you will never have the free feeling that comes from knowing you will not have to return home by a certain time. Then there is the thrown-together, messy, helter-skelter atmosphere sometimes found in rigs that are used solely for vacations. Things never seem to be stowed properly. When packing an RV for a trip, there is a tendency to cram things into any places that can be found for them. As a result, it is often difficult to locate what you want when you want it.

Sometimes equipment on an RV that hasn't been used for some time may not work as it should, or at all, just when you are counting on it. You might be able to fix the problem if you can remember where you stashed the needed tools — if you remembered to bring them in the first place. Food and other supplies may run out at inconvenient times, and extras may not be on hand as they would at home.

A vacation is a period of increased and pleasurable activity when your wife is at the seashore.

ELBERT HUBBURD

▼ ▼ ▼ ▼ ▼ ▼ ▼ ▼ ▼ ▼ ▼ ▼ ▼

When vacationing, your routine is not a normal one. Normal is when you are at home, where things are kept in specific places and where items that are used on a regular basis can be located easily. You know when you are running low on such things as flour or toothpaste, and you replenish them before the supply runs out. Your toothbrush is always where it belongs as well; it has never been left behind somewhere.

PHOTO: ROBERT J. SMITH

Figure 1.5
Morning finds a lone angler adrift at Crane Prairie Reservoir along the
Cascade Lakes Scenic Byway in Oregon. The reservoir is also one of the
few osprey nesting areas in the country. Fulltimers have the luxury of
spending a day or weeks at such areas.

When you are fulltiming, your RV is your home. It can be, and
should be, managed just as any other home. If it is, your fulltiming experience will become a positive one. There will be no
continuing, petty annoyances or inconvenient situations to put
up with, and you should never have to make do or rough it.

It may, however, take some time before you get your fulltiming lifestyle in order. The first day you set off you may think
that Murphy's Law—if something can go wrong it will—was
invented just for you.

Hang in there. You will have to give yourself time to settle into
the routines of this different lifestyle, time to get the feel of it. It
may be rocky at first, but eventually things will sort themselves
out, and you will be able to enjoy yourself to the fullest.

WHO ARE FULLTIMERS?

▼ ▼ ▼ ▼ ▼ ▼ ▼ ▼ ▼ ▼ ▼ ▼ ▼

Fulltimers are young, middle-aged, and old, those who are retired and those who are employed, parents with school-age children, those with no children, and those whose children are grown and on their own. Fulltimers are families, couples, and singles.

Some fulltimers live in their RVs year-round and travel much of the time, rarely spending more than a month in any one place. They have no home other than their RV. (This is the type of fulltiming we do.)

Others live exclusively in their RVs but spend the winter months in one location and the summer in another. The only major traveling they do is following the seasons twice a year. They often seasonally rent the same site in the same park year after year.

Others may travel during part of the year, living in their RVs while doing so, and return periodically to a fixed, permanent dwelling that is their primary home and where they live most of the time.

Some mild controversy has arisen over who can correctly and rightfully call themselves fulltimers. Whether someone qualifies in another's perception as a fulltimer is not important. Labels, names, and designations don't mean a thing as long as you are doing what you want and having fun.

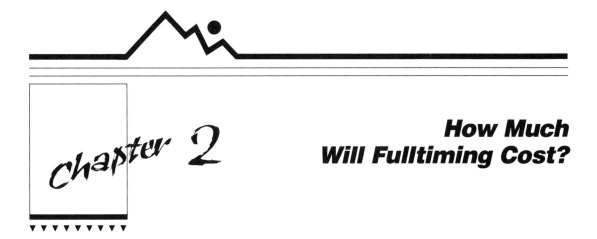

How Much Will Fulltiming Cost?

Fulltiming can be one of the most economical ways to live. Many expenses will be the same as those with a fixed residence; some will increase, and some will decrease. How much it costs can be controlled in large measure by the decisions you make before venturing into the lifestyle and when you are actually on the road.

THE FULL-TIMING RIG

Preliminary cost control begins with the selection of the full-timing rig. The would-be fulltimer has lots of options available when choosing the rig that will be an RV home: new or used, large or small, luxury or utilitarian model, motorhome, conventional or fifth-wheel trailer, pickup camper, or camping van conversion. For most of us, it first comes down to a choice between a trailer or a motorhome.

What you can afford to pay for the type of unit you want is the next consideration. If you purchase a used trailer and already own a proper tow vehicle, you can be on the road in a suitable, fairly recent RV home for around $10,000, or you can spend well into the six-figure range for a brand-new, luxurious motorhome.

Most new trailers cost much less than new motorhomes because they don't have an engine or a drivetrain. But if a tow vehicle must be purchased along with the trailer, the total cost of the combination can be comparable to that of a mid-priced motorhome.

▼ ▼ ▼ Preowned Units

For those who cannot afford new equipment, there is always a selection of good used rigs to choose from. Preowned motorhomes and trailers are available for prices ranging from one-third to one-half the cost of new units. Often a tow vehicle is offered with a trailer when sold by a private party.

The next thing to being rich is travelling as though you were.

STEPHEN BIRNBAUM

▼ ▼ ▼ ▼ ▼ ▼ ▼ ▼ ▼ ▼ ▼ ▼ ▼

Once we were parked in a site next to a new-looking, big, pricey motorhome in Skidaway Island State Park near Savannah, Georgia. During a conversation with Jack, the owner of the motorhome, he told us how he had acquired his impressive RV. "I certainly couldn't afford to buy this new," he said. The previous owner had spared no expense in having the motorhome customized just the way he wanted it. He had used it for a short time before his business failed at about the same time he was getting a divorce. He had to raise some cash quickly so he sold his motorhome for much less than it cost him. Jack was the happy buyer of a fantastic bargain.

Many preowned units, like Jack's, have been used only for vacations and occasional weekends, so they have low mileage and little actual wear, even though they may be many years old.

Some RVers who have been planning to fulltime may already have an adequate rig. One way or another, nearly everyone can find some sort of affordable rig in which to get started.

▼ ▼ ▼ Equipping the Tow Vehicle

When you take delivery of a new motorhome, it is ready for the road, but a new tow vehicle may not be outfitted with all, or any, of the equipment needed for pulling a trailer. Any tow vehicle that is ordered from the manufacturer should be ordered with the towing package. Before a trailer can be towed, a hitch of the proper type will be needed. A conventional trailer needs a load-distributing hitch and receiver and sway control. A fifth-wheel trailer requires a hitch that is mounted in the bed of the pickup-truck tow vehicle. The tow vehicle will need a trailer-brake control unit, and unless factory equipped with a towing package, a wiring harness, probably a heavy-duty transmission-oil cooler, and possibly heavy-duty shock absorbers.

The cost of the towing assembly and its installation is often offered as a package by the trailer dealer when a new trailer is purchased. If a tow vehicle is ordered from the factory, some of the equipment is offered as options.

If for any reason you do not want the trailer dealer to install the equipment, independent shops can do the job.

The day on which one starts out is not the time to start one's preparations.

NIGERIAN PROVERB

▼▼▼ What about Extra Equipment?

Motorhomes and trailers come equipped with just about everything needed to live comfortably. All modern units are completely furnished, tastefully decorated, and have the basic major appliances built in. You can add lots of other equipment or substitute deluxe items for standard ones on new units as your budget allows, but today's remarkable RVs are all set to go except for adding such items as pots and pans, dinnerware, flatware, linens, clothing, and personal items.

Some optional equipment will add to the enjoyment of fulltiming. The major and most expensive optional equipment items wanted by most fulltimers are an air conditioner—two of them may be needed if the unit is large—and an awning.

The fulltimer should have a few other miscellaneous items (these are discussed in the appropriate chapters), but none are especially costly, and their purchase shouldn't dent anyone's budget. Used units already may have many accessories and extra equipment.

▼▼▼

Those who opt for a motorhome probably will want an auxiliary vehicle so they can have alternate transportation. Once the motorhome is parked, whether for the night, week, month, or season, it is neither convenient nor practical to dismantle the campsite for short shopping or sightseeing trips.

The initial cost of an auxiliary vehicle is not as great a consideration as is the expense of operating it. Some people already own a suitable vehicle for this purpose. With the auxiliary vehicle and the motorhome, there will be two engines to be serviced, maintained, and repaired, and two sets of tires that will eventually need to be replaced.

Keep on truckin'.

ROBERT CRUMB

▼ ▼ ▼ ▼ ▼ ▼ ▼ ▼ ▼ ▼ ▼ ▼

Unless someone will be driving the auxiliary vehicle as you travel, a towing apparatus will have to be purchased. This can be a simple tow bar or a more elaborate and more expensive tow dolly. If a motorcycle is used as the auxiliary vehicle, it is usually stored in a convenient rack installed on the back of the motorhome.

▼ ▼ ▼ Operating Costs

Towing a car, just like towing a trailer, will increase the fuel consumption of the towing vehicle. Since fuel is one of the major expenditures for most traveling fulltimers, the miles per gallon are an important consideration when purchasing the rig.

If you have any doubts about the importance of this expenditure, take a careful look at Table 2.1. Obviously, having a motorhome or tow vehicle that is fuel efficient will result in significant savings.

It is, however, very difficult to determine what the fuel consumption will be for a particular rig. Miles-per-gallon figures are affected by so many variables—the driving habits of the driver, how a vehicle's engine is tuned, the condition of the engine, the weather and areas in which the vehicle or rig is driven, the loaded weight of the unit—that EPA ratings or the word of someone who is trying to sell you a unit give only an indication of what a particular unit might consume.

A fact that cannot be disputed is: The amount of fuel consumed increases in direct proportion to the size and dry weight of the unit (you have some control over the loaded and wet weight). Therefore, fuel expenses can be cut by purchasing a small or lightweight RV.

Table 2.1
A Comparison of RV Fuel Costs

MPG	Gallons to Travel 5,000 Miles	Cost per Gallon	Total Fuel Cost
16	312.5	$1.20	$ 375
12	416.7		500
9	555.5		666
6	833.4		1,000

Although motorhomes have a reputation for being fuel guzzlers—many average fewer than ten miles per gallon—a tow vehicle pulling a large, heavy trailer will also consume lots of fuel. If a truck is used as a tow vehicle, a half-ton truck will be the most economical as far as fuel is concerned, but a three-quarter-ton or a one-ton truck may be needed to pull a heavy trailer.

Vehicles with numerically high axle ratios are necessary for towing any type of heavy load. As the axle ratio is increased (numerically), the fuel consumption also increases.

In relation to operating costs, another point to consider is the number of wheels a unit may have. Some big trailers have three axles and six wheels instead of the two axles and four wheels found on smaller trailers. Large motorhomes may have some dual wheels. Eventually, all the tires on all the wheels will have to be replaced. In addition, there will be the continuing expenses of servicing all the wheel bearings and brakes.

The most economical traveling can be done in a unit that is easy on fuel, but much of the cost of fulltiming depends on the type of home base you maintain or whether you maintain one at all. If you have no home base, of course, you have nothing to maintain, so there will be no expenses connected with it. A home base should not be confused with a legal residence; for many they are one and the same, but a legal residence does not necessarily have to be your home base and vice versa. Actually, no one is required by law to have a legal residence or a home

SHOULD YOU KEEP A HOME BASE?

PHOTO: ROBERT J. SMITH

Figure 2.1
Fulltimers find Paulina Lake, cupped in the caldera of Newberry National Volcanic Monument in Oregon, is one of the best fishing lakes in the state because of its warm, nutrient-rich waters..

base. (Legal residences are discussed fully in Chapter 4, "Special Full-timing Situations and What to Do.")

Not having a home base is one of the reasons we have been able to live so economically as fulltimers. The only home we have anywhere, the only dwelling we own, is our trailer. In fact, we could not afford our RV home and travel as we do if we had the additional expense of maintaining a house or any other fixed home base. On our budget it has to be one or the other. We are perfectly content with our mobile dwelling and have never felt the need to have any place to go back to periodically.

The closest thing we have to a "home base" (the term is a misnomer because it is neither our home nor our base) is our mailing address, which is that of a relative. We visit this place infrequently, and, when we do, we continue to live in our trailer while we are there. In all the years we have been fulltiming, we have spent every night in our trailer except for one when the trailer was in a repair shop overnight.

One of the alluring aspects of fulltiming is the freedom it offers, but much of the freedom gained is eroded when you have a fixed-dwelling home base. In many ways, fulltimers with a home base have only a little more freedom than do full-time house dwellers going off on an annual vacation.

▼ ▼ ▼ More Costs, More Work

Many fulltimers and those contemplating the lifestyle feel they must have a place other than their RV that they can call home. This is unfortunate for those on tight budgets because keeping up such a place will be a burdensome extra expense. Fulltimers who maintain any sort of a permanent residence, unit, or site other than their RV home will spend more than those who do not. It doesn't matter whether it is a house, condominium, apartment, mobile home, park-model trailer, a campsite that is rented on an annual basis, or a campsite that is purchased outright. Certain expenses are incurred with all of them. A house or a fixed dwelling situated on a piece of land that you own or are paying for is the type of home base that will cost the most.

Three kinds of people die poor: those who divorce, those who incur debt, and those who move around too much.

SENEGALESE PROVERB

▼ ▼ ▼ ▼ ▼ ▼ ▼ ▼ ▼ ▼ ▼ ▼ ▼

▼ ▼ ▼ The Costs of a House

If you have a house you intend to keep as your home base, total up the amount you must pay for its annual upkeep: maintenance, repairs, insurance, taxes, mortgage payments. Can you afford to keep it if you are a fulltimer? If you can, will it be worth it? Or could the money spent on the house, which may be used for only a few weeks a year, be put to better use?

As long as you have the house, you will have to spend money to keep it up in order to protect your investment and have a decent place to come back to. Major repairs, such as replacing the roof, will have to be done as needed. When the washer or other major appliance gives up the ghost, it will have to be

▼ ▼ ▼

replaced. You will also have to allocate some funds for insurance and annual taxes. No real estate taxes are so low that they would be an insignificant amount to fulltimers who have to watch what they spend.

▼ ▼ ▼

Renting the house to defray expenses doesn't often work out because the rent that can be charged usually does not cover all the costs. In addition, if you are not there to oversee the property, you may have to pay someone to do the job.

It is one thing when you own property for the purpose of renting it; it is quite another matter when you are renting out your own home. Generally, tenants do not maintain the place as an owner would; bad tenants might neglect it to the point of ruin. Something else to consider: If the property is rented it may not be available for you to live in whenever you want to.

Each time you return to the house you will have to secure it before you leave again. All utilities will have to be shut off or disconnected; newspaper delivery may have to be canceled; windows and doors will have to be double-checked to be sure they are all closed and locked; chores, such as cleaning out the refrigerator, must be done; timers and alarms on security systems will have to be set and activated; arrangements will have to be made for the disposition of mail. If you will be away for some time during the warm months of the year, someone should come around periodically to take care of the yard work. And someone should be available to check on the house periodically when you are away.

▼ ▼ ▼

Is there anything as horrible as starting on a trip? Once you're off, that's all right, but the last moments are earthquake and convulsion, and the feeling that you are a snail being pulled off a rock.

ANNE MORROW LINDBERGH

▼ ▼ ▼ ▼ ▼ ▼ ▼ ▼ ▼ ▼ ▼ ▼ ▼

In addition to all these going-away preparations, dwellings in northern climates, those subject to freezing temperatures, will need to be winterized before you head for the Sunbelt. You will have to decide if you want the expense, and perhaps the danger, of leaving the furnace on, or if you would rather take the time to drain all the water lines and protect anything that needs it from freezing. If you have ever winterized an RV you know what a time-consuming job it is. The process is magnified tremendously when dealing with all the systems in a house. Arrangements should be made for someone to shovel the walkways in case of snow. Uncleared walks, like untended yards and any other indication that the house is vacant, would make it a prime target for thieves and vandals.

When you return, whatever the season, everything will have to be made livable for the time you will spend there before it has to be made secure again. It is an endless cycle.

You can only hope you never return to find the basement full of water, termites at work, the roof caved in, or the place stripped bare by thieves. If nothing so drastic happens, it will be amazing if reactivating the systems is all you have to do when you arrive. Some cleaning to get rid of accumulated dust almost certainly will be needed immediately. Something always needs to be done around a house if one is living in it full time; houses left unattended seem to need a lot more work, so you can count on doing the odd jobs and repairs that have piled up in your absence.

If you have a house, you will, in effect, be living in two places, so you will do a certain amount of packing and unpacking. Like the vacationer, you may find you have forgotten something you need and left it where you are not.

Traveling is not just seeing the new; it is also leaving behind. Not just opening doors; also closing them behind you, never to return. But the place you have left forever is always there for you to see whenever you shut your eyes. And the cities you see most clearly at night are the cities you have left and will never see again.

JAN MYRDAL

▼ ▼ ▼ What Price Security?

A while ago we read a survey that revealed most fulltimers who were holding onto a dwelling for a home base were doing so to have a place to return to when they could no longer fulltime or when they would voluntarily give up the lifestyle.

If this is the reason you want to keep a fixed dwelling, ask yourself: What could cause my fulltiming to come to an end?

Old age? What is old age in relation to fulltiming? Is it when you are so infirm that you cannot perform the functions needed for setting up a campsite? Is it when your driving abilities are no longer as good as they used to be? Speculate as to what age you will be when you consider yourself to be old.

We have met many fulltimers in their seventies and some in their eighties. If you can't manage to hook up your RV and take care of the little maintenance it requires, how will you ever take care of a house?

Bad health can be a valid reason for giving up fulltiming, but consider whether it would make sense to move back into a house because of what ails you. If heart trouble or emphysema is your problem and you cannot overtax yourself, who will take care of your house? On top of your medical expenses, you may have to pay for help to do all the maintenance you used to do.

If you need regular treatments that can be performed only at a hospital, you can find hospitals in places other than where the house is.

To bring up again a subject discussed on page 11, if you need a walker, crutches, or a cane to get around, why put yourself in the position of having to traverse the large rooms and perhaps stairways in a house when you could maneuver more quickly and easily in an RV? There are so many convenient handholds and supports in an RV that a walker might not be needed when moving around in it. This would not be the case in any average room in a house.

▼ ▼ ▼

[T ravel seems] not just a way of having a good time, but something that every self-respecting citizen ought to undertake, like a high-fiber diet, say, or a deodorant.

JAN MORRIS

▼ ▼ ▼ ▼ ▼ ▼ ▼ ▼ ▼ ▼ ▼ ▼

Conceivably, you could become tired or bored being a traveling fulltimer, but it is not necessary to have a house if you decide to settle down.

What we are getting at is something that evidently did not occur to any of the survey's respondents: If you stop fulltiming, for whatever reason, nothing requires you to give up living in an RV and go back to a fixed dwelling. Why not continue to live in the RV? If you have chosen well, it will be comfortable, efficiently designed, will require little maintenance, and will have storage space for everything you need and want.

If your traveling home has been a compromise between space and a larger unit's fuel consumption, you could purchase a larger unit to live in when you stop traveling. Miles-per-gallon figures won't be a concern if it is permanently parked or if it is driven infrequently.

As a permanent, full-time residence, an RV has a lot to recommend it over and above its being an inexpensive dwelling with low-cost, easy maintenance. No matter how long it is parked, it still retains much of its mobility and can be moved without too much trouble. This can be an advantage if, for instance, you find the RV park you have chosen has been built over a toxic waste dump, the neighborhood deteriorates or becomes the target of criminals, air pollution increases in the area, a superhighway is built adjacent to where you are parked, you need or want to move to another climate, or you just don't like the neighbors. If you are a working fulltimer who is out of a job, your home can be moved from a place of high unemployment to a better economic area. Moving an RV is a lot less trouble than moving roomfuls of furniture and having to sell one house to be able to buy another.

Many of the people who participated in the survey said that keeping a house gave them a feeling of security. Whether the mortgage is paid off or not, any house will continue to cost you money until it is sold. It doesn't matter whether the property is appreciating or depreciating, funds for it will come out of your pocket on a regular basis. What sort of security is that?

Some believe that owning a house provides security for the future, but real estate values never stay constant; they can go down as well as up. Counting on a house to be worth more in later years is unwise. And real estate can only be converted into cash when a buyer is found who is willing to pay the amount you will accept.

Here I am, safely returned over these peaks from a journey far more beautiful and strange than anything I had hoped for or imagined—how is it that this safe return brings such regret?

PETER MATTHIESSEN

▼ ▼ ▼ ▼ ▼ ▼ ▼ ▼ ▼ ▼ ▼ ▼

▼ ▼ ▼

All the foregoing won't make a bit of difference if you want to hang onto your house for sentimental reasons. Many cherished memories are associated with houses. They are places where children have grown up; they may be filled with things you have built with your own hands, or surrounded with plantings you have nurtured and watched grow from seedlings to maturity. For some, the house may not be as important as the possessions in it—family heirlooms, hobbyists' collections, or valuable furniture. Only you can decide if the emotional attachment is really worth the cost and time needed for keeping up a house.

It is true that when most people begin fulltiming, they maintain some sort of home base, many for the reason we mentioned earlier: to try out fulltiming while having a place to come back to in case it doesn't work out. But many soon find what an expense and nuisance having a home base is and get rid of it when they realize how much it directly affects and hinders their new way of living once they become committed to the full-timing life.

EXPENSES: A COMPARISON

▼ ▼ ▼ ▼ ▼ ▼ ▼ ▼ ▼ ▼ ▼ ▼ ▼

One important thing to remember, once you start fulltiming, is that it will be your everyday way of life. You will not be on vacation—even though it may seem like it—so, chances are, your budget will not stand the strain of spending money for extras and luxuries as you might when on a two-week trip.

Many people begin fulltiming with a being-on-holiday attitude. Why not celebrate such an event? But most of us have to come back to normal before we spend too many of our hard-earned dollars on vacation-type frivolities.

▼ ▼ ▼ Day-to-Day Expenses

Excluding this initial cutting-loose celebration, many of your expenses will be generally the same as when you lived in a fixed dwelling, unless the beginning of your fulltiming happens to coincide with a drop or increase in income and you need to revamp your budget. Being a fulltimer does not necessarily mean you will change all of your habits and priorities.

You aren't likely to alter your eating habits just because of your new lifestyle, so food expenditures will remain the same. Most likely, so will the number of times you eat out compared with the number of meals you will eat at home.

You probably will continue with any long-standing personal habits you have, such as smoking or drinking, to the same extent as prefulltiming, so the expenses connected with them will remain virtually the same.

Fulltiming will do nothing to affect what you normally spend for periodic medical and dental checkups.

Life- and medical-insurance costs will not change just because you are living in an RV; however, vehicle-insurance rates might increase if you have an expensive rig or if you drive more miles in a year than is considered average.

If you left a white-collar job, you may be able to save substantially on clothes since you won't have to maintain a business wardrobe. Casual wear is appropriate for fulltiming, and the lifestyle requires no special clothing. Selectivity about the climates in which you spend your time may enable you to do away with heavy winter clothing. No matter how sunny the clime, however, some cool- and cold-weather garments will be needed every now and then.

More money may be spent on vehicle fuel, maintenance, and repairs depending on the amount of traveling you do and when you do it.

Most of us like to do some sightseeing when we travel, and many tourist attractions charge admission fees. Entertainment expenses should depend on what you can afford.

Traveling is seeing; *it is the implicit that we travel by.*

CYNTHIA OZICK

▼ ▼ ▼ ▼ ▼ ▼ ▼ ▼ ▼ ▼ ▼ ▼

If these expenses were all that had to be considered, fulltiming could cost more than, or just as much as, other nonmobile lifestyles. But you may have noticed that two significant items are missing from the budget categories: taxes and shelter. These two items are what can make the lifestyle an inexpensive way to live. Both are affected by the fulltimer's mobility, and it is the mobility alone that can make the difference.

▼ ▼ ▼ Shelter and Taxes

Because fulltimers can choose where they want to register their vehicles, they can decide on a place where wheel taxes or personal-property taxes are low or nonexistent. They can also select a place with no sales tax or a low one for purchasing big-ticket items. If a state income tax must be paid, fulltimers can arrange to "live" in a state that takes less of a bite than others. A good possibility exists as well that some of the taxes a person paid before becoming a fulltimer may no longer be applicable. (See *Selecting an RV Home Base: State Tax & Registration Information,* Trailer Life Books, Camarillo, California.)

The budget category for a fulltimer's shelter is the rent paid for a place to park an RV home—in other words, campground fees. It's possible to spend much less on these fees than what might be spent for renting an apartment or maintaining a house, with or without attendant mortgage payments.

Let's say campground fees are $15 for overnight stays. At this rate the costs for an an entire year would be $5,475 or $456.25 a month. This is what might be paid for rent on a small apartment or for payments on a modest mortgage. Where do the full-timing savings come in? We used a $15 overnight fee for our example and, although plenty of campgrounds have fees of $15 or higher, just as many have fees that are much lower. Sometimes even a free campground can be found.

For the last year our rent has averaged almost $10 a night. This included a few stays in campgrounds that charged $15 or more, and one week where no fee was paid because we were parked in a friend's driveway. We were not making any special effort to economize, but we followed our usual practice: If there are several campgrounds in an area where we want to stay, we almost always patronize those with a price below that of the most expensive ones. Our total yearly expenditure for shelter was $3,538.83. In what other lifestyle would the amount spent for shelter be so low? It is lower still when you take into account that our campground fees included all utilities and sometimes cable television. If we had concentrated on spending as little as possible for each night's stay—which would have meant going out of our way in some instances, or doing without hookups for the sake of saving money—our annual expenditure for shelter would have been even lower.

COST-CUTTING TACTICS
▼ ▼ ▼ ▼ ▼ ▼ ▼ ▼ ▼ ▼ ▼ ▼ ▼ ▼

Once into the full-time way of life, there are additional ways to economize. Being a do-it-yourselfer for maintenance and repairs, for instance, will help in holding down expenses.

One of the best tactics for saving money is simply to cut down on traveling. Go somewhere and stay a while instead of spending each night at a different campground.

The immediate and considerable saving will be on fuel. Instead of fueling up once or twice a day, you may find as much as a week might go by before you need fuel. You will realize long-range savings because the regular maintenance of the vehicle will not have to be performed so often and, since there will be less wear and tear, the need for repairs and replacements will be lessened.

▼ ▼ ▼ Saving on Campground Fees

The other significant savings will be on campground fees. Most private campgrounds have weekly and monthly rates. When we pull into a place intending to stay overnight and find it has an especially attractive weekly rate and it is in a place we like, we often decide to stay over for a week, or sometimes longer. As a matter of fact, we are writing this chapter in a campground that we intended to use as just an overnight stop. It's a lovely public park on a lake, with wide sites in its well-maintained camping area, and, unusual for a public park, a weekly rate is offered. We have been here almost a week and will probably stay for another week. Some campgrounds also have seasonal and yearly rates. As might be expected, the price for overnighting is the highest.

Many weekly rates amount to receiving one night's stay free: Six nights are paid at the regular overnight rate and the seventh night is free—although some campgrounds may give more of a discount. Often we have found that the weekly rate is less than three or four days at the daily rate.

Monthly rates average less per day than weekly rates. How they are determined varies widely. We have stayed in places where the monthly charge was less than half the cost it would have been if we paid by the day; in other places the monthly rate was only slightly less than renting the site by the week. Yearly rates are the lowest of all, if they are available.

Generally, campgrounds in and around cities and large metropolitan areas are the most expensive and the most crowded.

Higher, in-season rates are usually in effect at RV parks in vacation areas and resort localities. Although staying for the season, in season, is cheaper than staying at these places on a shorter-term basis, such places may be much more expensive than a campground in a less-popular area.

For long-term stops most of us want all the hookups: electricity, water, and sewer, but for overnight or a few days, all these conveniences may not be needed. Many RV parks have a base rate for a site with no hookups and an individual charge for the electricity, water, or sewer. Each hookup may have a different charge; it generally ranges from one to three dollars. The higher figure is usually for the electrical hookup; sometimes water is

My heart is warm with
the friends I make,
And better friends
I'll not be knowing;
Yet there isn't a train
I wouldn't take.
No matter where it's going.

"TRAVEL"
EDNA ST. VINCENT MILLAY

▼ ▼ ▼ ▼ ▼ ▼ ▼ ▼ ▼ ▼ ▼ ▼

▼ ▼ ▼

*We're tenting tonight on
the old campground,
Give us a song to cheer
Our weary hearts, a song
of home
And friends we love so dear.*

WALTER KITTREDGE

▼ ▼ ▼ ▼ ▼ ▼ ▼ ▼ ▼ ▼ ▼ ▼ ▼

included with the electric charge. On top of this may be an additional charge of one to three dollars for running an electric heater or an air conditioner. To save money in places with individual charges, never pay for more than you will use, and never hook up to anything you don't need.

In campgrounds where each hookup carries an individual charge, we habitually only pay for an electrical hookup. If we have filled our water tank and dumped the holding tanks at the campground where we stayed the day before, we have no need for anything but electricity and sometimes not even that. Even if we are running low on water and the holding tanks need to be emptied, we often can take care of these things at no charge at a highway rest area. (Don't let the gray-water holding tank become too full or, as you travel, the motion may slosh the gray water up into the shower or sinks.)

We also frequent state, city, and county parks where we can dump on the way in, if we need to, and on the way out, at no charge. A little calculated planning often saves money. Not spending even so little as a dollar can add up to quite a bit if you do it often enough.

Another way to economize is to seek out places not advertised as resort campgrounds. Stay at campgrounds that do not have swimming pools, tennis courts, golf courses, stables, marinas or boat rentals, water slides, or saunas. All this fancy equipment has to be paid for and maintained, and these costs will be reflected in the rates.

▼ ▼ ▼

Staying in a campground miles from a place you want to visit or a town where you must shop for supplies just because it is inexpensive may be false economy. Calculate the amount of fuel it will take to make the round trip from the campground to your destination, and multiply that figure by the number of times you will make such a trip. It may be cheaper, in the long run, to pay a higher rate at a closer-in campground. For a long-term stay, the costs of going out for a daily newspaper, making regular trips to the post office, and, perhaps, having to drive a distance for a public telephone should be figured in. They can mount up. The attractive rate at an out-of-the-way campground wasn't nearly so appealing to us when we found we would have to make an eight-mile round trip to purchase a daily paper.

▼ ▼ ▼ Stay Longer, Save More

Staying a while in one place can lower your campground costs, but it can also aid in cutting costs in another way. You will be in an area long enough to take advantage of sales and specials on such things as groceries, clothing, vehicle maintenance and replacement items, hair care, meals, even entertainment. All you need to do is buy the local newspaper, pick up all the free "shoppers" and classified-ad publications you can find, then read the ads, and clip the coupons you might use. Also consult the telephone directory to locate such places as beauty and barber schools and medical and dental clinics, where you can receive the services you need at low cost.

The longer we stay in a place, the better we know it, and this too can help save money. We learn which places charge the highest prices, be they restaurants, supermarkets, or pharmacies, and we patronize other, lower-cost establishments. We have the time and opportunity to become acquainted with local people who often have information about where bargains can be found. Last week we were telling a local resident about a great lunch bargain we had found. She proceeded to tell us about an even better one in a restaurant we had avoided because we thought it was too expensive.

Travel is fatal to prejudice, bigotry, and narrowmindedness.

MARK TWAIN

▼ ▼ ▼ ▼ ▼ ▼ ▼ ▼ ▼ ▼ ▼ ▼

We vividly remember one day when we saved a whopping $101.19 over what we would have spent if we had done our shopping without the benefit of previous newspaper perusal. First, we saved money in the supermarket. We always buy the local newspaper on food day and Sunday for the manufacturers' coupons in it, and we never do any supermarket shopping without our coupon collection in hand. That day we had coupon savings of $7.30 because we learned from the newspaper that a

▼ ▼ ▼

particular supermarket was doubling manufacturers' coupons. The amount we saved with coupons was over and above any in-store specials we bought; we didn't keep a record of those.

At that time we were working on a project that required extensive photography. We had noticed a discount catalog store in town and thought it might be a good place to obtain some needed film-processing mailers. It was. We bought a quantity of them and saved $17.52 over the regular, or undiscounted, price. This turned out to be an especially fortunate purchase because with the amount of mailers we bought, we received a manufacturer's rebate form for five free mailers worth $29.25.

We had a newspaper coupon for air-conditioner servicing on our truck that allowed us to have this needed job done for less than half the usual price — $17 saved. We needed some reference books for our project and knew, again from a newspaper ad, that one of the bookstores in town was giving an across-the-board discount of 20 percent. This amounted to $5.17 on our purchases. We stumbled onto an apparel item for which we had been searching for some time. It was on a sale rack for less than half the regular price, resulting in another sizeable saving of $15. For lunch we used a buy-one-get-one-free coupon we had clipped, so the check for both of us was $7.95. On the way back to the RV park, we noticed a car wash that was having a special that day. We ran our filthy truck through and saved another $2.

It was unusual that we were able to save so much in just one day. Usually such an amount would have been spread over a number of days or weeks. We had not planned this bargain-finding onslaught; we were just going about our business as we normally do. True, it was just luck to receive the coupon for the free mailers and to find the garment we had been looking for, but if it happened to us, it could happen to you.

▼ ▼ ▼

Many papers and shoppers also carry ads for garage sales and flea markets where bargains often can be found. In addition to the restaurant coupons and specials that might appear, other establishments advertise such things as movies at reduced prices, "early-bird" dinner offerings, and senior-citizen discounts. Aside from advertising special grocery prices, supermarket ads often contain a number of coupons enabling you to double your manufacturers' coupons, or their ads might contain the valuable information that they double all coupons.

We know of many fulltimers who never buy or read any newspapers. One woman said she never reads them because they are full of bad news and they depress her. Another said, "I don't know any of the local people here, and I don't care about what goes on in this town." Some fulltimers believe that reading the newspaper is a chore and an infringement on their new-found full-timing freedom. But whether the news is read or not, the sum spent for a newspaper can often result in quite a return on the investment for those of us who have to watch what we spend. We don't use all the coupons in the Sunday paper, but we consider this paper to be free most times because the value of the coupons we do use usually exceeds the cost of the paper.

When we stay in one place for a while, we like to be in or near small towns with populations of about twenty to thirty thousand. Towns of this size have a variety of competing businesses that gives us a better opportunity for finding the lowest prices or the best deal. If you plant yourself in a town that has, for instance, one grocery store and one service station, you have no choice but to pay whatever is asked, no matter what the price. Big cities have more bargains than small towns, but the fuel used to cover the miles to reach them often offsets much of the savings. It is possible to walk to many places in small towns.

The traveler sees what he sees; the tripper sees what he has come to see.

G. K. CHESTERTON

▼ ▼ ▼ ▼ ▼ ▼ ▼ ▼ ▼ ▼ ▼ ▼ ▼

▼ ▼ ▼ Other Economies

Saving money results when you practice conservation of consumables. Propane expenses can be cut if:

▼ The water-heater thermostat is set low or just the pilot light is used to heat water.
▼ The RV is well insulated and has insulating window coverings so the furnace won't run as often.

▼ The furnace thermostat is set low at night and during the times the RV is unoccupied

▼ A catalytic heater is used instead of the furnace

▼ The refrigerator is run in the electric mode and cooking is done with a microwave oven or some other electric galley equipment.

Some campground fees for electricity can be avoided if you equip your unit with solar panels for battery charging and an inverter for running much of the 120-volt AC equipment in your RV. (See also pages 255–258.)

Figure 2.2
Normandy Farms Campground, located in Foxboro, Massachusetts, is one of over 1,500 Good Samparks located across the country. The property has been owned by the Daniels family since 1759.

Using solar panels and an inverter for electricity and water from the RV's tank will enable you to comfortably stay in campgrounds that have no hookups; such campgrounds usually have very low rates.

Arrange to have the water and holding tanks empty if you will be driving many miles. The less weight hauled around, the less fuel consumed.

We can estimate fairly accurately how long it will take us to use a cylinder of propane, so we usually put off filling the one empty one until necessary to avoid pulling the weight of two full cylinders.

It won't take more than a month or two of full-time living in your RV to learn how long you can expect a propane cylinder to last. You will also be able to quickly determine how long the water in the freshwater tank will last with normal use, and how many days can go by before the holding tanks need to be emptied. You will have to spend money for the propane eventually; however, at certain times you may not need to spend anything for water and sewer hookups or for a dumping fee if you have a basis on which to estimate how full the tanks are.

MEMBERSHIP CAMPGROUNDS: WORTH THE COST?

▼ ▼ ▼ ▼ ▼ ▼ ▼ ▼ ▼ ▼ ▼ ▼

When the membership campground association concept was in its heyday a few years back, many of these associations sprang up quickly and disappeared just as fast. Overbuilding and underfinancing were the main causes of many associations' failures. The more stable organizations often bought out the shaky ones, but even the stable companies were not immune to problems. Now just a few membership campground associations remain. They all operate in basically the same way. To join costs thousands of dollars. On the low side, the cost might be $5,000 but it can be as high as $10,000. This amount can be paid all at once or in periodic installments—with a finance charge added on, of course. In addition to the initial cost, members pay annual dues; a typical amount is $200.

For this money you have the opportunity to stay free at the campground where you joined—we'll call it the home campground—for a given amount of time each year. Depending on the individual campground or the association, this time period can range from as little as two weeks to much longer stays, all

Table 2.2
A Comparison of Campground Costs

Costs and Charges	Campground Stays to Equal Costs and Charges	
Membership $7,000 (Cost per year, amortized over 10 years)	$700	
Yearly dues	200	
Yearly base cost	$900 =	90 nights @ $10.00 a night
		−30 nights at home campground
		60 nights at affiliated campgrounds

subject to varying regulations and restrictions. You can stay at any other affiliated campground in the association for the same, or sometimes shorter, lengths of time. One association imposes a nominal cost of a dollar a night for such stays.

The associations have affiliated campgrounds all over the United States, which makes it seem as if joining might be worthwhile for a traveling fulltimer. A common problem, though, is that popular tourist areas are heavily saturated with these campgrounds — campgrounds in the same association might be just a few miles from one another — but in some states there may be just a few campgrounds, maybe even none, and they could be clustered in certain popular tourist areas rather than scattered throughout the state. If you can't count on staying at the campgrounds in your association a large percentage of the time as you travel, without having to drive many miles to do so, it will take you quite a few years to break even on your investment.

Table 2.2 shows an example of how a typical membership might work out. If you are considering joining a membership campground association, it may be of help in evaluating whether it will be worth it.

For simplicity's sake the following figures have been used in Table 2.2 (any or all of the figures given could be higher or lower): $7,000 as the initial membership cost, $200 for annual dues, $10 as a typical rate that might be paid for a night in a private campground that is not affiliated with a membership association, and thirty nights at the home campground.

Using the figures above, the membership cost amortized over ten years and combined with the annual dues bring the yearly base cost to $900. Using $10 as the average unaffiliated campground's rate, that means that you would have to stay ninety nights a year in a membership campground to get your money's worth. But if you stayed the thirty nights allowed at the home campground, you would have to spend only sixty nights of the ninety it takes to break even at other affiliated campgrounds. (If it cost you a dollar a night at these other affiliated campgrounds, $60 would have to be added to your yearly costs.)

For clarity we have made our example simple. We have not included finance charges, miscellaneous costs, or any assessments that might be made, so the picture is far from complete. What's more, expecting the annual dues to remain the same for ten years is unrealistic.

The campgrounds in membership associations are promoted as, to use the parlance of the salespeople, "destination resorts" — the sort of place at which one might spend an entire vacation. It is true that many of the campgrounds in each association have the amenities of a resort (but many do not) and are in desirable vacation areas (but many are not). If you prefer to regularly stay at a resort type of campground, which would cost more than the $10 used in Table 2.2 as the rate for an overnight stay in an unaffiliated campground, a membership in a campground association might be worth what it costs.

You might be able to buy a membership in a campground association at a bargain if it is offered for sale by an individual or through a broker. Such a membership can usually be purchased for 40 to 50 percent of its original cost or less. A transfer fee is always involved in a transaction of this sort and can be as much as 20 percent of the original owner's cost. (If you buy through a broker be sure you are dealing with a reputable one.)

▼ ▼ ▼

Aside from the costs, where you travel and where you want to spend time must be a prime consideration when deciding whether a campground membership will be worthwhile for you. Before signing on the dotted line, fulltimers will have to look at affiliated campground locations with a critical eye. Are they in places you would be likely to visit? Are there enough of them in the places where you intend to go? This is one of the reasons we don't belong to a membership campground association; we must go where our work takes us and, for the most part, that has been in areas where there is a dearth of membership campgrounds.

Be aware that we have not begun to cover all the ramifications of either buying or selling a campground membership. Various rules, regulations, and covenants will have to be abided by to use or sell your membership. If you default in any way you could lose your entire investment. The membership campground industry has been, and continues to be, rife with mergers, buy-outs, bankruptcies, and park closures. These factors can also adversely affect your investment.

Although many states strictly regulate the manner in which membership campground associations can operate, many others have no regulations at all. No matter in which state the membership is sold, buyers, for their own protection, must be able to read and throughly understand what they will have to sign. The saying "buyer beware" certainly applies to purchasing a campground membership.

LIVING WITHIN YOUR BUDGET
▼ ▼ ▼ ▼ ▼ ▼ ▼ ▼ ▼ ▼ ▼ ▼ ▼

As we have shown, some full-timing expenses will be the same, some will lessen, and some will increase. Figuring out the expenditures for those budget items remaining the same is no problem, but the expenses that will be less or more can only be determined by actually living for a few months as a fulltimer. Only then will you know if you are spending too much on items such as fuel or campground fees.

It is wise to be cautious in the the beginning if your funds are limited. For example, don't start off on a quick cross-country trip the first day you begin fulltiming unless you know you can afford it. Nothing is wrong with planning such a major trip across the United States, but do it in small sections at first to get the feel of where your money will be spent and how fast its outgo will be. If it is disappearing too quickly, slow down your traveling.

Where Will the Money Come from?

It requires money to be a fulltimer just as it does to live in any other way. You must either have an income of some sort, work as you go, or stop traveling for a while and work until you earn enough money to go again.

Many retirees can count on a monthly social security or pension check or income from investments. This is one of the reasons that retired persons, more than others, are fulltimers, as well as the reason that those who are not retired believe they cannot become fulltimers until they too have retired. This does not have to be the case. As we have shown, fulltiming can be much less expensive than a nonmobile lifestyle, so an early retirement with perhaps a little less money coming in might be considered.

If retirement is a long time away, as it was for us when we started fulltiming, it is conceivable that you could work for a few months and earn enough to tide you over to travel for several months. No matter what your age, it might be possible to earn a living by working as you travel.

WORK AWHILE, TRAVEL AWHILE
▼ ▼ ▼ ▼ ▼ ▼ ▼ ▼ ▼ ▼ ▼ ▼ ▼

Some occupations are ideal for those fulltimers who need to work for a time to earn traveling money: waiter, waitress, bartender, cook, construction worker, and many construction-related trades such as electrician, plumber, painter, mason, or carpenter. Many of these jobs can be seasonal or limited to a designated period of time, so they are inherently short term.

Nurses are in demand just about everywhere. It rarely matters whether they want to work for a few months or a year; most medical facilities are happy to have them for any length of time.

Fast-food restaurants offer job opportunities for those interested in short-term employment. No one expects employees of such establishments to stay on the job for very long unless they are interested in advancing to a management position.

Other work where a lengthy commitment is not required or expected is in general-maintenance jobs of any kind, such as lawn care, landscaping, janitorial jobs, or cleaning and readying new cars or RVs at a dealership.

If you don't do it excellently, don't do it at all. Because if it's not excellent, it won't be profitable or fun, and if you're not in business for fun or profit, what the hell are you doing there?

ROBERT TOWNSEND

▼ ▼ ▼ ▼ ▼ ▼ ▼ ▼ ▼ ▼ ▼ ▼

Working in orchards or on farms is another way to earn money seasonally. Once we were in Montana when the cherry growers had an exceptionally fruitful season. They needed more cherry pickers than they could find. Many had large signs next to the highway offering free RV space for anyone who would help them out. We were tempted to stop and pick up a few extra dollars, but right then the kitty was pretty full, so we just bought and ate the delicious fruit others had picked. Another year, in Virginia, we noticed strawberry pickers were in great demand. In some areas in certain seasons, huckleberries and some kinds of mushrooms can be gathered and sold to buyers who station themselves along the roadsides.

Before computers were common, someone once offered Jan a job doing some typing, assuming, incorrectly, that Jan was a typist. She declined the offer, but if you have typing, word-processing, or other office skills, they can be marketed through agencies that specialize in temporary employment, or you can contract for work on an independent basis.

Seasonal work is always available from concessioners who operate restaurants, gift shops, lodging facilities, stables, marinas, and the like in the national parks. Privately owned resorts have need for the same type of personnel, as well as instructors for activities such as scuba diving, horseback riding, swimming, tennis, and golf. There might be a need for qualified people to teach cooking, photography, crafts, and exercise classes.

Campground hosts are needed in the summer or year-round in some national parks, as well as in parks under the jurisdiction of the United States Forest Service, the Corps of Engineeers, and the Bureau of Land Management.

The best source of campground employment information is the publication *Workamper News*. This bimonthly newsletter, which serves as a clearinghouse of information on campground and resort jobs, also runs a referral system, collecting résumés and job-preference data from its subscribers and making them available to employers upon request. The service is free to subscribers. For information, write:

Workamper News
HCR 34, Box 125
Heber Springs, Arkansas 72543

A central source of information on concessioners in the national parks is:

National Parks Trade Journal
P.O. Box 2221
Wawona Station
Yosemite National Park, California 95389
(209) 375-6552

The Good Sam Club, a division of TL Enterprises, Inc., works closely with federal agencies to fill host positions, and, subsequently, a considerable number of hosts in government campgrounds are Good Sam members. Information about hosting in federal areas can be found in issues of the club magazine *Highways*. Host positions are also available in some state parks.

When hosts have more duties than just greeting campers and selling firewood, they may be paid something for their work, but often a free campsite is the only compensation for their services. Depending on the campground, the host's site may have no hookups, or just electricity, but some can be quite luxurious, having all hookups and a paved pad.

A demand exists for hosts in all areas of the country. It's possible to work in the mountains, the desert, and the forests, and you can count on every Corps of Engineers' campground to be on a body of water.

We have met many full-timing couples who manage private campgrounds on a seasonal basis. Positions of this sort are often advertised in the classified section of *Trailer Life, MotorHome,* and *Highways* magazines.

Varieties of other jobs present themselves around RV parks. The office has to be looked after, the buildings and grounds need maintenance, and equipment requires servicing and repair. If you have talents in copywriting, graphic design, illustration, or photography, you might be able to produce ads, brochures, letterheads, or design logos for campgrounds.

WORK AS YOU GO
▼ ▼ ▼ ▼ ▼ ▼ ▼ ▼ ▼ ▼ ▼ ▼ ▼

Once people find out we are fulltimers, the first thing they usually ask is if we are retired. When we tell them we are not, they are either discreetly or openly curious about how we earn the money on which to live. We are often tempted to tell the truth and say we live by our wits, but we know this wouldn't be satisfying, so we try to give them a little insight on our vocation: free-lance writing and photography. To many people this seems like a good way to travel and earn a living. It is, in respect to the working conditions. You can set your own hours and choose the place in which you want to work. But very few fulltimers, or nonfulltimers for that matter, can make their living as free-lance photographers or writers.

Income from Writing and Photography

Let's examine the writing first: If you intend to write articles about RV-related subjects, there are just two major magazines that might buy them: *Trailer Life* or *MotorHome.* The only other markets for such articles might be the regional newspaper-type RV publications that are sold or given away free in RV-oriented areas of the country. The magazines pay the most for articles. The other publications pay considerably less, often so little that it is not worth a serious writer's time to do a piece for them.

Regardless of what is paid for an RV article, consider how many you would need to publish to sustain your lifestyle. One each month? Even if this would provide you with enough money to live on (it wouldn't), the chances of selling an article for each issue of a magazine are practically nil. You would have to be very lucky and be a very good writer, penning articles the magazine could use, to sell even a few articles a year to one magazine. Other writers are also submitting articles all the time, so you might have yours rejected, no matter how good it is, because the magazine already has something scheduled on the same subject.

Okay, you might say, what if I write articles on subjects other than RVing for other magazines? If we were asked the question we would answer, "Try it." But we would also let you know about the results of a survey that was taken about income received from writing: If all the free-lance writers' incomes were lumped together and an average taken, each writer's earnings would be well below the poverty level. The survey took into account the hundreds of thousands of dollars earned by many best-selling authors. So don't be disappointed if your writing earnings don't begin to pay your way.

Writing is easy. All you do is stare at a blank sheet of paper until drops of blood form on your forehead.

GENE FOWLER

▼ ▼ ▼ ▼ ▼ ▼ ▼ ▼ ▼ ▼ ▼ ▼ ▼

It is certainly possible to earn some money by writing even if writing is not your occupation. If you write well and know your subject thoroughly enough to write about it with authority, you may be able to sell occasional articles. Anyone who wants to sell articles should be familiar with *Writer's Digest* (available in most libraries). It contains listings of publications and particulars about the articles they need.

If you want to pursue photography as a means of making money, the picture is even more gloomy (no pun intended). Whether you plan to specialize in art photography, the sort of pictures that would be framed and hung on a wall, or purely commercial work, you will be hard put to realize any decent return on the considerable investment of equipment, materials, and time it takes to produce a professional product.

It isn't possible to do professional-quality work with one 35-millimeter camera and a lens or two. You will need a variety of cameras, lenses, many other expensive accessories, and you will need to buy and shoot film in quantity.

Not everybody trusts paintings but people believe photographs.

ANSEL ADAMS

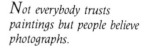

Installing a darkroom in an RV isn't easy, and even if it could be accomplished, it would not be practical for doing extensive

There is nothing worse than a brilliant image of a fuzzy concept.

ANSEL ADAMS

▼ ▼ ▼ ▼ ▼ ▼ ▼ ▼ ▼ ▼ ▼ ▼ ▼

professional work. You will need to have all your developing, processing, and printing done commercially. These costs will have to be figured into what you charge for your work.

If you have the equipment and the expertise for turning out top-quality photographs, where will you sell them? Articles accompanied by photographs usually are paid for at a somewhat higher rate than those without pictures. As we mentioned before, you might take advertising photos of a campground's facilities. Some RVers might like a picture of their rig. You could solicit work from businesses in the area where you are staying, but you will have stiff competition from established local photographers who need every job they can get to make a decent living. If your work is professional and the subject matter salable, you might be able to concentrate on doing work for a stock photo agency. To make any significant amount of money though, you would need to have thousands of photographs on file. No matter what you choose to do photographically, jobs are not plentiful, and the field is overcrowded.

In the position we are today — being fullltimers and being able to travel and earn enough to live on — is the result of years of work. We sell some articles, but the bulk of our income comes from royalties on books that sometimes take us years to compile. We derive additional earnings from photo sales that are made by us directly or through stock photo agencies with which we are affiliated. It took many years to build up the many thousands of photographs we, and the agencies, have on file.

▼ ▼ ▼

Although we enjoy our work, to keep producing material for future royalties and sales, we often work long hours and sometimes weeks go by before we have any days off. In order to count on bringing in enough to support our traveling lifestyle we must have a commitment to our projects and be willing to work as long as it takes in order to meet our deadlines. Other fulltimers who are self-employed and work at their businesses as they travel must be as committed as we are, although most of us think it is a fair trade-off for having the freedom to work when and where we please.

For our writing we use a computer. If much of what you do in your regular job is computer work, it can usually be done on any computer no matter where it is located. Many engineers, designers, word processors, and others do their work from a computer in their home. In the case of a fulltimer, the home would be an RV. Many recreational vehicles have space where a computer workstation can be installed (see Chapter 8, pages 192–194).

Every morning I take out my bankbook, stare at it, shudder—and turn quickly to my typewriter.

SYDNEY J. HARRIS

▼ ▼ ▼ Marketing Special Skills

Representatives for certain manufacturers' products often can work as they travel. If fulltimers want to do this, they usually think of representing an RV product, but the field does not have to be so limited; there are thousands of manufacturers that have nothing to do with the recreational vehicle business that need reps for their products.

As a rep you may not be able to travel when or where you want. Your traveling might be limited to a specific area of the country or a small territory. On the other hand, you might have to travel more than you would like. If you are repping an RV-related product, you may have to attend rallies and RV club get-togethers as well as visit RV-supply stores. This might mean you would be required to travel many miles on a tight schedule.

A friend of ours is a sales representative for a company that manufactures fishing rods and other anglers' equipment. This ties in nicely with his full-timing lifestyle and one of his favorite hobbies, which just happens to be fishing.

Another man works in an unusual way as he travels. We met Lowell several years ago in Florida. Then in his mid-thirties, he was fulltiming with his wife and two children and also supporting his family by working as a blacksmith as they traveled. Lowell specializes in horseshoeing. You might think this is a little-called-for skill nowadays, but there is work at racetracks, horse farms, and rodeos all over the country yearlong, so Lowell can count on being paid often and well for his valuable service in just about any place he chooses to go.

Since he works out of the back of his pickup truck, he can set up his portable forge and anvil in minutes and be ready for work.

*The man who lets himself
be bored is even more
contemptible than the bore.*

SAMUEL BUTLER

▼ ▼ ▼ ▼ ▼ ▼ ▼ ▼ ▼ ▼ ▼ ▼

The tools, equipment, and supplies for his trade take up only about a third of the space in the truck's bed.

In a Virginia campground, we met another man who is also a fulltimer and whose entire income comes from his work with horses. Judd is a horse dentist, an occupation we didn't know existed. He has a big, luxurious Class A motorhome (horse dentists, like people dentists, can make a good deal of money from their work) and tows a compact station wagon, which easily carries his dental equipment. Sometimes he parks his motorhome in a conveniently located campground and travels to his patients or customers (we didn't ask what he calls the horses he services) in the wagon. Other times he may park the motorhome at the horse farms and racetracks where he works. The owners of some of the farms on his regular circuit have installed a paved pad and hookups just for his use.

Judd only works the East Coast from New York to Florida, but he, like Lowell, could find work anywhere he wanted.

Some time ago in Montana we met Dave, a retiree who was fulltiming and still working at his trade—welding. He carried a portable welder in his pickup-truck tow vehicle. He occasionally made some money from other RVers who needed welding done, but he specialized in repairing heavy equipment. Dave would travel to farms and ranches in the area where he happened to be to see if any welding was needed. There was always work for him, he explained, because it was usually inconvenient to take large machinery to a shop where the welding could be done.

If Dave was going to be in one area for a while, he would post notices about his service with implement dealers, in feed stores, and in any other places where they would be seen by likely customers. He had arranged with the owner of the campground at which he was staying to use the park's telephone number on his notices, and the owner had agreed to take the calls he received. Even though Dave didn't get a lot of calls, he was lucky; most campground owners would not be so accommodating.

Dave did not earn enough to live on from his itinerant work. Perhaps he could have if he had pursued it more aggressively, but it was not necessary because he had a retirement income.

For twenty years, Fred, a professional bicycle mechanic, has been a fulltimer. He, like Dave, takes his services to those who need them, spending much of his time in small towns that do not have a bicycle-repair shop. The converted bus in which he and his wife, Jenna, live, has ample room for the necessary tools of his trade.

We heard about Cyril and Agnes, an ingenious full-timing couple who run an upholstery business from their RV. Their large trailer was originally built for hauling dune buggies. They have transformed the front of the trailer into living quarters and converted the rear into their shop. They specialize in RV products such as tire covers, screens, and shades.

▼ ▼ ▼

Those who need a workshop in their traveling home might investigate the Play-Mor Sport-model trailers, or the Alfa Toyhouse. The Play-Mors are fifth-wheel trailers available in 29-, 34-, and 37-foot lengths. The rear of the trailer is an open area designed for carrying such bulky items as motorcycles or a boat, but could be easily be converted into a workshop. The cargo area ranges from 11 feet, 7 inches to 19 feet, 7 inches in length. The balance of the trailer is the living area and has the floor plan of most fifth-wheels and all the amenities, including standing headroom in the bedroom.

The Alfa Toyhouse is available in either conventional or fifth-wheel models, in lengths of 24, 28, and 32 feet; fifth-wheels also are available in 35- and 40-foot lengths. The Toyhouse comes with bath and galley. The remainder of the trailer can be customized with or without furnishings and built-ins as desired.

If you have a skill that allows you to use portable tools or equipment, maybe you can think of a way to put it to good use for earning money while fulltiming.

Some fulltimers think about financing all their traveling by selling items they have handcrafted. A few manage to do this but they are in the minority.

It doesn't matter how unique or well done the product is or what it sells for, earning enough to live on may be impossible because of two factors: the logistics of selling the product and the competition you will encounter. You will have to travel to established flea markets and craft fairs to obtain maximum

Work expands to fill the time available for its completion.

C. NORTHCOTE PARKINSON

exposure for your wares. Even if you travel long hours and many miles, you won't have the time to cover all of the big events. If you try to, proportionately more of the money earned will be spent on traveling expenses. The fabrication of the item also enters into the logistics. If you are rushing off to market after market, you won't have much time left over to make more of the product.

Competition in all craft areas is keen. If the items you offer for sale are not top quality, not many of them will be sold. Many highly skilled people are turning out fine work, and some of them probably will be participating in the same events as you.

If you have visited any flea markets and craft fairs, you are probably aware that not much being offered today is unique. Unless you can come up with something that is truly different, you probably will have to settle for a minuscule share of the market.

When you are making an item just for fun or relaxation, you don't care how long it takes to complete it. If you are crafting articles to sell, such as elaborate wood carvings or quilts that are quite time consuming, you will have to sell them for a comparatively high price if you expect to be compensated for the time spent making them. The more costly the item, the narrower the market.

The higher-priced items need to be offered for sale in a marketplace where buyers will be avilable for them. To avoid wasting time, you will have to become familiar with the best outlets for your product. Some flea markets seem to attract a lot of junk sellers, whereas others have a reputation for offering higher-quality merchandise.

If you can turn out a quantity of items in a short time, and they can be sold for less, the market is wider, and you won't have to exercise so much selectivity about where the item is sold.

If you are one of those who can make a substantial amount of money from your handiwork, it may affect your full-timing lifestyle. You may need a larger place to store your project materials or for the equipment to make them. You might be faced with buying a larger RV or renting space and remaining in one location to do the work (See Figure 3.1).

We know of one talented man whose income is derived entirely from what he handcrafts. Some years ago Steve was living in a large town on Chesapeake Bay, working as an advertising artist and making scrimshaw items as a hobby. His work was so good he began to get orders from friends for custom-made

Figure 3.1
Home to professional artist Jeanne Dunne is a 36-foot custom-built Apeco trailer. Jeanne's trailer has allowed her to travel the nationwide art show circuit comfortably and sell many of her paintings across the country.

All the really good ideas I ever had came to me while I was milking a cow.

GRANT WOOD

▼ ▼ ▼ ▼ ▼ ▼ ▼ ▼ ▼ ▼ ▼ ▼

items. He eventually exhibited his work at a craft fair and sold nearly everything he had.

As is the case with many hobbyists, Steve enjoyed the time spent with his hobby as much as any work he did. As an artist creating for his own pleasure, he was free to do the sort of things he wanted; it was much more satisfying than doing the work his advertising clients demanded.

At one time or another most hobbyists wonder if they could make a living from their hobbies. Steve was no different, but he knew he would need a broader market than an occasional craft fair or show to make enough money to live on. He made some samples and took them around to places on or near the water that he thought might be possible outlets: marine-supply stores, nautical gift shops, even the several maritime museums in the bay area. Steve received so many orders he knew he would have a problem filling them if he worked only in his spare time, so he took the considerable gamble, quit his job, and began working on the scrimshaw full time. Now he is able to live on what he earns from his former hobby.

Scrimshaw, a one-of-a-kind work of art painstakingly carved on ivory, or, nowadays, on a synthetic lookalike, can command a high price. Steve was able to find proper outlets for his work because at the time he went into business for himself he lived in an area where there was always a market for this old sailors' art.

Now that Steve has enough established customers, he supplies them by mail. He can practice his craft wherever he wants and is free to travel whenever he desires.

The items Steve makes are relatively small—earrings, belt buckles, and other jewelry items, so he does not need storage space for a large amount of raw material. The equipment used for fabricating the items is also compact. A craft such as this fits nicely into the full-timing life since everything can be stored conveniently in an RV and not much work space is needed.

Steve does his own marketing and keeps all the money he makes, but other artists might want to become affiliated with a gallery that will display and sell their work (for which the gallery receives a commission). Most galleries will accept only the work of a superb artist who has either a reputation in his or her field or whose work is obviously marketable.

At the outset, most fulltimers with a craft skill should look upon selling the results of their talent as a means of earning a little extra money rather than counting on it to be their main or sole source of income.

▼ ▼ ▼ Making Products for RVers

It is not necessary to sell all or any of your products at flea markets or craft fairs. Often a market exists — it may be a limited one — right in the campground where you are staying. Selling in this market could put a few extra dollars in your pocket.

Dotty is a talented artist who combines her artistic skills with her lifestyle. She does portraits of people and drawings or paintings of RVs, which she sells. Depending on what is wanted by her customers, she will create the work in pencil, pen and ink, or acrylics. Once she received a commission from a proud RV owner to execute his rig in needlepoint. Fortunately, this too is one of her skills.

Dotty knows she can never earn even a modest living from this sort of work, but she enjoys doing it. It supplements her income and she welcomes the extra money.

Mary Jo has talents of a different sort; she can make the best homemade doughnuts anyone ever dunked into a cup of coffee. Often, when she and her husband, Dick, pull into a campground, she goes around to all the RVs in the park and leaves a simple little flyer that says she will take orders for fresh, homemade doughnuts. On the flyer are the prices and simple instructions for ordering.

All orders must be in by 6:00 P.M. This way Mary Jo, a habitual early riser, knows how early she will have to get up to prepare the number of doughnuts ordered. When she has orders to fill, she sets about mixing the dough and preparing the doughnuts long before most others are up and about. The doughnuts are delivered fresh to each customer's RV door in plenty of time to enjoy them for breakfast. All the work is done in Mary Jo's galley, which is no different from the size and type found in many RVs; she has not needed to make any modifications to it.

▼ ▼ ▼

▼ ▼ ▼ ▼ ▼ ▼ ▼ ▼ ▼ ▼ ▼ ▼

When she and Dick are staying in one place for some time, Mary Jo will take orders for fancy special-occasion cakes. Dick has a modest retirement income that is supplemented by the money from Mary Jo's bakery.

If you are a fulltimer who happens to be a good cook, it shouldn't take much imagination to see how extra money could be earned by putting this talent to work. Skilled bakers could specialize in cookies, brownies, pies, or Danish pastries. What RVer wouldn't like a fresh-from-the-oven loaf of homemade bread? Either plain ol' white bread or a specialty loaf would be welcome if it were homemade. If baking isn't your forte, how about making jams, jellies, specially flavored vinegars or mustards, sauces, pickles, relishes, or seasoned salts or peppers? All of these could be made in limited quantity in the galley of practically any RV.

Sewing skills could be put to good use to earn extra money. A small sewing machine that can be tucked away in a cabinet can be used to turn out a great many money-making items. Garments can be made, altered, or repaired for other RVers. Perhaps you can invent something specifically for RV use, such as pocketed shoebags to fit on the inside of RV cabinets or wardrobe doors (regular shoebags are usually too wide). How about making some of those decorative, multicolored wind socks in a size suitable for flying from an RV? Or you can apply the better mousetrap theory and come up with some sort of practical, easy-to-use laundry bag; dirty laundry storage is the bane of many fulltimers.

▼ ▼ ▼

Being an RVer and a fulltimer, you know from your own experience what products need to be invented or improved. If you are creative, you might be able to come up with something that would cause other RVers to beat a path to your door.

If you can't think of anything to make, any RV accessory catalog should provide a wealth of ideas. We looked through one of our catalogs and found many things that could be made using an ordinary sewing machine: covers for air conditioners, propane cylinders, or spare tires; folding-chair storage bags; picnic-table covers; protective wheel covers; curtains and draperies; electric jack covers; and vent covers. Any of these items lend themselves to customization.

Money-making activities, such as cooking and sewing, should not be considered only "women's work." Men can sew and cook, too. Bill uses the sewing machine more than Jan in our household. She freely admits that he turns out the best work and has infinitely more patience for it. Jan thought she was pushing her luck one day when she said to Bill, "As long as you have the machine set up why don't you run up that pair of culottes I cut out?" Bill thought for a moment, then, figuring he could certainly do something that simple, proceeded to turn out a creditable garment that Jan wore for many years.

A carpenter could do cabinetry for RVers who want more storage space; certain cabinets in RVs can become better storage areas with the addition of a shelf or a partition. A carpenter can build other items that cannot be purchased ready-made, such as a bookcase just for paperbacks. In fact, a person skilled in carpentry could do major custom work on RV interiors. Our first full-timing trailer had no specific place suitable for storing such books, so Bill made a bookcase for our paperpacks that fit neatly against one end of the galley counter. He later built another that was attached to the vanity in the bedroom. We collaborated on building and installing storage bins in the bed of our pickup truck. Jan designed, and Bill built, a gun case that fit into a small, odd corner that couldn't have been put to practical use for much else.

Any carpenter would also have the tools needed to make boards used for leveling RVs. The board needs only to be cut to the desired length and have its ends beveled. Tapered, wooden wheel chocks could also be fabricated easily.

▼ ▼ ▼ Sharing Your Skills for Money

Any of your own special skills can be used to teach others. You could hold classes in a campground recreation hall or perhaps in or outside your own RV for a limited number of people. You might instruct others in sewing, knitting, crocheting, needle-

If you know somethin' well, you can always paint it [but] people would be better off buyin' chickens.

GRANDMA MOSES

▼ ▼ ▼ ▼ ▼ ▼ ▼ ▼ ▼ ▼ ▼ ▼ ▼

work, carpentry, photography, writing, painting, drawing, or jewelrymaking, for example. Classes might be given in fly-casting, golf, or tennis techniques, or in any other art at which you excel. If you have traveled to interesting places, you could give talks and slide shows about your travels. Include a question-and-answer-period afterward so RVers who wish to make the same trip can learn how to prepare for it and how to handle any special problems they may encounter. Talks such as this might also be given to civic clubs and fraternal organizations. If your background is in finance, you could hold seminars on money management or investing. Specific fees should be set up for classes. Admission could be charged or donations accepted for talks and seminars.

Don't hide your skills or your desire to work. It is important to let others know what you can and are willing to do. If you want a job, advertise the fact as much as possible. If you expect to earn any money, it will be up to you to make the first move toward that end.

▼ ▼ ▼

No matter what you do, be sure you are not violating any campground rules. It is common to find rules posted in campgrounds prohibiting the selling or displaying of merchandise as well as banning solicitation of any type by outsiders or tenants of the park. Many campgrounds have restrictions against the washing or repairing of vehicles. We were told of a couple who earns money by washing RVs. We don't know how they conduct their business, but it must be with the cooperation of the campground owner. Perhaps they have an arrangement whereby they are the only ones permitted to do this work in the park, in which case they may have to pay the owner a certain percentage of their earnings for the water they use. Be certain you know the rules and regulations of a campground before you conduct any kind of business in it.

If you are selling a product, don't be surprised if other fulltimers are not your best customers. Many fulltimers are living on an income where pennies have to be watched; they cannot afford to buy many of the things they would like to have. If the money is available, fulltimers cannot collect too many purely decorative items; there simply is not enough space in an RV home to keep them. Even utilitarian items must be purchased with an eye toward their storage.

We have a saying about earning extra money. It certainly applies to us and may hold true for you: The easier it is to see the bottom of the barrel, the more inventive and imaginative you will become in putting your skills to work to earn money.

A PLAN FOR EARLY FULLTIMING

You might be able to become a fulltimer and not have to worry about earning money, even if you are too young to receive social security or if you opt for an early retirement and do not have enough equity in a pension fund to provide you with an adequate income.

When employed and earning a salary or wages, each paycheck you receive has a considerable amount deducted from it for income tax and social-security payments. And there are a lot of expenses connected with working at any job: parking fees, lunches and other meals eaten out because you don't have the time to shop for food and cook, a business wardrobe, dry cleaning, special tools or equipment used in your work, and any transportation costs incurred as a direct result of having to travel to the place where you earn your money. For instance, a typical, new, six-cylinder, four-door sedan, driven 15,000 miles a year, costs 32.7 cents a mile, or $4,908 a year to operate. If the vehicle is being financed, the costs escalate to 37.9 cents a mile and $5,686 a year. Often-overlooked expenses related to working include payment for those who perform maintenance work on your house, yard, or vehicles that you might otherwise do yourself if you had time.

If you have a house, the insurance, utilities, maintenance, and property taxes will take another large chunk from your income—lots more if you are making mortgage payments.

In fact, the taxes and social-security deductions from your paycheck, job-related expenses, and house payments and expenses can amount to as much as an astounding 80 percent of your gross income. So what is left over could be a mere 20 percent. This percentage represents the amount of money available for all other living expenses: food, clothing, insurance other

The more the gypsy leaves your soul, the more the money stays in your pocket. Flexibility and independence cost money.

GAIL RUBEN BERENY

than house insurance, transportation, entertainment, and miscellaneous items in your budget. It is just about *all* you will need to live on if you don't have a job or a house.

▼ ▼ ▼ Steps to Determine Your Full-timing Income

By following these steps and using Exhibit 3.1 as a general guide, you can get an idea about whether this plan would work for you:

1. Enter your yearly gross income.
2. Total your income taxes and your social security (FICA) paid, mortgage or rent payments, all house-related expenses, and all job-related expenses.
3. Subtract the total deductions from your yearly gross income.
4. This is the amount of money available for all other living expenses once the taxes and house and job-related expenses have been eliminated.
5. Calculate your net worth by computing what you could reasonably expect to receive if you converted your assets into cash by selling your house, cars, furniture, and other items not needed if you were living in an RV home. (If you have contributed to an employee pension plan and can take a lump-sum payment when you leave your job, add this cash to your net worth.)
6. Calculate how much the converted cash from assets' liquidation would produce if it were invested in U.S. bank certificates of deposit (CDs).*
7. Calculate the income taxes that will have to be paid on this interest income, and subtract the tax amount from the amount in Step 6.
8. This figure is the amount you will have available for your full-timing lifestyle.

---

*U.S. bank CDs are used for this example because, being federally insured, there is no risk of losing your money and they pay a guaranteed rate of interest. Investing in money market funds, annuities, mutual funds, or stocks and bonds might provide more income, but more risk is involved and no return is guaranteed.

▼ ▼ ▼

▼ ▼ ▼ ▼ ▼ ▼ ▼ ▼ ▼ ▼ ▼ ▼ ▼ ▼

Exhibit 3.1
8 Steps In Approximating
Your Annual Full-timing Income

Yearly Gross Income   **1** _____

   Income Taxes   _____

   Social Security   _____

   Mortgage/Rent Payments   _____

   House-related Expenses   _____

   Job-related Expenses   _____

Total Deductions   **2** (_____)   **3** _____

Funds Remaining after Deducting Above Expenses   **4** _____

Net Worth from All Convertible Assets   **5** _____

Estimated Income from Converted Net Worth   **6** _____

Income Taxes on Above Income   **7** _____

Total Estimated Full-timing Income   **8** _____

If the figure in Step 8 is close to the amount of the funds remaining after deduction of certain expenses in Step 4, you could seriously consider quitting your job, becoming a fulltimer, and living on your investment income.

Should you not come up with enough to sustain you, perhaps you could still have a full-timing lifestyle if your income were supplemented with part-time work.

If you don't have an RV suitable for fulltiming, the purchase of one could, in some cases, alter the figures so the plan would not

Well, I reckon I got to light out for the territory ahead of the rest because Aunt Sally she's going to adopt me and civilize me and I can't stand it. I been there before.

MARK TWAIN
Huckleberry Finn

▾ ▾ ▾ ▾ ▾ ▾ ▾ ▾ ▾ ▾ ▾ ▾ ▾

be feasible. But the purchase of an RV for your home could lower or eliminate any capital gains taxes you might have to pay if you sell your house at a profit. (See Avoiding Capital Gains Taxes, page 111.)

It may seem as if the preceding plan is too simple; there must be a catch in it somewhere. Certainly the plan won't work for everyone; some don't earn enough, haven't saved or invested enough, or may not have assets they can convert into the amount of cash needed. Others may have a large debt load or family financial obligations. But the only catch for lots of people stems from their attitudes — believing that something so simple and straightforward couldn't possibly work and being unable to break away from ingrained conventions.

If you think the plan has possibilities for you, don't do anything hastily. Carefully consider all the ramifications. Then, if you have calculated carefully and thought it through realistically — get the input of an accountant or financial planner if you feel you need it — you will have an accurate picture of your situation. And you might be able to become a fulltimer sooner than you ever dreamed.

Chapter 4

Special Situations and What to Do About Them

Traveling fulltimers are ignored when local, state, and federal rules, regulations, and laws are enacted. These rules are made for the majority who live in one place or whose dwelling is permanently affixed to one spot. In some instances, it is a test of our ingenuity as fulltimers to figure out how to live within these governmental frameworks while adapting them to our way of life without violating the rules or breaking laws.

Many fulltimers who travel extensively sometimes experience inconveniences in what are routine situations for those living a nonmobile life. These inconveniences are easily overcome, though, and the fun and benefits of fulltiming far outweigh any paltry annoyances that might crop up.

Before we go any further, let us introduce you to the Good Sam Club in case you are not familiar with it. It is advantageous for any RVer to join, but especially so for fulltimers. In the previous chapter we have already mentioned *Highways,* the informative, monthly magazine sent to members. Throughout the book we will referring to the Good Sam Club and its benefits. It will be obvious how worthwhile a membership will be for fulltimers.

THE GOOD SAM CLUB

One of the things we like best is the 10 percent discount we receive at the many Good Sam-affiliated campgrounds.

For information about joining, call (800) 234-3450, or write: Good Sam Club, 3601 Calle Tecate, Camarillo, California 93012.

MAIL FORWARDING

▼ ▼ ▼ ▼ ▼ ▼ ▼ ▼ ▼ ▼ ▼ ▼ ▼

Prospective fulltimers often think that receiving mail regularly will be their biggest problem. Actually, it is one of the least troublesome areas.

Most of us need to receive certain types of mail—insurance-premium notices, vehicle-license renewals, bank statements, and the like—and want to receive other kinds of mail, such as letters from family and friends. The mail must have an address, but not one that constantly changes. Even in these days of lightning-fast computers, it still takes a while for any organization to process a change of address. Your social correspondents won't even try to keep up with many address changes, so, if you are to receive mail, you must have a place where it can be sent and someone who is dependable to forward it on a schedule that is mutually convenient. The better your mail service, the freer you can be.

▼ ▼ ▼ Using the Services of Friends and Relatives

Friends or relatives are suitable as mail forwarders only if they are likely to remain at one address for some time and if they are responsible, organized, and understanding.

Depending on the amount of mail you engender, the forwarder should be paid something for the service, even if only a token amount. This puts what might be a casual arrangement on a somewhat more businesslike basis and might encourage the forwarder to do his or her job with dispatch. Of course, you will also need to make some arrangement to pay for any extra needed postage for forwarding.

Sometimes fulltimers are lucky enough to be able to work out an arrangement whereby the forwarder also pays their bills. If so, be sure the forwarder, in addition to being responsible, is trustworthy. In our case, the forwarder is a relative who pays our bills from a joint checking account we have just for this purpose.

We keep her informed about what bills to expect. If we have any credit-card purchases, we send her a list of the charges at the end of each month so she can check it against the bill. To avoid having to compile this list all at once, which can take hours if we have a lot of charges, we enter each charge, on the day we make it, on the list. We also telephone her on a regular, prearranged schedule so she can give us any telephone messages we may have received, to give her a forwarding address, or to discuss anything we may need to act on quickly without waiting for the mail to arrive.

When the mail is forwarded, it is marked so we know how many pieces to expect, such as: *1 of 4*. Then, if we don't receive them all, and we are leaving the area and can't wait for the delayed mail, we give the post office a change-of-address card (Form PS 3575) so it can be sent to our next stop.

▼ ▼ ▼

We often use overnight mail services from one major city to another (delivery to small towns takes two days). We like the U.S. Postal Service's Express Mail because the cost of insurance, up to $500 for merchandise, is included in the rate. The post office is very fussy about this type of mail and seeing that it arrives on schedule; the postage is refunded if it doesn't. Best of all, from our point of view, is that if there is someone at the post office, Express Mail can be picked up after hours and on weekends. We usually have a fair amount of accumulated mail sent to us whenever we use the express service. We are willing to pay the extra cost for the rapid delivery. In some cases, it almost pays for itself. If we happen to be stuck in a campground with a high rate, we spend less out of pocket by paying for the express postage than by paying for extra days in the campground waiting for mail.

I believe in opening mail once a month, whether it needs it or not.

BOB CONSIDINE

▼ ▼ ▼ ▼ ▼ ▼ ▼ ▼ ▼ ▼ ▼

Packages can be sent by Priority Mail, which is actually first class, at a cost less than that of Express Mail. Priority Mail is supposed to be delivered in two days, and we have found that Priority Mail packages usually arrive on time. Again, it takes longer when sent to smaller towns.

A first-class letter can be sent by Priority Mail at about one third the cost of the basic Express Mail rate.

▼ ▼ ▼ United Parcel Service

When we order something from a company that will ship only by United Parcel Service (we avoid this as much as possible), we use our regular mailing address, which happens to be a street address. UPS will not deliver to a post office box or General Delivery, and the post office will not accept anything from UPS because it is not mail. The package then is either mailed to us or held until we have an address acceptable for UPS delivery. Either way, we have to pay additional shipping charges.

▼ ▼ ▼ Mail-Forwarding Services

If you don't have a friend or relative you can depend on, using an established mail-forwarding service is probably the safest, most reliable, method of handling your mail. Several of these mail forwarders are always listed in *Trailer Life* and *MotorHome* magazines' classified ads under the "Services" heading.

These services all operate in basically the same way: They receive your mail and hold it until you notify them of the address to which you want it sent. This can be done by mail (some services provide a form for this purpose) or by telephone. More and more of these organizations are providing a toll-free telephone number for their customers' use. Some offer twenty-four-hour service.

Mail forwarders repackage the mail in their own envelopes and forward it. A flat fee, plus postage is charged. Some require a postage deposit.

If you provide the forwarding service with a copy of your itinerary, most will forward mail accordingly. Some mail forwarders offer a telephone-message service for a separate fee.

Privately owned mail and shipping services, located in many towns and cities, have mail boxes for rent and do limited mail forwarding for box renters. Such a service might fit the needs of certain fulltimers. Often these places also offer fax service, which we have used on occasion when we have needed to receive or send something immediately.

Members of the Good Sam Club can use its mail-forwarding service, but it is not as broad in scope as some of the other services. Most mail-forwarding services will send on anything they are told to forward, from packages to junk mail, but the Good Sam service will forward only first-and second-class mail. Members may also enroll in the separate Good Samantha Message Service. Those wishing to reach you call a special number to leave a message, and periodically you call the service to receive your messages. A basic fee is charged for the service, along with a per-minute rate.

▼▼▼ General Delivery and RV Parks

Our forwarded mail is addressed to:

Bill and Jan Moeller
c/o General Delivery
City, State, Zip Code.

When selecting a mail drop, we try to pick a small town with only one post office so we won't have to figure out which branch will be the most convenient for us. In many cities, though, General Delivery is sent only to one post office, no matter to which branch it is addressed.

Sometimes we send a postcard to the postmaster to let him know we are expecting mail. Doing this is not necessary, but when we notify the post office in advance we seem to receive more personalized service. The postal employees usually attach our card above the General Delivery mail slot, and they invariably recognize our name when we come in for our mail. We also have an index card with our names printed on it in large, legible letters. When we go in to pick up mail we show the card to the clerk so there won't be any misunderstanding about the spelling of our name. We started this practice after a clerk understood our name to be Moore and told us there was no mail for us; there *was* mail for Moeller, however.

General Delivery mail will be held for ten days after its arrival. If you will be delayed longer than this, or have a change in plans and won't be going to the post office where your mail has been sent, you can send a change-of-address form requesting the mail be sent to another post office. We keep a supply of these on

Letters are expectation packaged in an envelope.

SHANA ALEXANDER

Local radio stations dissolve in static every five miles; insects detonate against the windshield. He stops and has his oil checked. The American is in his seasonal migration.

TIME MAGAZINE

▼ ▼ ▼ ▼ ▼ ▼ ▼ ▼ ▼ ▼ ▼ ▼

hand; we obtain them at the post office. Depending on the post office branch, a phoned request asking them to hold your mail for a day or two longer than the limit also might work. If postal employees go strictly by the book, regulations forbid them to tell you, if you telephone, whether you have any mail waiting in General Delivery. Not all employees adhere to this, however, and some will tell you, especially if you are dealing with a small post office. Information about the arrival of Express Mail is always available by phoning. If your expected mail hasn't arrived, most postal clerks will inform you of the next Express Mail delivery time — there are often several deliveries a day — and suggest you call back then.

▼ ▼ ▼

The most inconvenience we have experienced from the with-holding-of-information regulation was when we were in a campground in the boondocks twenty miles from the nearest post office. Even after we explained by phone that we would have to drive forty miles round trip just to find out if our mail had arrived, the employee still would not tell us if it was there. Fortunately, our mail had arrived by the time we got to the post office, so the trip was not wasted.

If postal employees follow the rules, they must ask for identi-fication before releasing General Delivery mail. This is a postal regulation we thoroughly approve of. But only a few times have we ever had to produce any identification. It seems as though some employees pick and choose the regulations they want to enforce.

Most postal employees are generally quite helpful and under-standing and will give you the information you need over the telephone. Most of them will also hold your mail beyond the prescribed limit if you have taken the trouble to let them know your situation.

We never have mail forwarded to the main post office in a large city. We believe mail has more of a chance of being mis-placed or lost in a high-volume post office, there are longer lines and fewer places to park, and it is not convenient because the heart of town, where most main post offices are, is not anywhere near the location of most RV parks. We have always been able to find a post office in a small town or a substation in larger cities where we can have our mail sent.

We prefer to receive our mail at a post office unless we can have it sent to an RV park where we know the manager and the manager knows us. Even then, if the mail is routinely placed where other tenants have access to it, rather than being distributed by the manager, we will not have it sent there.

SUBSCRIPTIONS

▼ ▼ ▼ ▼ ▼ ▼ ▼ ▼ ▼ ▼ ▼ ▼ ▼

When traveling full time, it will be simpler and less expensive if you cancel subscriptions to any periodicals that are readily available on newsstands in the areas where you will be traveling. You will not have to worry about receiving issues, and you will not have to pay for forwarding postage, which will always cost more for any class of mail than the newsstand price. We have never missed an issue of any of the periodicals we read regularly, although occasionally we have had to go to some lengths to find them when we have been in places off the beaten path. Some full-timing Good Sam members, though, might want to take advantage of the club's Snowbird Service. Subscribers to *Trailer Life* and *MotorHome* magazines can have their copies sent to one address during the summer months and another address during the winter.

**FULLTIMERS
AND TELEPHONES**

▼ ▼ ▼ ▼ ▼ ▼ ▼ ▼ ▼ ▼ ▼ ▼ ▼

As a fulltimer you probably won't have a telephone in your rig unless you are parked for a considerable length of time in one place, and maybe not even then, so you will be forced to use pay phones for all your calls, many of which will probably be long-distance calls to friends and family.

It used to be that this was pretty straightforward when it was done by charging the call using a telephone credit card: you dialed your number, were connected with your party, and later were billed a reasonable amount for the call. Not anymore. Making a long-distance call from a pay phone these days is fraught with pitfalls for the unwary.

Since the breakup of AT&T, many other telephone companies have gotten into the business. After AT&T, MCI and Sprint are the largest and best known. But numerous other small companies, called alternate operator services (AOS), have proliferated. These AOS companies market their services to private businesses—campgrounds or convenience stores, to cite a couple of examples—which then receive a percentage of the charge for each call made through the AOS. If you use such a phone you will most certainly be charged a high rate for any long-distance calls, and you may be charged for all calls made, whether answered or not. One fulltimer, using a campground phone, had to make four calls to the same number before reaching his party on the fifth try. When he received his bill, he found he had been charged almost five dollars for the four uncompleted calls and much more than he expected for the fifth.

To avoid such charges you will have to be selective about the pay phones from which you make calls. The calling information card on the phone will often, but not always, indicate which long-distance carrier services the phone. Most fulltimers who regularly make long-distance calls have a telephone credit or calling card issued by either AT&T, MCI, or Sprint. If your carrier's name is on the phone's information card, you can make your call in the usual way. If it is some other carrier, you will have to do some extra dialing to reach the carrier desired: 10-288-0 will access the AT&T system. For MCI access, dial (800) 444-4444 and, for Sprint, (800) 877-8000.

▼ ▼ ▼

To place a call using MCI or Sprint, dial the 800 number, wait for a tone, and dial the number you are calling; after another tone, dial your calling-card number. For AT&T calls, dial the access number and immediately follow it with the number you are calling; there is no tone between these two numbers. After the access and calling numbers are dialed, there will be a tone. After this tone, dial your credit-card number. In some instances, when trying to access AT&T, after you have dialed the first digits of the number you are calling, you will be interrupted by a recording that tells you that your call cannot be completed as dialed, or that the number you have dialed is not a working number. When this happens, dial only the access code; this should connect you with the AT&T operator who will then handle the call for you—at operator-assisted rates instead of the cheaper direct-dial rates, but still much lower than AOS rates.

There may be times when you cannot access AT&T. Sometimes, after you have dialed the first few digits of the access code, you will be informed that the number you are dialing is not a recognized number. If this happens, dial O and ask the operator how you can access AT&T; chances are, on a phone like this, you will be told you cannot (once we were told we could be connected with AT&T if we deposited fifty cents).

When this call blocking happens to us, we go to another phone, which might be next door, in the same block, or some distance away, but, as a matter of principle and to be easy on our pocketbook, we refuse to use a phone on which we cannot access the carrier we want.

Eventually call blocking will be against the law. Legislation about the practice is on the agenda in Congress, but it could be years before any action is taken.

If you do not have a calling card and must use coins for your long-distance calls, you will have to pay the rate set by the long-distance carrier that services the phone you are using or locate another phone. This might be worth the time and effort, especially if the information card states that no coins will be returned. If you use such a phone and get a busy signal after dialing your number, you won't get a second chance unless you deposit the same amount of money again.

I've suffered from all of the hang-ups known,
And none is as bad as the telephone.

RICHARD ARMOUR

▼ ▼ ▼

Cellular phones? On the surface, it seems as though having a handy phone in your rig would be the perfect way for fulltimers to call from wherever they happen to be. That's the catch—wherever they happen to be may not be an area, a cell, served by a cellular phone system, since, at present, the services are concentrated in urban areas. In some of the scenic areas of the Rocky Mountains, for example, where many fulltimers like to go, a cellular phone would be unusable. Even so, with its limited-use areas and relatively high cost for calls, some fulltimers have their rig equipped with a cellular phone.

With improvements in technology, with more areas being covered, and with call charges and equipment costs coming down, it is inevitable that eventually a cellular phone will become a practical piece of basic equipment for those fulltimers who want it. We have mixed emotions about having a cellular phone. On the one hand, it would be a great convenience at certain times; on the other hand, we have come to enjoy not having a phone. We don't know—like Scarlett O'Hara, we'll think about it tomorrow.

▼ ▼ ▼

E.T., *phone home.*

MELINDA MATTHISON

▼ ▼ ▼ ▼ ▼ ▼ ▼ ▼ ▼ ▼ ▼ ▼ ▼

Before becoming fulltimers, many are accustomed to having two or more people participate in a phone call by using extension phones. After becoming fulltimers, some may find it frustrating that only one person can be in on the conversation when using a pay phone. There is a solution for half the problem at least: a device called a "telephone listener," which is nothing more than a suction cup on a wire connected to a slightly larger than palm-sized battery-powered amplifier. To use it, the suction cup is placed on the back of the receiver on the earpiece end, the wire is connected by inserting the plug, and the amplifier is switched on. Another person besides the one on the phone can then hear the conversation. The device has an adjustable volume control and uses a nine-volt battery. It can be obtained at Radio Shack for about $10.

The listening device works well. We discovered it by chance as we waited one day to use a pay phone in a campground. Although we were some distance away, we were surprised to hear every word of the conversation from where we were — the couple at the phone were making arrangements to meet a friend for dinner. As soon as the caller hung up we inquired about the device and next day we bought one.

We keep the listening device and a spare battery in a drawstring camera-lens bag and store it in our tow vehicle instead of our trailer. If we use a campground phone, we take it from the truck, parked adjacent to the trailer. When we must drive to a phone or use the truck without the trailer in tow, it is always with us; we don't have to remember to take it from the trailer.

When traveling, operating capital is available from several sources. The choice is personal, and perhaps several of them might be used over a period of time.

OPERATING CAPITAL

▼ ▼ ▼ ▼ ▼ ▼ ▼ ▼ ▼ ▼ ▼ ▼

▼ ▼ ▼ **Credit Cards**

Before we became fulltimers, we had the usual plethora of credit cards. We soon found our full-timing life was made simpler by eliminating many of them. Our advice is, keep only those credit cards you know you will use and that can be used all over the country. A charge card from a local department store will not be useful and, until you close the account, you will receive monthly or more frequent mailings about sales and specials whether you have charged anything or not.

Many nationwide chain stores that issue their own credit cards, such as J.C. Penney and Montgomery Ward, will also accept Visa and MasterCard (sometimes others, as well), so you do not need separate cards from such stores. Sears Roebuck, however, will accept only its own card or the Discover card.

Charging fuel with an oil company credit card means you will receive another bill or two each month. If you prefer to charge your gas or diesel purchases, you might consider patronizing the many service-station chains that allow you to use a card other than their own. If you want to save money, watch out for those stations that charge a few cents more per gallon when the purchase is paid for by credit card.

The idea is to consolidate and condense in order to reduce the amount of mail you will receive and, in the process, to simplify the paying of bills. We use our credit cards as little as possible because it makes less work for our "business manager." But if we took care of paying the bills ourselves, we would follow the same procedure. We also try to use just one card for any one month's charges. That way only one bill is received, which cuts down on paperwork and saves on check charges and postage. In addition, the less you charge, the less chance for errors. One frustrating experience in trying to explain a billing mistake to a computer is enough to make you want to tear up your credit cards and never use them again.

In a world where the time it takes to travel (supersonic) or to bake a potato (microwave) or to process a million calculations (microchip) shrinks inexorably, only three things have remained constant and unrushed: the nine months it takes to have a baby, the nine months it takes to untangle a credit card dispute and the nine months it takes to publish a hardcover book.

ANDREW TOBIAS

▼ ▼ ▼ ▼ ▼ ▼ ▼ ▼ ▼ ▼ ▼ ▼

▾ ▾ ▾

American Express and Carte Blanche memberships have rather high-priced annual dues. Only the user can decide if it is worth the cost to have the use of these cards. The annual fees charged by most Visa and MasterCard issuers are not nearly as high, and for fulltimers they are well worth the cost. The Discover card, issued by Sears Roebuck, has no annual fee and even pays you back a small amount each time you charge with it. Visa and MasterCard are accepted almost universally wherever credit cards can be used; the Discover card is more limited in acceptance. Having a couple of credit cards makes some aspects of fulltiming easier and more convenient.

A Visa card that is available to Good Sam Club members would also be good for fulltimers. Card holders can conveniently arrange to have each month's bill paid automatically from their bank account.

We have a MasterCard issued by AT&T (when you sign up, you can select either MasterCard or Visa), which can be used like any MasterCard but is also a telephone credit card. Having this card works well for us because the bill contains both the charges and an itemized list of all phone calls. We use this card whenever we make other than local calls. Before we had the AT&T card, our telephone credit card was issued for the number of our mail forwarder. Each month she had to go through the bill and separate her calls from ours. Now all our calls are on a separate bill. With the AT&T card, charge purchases can be paid in monthly installments, as can be done with all Visa, MasterCard, and Discover bills, but all telephone charges must be paid each month, just as any phone bill.

▾ ▾ ▾ Personal Checks

A problem encountered by nearly everyone who travels is how to pay for services and needed items without carrying too much cash. Solutions do exist, but using personal checks is not one of them.

Few businesses will accept checks that are not drawn on a local bank. You can pay by check for overnight stays in some RV parks and campgrounds, depending on the policy of the management and, often, the nearness of the bank where you have your account. Checks will almost always be accepted for a week's stay or longer because the check will have a chance to clear before you are due to leave. Most restaurants will not accept checks—even those from a local bank.

Supermarkets have varying policies; their rules are sometimes lenient for those with an account in a local bank but much more strict for others. Sometimes it's possible to write a check for groceries when caught short of cash, but we've always found some hesitancy on the part of supermarket managers when we requested this service. In the very few instances when we've done this, we were not able to write the check for more than the cost of the groceries.

▼ ▼ ▼

A personal check is worthless for obtaining cash because one written solely for that purpose can rarely be cashed in any place other than the bank where you have an account.

Even with all these restrictions you should maintain a checking account somewhere. A check is the most convenient way to pay bills by mail.

It might be worthwhile to have several checking accounts, each in a locality that you frequent regularly—or even occasionally. In the days when there were no service charges on checking accounts, we had accounts with six different banks in six different states. We kept just enough in each account to pay for expenses we might incur when in each bank's area, except for one—our major account in which we kept the largest amount of money to use for paying bills. If having more than one checking account would be useful to you, shop around for the banks that allow you to maintain the smallest balance for the lowest monthly service charge. Know the charges, if any, for all transactions. Some banks offer free or low-cost checking accounts to seniors. Don't overlook interest-paying accounts. If you will be banking by mail, request a supply of bank-by-mail envelopes. A few banks still provide envelopes with prepaid postage.

No matter where you open an account, your regular mailing address should be used. Your statements and other bank correspondence will be sent there, whether it is across town or across the country. Banks are usually happy to have new accounts.

Canceled checks . . . will be to future historians and cultural anthropologists what the Dead Sea Scrolls and hieroglyphics are to us.

BRENT STAPLES

▼ ▼ ▼ ▼ ▼ ▼ ▼ ▼ ▼ ▼ ▼ ▼

If the bank's policy allows, we don't have an address imprinted on our checks; we use only our names and social security numbers. Then, if we present a check to a local business, it won't have an address on it from another state and perhaps raise questions about its acceptance.

Once you get into fulltiming, you may accumulate various pieces of perfectly legal identification that have different addresses on them. Our mailing address is located in a state hundreds of miles from the address on our drivers' licenses.

If you travel mainly in the western half of the country, a checking account at a First Interstate, Norwest, or Bank of America might be the one to have. These banks have numerous offices in western and midwestern states. Most banking transactions, except deposits which can only be made intrastate, can be done in any of these locations just as if it were your local branch, including writing a personal check for cash. The maximum amount the check can be written for depends on the type of account you have and the individual bank's rules.

Some fulltimers might want to take advantage of the direct-deposit feature offered by most banks. You may instruct the issuers of any checks that you regularly receive to send these checks directly to your bank where they will be deposited into your account.

*Travelling may be . . .
an experience we shall
always remember, or an
experience which, alas, we
shall never forget.*

J. GORDON

▼ ▼ ▼ ▼ ▼ ▼ ▼ ▼ ▼ ▼ ▼ ▼ ▼ ▼

▼ ▼ ▼ Automatic Teller Machines (ATMs)

One good reason for having a checking account is that it allows you to use your bank's automatic teller machine (ATM) or other ATMs with which your bank may be affiliated.

ATMs can be used for nearly all banking transactions, but the most important use, for us at least, is to obtain cash. If your bank belongs to one of the two nationwide ATM systems — Plus or Cirrus — you can obtain ready cash (up to $200 in any twenty-four-hour period, generally) anytime (ATMs are "open" twenty-four hours a day) and nearly anywhere. At many banks both Plus and Cirrus cards can be used in their ATMs. Systems in use at an ATM are indicated by signs or labels on the ATM itself and often on the bank's street sign.

Your bank will issue you a card to use in its ATMs or other ATMs in the same system. Along with the card, you will be given a personal identification number (PIN) that must be used with the card for each transaction.

Before some people begin fulltiming and traveling, they may have never had a reason to use an ATM. The procedure is simple, and step-by-step instructions are displayed on the ATM's computer-like screen. You are allowed more than enough time to complete each step. The ATM even tells you what to do if you make a mistake or change your mind about your transaction. There may be a charge each time you use the machine for a withdrawal (which will be reflected on your monthly statement), but it is usually a small price to pay for the convenience.

Some banks provide a directory of all locations where its ATM card can be used or a toll-free number to call for the nearest location.

▼ ▼ ▼

Most Visa, MasterCard, and Discover cards can be used to obtain cash from ATMs. If Visa and MasterCard are used in this way, the amount received from the ATM, plus interest and maybe a service charge, will appear on the monthly bill. When using the Good Sam Visa or Discover card for cash from an ATM, however, there is no interest if the bill is paid within twenty-five days, and no service charge on the Good Sam Visa transaction unless the bank whose ATM you are using imposes a service charge. A small service charge is added to Discover-card cash advances.

American Express cards can be used for obtaining cash through ATMs in the Plus and certain other systems. A PIN number will be have to be requested for using the American Express green, gold, or platinum card in an ATM. In addition, a form must be signed that permits immediate withdrawal of the amount of money received from the ATM, plus a service charge, from your account in a designated bank; those holding a green, gold, or platinum American Express card will not be billed for ATM withdrawals. Holders of an Optima card issued by American Express, which is much like the Visa, MasterCard, and

Discover cards in that bills can be paid off in monthly installments if desired, will find ATM withdrawals included on their monthly statements along with interest and a service charge for such transactions.

▼▼▼ Credit-Card Cash Advances

An ATM isn't the only way to obtain cash by using Visa or MasterCard. During banking hours you can go to a teller and receive a cash advance for as much as your credit line allows, less any outstanding charges.

Upon issuance of most Visa and MasterCards to someone who has not been a cardholder before, the credit limit may be as low as $500. This means the combination of all charges and cash advances cannot exceed $500 during each monthly billing period. These days $500 doesn't go very far, so it will be in your best interest to have the credit limit raised. This is easily done by charging a few items for two or three successive months and paying the bills promptly. Having thus established that you are a responsible person who pays bills on time, you can request a greater line of credit; such a request is rarely refused.

Unless you are a credit cardoholic, unable to control what you charge, try to get the limit raised as high as you can. Then, should you need extra money for an emergency, it will be available. If you have both a Visa and MasterCard, you can charge or obtain cash up to the credit limit on each. If you are prompt about paying monthly bills, your credit limit may be automatically increased periodically.

Cash advances and charge purchases are billed each month. If the bill is paid on time, you will have no finance charge, but you will be charged interest on the cash advance because you have, in effect, borrowed money. The amount varies according to how much money is advanced.

Being able to avoid the steep finance charges of credit-card use is something you should consider when setting up your mail-handling system. If you are paying your own bills, you will

Life was a lot simpler when what we honored was father and mother rather than all major credit cards.

ROBERT ORBEN

▼ ▼ ▼ ▼ ▼ ▼ ▼ ▼ ▼ ▼ ▼ ▼ ▼

have to receive your mail regularly and in time enough to pay the bills before they become past due.

Incidentally, because of credit-card fraud, it is prudent to collect all carbons from the form used when you get a cash advance from a bank or when you charge anything with a credit card. Take the carbons home and, before disposing of them, obliterate them so your credit-card number, name, and signature are unreadable. This will insure that no one can use your name and number to charge items by telephone. Having a salesperson or bank teller merely tear the carbons in half and toss them into a wastebasket is not good enough. The waste passes through many hands between its point of origin and a landfill or incinerator.

There are other more complicated and less desirable ways to obtain cash when you are traveling. When we began fulltiming years ago, it was rather difficult to arrange to have cash when and where we needed it. ATMs did not exist and cash advances were not as common as they are today.

▾ ▾ ▾ Traveler's Checks

We started our fulltiming with a fat wallet full of traveler's checks but soon realized that even though this is one of the safest ways to carry cash, it does not work out well when you are constantly traveling. The problem is not so much the cost of the checks as how you can obtain more when your supply runs out. What should you do then? Try to purchase them from an issuing bank and pay for them with your personal check from an out-of-town bank? Usually it can't be done unless you want to wait for however long it takes for your check to clear. You could get a cash advance and convert the cash into traveler's checks, but this is really going the long way around because if you don't want to carry a large amount of cash you could get smaller advances more often.

The Good Sam Club provides members with free traveler's checks if the amount ordered is $1,000 or more; a small service charge is added for lesser amounts. They can be ordered by phone using a toll-free number and charged to your Visa or MasterCard. Orders should be called in by Thursday, since each Friday the traveler's check orders for that week are mailed by Priority Mail; they should arrive at their destination no later than Tuesday of the following week in most parts of the country. You would have to stay at a place until your traveler's checks arrived, or be sure you would be at an advance address when they were scheduled to arrive. On a continuing basis this might not be convenient.

Traveler's checks are supposed to be as good as cash, but many retail clerks do not recognize this. More than once, when we tried to pay for groceries or merchandise with a traveler's check, we had to go through the process of having it okayed by the manager just as if it were a personal check. We know of one RVer who wanted to purchase five dollars worth of stamps from the post office. The only money he had was a fifty-dollar traveler's check. The postal clerk told him they would not accept the traveler's check unless 50 percent of its value was spent for postal services or supplies. We confirmed this, and it's true.

In the beginning, we experimented with certified checks, postal money orders, registered mail, and Western Union as a means of receiving cash and found them all generally unsuitable for our purposes.

▼ ▼ ▼ Certified Checks

Certified checks presented the most problems, but we didn't know that until we tried to cash one. Since a certified check, or bank draft, is paid for before it is issued, we assumed it would be the easiest type of check to cash. We had a certified check sent to us by our mail forwarder. We told her to have it made out in both our names, thinking it would make it more difficult for anyone other than ourselves to cash if it were lost or stolen. With double identification, we also thought it would be easier to prove we were the legitimate payees. The banks we dealt with, however, didn't much care whether we could prove who we were. They were concerned only about the check being a forgery. We offered to pay for a call to the issuing bank, but that was not satisfactory. A forger, we were told by one bank officer, might have one good check with a verifiable number and make copies of the check, using the same number and making each for the same amount as the one good check. It would be verified as genuine every time until the original, or one of the forgeries, made its way back to the issuing bank. So much for that idea.

▼ ▼ ▼ Postal Money Orders

A postal money order is easily cashed at a post office, but it may be several days in arriving unless one of the fast mail services is used. If you pick up your mail at the post office, all you need do to cash it is open the envelope, endorse the money order, and present it to the postal clerk. The maximum amount for which a postal money order can be purchased is $700.

▼ ▼ ▼ Cash by Registered or Express Mail

Cash can be sent safely by registered mail. The fee is based on the valuation of the material being sent, and insurance is included in the fee. If the registered mail should be lost, reimbursement will be for whatever value was declared. Express Mail should not be used for sending cash since the maximum indemnity for any negotiable item is only fifteen dollars.

▼ ▼ ▼ Cash by Wire

Money can be obtained within hours, even minutes, when it is sent through Western Union, but you pay dearly for the speed. It is sometimes difficult to locate a Western Union office; they aren't nearly as common as they once were, though in our travels, we have noticed that many of the private mail and shipping services are also Western Union offices.

Any of these cash-obtaining methods—certified checks, postal money orders, registered mail, and wired cash—require someone on the other end to send you the money.

▼ ▼ ▼ Money Market Funds

If you want your money to earn interest and still be readily available, you might consider one of two kinds of money market funds (not to be confused with mutual funds) instead of, or in addition to, an interest-paying checking account. One type requires a small amount for initially opening the account; $2,500 is a common figure. Smaller deposits thereafter can be for as little as $100. With most funds of this type, free checks are provided that can be used like any other personal check to pay for goods or services, but each check written can be for no less than $500, or in some funds, $250. This won't do you much good if you need ready cash, since it is highly unlikely that a bank other than your own would cash such a check. One way to get around this situation would be to write the check before the cash will be needed, deposit it in your checking account, and then use your ATM card for cash withdrawals.

The other type of money market fund requires an initial investment of, usually, $20,000, which puts it out of the reach of many. One of the better-known funds of this type is Merrill Lynch's Cash Management Account (CMA). Once the initial investment is made, it doesn't matter to what level the subsequent balance falls. The folks at Merrill Lynch hope you will use some of that money to puchase stocks and bonds through their firm, paying them the usual commissions, but you are not required to do so.

Free checks and a Visa card are issued to holders of a CMA. The card can be used just like any other Visa card for cash advances and to charge purchases. The CMA Visa card, however, like the cards issued by similar-type funds, is not a credit card; it is a debit card. It has no credit limit other than what you have in your account. You will never be charged for a cash advance from a teller (unless the bank itself charges a fee for handling such transactions), since you are not borrowing money, you are withdrawing it from your account. If you wish, you can withdraw as much as you have in the account, all at once, at any time, allowing for any charges you may have made but which have not yet been debited. Of course, you never receive a bill to pay. Instead, a detailed statement showing each transaction is sent to you monthly.

Unlike the first type of money market fund, CMA checks can be written for any amount. It is just like a regular bank checking account in this respect. These checks also have the same disadvantages as bank checks for the fulltimer: They are personal checks written on an out-of-town "bank."

Money-market funds usually pay a higher rate of interest than bank savings accounts and some certificates of deposit. Bank funds are usually insured against loss, up to a certain amount, by the Federal Deposit Insurance Corporation (FDIC) or the Federal Deposit Savings and Loan Insurance Corporation (FDSLIC). Funds with brokerage houses may not be insured.

▼▼▼ Dealing with Banks – and Bankers

When dealing with banks, we never volunteer any more information about ourselves or our lifestyle than we have to. As a rule, bankers simply do not understand fulltiming and its ramifications.

We learned this the hard way. When nationwide ATM service first became available, we wanted to open a checking account in a bank affiliated with one of the nationwide systems. We located a bank in the area in which we happened to be at the time. We sat down across the desk from the friendly, polite, and efficient new-account person and chatted freely with her, explaining why it would be convenient for us to have an account with the bank. She seemed to understand and agreed that it was a good idea. After all the paperwork was completed, she took it to be okayed by an officer. She shortly returned to her desk in the company of a woman who didn't look friendly at all. Unsmiling, she asked why we wanted to open an account. We retold our story, the upshot of which was that the bank officer would not allow us to open an account. When we asked why she refused us, she could not give any specific reason. She hedged, using phrases that implied we were trying to pull a fast one or some sort of scam. She was unnecessarily insulting. The person who had tried to open the account for us was obviously embarrassed by her superior's actions and apologized profusely after "Old Grumpy" had left.

Except for the con men borrowing money they shouldn't get and the widows who have to visit with the handsome young men in the trust department, no sane person ever enjoyed visiting a bank.

MARTIN MAYER

▼ ▼ ▼ ▼ ▼ ▼ ▼ ▼ ▼ ▼ ▼ ▼

We didn't give up in our quest, but we changed our tactics. Within an hour we had an account with a different bank and an application in the works for an ATM card. While opening the account, we were friendly and answered all the questions we were asked, but we did not elaborate on our full-timing lifestyle.

Since being totally honest and aboveboard can work against you, especially when dealing with banks, fulltimers might temper what they reveal to them and other strangers with whom they have to conduct business.

It never hurts, and it might help, to dress in clothes that give you a businesslike appearance when dealing with banks for other than ordinary teller transactions. Try to project a solid-citizen look (which shouldn't be difficult for most fulltimers), and bankers will be more comfortable dealing with you—even if they do find out about your lifestyle.

If your identification doesn't all match, here's another tip: When getting a cash advance from a teller, you are usually asked to present some identification other than the credit card. We use our drivers' licenses but, as we mentioned, they have a different address than our mailing address—the one that should be entered on the Visa or MasterCard form. The instant the questioning eyebrows are raised, we volunteer the information that the address for the credit-card account is a business address that is different than our home address. This plausible, but not completely true, explanation seems to satisfy most suspicious tellers.

To give bankers their rightful due, we must admit that they, as a group, are not as hard-nosed, unbending, and inflexible as they were in the past.

More information about money matters can be found in *The RVer's Money Book* by Bob Howells, from Trailer Life Books, 3601 Calle Tecate, Camarillo, California 93012.

VEHICLE REGISTRATION AND LICENSES

▼ ▼ ▼ ▼ ▼ ▼ ▼ ▼ ▼ ▼ ▼ ▼ ▼

Vehicle licensing is a thorny situation. Each state has its own regulations for the procedure, many of which seem designed to foil the traveling fulltimer. Almost half the states require an annual inspection of vehicles, and about one-quarter of the states require a vehicle be equipped with a state-approved smog device. Before a vehicle can be registered, some states demand a special proof-of-insurance form, filled out by the insurance company, not you, before plates will be issued. Others need proof that certain local taxes have been paid. Various states probably have many other legal idiosyncracies we have not yet had the displeasure of finding out about. (See *Selecting an RV Home Base: State Tax and Registration Information* for complete registration, inspection, and insurance data.)

Each state's laws are precise about when you must purchase license plates. For example, they may be required if you are employed in the state or after you have resided in the state for a certain period of time, but these laws ignore people like traveling fulltimers who don't really reside in any one state. Some don't even want your money unless you are a bona fide resident of the state.

Since we have been fulltiming, we have had vehicles licensed in several states. If the initial registration turns out to be easy, the renewals rarely are. At one time, when we were still in the West after spending the better part of the year there, the registrations on our truck and trailer from an East Coast state were close to expiring. We had long since abandoned any East Coast mailing address, so there was no way we could have renewed the registrations by mail. We could not get by for long driving with expired plates. Even if we were not stopped for out-of-date license plates, we would have had some awkward explaining to do if we had been involved in an accident.

We did what we had done before. We found an RV park in the community where we wanted to license our truck and trailer and checked in for a month. We then went to the motor-vehicle office and applied for registration using the park's address as our address, which it was at the time. The plates were issued on the spot, but we were given temporary registrations. The permanent documents were to be sent to us from the main office in the state capital. Explaining that we were leaving on an extended trip and probably would not be at "our address" when the documents arrived, we asked if they could be sent to another address out of state. This was possible, so we had the registrations sent to the address from which all our mail is forwarded. They arrived in due time and we were officially, but perhaps not quite legally, licensed.

One of the problems with this procedure is that someone along the line may not follow your instructions about where to send the documents. A lot of follow-up writing or telephoning might have to be done while the time runs out on the temporary registration, which is good for only a limited number of days.

To cover your bases, you could leave a self-addressed, stamped envelope with the manager of the RV park you used for your address, trusting he or she would forward it in the event it was mistakenly sent there, and hoping he or she won't think you are up to something shady. Or you could stay put until the license did arrive, hoping the delay wouldn't be long enough to interfere with your traveling plans.

We recommend using a self-addressed, stamped envelope whenever you expect to have someone send along anything in an envelope that comes from a motor-vehicle division. Most such envelopes are imprinted with the words DO NOT FORWARD.

Be aware that many states will not send anything dealing with registrations or drivers' licenses to a post office box; a street address is required. Or, in some states, documents will be sent to a post office box only if it can be verified that you also have a street address. A street address is required when you rent a box from the post office; it may not be a requirement when renting a box from a private mail service.

If you use a mail-forwarding service you can use the address of the service for your registration address as long as the service is in the same state as the vehicle registration. Probably no service will handle just your vehicle registrations for you. Check to see if there are any problems that might arise if your vehicle registrations are handled by the service.

▼ ▼ ▼

Each time we relicensed our vehicles we were not financing them, so we had the titles in our possession. Most states will not register vehicles unless the original title can be produced; a copy will not do. Imagine the complications if you have to make this request of the lending institution holding your papers. Lenders don't approve of financed vehicles being permanently removed from their state (see also page 151).

Even if we could have successfully renewed our East Coast registration by mail we might have had another problem: If we had crossed that state's borders with our valid, renewed license plates and current registration, we might have been cited for having an outdated inspection sticker; an annual inspection is necessary in that state. We cannot register our vehicles in the state of our mail-forwarding address because that state requires an annual inspection, and we are rarely ever physically there.

▼ ▼ ▼

Another aspect of the licensing process may create a problem. Every state will allow registration renewal by mail. The renewal form is mailed, you fill it out, enclose the required payment, and return it. After it is received and processed by the motor-vehicle department, the renewal license-plate stickers (or new plates) and registration are sent to you. Some states mail the renewal forms uncomfortably close to the registration's expiration date. Fortunately, the majority of states allow at least a month for renewals, but our former state allowed only ten days for all this mailing back and forth.

Another complication presented itself when we found our truck registration would expire in a different month than our trailer registration, even though both had initially been regis-tered at the same time.

It may not be possible to have all registrations with the same expiration date unless all vehicles are purchased and registered at the same time, or all are reregistered in a new state at the same time. Those who fulltime in a motorhome and tow an auxiliary vehicle may have to contend with differing registration dates. In the last few years, our truck and trailer registration dates fell in the same month until we got them out of whack by buying a new trailer four months before the truck registration was due to be renewed. Now we must contend with two separate registrations each year. This is enough of a nuisance that when we buy a new truck, it will be purchased in the same month as our trailer.

Registration by mail presents no problem for the nonmobile person who receives mail at a home address. Traveling people will need to have the forms forwarded to them; no one else can take care of this for you because the forms will have to be signed by the owner of the vehicle. Then, later, the new stickers and registration will also have to be forwarded. Depending on your state's policy about how soon the forms are mailed out, you may have to remain in one place until you have the proper documents in hand.

This vexation must be faced annually unless you are able to license your vehicles in Oregon — the only state where plates and registrations are valid for two years on both passenger vehicles and recreation vehicles. The residency requirements for vehicle registration in Oregon are very strict, and it is rumored that the two-year registration may be changed to annual registration.

Vehicles can be preregistered before "entry" (our quotation marks) in many states, but some states require the vehicle to be in the state before it can be registered.

▼ ▼ ▼ Drivers' Licenses

For fulltimers, the matter of their drivers' licenses must be considered. There is nothing illegal about driving a vehicle with plates from one state while holding a driver's license from another; those who rent cars do it all the time. As far as we can determine, there is also nothing illegal about driving your own vehicle with the registration in your name but an address different from that of your driver's license. This circumstance could happen to nonfulltimers if a business vehicle were registered in the name of the business' owner and carried the business' address while the driver's license of the owner had his or her home address. It could, however, raise some questionable issues if you were ever stopped by the police. You may or may not be able to explain the situation satisfactorily.

When we registered our vehicles in a western state, we also got new drivers' licenses even though our East Coast licenses were good for two more years. (Other complications could have arisen because we each happened to have a license from a different East Coast state.) We figured the fees involved were a small price to pay to keep the situation as close to the norm as possible.

The norm, however, can be elusive for the fulltimer. Consider how the following might apply to you, as it once did to us: We had drivers' licenses that carried the same address as our vehicle registration: the address of the RV park where we were staying at the time we acquired them. We only stayed at the park for a month and never returned during that year, so we could not be reached at that address. Even though we were still in the state, we could not change our address to our current one because it was always changing; we moved from campground to campground and rarely stayed in any one place for longer than a week. The Department of Motor Vehicles wouldn't appreciate continual address changes. We certainly could not use our mail-forwarding address in another state, where we could be reached at any time. What did we do? Then, as now, we drove very carefully, obeying all laws, hoping we wouldn't be stopped for any reason that would require us to explain why we could not be reached at the address on our license and registration. We have since made arrangements with a private party to handle our motor-vehicle mail, so as far as our registration and drivers' licenses are concerned, we have a legitimate address.

You may be asked to present identification when applying for a driver's license. Sometimes a birth certificate is all that is needed, but some states require three separate pieces of identification. Unless a birth certificate is used, the addresses on the IDs had better match.

If examinations or tests are needed for driver's-license renewal, you will have to be in the state for them. If your state's licenses expire on the driver's birthday and your spouse or partner has a different birthday, the logistics can become tricky.

▼ ▼ ▼

The following illustrates another situation that fulltimers might experience: Jan's license expires on her birth date in November. One year, in June, we were about to leave the state where her driver's license was issued, and there was no chance we would be back in the state in time to renew it. We waited until the day before we were going to leave the state to ask if she could renew it that far in advance. We found she could, but just a week before, the computer would have rejected the request, we were told by the clerk at the motor-vehicle office. If Jan's license could not have been renewed so early, she would have had to apply for a driver's license in the state where we happened to be when the other expired. Either that or drive without a license (for the better part of a year as it turned out) and risk the consequences.

Fulltimers who live in, or regularly visit, a specific place will not have to face such complicated registration-licensing situations as we do.

When you begin fulltiming, you will have to work out the procedure for getting your registration, plates, and driver's license in a way that is convenient for you while complying with the issuing state's laws. To a great degree the problems you will have to face to establish your home residency are individual and so are the solutions.

Would that there were a state whose officials understood fulltimers and had laws flexible enough to accommodate those who have an address problem because they travel the year-round. We would rush to that state and gladly pay any fees imposed.

▼ ▼ ▼ Legal Residency

Being able to choose the state in which to "live" gives fulltimers a definite advantage over those who are not mobile. Fulltimers can select the state that is the most beneficial and least expensive for them. They can select one without a state income tax or one where the personal property tax is low. Vehicle insurance rates vary greatly from state to state, and this, too, can be a factor in their decision.

Many people think being a fulltimer is a good way to escape paying taxes, but this is not true. As we mentioned earlier, we fulltimers can only avoid paying stiff local and state taxes by deciding to "live" where the tax rates are lower or, in some cases, nonexistent.

This brings us to the question of legal residency. Most of us feel more comfortable if we have some place that we can call our legal residence, but nowhere is it written that we absolutely *must* establish one.

Depending on who is defining it, legal residency can be one or more of the following: the state in which you are licensed to drive, in which your vehicles are registered, where you have your permanent mailing address, where you are employed, where you have your bank accounts, where you own property, or where you are registered to vote. Other definitions are even more vague. A legal residence might be where your closest relatives reside, or the state where you would choose to reside on a permanent basis if you were to stop traveling. (This would never work for us because we haven't yet explored all the places we want to see). You will find as many opinions about what constitutes legal residency as there are state agencies.

There probably will never be a uniform, standard definition of legal residency, but as far as we are concerned, our properly licensed and registered trailer is our legal residence, wherever it happens to be. So far we have had no problem operating this way. If and when we do, we will handle it as best we can at the time. Generally, it is necessary to prove that you are, or are not, a legal resident of a particular place only when payment or non-payment of some kind of tax is in question.

We will travel as far as we can, but we cannot in one lifetime see all that we would see or learn all that we hunger to know.

LOREN EISELEY

▼ ▼ ▼ ▼ ▼ ▼ ▼ ▼ ▼ ▼ ▼ ▼

▼ ▼ ▼

Some people mistakenly believe that the Internal Revenue Service requires you to have a permanent, legal address for filing your income taxes. This is not so. Actually, the IRS doesn't care a whit where you file from as long as they get their money. It will benefit you, however, to have an address, permanent or not, legal or not, to which a refund can be sent if one is due.

Here is some information about state taxes that may be useful: If you work less than an entire calendar year in a state and you must pay state taxes on your earnings for that period, you may have to use a special state-tax form. Once, just before we left a state in which we had been employed for a short time, we dutifully picked up the state income tax form before we left. It wasn't until weeks later, when we were filling out the form, that we found we didn't have the proper one for part-year residents.

VOTING

▼ ▼ ▼ ▼ ▼ ▼ ▼ ▼ ▼ ▼ ▼ ▼ ▼

Fulltimers are frequently confused about voting, especially about when and how to use absentee ballots. It might be clearer if you take into account that two separate procedures are involved before anyone can vote. First, you must register. Second, you must have a ballot for casting your vote. Each state has its own requirements for voter registration with one regulation common to most: Each registrant must provide a street address so he or she can be assigned to a voting precinct. It is not necessary to be residing at the address. When you register, you can specify another address to which an absentee ballot can be sent. This mailing address can be your own post office box, that of your mail forwarder, or any other address where you have your mail sent. The street address is required only for registration. A post office box will not suffice for an address unless registering in Delaware, Georgia, Iowa, or South Carolina, where a post office box is an acceptable address. Registration can be done by mail in many states.

HEALTH ASSISTANCE

▼ ▼ ▼ ▼ ▼ ▼ ▼ ▼ ▼ ▼ ▼ ▼ ▼

The itinerant lifestyle must be good for people because most of the fulltimers we know are basically a pretty healthy group. Even so, we all have to see a doctor or dentist occasionally. Periodic checkups can be done by your regular doctor or dentist if you can arrange the appointments to fit your schedule. Sometimes, though, we need the services of these professionals when we are in an unfamiliar area.

▼ ▼ ▼ Referrals

How do we go about finding health-care professionals? We first ask the RV park manager to recommend someone. In nearly every instance we have been satisfied with the people to whom we have been referred. If the manager can't help us for one reason or another (one woman couldn't recommend a dentist because she had never had a cavity in her life), he or she will often give us the name of another local person who can. Perhaps we might call a local hospital or medical group for referrals.

Once, when we were parked for lunch in Wyoming, Bill broke a cap on one of his teeth. We decided to stop in the next town to see if we could find a dentist who could glue the broken piece back on. The next town was the tiny one of Lyman. Using the telephone book, we located the two dentists in town; they were in the same building. Since we were not planning to stay over, we drove there with our trailer and parked in a big lot across the street from the dentists' offices.

Both offices were closed. We assumed the dentists were out to lunch, so we waited around for a few minutes. A woman returning to an adjacent insurance office told us that one dentist was out of town and the other was gone for the day. We explained our problem—not much explanation was needed because when Bill smiled, it was plain to see a great empty space where a front tooth should have been. We mentioned that we were headed for another small town about forty miles away. The woman invited us into her office and voluntarily telephoned dentists at our next stop until she found one who could see Bill. After thanking her for her generous help, we left for our prearranged appointment.

The dentist glued the piece on, but it fell off the next morning soon after we were under way. We were less than 100 miles from where we were going to stay the night. On the way we stopped at a tourist information center. Bill asked the woman employed there if she could recommend a dentist. She unhesitatingly gave us a name. As soon as we got to the town we called for an appointment and were told to come right over. This dentist did the job successfully.

Another time a helpful campground owner in Idaho recommended his dentist, whom Bill liked so much that we will make an effort to go back and see him should we need any major dental work done.

▼ ▼ ▼

For years I have let dentists ride roughshod over my teeth; I have been sawed, hacked, chopped, whittled, bewitched, bewildered, tattooed, and signed on again; but this is cuspid's last stand.

S. J. PERELMAN

▼ ▼ ▼ ▼ ▼ ▼ ▼ ▼ ▼ ▼ ▼ ▼

We know you don't care about the condition of our teeth— though you may have deduced that Bill has more problems than Jan—but the anecdotes make some useful points: You usually can count on local sources for recommendations about qualified medical personnel, people are generally friendly and helpful when you are from out of town and have a problem, and, more often than not, doctors and dentists will find room to squeeze you in quickly if you are just passing through.

Throughout the years we have collected doctors and dentists in various states from coast to coast. These scattered individuals are the ones we see "regularly" when we need a checkup or if a medical problem arises when we are in their areas. If we aren't near one of the "regulars," we are confident we will find another to add to our list. You can usually establish an instant rapport with health-care professionals because most of them are fascinated by a fulltimer's lifestyle. They want to know where you have been and where you are going. They invariably remember you no matter how long you have been away. Because of the way you live, you are one of their most interesting patients.

▼ ▼ ▼ Medical Records

If you have a full set of current dental X-rays, carry them with you so you won't have to keep paying for new ones. A dentist cannot justifiably refuse to let you have them. You paid for them; they are yours, although some dentists might rightfully insist on keeping X-rays of the teeth they have worked on.

In addition, keep a careful record of the names of any prescription medications you take regularly so you can inform those who need to know.

▼ ▼ ▼ Surgery

If you need elective or minor surgery, it might be worthwhile to do a little investigating and have it done in an area where hospital costs are the most reasonable yet medical standards are still high. Rates vary widely across the country. More and more hospitals have places where RVs can be parked, often with hookups.

VEHICLE RIG REPAIR
▼ ▼ ▼ ▼ ▼ ▼ ▼ ▼ ▼ ▼ ▼ ▼

When it comes to having your vehicles taken care of when they are "sick," fulltimers cannot count so much on local referrals. The mechanic who has solved a problem on one type of vehicle may know nothing about the make and model you have. Mechanics in their own way are more specialized than doctors. A human is a human, but each make of vehicle is a completely different breed.

▼ ▼ ▼ Reputable Sources for Repair

There is no guaranteed way to locate a qualified mechanic who will be able to solve your particular problem, but you can do a few things to improve your chances of finding a good one. If you are enrolled in the Good Sam Emergency Road Service plan, you can draw on its nationwide network of mechanics who are chosen for their ability to handle RV repairs. What's more, it is the only emergency service that provides towing for all types of RV rigs.

Members of the American Automobile Association (AAA) can call a toll-free number to locate an AAA-approved repair facility in their area. Such a facility will have a record of providing consistent high-quality work, and their work is guaranteed to members. Should a dispute arise, AAA is the final authority for resolving it. Not all of these AAA-approved facilities can handle RV repairs, however.

The service department at a dealership for your make of vehicle is another possibility for having competent work done.

If none of these options is open to you, you might call the Better Business Bureau to find out if it has received any complaints about the place you have selected to do the work.

Repair work on motorhomes or trailers cannot be done in many auto shops because they don't have the necessary specialized equipment.

▼ ▼ ▼ Repair Precautions

Although many travelers already know this, it bears mentioning: Never leave your vehicle unattended in an unfamiliar service station while you are fueling or having its fluid levels checked. Watch carefully to see that only what you ask to be done is done.

Check all dipsticks yourself before authorizing anything to be added. When it is obvious that you are traveling through, you are in a very vulnerable position; mechanics in lots of places can and will take advantage of you.

We carry this a step farther and make it a practice to never leave the repair shop when our truck or trailer is being worked on (except in the one instance where we had to leave the trailer overnight; we removed some of the most valuable items from it before we took it to the shop, however). We stay there and wait for it no matter how long it takes. Most times we really don't have much choice because if we don't have our truck available, we have no other way of getting around. We always take lots of reading material, and once we did our wash in an adjacent laundromat we spied the day before when we made the appointment for the repair.

We believe our presence speeds things up to some degree. Also, we want to be on hand in case any problems are encountered. If we can get away with it, we periodically stroll into the repair area to see how things are coming along. In places with not-too-strict rules we can often talk to the mechanic, which helps us learn more about our vehicles. Of course, be aware that many places, for legal reasons or otherwise, will not allow any unauthorized people in the work area.

▼ ▼ ▼

Unfortunately, some dishonest mechanics, if left alone, will find other things that need to be "fixed." They might dutifully call your attention to a fan belt or hose with a split in it or perhaps point out a damaged tire, none of which needed fixing when the vehicle was brought in. Strange how such incidents occur in some repair shops *after* the vehicle is in the shop.

All too many of this same type of mechanic realize that their mistakes will not come back to haunt them if you are just passing through. When we are having repair work done, we never reveal this information if we can avoid it. If someone comments on our out-of-state plates, we say we are on an extended stay in town visiting relatives. This lets the mechanic know that if the work is not done satisfactorily, we can come back. This does not turn a bad mechanic into a good one, however. If we have any major repair work done, we do try to stay in the area long enough to be sure everything that was fixed is working properly.

If repairs are done at vehicle dealerships, they are often warranted for a given period. It might be possible that other dealerships would honor the warranty even though the work was not performed there. If a franchised shop of a nationwide chain such as Aamco, Goodyear, Midas, and the like does the repair, most likely they will also provide a warranty that is good in any of their affiliated shops.

Keep this in mind when buying tires or batteries or any other warranted item: If you purchase the item from a nationwide chain, warranty problems can be taken care of in many locations across the country.

VEHICLE INSURANCE

▼ ▼ ▼ ▼ ▼ ▼ ▼ ▼ ▼ ▼ ▼ ▼

It is important to have your RV rig insured by a company that understands fulltiming. Most do not, or if they claim they do, have some faulty, preconceived ideas about it. The carrier that provides group insurance for members of the Good Sam Club, National General Insurance Company, is a very understanding insurance company. They know that fulltimers may have their vehicles licensed in one state and have a mailing address in another. They also know that insuring a fulltimer's "house" is a good risk. When danger threatens a fulltimer's dwelling, be it hurricane, brush fire, or flood, National General knows that, unlike fixed dwellings, the fulltimer's home can usually be moved out of harm's way. Most other insurance companies haven't tumbled to this yet.

We know from our own and others' experience that their claim service is superb. One example: A couple with their rig, a truck and trailer, traveling with a caravan, was involved in an accident that didn't seriously injure them but wrecked their rig beyond the point of cost-effective repair. Within a week they had a new rig and were able to rejoin the caravan.

When you join the Good Sam Club you will be provided with information on the Good Sam Vehicle Insurance Plan (VIP), but if you are already a member and want information about vehicle insurance, contact:

Good Sam Vehicle Insurance Plan
P.O. Box 66937
St. Louis, Missouri 63166-6937
(800) VIP-AUTO; (800) 847-2886.

▼▼▼ Personal Liability

Personal liability insurance is one type of often-overlooked coverage. Fulltimers should have this coverage — just as they might have had when they were living in a house and had homeowners' insurance — in addition to rig insurance.

The liabilty insurance that is included in most vehicle coverage is intended to cover situations that arise as a result of the vehicle's being driven, or in the case of a trailer, while it is being towed. Another type of liablility insurance is needed to cover the vehicle when it is parked. A fulltimer's personal liability policy, like a homeowner's policy, will protect you if someone should be injured in or on your property: in the case of a fulltimer, your rig or your campsite. Even though you don't own your campsite, you may have a hose, electrical cords, or a doormat that someone could trip over.

We know of an instance where a motorhome's propane tank exploded, virtually destroying the motorhome, and the flying debris damaged two other RVs in adjacent sites. The motorhome's owner, who was not a fulltimer, didn't have this sort of liability coverage and his insurance company was balking at paying for damages since the accident occurred when the vehicle was parked.

Besides National General, only three other companies are on the RV insurance bandwagon:

Alexander & Alexander, Attn: RV Department, 700 Fisher Building, Detroit, Michigan 48202, (800) 521-2942, is, at this time, the only company offering a replacement-cost endorsement. Although the company will insure all types of RVs, the endorsement is limited to only motorhomes at this time. With this insurance, a destroyed motorhome will be replaced by a new motorhome of the same brand and model.

Caravanner Insurance, 14805 North 73rd Street, Scottsdale, Arizona 85260, (800) 423-4403, insures only trailers, no other vehicles with engines, and the policies are designed primarily for fulltimers.

The policies from Foremost Insurance Company, P.O. Box 3357, Grand Rapids, Michigan 59501, (800) 237-2060, can be purchased directly from the company or through many independent agents. In the last few years, this company has been one of the few general insurance companies that has recognized the need for insurance tailored to all aspects of RVing, including fulltiming.

If you're among the growing numbers of RVers who travel with a personal computer, consider signing up with one of the database services such as Prodigy or CompuServe. These give you access to a wealth of information and services that can assist you in travel planning and managing your finances. They also provide the convenience of electronic mail, allowing you to communicate instantly with other members of the service. Other services are just for fun or information: computer games and movie reviews, and articles on health, exercise, and recreation.

Prodigy members can do home banking and bill-paying through their computers. CompuServe members can tie into a number of travel forums that allow a sharing of travel tips with other members around the country. Both Prodigy and CompuServe have encyclopedia services and computer bulletin boards that tie you in with hundreds or thousands of special-interest enthusiasts.

To utilize one of these services, you'll need a personal computer (or a briefcase or notebook computer) with a modem, which allows you to tie into a telephone line. You must be able to plug into a telephone jack, which is generally only available on a private phone line. The services charge a basic membership rate, plus a monthly or by-use rate, and, of course, you will have to pay telephone time. For more information, call Prodigy at (800) PRODIGY, or CompuServe at (800) 848-8199.

COMPUSERVE AND PRODIGY

▼ ▼ ▼ ▼ ▼ ▼ ▼ ▼ ▼ ▼ ▼ ▼

Chapter 5

Getting Started

Preparations for fulltiming can either begin many years before the event, keeping in mind what can happen to long-
range plans, or the switch from one lifestyle to another can be
made within weeks, depending on individual situations. Although fulltiming should not be jumped into with reckless
abandon, neither should it be postponed if it is something you
want to do now and your circumstances allow it.

It is risky to venture into fulltiming if you have no RV experience at all. Having to learn about RVs at the same time you are
learning about fulltiming could be exasperating and discourag-
ing. Some people manage to handle both with equanimity, but
other neophyte fulltimers might become soured on the lifestyle
without giving it a fair chance.

READ ABOUT
THE LIFESTYLE

One of the best ways to get a handle on what fulltiming is all
about is by reading *Trailer Life* and *MotorHome* magazines every
month. These magazines are the only monthly RV publications
available throughout the United States and Canada. More im-
portantly, they are the only publications that regularly have
information about fulltiming. They often publish articles about
the full-timing lifestyle, news columns that report on legislation

or regulations that affect all RVers, as well as letters to the editor and "action" line and troubleshooting columns.

Information in these magazines not specifically related to fulltiming may still be of use. For instance, both publications contain many articles on general maintenance of trailers, tow vehicles, and motorhomes. Reports about tests and evaluations of new units may help in selecting a rig for fulltiming. Travel articles, written by people who have actually been to the places they are writing about, are valuable if your fulltiming will include traveling. Many RVers collect articles about places in which they are interested and keep them in a file or scrapbook for future reference.

Members of the Good Sam Club receive the magazine *Highways* each month. This publication is also of much interest to fulltimers. For example, most issues contain items about parks that need campground hosts.

A few other publications might be found in campgrounds or RV-supply stores. These are generally regional bimonthly or quarterly periodicals, often distributed free of charge. In them you will rarely find articles directed exclusively to the fulltimer; nevertheless, they are worth reading. For instance, we recently found an informative piece in one of them about how a popular brand of RV is constructed.

▼ ▼ ▼ Talk to People Living the Full-timing Life

Talking to fulltimers can be helpful. When we began, we purposely sought out fulltimers in order to get an insight into the lifestyle. Those we encountered were all enthusiastic about fulltiming. But later, when we were fulltimers, we had a conversation that made us realize the picture of the lifestyle is colored by the experiences of those you talk to.

▼ ▼ ▼

We happened to meet a couple who were suspicious and distrustful of just about everything: They didn't like driving on highways because of potential dangers. They found something to complain about in almost every campground they visited. They lived in constant fear of having things stolen by intruders and even worried about being ripped off by the management of campgrounds. They rarely left a campsite after they were parked because they felt it necessary to be on guard constantly against people who were up to no good; in their opinion, this included just about everyone. Throughout our conversation, all these two did was voice their fears and complain. We marveled that they revealed so much to us—a couple of strangers.

These people didn't enjoy fulltiming, but with their attitude they probably couldn't enjoy life in *any* style. Had a novice or prospective fulltimer encountered this couple, he or she might understandably have had qualms about the lifestyle.

A traveler. I love his title. A traveler is to be reverenced as such. His profession is the best symbol of our life. Going from—toward; it is the history of every one of us.

HENRY DAVID THOREAU

▼ ▼ ▼ ▼ ▼ ▼ ▼ ▼ ▼ ▼ ▼ ▼ ▼

Beware of those who paint an excessively gloomy picture of fulltiming. Also take with a grain of salt those who say the lifestyle has no problems at all. No way of living is totally trouble free. It's best to talk to as many fulltimers as you can, weigh their opinions, and then formulate your own ideas.

You can easily find people to talk to who are engaged in fulltiming. When you are camping, ask others in the park if they are fulltimers. If you don't have an RV, you can still visit campgrounds and talk to campers. Whether or not you are camping, stroll around the sites. Conversations can be started by noting license plates and asking where in that state the people are from. Other good opening questions are those about a particular rig: How do you like your diesel? Do you find a fifth-wheel easy to tow? Do those automatic levelers you have on your motorhome work well?

Most RVers are friendly folk, and fulltimers are happy to talk about their lifestyle, so much so that you should allow a few hours for this. Time seems to fly by as effusive RVers willingly tell you about interesting places they have visited, campgrounds they like or don't like, how they live the full-timing life, how their rigs are working out, if they have gone from a smaller unit to a larger one or vice versa, and more. Often lifelong friendships are formed from these encounters.

When fulltimers are enjoying themselves and paint a glowing picture of the lifestyle, you will have to sift through the information you receive and apply it to your own situation. Your fulltiming will not be exactly like anyone else's, so what suits others may not be right for you.

Fulltiming should not be undertaken if you have never driven a rig or stayed overnight in an RV. Without these experiences, you will have no basis on which to select a rig, and you will be unable to adequately judge how you will like spending time in an RV.

**TRY RVING
BEFORE BUYING**

▼ ▼ ▼ ▼ ▼ ▼ ▼ ▼ ▼ ▼ ▼ ▼

▼ ▼ ▼ Renting an RV

If you have no RVing experience, it will be much better for you, and perhaps less expensive in the long run, if you rent an RV for a vacation to see if the lifestyle is right for you. Even a weekend vacation is better than nothing. As we explained before, a vacation in an RV is not at all the same as living in one all the time, but it will give you some idea of what it is like.

When it comes to renting an RV, however, only motorhomes are generally available. Sometimes very small trailers, under twenty feet, are offered as rental units. Rental trailers are small because they can be towed with a simple, easy-to-install bumper hitch. Other trailers require a large hitch assembly where the hitch receiver is bolted or welded to the tow vehicle's frame. It would not be practical to install a hitch of this type each time a trailer was rented.

Renting a motorhome is a good idea, even if you think you will want a trailer for fulltiming. Living in a motorhome and hooking it up in campgrounds is virtually the same as living in or hooking up a trailer.

Renting too small a unit for a short period of time will not provide you with a realistic full-time experience, but time spent in any size RV would be better than having no RVing experience at all.

Two RV-rental companies with branches throughout the country are Cruise America and Go Vacations. They, and other companies that rent RVs, can be located in the Yellow Pages under the heading "Recreational Vehicles — Leasing and Rental."

We have come across a few places that rent stationary trailers. These units are usually travel trailers that serve as cottages or cabins in vacation areas and are permanently parked and hooked up to all utilities. By renting one of these units you would not gain any driving or parking experience, but you would get the feeling of living in a trailer.

People who have done some RVing know a little of what will be encountered when they begin fulltiming. They have driven their rig somewhere, parked it in a campsite, and perhaps have hooked it up to various utilities. The broader their RV experience, and the more they have traveled, the better and the quicker they will adapt to fulltiming.

▼ ▼ ▼ First-day Experiences

Those who start fulltiming without some earlier experience will probably be faced with lots of worries along with the excitement and anticipation of starting out. A typical first day might include at least the following concerns:

Everything must be loaded, stowed, and secured so that during the day's travel there won't be any breakage.

If the rig is a trailer, it will have to be hitched properly. Don't pull away without raising the hitch jack. If a car is to be towed behind a motorhome, it will have to be hitched. Be sure nothing is left behind on the ground.

After successfully navigating city traffic before reaching the highway, next comes the concern about how the rig will handle when being passed by large trucks. Aside from the suction the trucks create, will the drivers try to give you a hard time?

If fuel is needed, you will have to maneuver the rig next to a fuel pump; there must be sufficient overhead clearance. Will you find an empty parking space large enough for your rig in a rest area if you want to stop there? How will your rig handle going up or down steep grades? If you run into rain, snow, sleet, or fog, will it create problems? You will have to determine the best speed for your rig under any conditions encountered without having any previous experience on which to base your determinations.

Throughout history it has been man who worships and polishes the vehicle, and woman who packs the suitcases.

JOHN FOWLES

▼ ▼ ▼ ▼ ▼ ▼ ▼ ▼ ▼ ▼ ▼ ▼

You may have to drive through an unfamiliar town or city to find a campground. Will you get there before rush-hour traffic starts? Will the campground you selected have space for you? Have you allowed enough time so you will not be driving after dark? It's not an uncommon tendency to drive too many miles on the first day.

If no pull-through spaces are available in the campground, the rig must be backed into a site. A towed car will have to be unhitched before the motorhome can be backed. Perhaps the site will not be level, and you will have to undertake leveling. You will probably want to hook up the electricity and maybe the water and sewer. When you finish with these duties, it will be necessary to get the appliances going. In many new RVs, the refrigerator, water heater, and furnace are turned on simply by using a switch. In older RVs, a little more effort may be required. The owner's manual may have to be located and consulted.

Only when this is all taken care of, can you raise the television antenna and relax—relax, that is if everything has gone smoothly. Simple hookups may not seem as if they would present any problems, and usually they won't, but when you arrive in a campground, tired after a long day of driving, you may find your thinking becomes cloudy and your actions less efficient.

We saw this phenomenon late one night when a motorhome pulled into the site next to us. A man got out, gave his site a cursory glance, then headed for our trailer. We were the only others in the campground; the manager had locked the office and gone home. The man wanted to know where he could get some electricity; he said there was none at his site. We showed him his outlet—identical to ours and in the same location—which was in a common gray enamel electrical box with a hinged lid that lifted up to expose the receptacles. The man had seen the box but hadn't thought to lift the lid. He sheepishly explained away his oversight by telling us he was tired because he had been on the road since early morning.

Another time, a couple parked next to us in a Wyoming campground. We noticed they were spending an inordinate amount of time doing something to their water heater. We went over to see if we could help. Between the two of them they simply couldn't figure out how to light the water heater.

On the old highway maps of America, the main routes were red and the back roads blue. Now even the colors are changing. But in those brevities just before dawn and a little after dark—times neither day nor night—the old roads return to the sky some of its color. Then, in truth, they cast a mysterious shadow of blue, and it's that time when the pull of the blue highway is strongest, when the open road is a beckoning, a strangeness, a place where a man can lose himself.

WILLIAM LEAST HEAT-MOON

▼ ▼ ▼ ▼ ▼ ▼ ▼ ▼ ▼ ▼ ▼ ▼

After we showed them what to do, they told us they had taken delivery of their rig — a used one, but a recent model — the previous day. They had left their home in Missouri and had driven 700 miles on their first day out. They had no RV experience whatsoever. The dealer from whom they purchased their rig evidently had not gone over the systems to show the new owners how to operate them — not an accidental oversight of the dealer, we suspected.

As long as we were being so accommodating, the couple asked us to help them with some other problems. We showed them how to light the burners on their range; this was a complete mystery to them. They had managed to light the pilot on the furnace but they hadn't deduced how to make the furnace burner go on. We showed them the thermostat; they hadn't realized they even had one.

Those who have no RVing experience before taking off in their rigs could find themselves in situations like this, or worse. Just a little practice will go a long way toward solving these problems when they arise.

▼ ▼ ▼ Experiment First

Even if you have been RVing for years but will be fulltiming in a new-to-you rig, a little experimentation to familiarize yourself with your rig and its equipment before you take off will smooth your way and bring to light any problems so they can be corrected before you leave.

When we went from a conventional to a fifth-wheel trailer, we had to learn an entirely new way of hitching. This was not made easy for us because we had a defective hitch, but we weren't aware of it at the time. We struggled with it, trying to make it work properly, all the while wondering how fifth-wheels had gotten the reputation for being easy to hitch. We had no previous experience with hitching fifth-wheels, or we would have known immediately we weren't doing anything wrong; it was the simply the equipment causing the problem.

Practice hitching and unhitching either the trailer to the tow vehicle or the auxiliary car to the motorhome. It shouldn't require more than a half-dozen tries to make you a virtual pro at it, unless you, too, have some equipment that won't work right. Once you develop a routine for hitching and unhitching, you will find the procedure to be quite simple.

Once hitched, drive the rig on streets that have little traffic and few or no hills, if possible. Turn corners to find out how wide the rig must swing and in how narrow a space it can be turned safely. Notice the tracking. Be aware of the distance needed to stop when braking. Take the rig to a large, nearly empty parking lot, preferably when the stores are closed, and practice backing and parking.

Try all the basic systems — water heater, refrigerator, water pump, range, furnace, electricity — and any others you may have on your rig, to find out how they work. Read the instructions for use and apply them until you are completely familiar with each system's operation. Experiment with these simple procedures one at a time. Don't put yourself in the position of having to learn the operation of everything all at once.

Make a short trip to a nearby campground to get some actual field experience. Even if it is an RV park in your town and you only stay overnight, you will benefit from the experience. If you can't do this, live and sleep in your RV home in your own driveway for a day or two.

If it is impossible to arrange for some practice before actually starting your fulltiming, don't plan to drive for more than a few hours the first day. Making this initial day a short one in miles traveled should help you avoid feeling too pressured or harried. You will give yourself a better chance to enjoy the beginning of your fulltiming adventure, and you may escape doubts about whether you have done the right thing.

I often tire of myself and I have a notion that by travel I can add to my personality and so change myself a little.

W. SOMERSET MAUGHAM

▼ ▼ ▼ ▼ ▼ ▼ ▼ ▼ ▼ ▼ ▼ ▼

The most definitive step toward a total commitment to fulltiming is selling your house. This is the biggest decision that will have to be made, except, perhaps, the initial one to become a fulltimer, because once the house is sold, any change of mind about going back to live in a fixed dwelling certainly will be an expensive one.

Should you sell your house?

TO SELL OR NOT TO SELL YOUR HOUSE

▼ ▼ ▼ ▼ ▼ ▼ ▼ ▼ ▼ ▼ ▼

Probably not if you or your partner have doubts about whether you will like the lifestyle.

Definitely not if you plan on using it as your home base.

Maybe not if you are planning to fulltime for a few years and then return to living in a fixed dwelling.

If retirement coincides with fulltiming, it may be an opportune time to sell a large family house, experiment with fulltiming, and then perhaps purchase a smaller, fixed dwelling later to use as a home base. Only you are in a position to know what you want to do; what you actually can do often depends on your financial situation.

▼ ▼ ▼

For many, the decision to become fulltimers means they will have to sell their house in order to have the money to purchase a recreational vehicle. This was our situation. Making up our minds to sell our house was not difficult for us. We were disenchanted with the responsibilities of home ownership and anxious to be free of the expenses and never-ending chores of keeping it up. In fact, we were so eager to be rid of our house, we placed an ad offering it for sale the Sunday after we made our full-timing decision.

January in Connecticut is not the ideal time to sell houses; they are hardly at their best when buried in snow with ice-covered driveways. But we thought running an ad might give us an idea of what to expect in the spring, when serious buyers would be out looking. It would be interesting to see if we got any nibbles. As it turned out, we could have sold the house five times over that day, and indeed, did sell it to one couple. There was no turning back for us at that point.

We were lucky to find a buyer so quickly, but years ago the real estate market was much healthier than it is now. If houses aren't selling in your area, you might not be able to begin fulltiming when you want to. If you need to sell your house to buy your rig, put it on the market as soon as possible. If you aren't quite ready to start fulltiming when you find a buyer, perhaps the closing date can be set some months ahead to give you ample time to make all the arrangements for your change in lifestyle.

Apartment dwellers don't have this problem. They can schedule their fulltiming to begin when their lease runs out. They have a definite date to work with. You cannot count on selling a house precisely when you want to.

▼ ▼ ▼ Avoiding Capital-Gains Taxes

If you sell your house for more than you paid for it, you may be subject to paying capital-gains taxes on the profit. One way to avoid this is to purchase an RV that costs as much or more as what the house sold for. For tax purposes, an RV qualifies as a house if it is your only or primary residence. Taxpayers aged fifty-five or older can elect to take a one-time deduction of $125,000 from the sale of a house. Capital-gains taxes would be due on only the amount over $125,000 for which the house was sold. This rule was written with older housesellers in mind. When older people sell a house, it is often because their children have grown and moved away or they want something smaller to keep up; they don't often reinvest the money realized from the sale in a larger, more expensive, house.

▼ ▼ ▼ Dealing with Your Possessions

Once the house is sold or before the apartment lease runs out, you will have to make some crucial decisions about many of your possessions. When you go from living in any kind of a fixed dwelling to an RV home, you will not have room to store everything you own no matter what size the RV.

Those who will be living exclusively in an RV home have two choices regarding the items they will not be taking with them: dispose of the items or store them. Some possessions can be disposed of by selling them or giving them away. They can be stored either by renting storage space or by lending them temporarily to family or friends, perhaps with the understanding that if, in the future, the things are wanted, they will be given back.

It's difficult to give up one's possessions — often so difficult for some that they never become true fulltimers, even though the

If you want a golden rule that will fit everybody, this is it: Have nothing in your houses that you do not know to be useful, or believe to be beautiful.

WILLIAM MORRIS

desire is there; they cannot bear to part with most of the things they have accumulated over the years.

Deciding what to keep hinges on two words: want and need. We truly need only a few things to live, but we always want more than just the basics. Life really wouldn't be much fun if we had to limit ourselves to just necessities, so a happy balance has to be found between the needed items and the wanted ones.

On a long journey even a straw weighs heavy.

SPANISH PROVERB

Since all RVs suitable for fulltiming are completely furnished, you will not need any of the furniture you now own—not one stick of it. Even though we had some good furniture and a few antique pieces, we sold every bit of it. We didn't want the bother of receiving a regular bill for storage, and we also figured we could put to better use any money we would have spent on storage.

Also, you will probably need fewer dishes, flatware, and linens in your new life. Cooking utensils, appliances, and tools will have to be judiciously sorted according to what you will need and what you will have room for. As you are sorting and considering what to take with you, think about how certain items can do double duty; special-purpose and one-purpose kitchen equipment will not be needed if other equipment can do the same job. As an example, before we became fulltimers, we had always done a lot of baking and saw no reason to discontinue the practice just because we would be living in a trailer. We kept our cookie press, which weighed little, but got rid of our heavy rolling pin. The cylinder of the cookie press is now used as a rolling pin. Hot dogs can be cooked in something other than a hot dog cooker; vegetables can be sliced by hand instead of using a special slicing gadget; an electric skillet is really not needed if there is a same-size skillet that can be used on the range top. Food cooked on a square griddle can be cooked just as well in a large skillet.

Many RVs suitable for fulltiming will have plenty of galley storage space, so equipment that is regularly used should be kept. *Regularly* is the key word; when weighing what to keep and what to get rid of, ask yourself: How many times did I use this last year? If the answer is once or twice or not at all, the item can probably be disposed of without your missing it.

Most of us have to pare down our wardrobes to fit into an RV's storage space. Most RVs have room for all the clothing you will need, but nearly everyone has more than just basic clothing, so some weeding out will have to be done. A heavy coat might be eliminated if you have a lightweight coat and sweater that can be worn together or separately according to the weather. The lightweight coat might be a parka that could also double as a raincoat.

Don't make the common mistake of chucking out too many clothes. Some about-to-be-fulltimers who plan to follow the sun eliminate all items of winter clothing from their wardrobes. In the United States, no matter how far south you go in the winter, jackets and sweaters, even coats, will be needed occasionally.

Collections—books, glassware, clocks, guns, antique items—and other accumulations of prized possessions may have to be sold, stored, or reduced to a size or number that will fit into your RV. Often the hardest choices to make are in this area.

Every increased possession loads us with a new weariness.

JOHN RUSKIN

We had a difficult time deciding which books to keep from our sizable library. We were faced with a problem not common to most fulltimers: Because of our writing, we needed to keep our large, hardcover dictionary and equally large encyclopedia. We replaced certain other hardbound reference books with lighter, smaller paperback editions. These included a thesaurus, an atlas, identification books for wildflowers, birds, trees, and rocks—even a few favorite novels we wanted to reread.

We had a large record collection that we could not bear to give up but would not fit into our RV home, so we transferred it all to tape cassettes and bought a good quality car stereo for the trailer to replace our large home-stereo system.

We also had some favorite paintings. To take them with us, we photographed them, then had prints made in a size that would fit the wall spaces in our RV.

Even when you have no sentimental attachment to possessions, you may find it difficult to know what to keep and what to eliminate. When in doubt, keep the item if there is room to store it in your unit. Eliminating such an item later will be less costly than having to repurchase it should you find you need it.

MOVING INTO AN RV: THE TRANSITION

Moving from one fixed dwelling to another is not easy. Moving from a fixed dwelling to an RV home, which is bound to be smaller, can be difficult and complicated.

Our move would have been simpler if we could have purchased our RV before moving out of our house. If you need to realize the money from the sale of your house to buy your rig as we did, perhaps our experiences will point up difficulties that might arise.

We began the process of disposing of our things the day after the buyers put a deposit on our house. We didn't have the deposit money to spend because it was being held in escrow by our attorney, but we knew, unless something out of the ordinary happened, the house sale would be finalized. The couple who bought our house couldn't have the closing until the first of May. Since January was nearly gone, that gave us just over three months to find a suitable RV and to get rid of everything we wouldn't be taking with us. Three months, we quickly found, was not an excessive amount of time for accomplishing what we had to do.

Although we had only a five-room house, and Bill's pack-rat tendencies had always been more than offset by Jan's penchant for not collecting things, it still seemed as if we had an uncommonly large number of items to eliminate.

We couldn't afford to give away much since we needed any money we could get from selling our possessions. The weather was not suitable for holding a yard sale, so we began the disposal process by running classified ads for some of our big furniture items, a car, a van, our small RV, power tools, and yard equipment. It was a rare evening that someone didn't come to look at what we had advertised. Little by little we saw the rooms empty, although a lot of items remained. Between phone calls and visitors, we tackled the sizable jobs of cleaning out closets and cabinets, setting aside items we would keep and other items to be included in yard sales later.

We wondered how we would ever find the time to shop for a rig, sell everything we wanted to sell, empty out the house, and move into our new RV home in the time we had before the closing. We were already weary from juggling schedules and appointments, and our lives were becoming more chaotic daily. Our usually neat house had become an unorganized mess.

A spring thaw finally melted the snow in the yard and the ice in the driveway. As soon as the resultant mud had dried up somewhat, we held our first yard sale. We had a sale every weekend for the following three weeks.

During this time we did manage to locate a travel trailer we liked and a truck with which to tow it. We had enough money in our savings account to put a deposit on the units we wanted, but, since we were not financing them, we could not take possession until they were paid for. We would not have the money for this until we had the check for the house, and we could not use the house proceeds until the check had cleared. In those days it took ten days for checks to clear. As it happened, the new owner of our house had the canceled check in his possession fully two days before it was "cleared" by our bank. Because we were victims of this then-existing banking regulation, we had to move into a motel for a week and rent a storage unit (monthly rates were all that were available) to temporarily keep everything we were going to take with us in our RV home. When the check cleared, we paid the balances due and moved into our trailer the same day.

That day we also rented a space in an RV park for a month so we could get settled. As long as we had to pay a month's rent on a storage unit, we could move our things in gradually. Having a whole month to do this was quite a luxury after the hustle and bustle of the previous three months. During this time we were able to thoroughly check out all the trailer's systems to see if they were functioning properly before leaving our dealer's area.

We haven't the time to take our time.

EUGÈNE IONESCO

▼ ▼ ▼ ▼ ▼ ▼ ▼ ▼ ▼ ▼ ▼ ▼ ▼

DELAYED FULLTIMING

▼ ▼ ▼ ▼ ▼ ▼ ▼ ▼ ▼ ▼ ▼ ▼ ▼

If your plans for taking to the open road are slated for some time well into the future, there is no reason to delay disposing of items you will not need for fulltiming. Any work you can do in advance will make the actual transition that much easier.

▼ ▼ ▼ Clearing the Closets

One of the best places to start clearing out "stuff" is in the closet. We doubt that anyone living in a fixed dwelling doesn't have some clothing that is rarely or never worn. People tend to hang on to such items as long as a place exists for storing them. You will not have such extra space in an RV. It should be easy to eliminate all the clothes that you don't wear, that have been relegated to the far reaches of the closet because they didn't fit properly, are no longer fashionable, or because you simply tired of them. Any item that falls into these categories should be sold or given away.

STREAMLINING YOUR WARDROBE

▼ ▼ ▼ ▼ ▼ ▼ ▼ ▼ ▼ ▼ ▼ ▼ ▼

Delayed fulltiming may give you time to adjust your wardrobe for the lifestyle. If you need additions to your wardrobe, it would be wise to buy only clothes that are classic in style so you won't be stuck with faddish items. Both men and women might think about settling on a color scheme for all their clothes and sticking to it, so nearly everything will go together. When all clothes are color-coordinated, fewer garments will be needed because items will mix and match. Try to purchase clothes that can be worn in all seasons. To keep things simple, we buy only clothing that doesn't require special care when laundering so that all items can be washed in the same water temperature using the same setting on the washer. We have only a few items in our wardrobe that need to be dry cleaned.

The closer you get to your full-timing date, the more wardrobe items you can dispense with. Formal clothing will not be neeeded in your new lifestyle. One woman's or man's business suit might be kept, but it is unlikely you will need any sort of business wardrobe unless you plan to continue working as you fulltime and your job will require business clothes. Neckties have no place in full-timing activities. A few years ago we were attending a get-together of campground residents in the campground's recreation hall. One man showed up in a suit and tie. He was jokingly told he would not be allowed to participate unless he wore clothes more suitable to the occasion. He promised he would never make such a fashion gaffe again.

Women rarely need dresses; separates suffice for nearly every occasion. A friend of ours has kept one dress, "Old Blue" she calls it, in case she has to attend any weddings or funerals.

She travels grubbiest who travels light.

ERMA BOMBECK

▼ ▼ ▼ ▼ ▼ ▼ ▼ ▼ ▼ ▼ ▼ ▼ ▼

▼ ▼ ▼ Cleaning Out Packed-away Items

Next easiest to get rid of, after clothes, are items stored away in the attic, basement, garage, storage shed, and unused rooms. Most people have boxes and cartons of things squirreled away in places such as these. Just about anything that is packed away can be eliminated. If the things are stored, they are not being used, so why keep them? If these repositories of unused items are cleaned out, a monumental job will be over with by the time you are ready to begin fulltiming.

▼ ▼ ▼ Now for the Furniture

It is a common tendency to fill all empty rooms in a fixed dwelling with furniture; many of these rooms seem to serve no purpose other than to hold furniture. They might have been in use at some time as bedrooms when children lived at home, or they might be furnished, but rarely used, sewing rooms, dens, or game rooms. Many dining rooms are not often used for dining when a family room or kitchen contains a suitable dining area. If you have rooms in your house that are not used regularly, you could dispose of the furniture in them now and have much less to do later. Even certain tables, chairs, lamps, pictures, and rugs in rooms that are used all the time could be eliminated without causing any real inconvenience.

I never gave away anything without wishing I had kept it; nor kept it without wishing I had given it away.

LOUISE BROOKS

Since disposing of possessions is one of the biggest hassles faced by those who are about to be fulltimers, anything that can be done in advance to get rid of what is unneeded and unwanted will make the final elimination much easier.

Chapter 6

Selecting the Full-timing Rig

Fulltiming can be done in any type of recreational vehicle. Some people are participating in the lifestyle in van campers, mini-motorhomes, tent trailers, pickup campers, and converted buses. With the possible exception of single fulltimers who need room only for themselves, most people who live in RVs of these types are doing so because they cannot afford to buy a larger or more practical unit. Having a home on wheels is more important to them than practicality — even comfort. They make do with their RVs because it is the only way they *can* fulltime.

FOUR BASIC TYPES OF RVS

Finances permitting, most of these determined fulltimers would probably prefer to live in an RV that had all the comforts and conveniences of a real home. The types of RVs that can be homes of this sort are described in this chapter: Class A and Class C motorhomes, which are self-propelled, and conventional and fifth-wheel trailers, which have to be towed (Figures 6.1, 6.2, 6.3, and 6.4). One of these RVs is the choice of the majority of fulltimers.

The difference between a conventional and a fifth-wheel trailer is that the front section of the fifth-wheel trailer, the

PHOTO: FORETRAVEL

Figure 6.1
The Class A motorhome is built on a rail chassis and is available in
lengths from 18 to 40 feet.

gooseneck, extends over the bed of the pickup truck tow vehicle,
and the hitch is located in the center of the truck's bed. Obviously, a truck is the only type of vehicle that can be used for
towing a fifth-wheel trailer. Most conventional trailers are
towed with trucks, but some passenger cars can be the tow
vehicles for conventional trailers if the trailer is not too heavy.

Class A motorhomes resemble buses in shape although many
models are sleeker and more streamlined.

Class C motorhomes are built on a van cutaway chassis and
have a van cab with the engine located under an extended hood.
The distinguishing feature of all Class Cs is the cabover bed.

Within these four basic types, a rig should be selected according to how it will be used and in a size that is right for you and
your full-timing companions.

Figure 6.2
The Class C motorhome is built on a van cutaway chassis and includes a cabover bed in the coach.

PHOTO: FLEETWOOD

Figure 6.3
The conventional trailer allows the living and driving areas to be separate and offers optimum storage space. It may be towed with either a pickup truck or passenger car.

PHOTO: NEWMAR

PHOTO: WESTERN RV

Figure 6.4
The fifth-wheel trailer has a front section that extends over the bed of the pickup tow vehicle; the trailer hitch is located in the center of the truck's bed.

The size and type of RV needed depend on how and where your fulltiming will be done. For instance, those who intend to do a lot of backcountry camping might want a smaller, different type of rig than those who will be staying in established campgrounds with designated sites. Those who travel more than just taking their rig south for the winter and north for the summer will want a maneuverable rig that is easy to drive and park in a variety of different campground situations—and one that doesn't require much setup time.

The climates in which the unit is to be used may also have some bearing on the rig's selection. Many, but not all, of today's RVs are well insulated, and on some the plumbing can withstand even below-zero temperatures without freezing.

SELECTING AN RV TO SUIT YOUR LIFESTYLE

▼ ▼ ▼ ▼ ▼ ▼ ▼ ▼ ▼ ▼ ▼ ▼

▼ ▼ ▼

Very few fulltimers engage in just one kind of camping. We have stayed in many places far off the beaten track with no utility hookups whatsoever, and we have spent a good share of our time in campgrounds with paved sites and all hookups. We like a change of seasons; winter usually finds us in places where the temperature often falls below freezing. We enjoy all types of camping, so we wanted a rig that would be as versatile as possible. Your own camping habits should figure in your RV selection.

When it comes to the rig itself, either a motorhome with a towed car or a trailer with a towing vehicle, those RVers who have experimented with different types and sizes will have a good idea of the combination that will be best for them as fulltimers. As for the motorhome or trailer itself, you will find soon after you have begun seriously shopping for a full-timing RV that no one unit will be absolutely right for all your needs. You will have to make compromises — perhaps many.

Many factors, in addition to those previously mentioned, must be considered when buying a rig for fulltiming. We hope the following information will help in your decision. The selection of an RV home that is not right for your needs can be costly. It can also negatively affect your feelings about fulltiming.

LOOKING FOR AN RV

▼ ▼ ▼ ▼ ▼ ▼ ▼ ▼ ▼ ▼ ▼ ▼ ▼ ▼

You probably will have to do a lot of looking before you can make a reasonably intelligent choice about a full-timing rig. Where to start?

Perhaps the best place is to first talk with other RVers and learn from their experiences. Joining an RV association, such as the Good Sam Club, and attending your local chapter's meetings will put you in touch with others who will be happy to tell you what they like or don't like about their rigs.

RV shows, which are held regularly in all parts of the country, afford excellent opportunities to see and compare many different brands and types of RVs. Announcements of many of these shows appear in local newspapers, *Trailer Life* and *MotorHome* magazines, and are often posted at RV dealers or RV-supply stores.

Visit as many dealers as you can and look at every model they have to offer that you think might fit your needs. Salespeople are helpful later, but you should do the initial looking on your own. You do not want to be high-pressured into anything. You need to poke around in the units and spend quite a bit of time going over them. Let the salespeople know you are doing some preliminary looking. You may still receive the high-pressure treatment, but at least you will have been honest about not being ready to buy.

We doubt that salespeople can help you decide whether a motorhome or trailer is best for you. Unless they have both types for sale, they will try to convince you that what they are selling is the best choice. Don't expect salespeople to say anything negative about the products they are selling, either. About the only time they will downplay one unit is when they are trying to sell you a larger, more expensive model.

▼ ▼ ▼

We don't mean to imply that salespeople are doing anything wrong or dishonest. On the contrary, these tactics are just good salesmanship, but you do have to be fairly certain about the type and size of RV you want before the salesperson can be of much help. Then, a good salesperson can be invaluable.

When you are ready to buy and are down to the final comparisons among several units, never feel guilty about taking up too much of a salesperson's time. Ask every question you can think of about the unit you are considering. Making the right selection takes time and should not be rushed under any circumstance.

Inequality of knowledge is the key to a sale.

DEIL O. GUSTAFSON

▼ ▼ ▼ ▼ ▼ ▼ ▼ ▼ ▼ ▼ ▼ ▼

No matter what size or type of unit you choose, you will be spending thousands of dollars. Because so much money is involved, it may be worth your while to travel some miles from home to look at units you are interested in. We had to travel more than 300 miles on different trips to see brands of RVs that were not sold in our immediate area.

Your local library should have phone books for your part of the country with listings of dealers and the brands they carry.

Advertisements in *Trailer Life* and *MotorHome* magazines may be helpful in finding units and dealers. Information on specific units and the dealer nearest you can be obtained by writing directly to the manufacturer or by circling the appropriate number on the reader service card (this number usually appears at the bottom or side of the advertisement). Some ads include a toll-free number that can be used for locating dealers or for asking questions you might have about the product.

▼ ▼ ▼ Consider a Customized Unit

A travel adventure has no substitute. It is the ultimate experience, your one big opportunity for flair.

ROSALIND MASSOW

▼ ▼ ▼ ▼ ▼ ▼ ▼ ▼ ▼ ▼ ▼ ▼ ▼

Don't overlook customized units in your search for the right RV home, but don't expect to find many manufacturers that will do customizing. Beyond the standard options offered, only a few manufacturers will do customizing any more, as we found when we were looking for our second full-timing trailer not long ago. If manufacturers customize, most likely it will be on only the largest, most expensive units they build. Fewer of these are built so there is time for some out-of-the-ordinary work on the assembly line.

If you want customizing done, be wary of the salesperson who assures you that "we can take care of it here." Salespeople don't want to let potential buyers get away so they may promise more than they are capable of delivering. It is difficult to make alterations to a finished unit and have the job look as if it were done at the factory. Very few dealers have the either the tools needed for doing much custom work on their premises or employ craftspeople that can do such work.

Should your customizing desires be nothing more than having something omitted, you may be unsuccessful in getting the factory to do even this. When we ordered our trailer we did not want the manufacturer to install a dinky, dust-catching, useless spice shelf in the galley and an unreachable-from-the-shower towel ring in the bath. We did not want to patch the holes that would be left when we removed the items, as we certainly would do if they were put on. When we were told that the worker on the assembly line who would install these items would be idle for a time, we suggested that he be given an extra coffee break. Whether he got an extra break we don't know, but the spice shelf and the towel ring were omitted.

We know of a couple who wanted the built-in dinette omitted on their unit, but the factory ignored their wishes and the dinette was installed in the usual way.

We managed to have some customization done because much of what we wanted amounted to taking pieces of furniture from other models and putting them in ours. Nothing was specially built just for us. We persuaded the sales manager at the plant to have the workers install a TV console and a cabinet used in their 32-foot model and a bank of cabinets used in another model. We also wanted a folding table installed from their 27-foot model. We got the table, but it was not installed; we had to put it in ourselves.

A few companies do nothing but build custom units; these might be explored. Some custom units don't cost much more than certain production models.

Whatever type of RV you decide on, it will be wise to purchase your unit from an established company and, if you intend to do much traveling, one with an extensive dealer network so you can count on having warranty work conveniently taken care of and other servicing done.

At the beginning, faced with selecting an RV for fulltiming, we were not absolutely sure whether a trailer or motorhome would be best for us. We weighed all the pros and cons many times over and decided on a conventional trailer.

WHY WE SELECTED OUR RIG
▾ ▾ ▾ ▾ ▾ ▾ ▾ ▾ ▾ ▾ ▾ ▾

We ended up choosing a trailer because it seemed to be the most versatile RV for what we planned to do, and its initial cost and projected future upkeep was affordable for us.

The amount we had to spend was not quite enough for the size motorhome we would need. We did not have a small car, which we anticipated we would need when the motorhome was parked, so this would have to have been purchased as well. We didn't want to be faced with spending money for the continuing maintenance and insurance for two motorized vehicles, and we did not want the bother.

More to the point, our work can take us over back roads that could not be negotiated in a cumbersome motorhome or low-clearance vehicle, so we needed a pickup truck.

When we started, we were lucky and made the right rig choice. We fulltimed happily in our trailer for many years, and when we needed a new RV home, we again purchased a trailer.

Your fulltiming will not be just like ours or anyone else's, so your choice of a rig may be entirely different than ours.

A MOTORHOME OR A TRAILER

There can be no accurate comparison of motorhomes against trailers because it would be like comparing apples to oranges. The two are both fruits, just as motorhomes and trailers are both RVs, but beyond this, the differences between the two are great. We will simply point out facts about trailers and motorhomes. It is not our intent to influence you to buy one type of unit over another.

Although the majority of fulltimers live in trailers, the initial tendency of those considering an RV home is to go with a motorhome. Perhaps they have used a motorhome for vacations and it is what they are used to. Some may feel they will not be able to handle a trailer, and there is often concern about the hitching procedure as well. Undoubtedly, what puts off many people about trailers is the impression that hitching, unhitching, backing, and parking a trailer are mysterious, hard-to-learn procedures. They are not, of course. Otherwise there would not be so many trailerists. These people are no smarter or more skilled than you are.

Towing a trailer is also often thought to be difficult. This, too, is a misconception. When a tow vehicle is properly matched to a trailer and fitted with the right hitch equipment, you will hardly know the trailer is behind you.

▼ ▼ ▼ Auxiliary Transportation

Almost all fulltimers who live in motorhomes have auxiliary transportation of some sort, usually a small car towed behind. It may seem as if we are putting the cart before the horse to discuss this auxiliary transportation before the motorhome itself, but towing a car — dinghy towing as it is sometimes called — is not as straightforward as merely attaching it to the motorhome and taking off. Knowing what is involved might affect your decision as to whether you want to fulltime in a trailer or motorhome.

Do Your Research

There are so many aspects to be considered about auxiliary towing it requires much research about the car to be used and the motorhome itself to be sure both are suitable and compatible. Two valuable resources are *Trailer Life's Towing Guide* (see page 147 for ordering information) and the annual February or March issue of *Trailer Life.*

We will cover only the main points of dinghy towing, but you should do your own thorough research before attempting to tow an auxiliary vehicle.

The research begins with the owner's manual. If you own a car to be used as auxiliary transporation or plan to buy one, consult the owner's manual for the manufacturer's recommendations about whether or not the the car can be towed, and, if it can, the restrictions, if any, regarding towing. Many manufacturers will not authorize towing. Those that do may have limitations on the distance and the speed at which the vehicle can be towed. Don't take the word of salespersons about the suitability of a vehicle for being towed; they often don't know. Use only the owner's manual as your authority so there will be no question about the warranty being honored in case of problems.

Towing Equipment Depending on the manufacturer's recommendations and the towed vehicle's transmission type (manual or automatic), the dinghy can be towed on all four wheels with a tow-bar arrangement, on a dolly that removes the drive wheels from the ground, or on a trailer, which carries the car. A tow bar is the simplest and least expensive towing apparatus; a trailer, the most expensive. But if a tow bar is used, you may need to purchase additional equipment: a device to disconnect the drive shaft, or with an automatic transmission car, a pump to lubricate the car's transmission.

▼ ▼ ▼

Towing Weights The weight of the vehicle you select, the weight of the towing equipment, and the total weight of the motorhome cannot exceed the motorhome's gross combined weight rating (GCWR). Most motorhomes of a size suitable for fulltiming can tow from 3,500 to 4,500 pounds. (See also pages 139–145.)

All states have different regulations regarding the licensing and titling of tow dollies. The regulations are often so ambiguous and bewildering that even the clerks in the motor vehicle departments can't give correct answers to questions you may have about them, so you may have to persevere in your research in this area too.

For my part, I travel not to go anywhere, but to go. I travel for travel's sake. The great affair is to move.

ROBERT LOUIS STEVENSON

▼ ▼ ▼ ▼ ▼ ▼ ▼ ▼ ▼ ▼ ▼ ▼ ▼ ▼

Towing Situations When deciding whether a trailer or motorhome is wanted for fulltiming, the situations that will be encountered with the car must be considered. Taking along this extra vehicle means that those with motorhomes will also have to do a fair amount of towing, hitching, and unhitching.

A motorhome with a small car hitched behind, whether by means of a simple tow-bar arrangement or with a tow dolly, is more difficult to back than a trailer. The car or dolly turns so quickly that there is little the driver can do to control it. The car can jackknife rapidly to the point where damage may be done to the car or the hitch.

Compared with hitching a trailer, hitching a car to a motorhome has fewer steps, which is fortunate because the car cannot be backed more than a few feet. The car or dolly wheels turn the wrong direction during backing. The result is that the tires are dragged sideways, causing undue stress on towbar components and on the car itself. Some campsites are so small that room for a dolly is not available in the site itself.

A towed car is difficult to see while turning corners because of its size and because it follows in the motorhome's path more than a trailer would.

Conventional and fifth-wheel trailers have their own brakes, which are activated when the tow vehicle is braked. When a car is towed without a dolly, the motorhome's brakes alone will have to provide the stopping power for itself and the ton or more the car weighs. Tow dollies may or may not have their own brakes.

Before any towing can be done, the motorhome's hitch arrangement should be inspected. A frame-mounted hitch receiver should be used; never use the bumper for towing.

If you don't want the bother of towing a small car, the motorhome will have to be used for all transportation, sightseeing, shopping, and errand running. Aside from this being impractical, if the motorhome is the sole means of transportation, it could conceivably have to be parked in places where it might be an easy mark for thieves. Motorhome owners are presumed, falsely in many cases, to have more money than other RVers and hence have more valuables stored in the motorhome. With a small car or a trailer's tow vehicle, you can leave your home, with all its valuables, in a campground or RV park where there is usually more security than in unattended parking lots or on the streets.

Without a car for auxiliary transportation, you will be hauling around the heavy weight of everything you own each time you go anywhere. You'll either stay put a lot, or your fuel expenditures will be very high.

If you are the type of fulltimer who stays in one place for months at a time, you could eliminate any auxiliary towing problems by leasing a car for the time you are in one area. This just might prove to be as cost effective as owning a car.

▼ ▼ ▼ Repairs and Servicing

As we see it, one of the biggest drawbacks to having a motorhome is that when the vehicle is in the shop for repair or even routine servicing, so are your possessions and living quarters. Other lodging will have to be arranged if the motorhome is in a shop overnight. No matter how long it remains in the shop there is the likely possibility that mechanics in dirty clothes and shoes will be tracking through your home, and some might take advantage of the situation and relieve you of possessions that are there for the taking. That such incidents occur is evident because it is the rare repair shop that doesn't have a sign posted somewhere stating that the management is not responsible for theft, among other things.

Some shops do not have enough overhead clearance for repairs that would require a motorhome to be raised on a hydraulic lift. What's more, many lifts are not capable of raising the weight of a motorhome.

▼ ▼ ▼

Having warranty work taken care of on motorhomes is sometimes a problem. Motorhomes have an engine and chassis from one manufacturer and the body and interior from another. We have heard many stories about how neither manufacturer would take responsibility when it came to honoring the warranty. In these cases, the motorhome owner is usually bounced from one manufacturer to the other, so it may take some time for even simple problems to be resolved. This would be an annoyance if you were staying put somewhere, but if you were traveling, the possibly complicated logistics and the time and effort spent to get satisfaction could cause considerable frustration. Although a dealership for the brand of engine in the motorhome might be found in most towns, dealers for the make of the motorhome will not be nearly so plentiful.

▼ ▼ ▼ Handling

In handling, motorhomes are the most like driving a car or pickup truck because they are one unit. They can be backed easily, and if designed well and equipped with items such as suitable shock absorbers or an air-bag suspension system they generally have little sway and body roll. Fifth-wheel trailers are the next best for ease of handling. They track well, sway is almost nonexistent, and backing and maneuvering is not difficult. The handling of a conventional trailer is largely dependent on the hitching apparatus and whether it is installed and used properly. The hitch and receiver must be sturdy enough for the weight of the trailer being pulled. Full-timing trailers will be heavy enough to require a weight-distributing hitch that has two equalizer, or leveling, bars. One sway control, perhaps two if the trailer is long, will also be needed. If the equalizer bars, which are adjustable, are attached so that both the trailer and the truck are on a level plane with the ground, there should be no problem with towing or tracking.

When driving in high winds, even when a sway control is used, there is more of a chance of sway with a conventional trailer than with a fifth-wheel or a motorhome. When we had a conventional trailer, we usually did not travel when it was extremely windy, although we did tow it several times in fifty-mile-per-hour winds with no problems. The effects of strong winds on the twenty-nine-foot fifth-wheel trailer we now have are minimal or nonexistent.

Head winds don't affect the stability of any RV, but when driving into a strong wind, fuel consumption goes up considerably, and we have found that sometimes we can't get up to the speed at which we want to travel. Going west on Interstate 80 across southern Wyoming is where this has repeatedly happened to us. The highway runs along at an altitude of 6,000 feet for much of its distance in Wyoming, and the head winds are fierce.

Nature, with equal mind,
Sees all her sons at play;
Sees man control the wind,
The wind sweep man away.
MATTHEW ARNOLD

The tendency of an RV to pull or swerve when being passed by large trucks is greatest with conventional trailers; longer trailers are more affected than shorter ones. The pull is negligible with motorhomes and fifth-wheel trailers. Although we felt the pull in varying degrees each time we were passed by a big truck when we were towing a conventional trailer, we never once thought that we were in danger of losing control of the rig.

Backing trailers, although not as straightforward a process as backing motorhomes (without a car behind), can be learned quickly; once learned, the maneuver can be handled with ease.

▼ ▼ ▼ Storage Space

On average, foot for foot, trailers have more living area and storage space, inside and out, than most motorhomes. As near as we can determine, a motorhome would have to be a minimum of four feet longer than a trailer to have an equal amount of storage space. The storage area in a motorhome cannot compare with that of a conventional trailer towed with a pickup truck with a canopy-covered bed. General lack of storage space may be why so many motorhomes have roof-mounted storage pods.

In recent years, however, storage in some motorhomes has been considerably expanded; basement-model motorhomes have huge storage areas that run the width of the motorhome under most of the floor area. Certain large trailers also have this basement feature.

Having a fifth-wheel trailer means that a portion of the pickup's bed cannot be used for permanent storage because of the hitch location. The front of the bed, ahead of the hitch, however, can be fitted with a weatherproof storage unit if desired. With fifth-wheels, any storage space lost from the pickup bed is regained on the trailer because of the capacious storage area under the gooseneck on most fifth-wheels.

A drawback to having no bed cover or just a forward storage compartment is that groceries, other purchases, and laundry will have to be brought home in the open truck bed, unless the truck is an extended-cab model. The problem with this is items could easily be stolen from the open bed of a truck.

When traveling, an open bed creates considerable drag. This can be minimized by utilizing a total bed cover or by removing the tailgate. Some fifth-wheel owners replace the solid tailgate with a net or mesh tailgate.

▼ ▼ ▼ Climate Control

In any size Class A or Class C motorhome, the dashboard air conditioner is not enough for adequate cooling. If the unit is to be cooled while under way, it must have a roof-mounted air conditioner. Some large motorhomes need two air conditioners to achieve proper cooling. The only way to run such an air conditioner while traveling is with a 120-volt AC generator.

Natural ventilation is better in trailers than in motorhomes. Many trailers have opening windows on all four sides, an arrangement that admits the breeze no matter which direction it is coming from. The front window on motorhomes, which is the windshield, does not open, and few motorhomes have any sort of opening window in the back.

Some trailer manufacturers are doing away with rear windows if the unit is a rear-bath model. Finding a front window on any recent-model fifth-wheel trailer is a rarity unless the living room is in the gooseneck. But even some of these front-living-room models don't have a front window.

Louvered windows are the most efficient because they can be left open in all but a driving rain and angled to catch the slightest breeze. No motorhome model has louvered windows throughout and very few models have them at all. Most opening windows on motorhomes are the sliding type; louvered windows are found on most trailers.

▼ ▼ ▼ Leveling

Most RVers know that it is necessary to have the unit level when parked for an extended period of time. This is mainly because the absorption-type refrigerators used in RVs may not work if they are too much off level. A level trailer or motorhome is also more comfortable for sleeping and eating. And doors on cabinets, wardrobes, refrigerators, or the bathroom will stay open and not swing shut.

In those campsites that are not level, and many are not, leveling a trailer is usually a simple matter. Side-to-side leveling is accomplished by running the wheels on the lower side up onto a leveling board of the needed height before unhitching. Front-to-back leveling is done simply by raising or lowering the hitch jack, or the front jacks on a fifth-wheel, after unhitching.

A motorhome might need to have boards placed under three wheels to level it fore and aft and sideways. We have seen many motorhomes that have been leveled, laboriously no doubt, by stuffing all sorts of various-sized pieces of lumber under the front and/or rear wheels. Often leveling a motorhome takes more time than unhitching and leveling a trailer.

The most effortless method of leveling is to have it done automatically. Top-of-the-line luxury motorhomes usually come equipped with automatic levelers, but they can be purchased, although not cheaply, for use on nearly any motorhome. Some trailers can also be equipped with automatic levelers.

▼▼▼ Living Areas

Again, each type of RV has particular advantages. We like a trailer because our driving and living areas are separate. Sitting in the same seat for driving and relaxing is not appealing to us, no matter how comfortable the seat is. We prefer more spatial variety than can be achieved merely by swiveling around the front seats of a motorhome to make a temporary living room. Others like this feature because once they are parked in a campsite they are inside their home. If, for instance, they have arrived in a pouring rain, they can delay going outside to attach the hookups or take care of other outside duties until the rain stops.

One fulltimer we know who sometimes overnights in highway rest areas likes his motorhome because he can leave the area without going outside, as he might want to do if suspicious characters were lurking about his rig.

With a motorhome, snacks and even meals can be prepared without stopping. If you are the type of person who becomes bored with watching the scenery go by, you can nap or watch television—as long as you are not the driver, that is. A great convenience is being able to use the motorhome's toilet facilities without having to stop. Be sure you're aware of any local seatbelt regulations or other restrictions before moving around in a vehicle that's under way. It's also a good idea to stay buckled up if the weather or road conditions are less than good.

▼▼▼ Other Points About Motorhomes and Trailers

Unlike trucks, cars, and Class C motorhomes, Class A motorhomes may not have a door on either the passenger side or the driver side of the cockpit. Many such motorhomes have only one central door on the curb side of the unit. After numerous complaints about this, some manufacturers are now installing a door on the driver's side. But most of these doors are located so high off the ground, usually right above the front wheel, that they may be difficult to use. They would provide a daily dose of exercise, though, for anyone who used them regularly.

This situation does not exist on Class C motorhomes because the living accommodations are installed behind a conventional van cab, and the door on each side of the cab has been retained.

A disadvantage of motorhomes is that the propane tank is not removable. When it needs to be filled, the motorhome must be driven to the propane supplier. It would be better if the supplier could come to the motorhome, but we have stayed in only a few RV parks where propane was delivered regularly.

When it comes time to replace either the trailer or the tow vehicle, you have the option of replacing just one unit. With a motorhome you have no choice; the whole unit must be replaced.

CHOOSING A PROPER RV SIZE

▼ ▼ ▼ ▼ ▼ ▼ ▼ ▼ ▼ ▼ ▼ ▼ ▼ ▼

Selecting the proper size RV home is as difficult as deciding what type of rig you need. Aside from the important consideration of its having enough storage space for your and others' needs, how and where you will use your rig also figures in the size selection, as it does in the type of RV chosen.

If you will be moving from a fixed dwelling to an RV home, don't even think about buying an RV large enough to hold everything you now own, even minus furniture. If such a rig existed, and you could afford it, it would not be much fun to haul all your possessions around with you all the time. It seems that some fulltimers, however, are trying to prove that you can take it all with you. We came across an extreme example of this in Texas where we saw a huge motorhome, with several roof storage pods, towing a double-deck flatbed trailer. The lower trailer level held a full-size pickup truck; on the upper level was a sizable boat with a large outboard motor on its own trailer.

▼ ▼ ▼ Think Small

The smaller the rig, the more places you will find to park it, not only in campgrounds, many of which have limitations as to what size RV can be accommodated in their sites, but in shopping center lots or on the street. We like to camp in national forest campgrounds. Many of the sites in these campgrounds

I'm as self-contained as a turtle. When I put my key in the ignition, I have my home right behind me.

ESTHER TALLAMY

can only accommodate small units. Size limitations, if they exist, are noted in the campground listings in the *Trailer Life Campground & RV Services Directory.* Before we bought our first full-timing trailer we checked through the listings of national forest campgrounds in states we planned to visit. The small RV sizes the majority of these campgrounds could accommodate had a direct effect on the size unit we chose then and the size we selected for the second full-timing trailer we bought.

National forest campgrounds are not the only ones that have size limitations. Restrictions on size may be encountered in state parks and even in some private campgrounds. It isn't that they consider big RVs undesirable, it's just that their sites are not large enough to accommodate them.

If you plan to do a lot of boondocking (primitive camping where hookups or even a potable water supply is not available), the capacity of the freshwater and holding tanks will be important. We mention this here because the size of these tanks does not necessarily increase in proportion to the size of the trailer or motorhome.

After looking at many trailers, we settled on a 23-foot trailer for our first full-timing RV. This particular model had more space than most of the 25-footers we had seen. We seriously considered a 20-foot trailer that was a scaled-down version of the 23-foot unit we finally bought. Later, we came to realize the 20-footer would have been too small for us and our needs. It is our opinion that for two people to fulltime comfortably and conveniently, a 23-foot trailer and a somewhat larger motorhome are about the smallest that should be considered. A conventional trailer's size designation includes the tongue, which is about 3½ feet long, so a 23-foot conventional trailer has only about 20 feet of actual living space. A 23-foot fifth-wheel, however, having no hitch protruding from the front, has a full 23 feet of living space.

We lived comfortably in our 23-footer for many years before we traded it in on the 29-foot fifth-wheel we now have.

Fifth-wheels had always attracted us, but when we bought our first RV for fulltiming, pickup-bed covers for use with a fifth-wheel hitch were unknown to us; perhaps they didn't even exist then. Knowing we would need the pickup bed for storage, we opted for a conventional trailer with a canopy for the pickup.

Nowadays with the availability of many pickup-bed covers in various designs and materials, we had no hesitation about purchasing a fifth-wheel trailer.

It had become necessary for us to have a slightly larger trailer because our files and reference materials, which we need for our work, have expanded steadily since we first began fulltiming, and we also needed space where we could comfortably work with our computers (we each have a laptop that we don't always use on our laps).

We didn't need or want a very large trailer; for our way of fulltiming it's just too restrictive. We didn't want a unit that would cramp our style, so we looked at fifth-wheels in the 26- to 30-foot range. We had found the total combined length of our first rig to be a convenient size and we didn't want to increase it too much. We were delighted to discover that our 29-footer, when hitched to our truck, measures exactly one inch less in length than the total length of our first rig because 6 of the 29 feet are over the truck's bed when hitched.

Methods of locomotion have improved greatly in recent years, but places to go remain about the same.

DON HEROLD

▼ ▼ ▼ ▼ ▼ ▼ ▼ ▼ ▼ ▼ ▼ ▼ ▼

We like as small a trailer as possible for a number of reasons: it doesn't require as much fuel to haul it around as does a larger, hence heavier, trailer. It costs less to heat when using the propane furnace, and a small RV doesn't need two furnaces to heat it properly or two air conditioners to cool it. Housekeeping and cleaning do not take as much time, and it can be taken more places because it is easier to drive, park, and maneuver. We once watched a couple try to park their 40-foot fifth-wheel behemoth in an ordinary, well-laid-out campsite. They managed it only after many attempts that included much turning, pulling forward, and backing. They almost went into a ditch at the campground's entrance because they could not turn sharply enough. Just yesterday in the campground where we are staying, we watched as another large trailer couldn't negotiate a turn and ended up off the road in the mud.

Drivers of large RVs will always have to be conscious of routes where they might encounter sharp curves, steep grades, low clearances, and other obstacles. To be safe, they will have to keep to interstates, freeways, and main highways using routes suitable for trucks. We know of one couple who took their 35-foot fifth-wheel trailer on a secondary highway and lost their air conditioner and a roof storage pod when they went under too-low an overpass.

We opted for a raised roof in our gooseneck bedroom so we would have standing headroom. This makes our fifth-wheel fourteen inches taller than our conventional trailer. More than once we have had to reject staying in certain campsites, even campgrounds, because of trees with too-low branches.

Traveling is the main reason we are fulltimers, as it is for many others as well. We've noticed those with large rigs don't travel as much as those with small rigs because, no doubt, there is more to do to get ready with a large rig. This is something to keep in mind if you intend to do a lot of traveling.

Because our RV is our only home, we need to have a rig capable of carrying everything we own; we have no home base where anything can be stored. If you have a place where you can seasonally store items you are not using, your rig will not have to be large enough to hold all your worldly goods.

It is sensible to purchase a trailer or motorhome that has sleeping accommodations for only the number of people who will be regularly living in the unit. Every extra bed or bunk takes up space that could be better used for storage.

THE WEIGHT FACTOR
▼ ▼ ▼ ▼ ▼ ▼ ▼ ▼ ▼ ▼ ▼ ▼ ▼

Most RV buyers are little concerned with the weight of the unit, its weight-carrying capacity, and the tank capacity of the unit, but these should be some of the primary concerns for fulltimers since they need to carry so much in their units. By doing some simple calculations using the figures contained in the unit's brochure you will know how much cargo the unit can hold without being overloaded.

How an RV is constructed affects its weight. Some have a lightweight aluminum framework; others are constructed with wood, which is heavier. Because of this, many units of the same size may have widely differing weights. Same-sized units from different manufacturers also may have dissimilar weights, so size is not always an indication of what a unit will weigh.

Keeping weight down aids in fuel conservation; every hundred pounds of added weight increases fuel consumption by about 2 percent. Reducing weight means that there will be less wear on the engine and other moving parts of a vehicle. The less weight tires carry, the longer they will last. Overloading an RV can void its warranty and can contribute to unsafe conditions, so fuel economy is not the only reason for keeping weight down.

▼ ▼ ▼ Motorhome Weights

The weights that must be considered with a motorhome are the dry and wet weights, the gross vehicle weight rating (GVWR), and the gross combined weight rating (GCWR) if an auxiliary vehicle is to be towed. *Dry weight* is the total weight of the vehicle with all tanks — fuel, water, propane — empty and no passengers or cargo aboard. (We use the word *cargo* as a catchall term to define any items that might be put aboard a unit other than what is put into the tanks.) *Wet weight* is the weight with all tanks filled except holding tanks. The *GVWR* is the maximum loaded weight the vehicle can safely carry. On motorhomes this is determined by the chassis manufacturer. It is up to the manufacturer of the body to build a unit that will be functional within the established GVWR. Some manufacturers do this better than others, as you will see.

Here is where things become complicated, as if they weren't already. You might think that motorhomes with the same GVWR, whatever the size, would have approximately the same dry weights. This is not the case. We have surveyed eighteen motorhomes, ranging in size from 28 feet to just under 35 feet, all with a GVWR of 16,000 pounds. The size differential was not surprising since some units were lightweight models. What was unexpected was the extreme variance between the gross weights and the dry weights. The highest dry weight was 15,100 pounds, and the lowest was 10,921. This means that 5,079 additional pounds of passengers, cargo, and wet consumables can be added

Table 6.1
Weight of Wet Consumables

Wet Consumables	Pounds per Gallon
Gasoline	6.15
Diesel	7.10
Water	8.30
Propane	4.25

to the unit that weighs 10,921 pounds dry, but only 900 pounds can be added to the one with the dry weight of 15,100 pounds.

Fuel, water, and propane must be carried, and their added weights will significantly reduce the difference beween the dry weight and the gross weight. Table 6.1 gives the weight of all wet consumables.

Table 6.2 is a comparison between two motorhomes, each with a GVWR of 16,000 pounds. There is a difference of 3 feet, 4 inches in length between the two, Motorhome B being the smaller. The total capacity of all tanks, including holding tanks, of Motorhome B is ten gallons less than in Motorhome A. Note the larger Motorhome A has a negative figure of 192 pounds, which means when all tanks, except holding tanks, are full, it will be 192 pounds *over* its GVWR, while Motorhome B can carry 4,132 additional pounds when water, propane, and fuel tanks are full.

RVers don't usually travel with full holding tanks, but sometimes it's necessary to haul waste around for a few miles. Motorhome A has two holding tanks with a total capacity of 66 gallons. Full, these would weigh 548 pounds. With the other tanks full and no cargo at all and no passengers, this comes to 740 pounds *more* than the GVWR.

Table 6.2
Weights and Cargo Capacities of Motorhomes with Equal GVWR*

	Motorhome A (33'9")	Motorhome B (30'5")
Dry weight (lbs.)	15,100	10,921
Engine fuel	492 (80 gals.)	480 (78 gals.)
Fresh water	515 (62 gals.)	407 (49 gals.)
Propane	85 (20 gals.)	60 (14 gals.)
Total wet weight (lbs.)	16,192	11,868
GVWR*	16,000	16,000
Total wet weight (lbs.)	− 16,192	− 11,868
Cargo weight allowance (lbs.)	(192)	4,132
Holding tank, full	− 548 (66 gals.)	638 (77 gals.)
Adj. cargo weight allowance	(740)	3,493

*Gross Vehicle Weight Rating

Motorhome B, with its 77-gallon-capacity holding tanks, can have them full at 639 pounds and still have 3,493 pounds to go before reaching the GVWR. Which one would you want for fulltiming?

The difference between the wet weight and the GVWR is what you will have to work with when adding all your belongings: clothing and other personal items, kitchenware, linens, a television (30 pounds), food, water hose, tools, folding chairs (8 pounds each), hobby and recreation equipment, and optional added equipment such as an awning (80 to 135 pounds), air conditioner (100 pounds), microwave oven (50 pounds or more), generator (50 to 250 pounds), automatic levelers (250 pounds), even the coach batteries and spare tire, plus the 50-pound weight of the water in a 6-gallon water heater (not included in the tank-capacity figures in Table 6.2, and rarely included in the specifications in manufacturers' brochures). Often forgotten in cargo-weight calculation is your own weight along with the weight of others who will be riding in your motorhome.

While there is a safety factor built into the GVWR that allows for a certain number of pounds over the given weight rating, it is not sensible or safe to push the weight too high.

To further help (or confuse) you, Table 6.3 compares cargo capacity and tank capacity in twenty-two motorhomes with lengths ranging from 31 feet, 4 inches to 33 feet, 10 inches. The difference in length between the longest and shortest of these units is only 2.6 feet, but notice the extreme variations between the GVWR and the dry weights. We have included the tank capacity for all units to give some indication of how motorhomes of this size are equipped. Notice the differences here too.

Even if the unit you buy is not a 31- to 33-foot motorhome, Table 6.3 should make you aware of how cargo and tank capacities can vary in units that are nearly the same length.

▼ ▼ ▼ Trailer Weights

Those who want a trailer for fulltiming have to be concerned with the weight issue too. All trailers have a GVWR, a dry weight, and a wet weight. The differences between the three are

Table 6.3
Selected Class "A" Motorhome Weights and Tank Capacities

Length	Dry weight* (lbs.)	Fuel tank (gals.)	LP tanks (gals.)	Water tank (gals.)	Total wet weight (lbs.)	GVWR (lbs.)	Cargo-capacity holding tanks empty (lbs.)	Total holding tanks (gals.)	Cargo-capacity holding tanks full** (lbs.)
31'4"	10,573	80	20	50	11,565.0	14,500	2,935.0	64	2,403.8
31'4"	12,936	60	22	42	13,747.1	16,000	2,252.9	100	1,422.9
31'6"	11,200	60	25	50	12,090.2	14,500	2,409.7	80	1,745.7
31'7"	12,900	90	25	57	14,032.8	16,000	1,967.1	101	1,128.8
31'9"	12,750	75	21	55	13,757.0	17,000	3,243.0	80	2,579.0
31'10"	12,265	78	18	66	13,369.0	16,000	2,631.0	81	1,958.7
31'11"	10,785	60	20	65	11,778.5	15,000	3,221.5	74	2,607.3
31'11"	12,413	78	18	41	13,309.5	16,000	2,690.5	72	2,092.9
32'	11,975	60	20	86	13,142.8	15,000	1,857.2	68	1,292.8
32'2"	11,886	75	20	60	12,930.2	16,000	3,069.7	90	2,322.7
32'2"	13,800	60	20	46	14,635.8	14,500	(−135.8)	90	(−882.8)
32'4"	10,940	85	22	40	11,888.2	16,000	4,111.8	40	3,779.8
32'6"	12,620	80	15	30	13,424.7	16,000	2,575.2	58	2,093.8
32'7"	13,000	80	20	60	14,075.0	17,000	2,925.0	64	2,393.8
32'10"	14,200	60	23	80	15,330.7	17,000	1,669.2	88	938.8
33'4"	13,250	75	20	75	14,418.7	17,000	2,581.2	76	1,950.4
33'6"	13,500	90	48	85	14,963.0	16,000	1,037.0	84	339.8
33'8"	12,733	78	23	66	13,858.2	16,000	2,141.7	77	1,502.6
33'8"	13,250	80	25	70	14,429.2	15,000	570.7	74	(−43.4)
33'9"	12,475	80	27	70	13,662.7	17,200	3,537.2	94	2,757.0
33'9"	15,100	80	20	62	16,191.6	16,000	(−191.6)	66	(−739.4)
33'10"	12,776	78	23.5	70	13,936.5	16,000	2,063.4	84	1,366.2

*All motorhomes used in table have a gasoline engine.
**Weight of water used to calculate weight of holding tanks' contents

just as important as they are on motorhomes. The trailer must have enough pound leeway so it will not be overloaded when tanks are full and cargo is aboard. A trailer's weight factor, however, differs from that of a motorhome in two ways: passengers do not ride in trailers, so their weights do not need to be considered; and engine fuel is not a factor.

As we noted, some motorhome manufacturers are not successful in building livable units within the limitations of the GVWR set by the chassis manufacturer. Trailer manufacturers either construct their chassis themselves or have them made to their specifications. Since they establish the GVWR, it is designed into each individual model. This enables them to build a unit that has an adequate GVWR in relation to the dry and wet weights. Whether they *do* build them properly is something else again. As with motorhomes, we found some disturbing facts about weights.

For a survey on conventional trailers we selected twenty-three units, ranging from 29 feet to 31 feet, 7 inches, with the greatest length difference being 2 feet, 7 inches. Table 6.4 lists their weights and tank capacities, and Table 6.5 gives a breakdown of two trailers of the same length but with considerable differences in the GVWR and dry and wet weights.

The trailers' figures are somewhat better than those for the motorhome examples, but Trailer A, in Table 6.5, has a ridiculously low cargo capacity with the holding tanks full and an impractical cargo capacity with them empty.

Since fifth-wheel trailers are among the most popular full-timing RVs, Table 6.6 illustrates the weights and tank capacities of eighteen fifth-wheels ranging in length from 29 feet, 6 inches to 31 feet, 6 inches — 2 feet being the greatest length difference.

Be sure any motorhome or trailer you purchase will allow you to safely carry all the supplies and other things you need. When totaling up the pounds, don't forget to add in the weights of any optional equipment. If you can't determine actual weights, they will have to be estimated. (A few manufacturers deliver their units equipped with what other manufacturers offer as options — air conditioners, batteries, spare tires — and include the weight for all this equipment in the unit's dry weight.)

[A driver] is a king on a vinyl bucket-seat throne, changing direction with the turn of a wheel, changing the climate with a flick of the button, changing the music with the switch of a dial.

ANDREW H. MALCOLM

▼ ▼ ▼ ▼ ▼ ▼ ▼ ▼ ▼ ▼ ▼ ▼

Table 6.4
Selected Conventional Trailer Weights and Tank Capacities

Length	Dry weight* (lbs.)	LP tanks (gals.)	Water tank (gals.)	Total wet weight (lbs.)	GVWR (lbs.)	Cargo-capacity holding tanks empty (lbs.)	Total holding tanks (gals.)	Cargo-capacity holding tanks, full** (lbs.)
29'	4,800	14	30	5,108.5	7,000	1,891.5	60	1,393.5
29'10"	4,800	20	39	5,183.2	7,000	1,816.8	60	1,318.8
29'10"	5,570	14	50	6,044.5	7,900	1,855.5	66	1,307.7
29'10"	5,250	14	56	5,774.3	7,792	2,017.7	65	1,478.2
29'11"	4,980	14	36	5,338.3	7,000	1,661.7	70	1,080.7
29'11"	4,450	14	54	4,957.7	8,000	3,042.3	70	2,461.3
30'	4,445	14	32	4,770.1	7,000	2,229.9	54	1,781.7
30'4"	4,210	14	35	4,560.0	7,000	2,440.0	70	1,859.0
30'6"	5,300	14	40	5,691.5	8,800	3,108.5	60	2,610.5
30'7"	5,347	14	30	5,655.5	7,500	1,844.5	60	1,346.5
30'7"	5,922	14	50	6,396.5	7,750	1,353.5	60	855.5
30'7"	5,235	14	40	5,626.5	7,500	1,873.5	80	1,209.5
30'7"	4,710	10	30	5,001.5	7,000	1,998.5	60	1,500.5
30'8"	5,247	14	40	5,638.5	7,500	1,861.5	96	1,064.7
30'10"	5,150	14	42	5,558.1	7,000	1,441.9	60	943.9
30'11"	5,420	14	30	5,728.5	7,000	1,271.5	70	690.5
30'11"	5,455	14	40	5,846.5	7,700	1,853.5	65	1,314.0
31'	5,625	10	30	5,916.5	7,340	1,423.5	96	626.7
31'	5,550	10	30	5,841.5	7,340	1,498.5	96	701.7
31'2"	6,120	14	100	7,009.5	9,240	2,230.5	80	1,566.5
31'2"	5,660	14	38	6,034.9	7,000	965.1	75	342.6
31'6"	4,850	14	30	5,158.5	7,000	1,841.5	70	1,260.5
31'7"	4,625	14	32	4,950.1	7,000	2,049.9	54	1,601.7

*Dry weight includes hitch weight.
**Weight of water used to calculate weight of holding tanks' contents

Table 6.5
Weights and Cargo Capacities of Two 31'2" Trailers

	Trailer A	*Trailer B*
Dry weight (lbs.)	5660	6120
Fresh water	315 (38 gals.)	830 (10 gals.)
Propane	60 (14 gals.)	60 (14 gals.)
Total wet weight (lbs.)	6035	7010
GVWR*	7000	9240
Total wet weight (lbs.)	−6035	−7010
Cargo weight allowance (lbs.)	965	2230
Holding tank full	−623 (75 gals.)	−664 (80 gals.)
Adj. cargo weight allowance	342	1566

*Gross Vehicle Weight Rating

To keep our trailer weight down and to keep our storage areas from becoming overcrowded, we continually clean out cabinets and storage areas and don't carry anything with us unless we need it frequently. We consider weight when we purchase non-consumables and sometimes with consumables as well. Once when we were out of potatoes and sugar, we delayed purchasing them by a day. And, on the same day, we did not refill one of our empty propane cylinders. Our next day's run was to be fairly long by our standards—close to 200 miles—and we knew there would be several grades along the way. Since we made it a point to have little water in our tank as well, we lightened our load that day by about 450 pounds.

THE TOW-VEHICLE FACTOR

If a trailer is selected for fulltiming, it is important to have a suitable tow vehicle, one that is heavy-duty enough to pull the loaded trailer. The engine size and rear axle ratio are the prime factors to consider when purchasing a tow vehicle. Powerful vehicles capable of pulling heavy loads have higher (numerical) axle ratios and high-liter displacement engines. Such equipment is usually standard on three-quarter-ton and one-ton trucks. A half-ton truck can sometimes have a more powerful rear axle and engine installed if the truck is ordered from the factory.

Table 6.6

Selected Fifth-wheel Trailer Weights and Tank Capacities

Length	Dry weight* (lbs.)	LP tanks (gals.)	Water tank (gals.)	Total wet weight (lbs.)	GVWR (lbs.)	Cargo-capacity holding tanks empty (lbs.)	Total holding tanks (gals.)	Cargo-capacity holding tanks full** (lbs.)
29'6"	5,600	14	42	6,008.1	7,000	991.9	60	493.9
29'8"	6,875	14	42	7,283.1	10,500	3,216.9	60	2,718.9
29'10"	8,010	14	50	8,484.5	10,600	2,115.5	80	1,451.5
29'10"	8,870	14	100	9,759.5	13,500	3,740.5	136	2,611.7
29'11"	6,500	14	50	6,974.5	9,700	2,725.5	80	2,061.5
29'11"	7,905	20	55	8,446.5	9,820	1,373.5	85	668.0
29'11"	7,895	23	56	8,457.6	11,320	2,862.5	80	2,198.5
30'	6,855	14	50	7,329.5	9,295	1,965.5	76	1,334.7
30'2"	5,765	14	32	6,090.1	8,000	1,909.9	54	1,461.7
30'3"	7,880	14	55	8,396.0	12,115	3,719.0	130	2,640.0
30'4"	7,800	14	52	8,291.1	10,500	2,208.9	100	1,378.9
30'6"	6,270	14	38	6,644.9	8,500	1,855.1	54	1,406.9
30'10"	6,862	14	50	7,336.5	9,500	2,163.5	74	1,549.3
30'10"	7,400	16	50	7,883.0	9,700	1,817.0	80	1,153.0
30'11"	6,000	14	30	6,308.5	7,000	691.5	60	193.5
31'	6,550	14	36	6,908.3	9,090	2,181.7	62	1,667.1
31'5"	5,610	14	50	6,084.5	8,700	2,615.5	66	2,067.7
31'6"	6,700	14	54	7,207.7	7,000	−207.7	56	−672.5

*Dry weight includes hitch weight.
**Weight of water used to calculate weight of holding tanks' contents

In selecting a tow vehicle and trailer, remember that the loaded weight of the truck and trailer combined, plus passenger weights, must not exceed the tow-vehicle manufacturer's recommendations for the gross combined weight rating (GCWR). For any given tow vehicle, this rating will vary depending on the size of the engine and the ratio of the rear axle. Thus it is possible to have different GCWRs within the same vehicle model by selecting a larger engine and/or higher (numerical) axle ratio than is offered with the standard model.

To calculate the proper size truck for towing a fifth-wheel trailer, the payload rating (cargo-carrying capacity) of the truck must be higher than the hitch weight of the trailer plus the weight of the passengers and any of the equipment carried in the truck.

All major tow-vehicle manufacturers publish a trailering guide that should be consulted before making any decisions about a tow vehicle. Study the guide carefully so the best tow vehicle properly equipped for your purposes will be selected.

Trailer Life magazine publishes a towing guide annually in its February or March issue. The guide covers ratings and specifications for tow automobiles, trucks, and vans for the past five years. Likewise, *MotorHome* publishes ratings for towed, "dingy," vehicles in its March issue each year.

TL Enterprises, Inc. also publishes *Trailer Life's Towing Guide* on a regular basis. This booklet includes specifications for towing vehicles, the suitability of vehicles for towing behind motorhomes, and Class A motorhome chassis specifications. This publication sells for $7.95 and is available from Trailer Life Books, 3601 Calle Tecate, Camarillo, California 93012 or by calling (800) 234-3450.

▼ ▼ ▼

Once again, don't depend on salespeople to give you accurate, correct information. Unfortunately, most of them know next to nothing about the vehicles they sell when it comes to using them as tow vehicles. You probably will find, as we did, that after studying the trailering guides, you will be able to talk more intelligently about the matter than any salesperson you deal

▼ ▼ ▼

with. If we had applied information we obtained from various salespeople, we would have purchased a tow vehicle entirely unsuited for pulling our trailer.

▼ ▼ ▼ Trailer Tongue Weight Considerations

The tongues of conventional trailers are designed to bear a specific weight. This weight must be considered when fitting the tow vehicle with a hitch; the hitch assembly must be strong enough to take the tongue weight. Tongue weight affects the towing properties of a trailer. The heavier the weight, the better the trailer will track. It will be more stable, and less fishtailing will occur. If you have a trailer, and it has any of these problems, perhaps shifting some weight to the front will alleviate them. The tongue weight, which is listed among the specifications on the manufacturer's brochure, should be no less than 11 percent of the loaded weight of the trailer.

The proper combination of trailer hitch and tow vehicle can make pulling a trailer an enjoyable task instead of a chore.

TRUCKS AND OTHER TOW VEHICLES
▼ ▼ ▼ ▼ ▼ ▼ ▼ ▼ ▼ ▼ ▼ ▼ ▼

Aside from certain specially designed vehicles, a pickup truck is the only type of vehicle that can be used to pull a fifth-wheel trailer. Although pickups are the most commonly used tow vehicles for conventional trailers, such trailers, in the medium-size range, can be pulled by passenger cars, wagons, and vans. (For specifications and more technical information on weight ratings, towing packages, axle ratios, and the like, *The RV Handbook* by Bill Estes from Trailer Life Books, 3601 Calle Tecate, Camarillo, California 93012 has comprehensive information.)

SLIDE-OUT ROOMS
▼ ▼ ▼ ▼ ▼ ▼ ▼ ▼ ▼ ▼ ▼ ▼ ▼

Slide-out rooms are available on many trailers and a few motorhomes. They are often offered as an option rather than standard equipment and will add significantly to the weight (and price) of an RV. (A slide-out can weigh from 300 to about 800 pounds.) Some units are offered with the option of three slide-outs, one in the galley, one in the living room, and another in the bedroom. Some may have one long slide-out that holds both the sofa and the dinette.

Because slide-outs are so heavy, manufacturers don't usually include their weight in brochures. Salespeople we have questioned about slide-outs can't seem to provide us with accurate weights either. If you want an RV with a slide-out, you should make every effort to determine how much the unit's weight will be increased, since it will definitely cut down on your cargo capacity and fuel economy.

Besides the additional weight, another aspect of slide-outs should be considered. If you travel a lot, will you want to deal with the slide-out(s) each time you are setting up camp for overnight — it takes one to two minutes to extend a slide-out — or will you leave it unextended and stumble around its walls for the evening? A slide-out often blocks access to cabinets behind its walls until it is extended. Dealers are careful to display units with slide-outs extended for good reason. Such trailers look, and are, cramped and crowded otherwise. Because of the way slide-outs must be constructed, they also have the potential for developing leaks.

Fulltimers who travel to a place and stay there for weeks or months might find the slide-out concept practical since they will not have frequent set-ups to contend with.

Having a slide-out can limit where you can stay. Some campgrounds have sites too narrow to accommodate them. Keeping up with the times, *Trailer Life Campground & RV Services Directory* now includes campgrounds that cannot accommodate units with slide-outs.

A USED RIG?

▼ ▼ ▼ ▼ ▼ ▼ ▼ ▼ ▼ ▼ ▼ ▼ ▼

Many RVers may already own rigs they could use for fulltiming. Indeed, many people purchase their vacation RVs with an eye toward future fulltiming.

But if you do not own a rig, a new one is not essential for fulltiming. In many ways a used one might be better: It will either cost less than a new unit or you will be able to get more rig for your money. What's more, the previous owner should have gotten all the bugs out of it.

Preowned RVs are usually a good buy. Rarely are they traded in or sold because they are worn out. The most common reasons they are on the market are that the previous owner wanted a different size or type of RV, a death or illness occurred in the family, or the RV owner just wanted a new model of the same unit.

Nevertheless, check over a used unit carefully. With a motorhome, a primary concern will have to be that the engine and drivetrain are in good condition.

When inspecting the RV itself, on both trailers and motorhomes, look for cracks in the wheel wells and around pipes. Especially examine the unit for evidence of leakage. Look for water-stain marks or a rippled wall surface around windows and doors and where the roof joins the sides. Note if caulking has been used on roof and side seams and around the outside of window frames. A leak that has not been taken care of may be an indication of dry rot in the structural members if the RV's frame is wood.

Sponginess in floors may also mean dry rot is present. The floors in many trailers will give a little in spots; our first full-timing trailer was purchsed new, but we noticed some give from the first day we lived in it. A distinctive, musty smell often accompanies dry rot.

Used RVs with worn or faded carpeting, upholstery, and draperies are often attractively priced. If such a motorhome or trailer is from a manufacturer that has a reputation for building solid, long-lasting units, it might be worth considering. Any money saved might allow you to refurbish the unit yourself or have it done by one of the many companies specializing in this work.

Although some of the scaled-down or special-purpose furniture used in RVs can't often be found at regular furniture stores, there are certain RV-supply stores that sell RV furniture, so replacements can be found, if needed.

FINANCING THE RV

We mentioned earlier the problem that might be encountered with registering an RV that was being financed in a state other than the one in which the lender was located. If you should want to finance your RV and are a Good Sam Club member, this problem can be avoided by working through the SamCash financing plan, which is handled by the Ganis Corporation. Ganis regularly makes loans for RV purchases to Good Sam members throughout the country. It doesn't matter to them in which state the vehicle is registered.

A minimum downpayment of 15 percent of the cash selling price is required (included within this amount can be costs for tax, license, extended warranties, credit life and disability insurance, and optional equipment.) Loan amounts range from $15,000 to $100,000 or more for terms of ten to fifteen years. Loans are also made on tow or auxiliary vehicles.

Compared with other lenders, interest rates are low and the service is quick. Loan approval is generally within forty-eight hours of receiving a fully completed loan application. For information, write: Ganis Corporation, 660 Newport Center Drive, Newport Beach, California 92660, (800) 234-2647.

SHOPPING TIPS

▼ ▼ ▼ ▼ ▼ ▼ ▼ ▼ ▼ ▼ ▼ ▼ ▼

It won't take much shopping before you are hopelessly confused about the various units you have looked at. If you go about your looking in an organized fashion, it will help to keep the task in perspective.

Make a list of what you want in an RV and what you need (See Exhibit 6.1). Some of the things on our list of wants were a battery box that would hold two good-sized batteries, and, since we had decided on a fifth-wheel, ducted air conditioning to the bedroom in the gooseneck, and an area we could use for a computer work station. Another's list might include such items as storage space for fishing rods or golf clubs. (Many of the following chapters in this book contain information that may aid you in making your list.) Take a small notebook or steno pad along when shopping so you can write down comments and make notes.

▼ ▼ ▼

After some preliminary looking at an array of units, from small to large, you should have an idea of what size RV you need. Since all RVs in a size suitable for fulltiming will have a galley, bath,

▼ ▼ ▼ ▼ ▼ ▼ ▼ ▼ ▼ ▼ ▼ ▼ ▼ ▼

Exhibit 6.1
An RV-Buyer's Scoring Sheet

Items may be graded with an A, B, or C, or graded numerically from 1 to 10, with 10 being the best. Other items are simply scored yes or no, or OK or not OK. Wardrobes, beds, and dinettes should be measured and the dimensions recorded.

Model _____

Dealer _____

Manufacturer _____

Date _____

LIVING ROOM

Couch

   Comfort/sitting _____

   As bed _____

Color/design _____

Storage _____

TV antenna/shelf _____

Carpet/floor _____

Chair/comfort _____

Woodwork quality _____

Lights _____

Curtains/blinds _____

Like best _____

Like least _____

GALLEY

Sink _____

Stove _____

Oven _____

Microwave _____

Refrigerator/make/size _____

Storage/undersink _____

Pantry _____

Woodwork/trim _____

Drawers _____

Overhead cabinets _____

Dinette/comfort _____

Like best _____

Like least _____

BEDROOM

Mattress type _____

Under-bed storage _____

Additional storage _____

Ventilation _____

Woodwork/trim _____

Nightstands _____ Lights _____

Walking room/bed-making ease _____

Like best _____

Like least _____

BATH

Basin/counter _____

Shower _____

Window _____

Woodwork/trim _____

Mirror/lights _____

Medicine cabinet _____

Power vent _____

Storage _____

Like best _____

Like least _____

MEASUREMENTS

Bed #1 _____ Bed #2 _____

Dinette _____

Galley counter _____

Dry weight _____

Wardrobe(s) _____

Couch _____

Shower _____

Outside storage _____ GVWR _____

OUTSIDE

Color _____ Trim _____

Overall attractiveness _____

Floorplan _____ Lights _____

Dead bolt _____

Extras _____

Like best _____

Like least _____

COST

List price _____

Advertised price _____

Air-conditioner _____

Awning _____

Hitch _____

Other _____

Total cost _____

EXTRAS

_____

_____

_____

_____

_____

_____

_____

OVERALL EVALUATION

_____

_____

_____

_____

_____

_____

_____

_____

_____

Source: Adapted from "How to Pick a Winner," O.T. Anderson, *1990 RV Buyers Guide,* TL Enterprises, Camarillo, California.

eating area, and sleeping accommodations, it comes down to finding a size that will comfortably sleep the number of people who will be your full-timing companions and one that has enough storage space for what you will be carrying with you. Limit your looking to RVs in this size. You will save time by ignoring those RVs that are too big or too small for your needs. Once we got down to serious shopping, many of the salespeople we dealt with couldn't understand why we wouldn't even look at any units over thirty feet. We knew we would not purchase a large trailer even if we liked it, so why should we waste time looking at such units? Besides we had already seen lots of large units when we did our preliminary looking to determine the size we needed.

Pick up a brochure on the RV before looking at the unit, not afterwards. As you are going through it, make notes on the brochure or in your notebook about its good and bad points, and write down questions you want answered. You might even rate the RVs you look at with a simple number or letter system.

A sheet listing each option on a particular unit, its individual price, and the total cost can be found in many RVs. If this is not displayed, get the base price of the unit from the salesperson and the cost of the options you want. The option list should be in the brochure. Jot down all this information, even though the dealer will probably offer you a deal at a lower price if you decide to buy.

When you go home to consider which units you like with the brochures and the notes you made at hand, you will have a clearer picture of each individual unit and be able to remember more about it.

Each succeeding visit to dealers should narrow the choices until you are down to just two or three to decide from. We made six visits to one dealer before we finally decided to purchase our trailer from him.

Chapter 7

Selecting a Full-timing RV: Interiors

▼ ▼ ▼ ▼ ▼ ▼ ▼ ▼ ▼

A unit for fulltiming must be considered in a different light than a vacation RV. Fulltimers' needs and requirements are much different from those who live in their RVs only occasionally and for short periods of time.

The actual living that is done in an RV home should not differ appreciably from the living that is done in a fixed dwelling. The closer the two lifestyles are, the more satisfaction you will receive from fulltiming and from the RV you have selected.

When looking for an RV home, don't be overwhelmed by the decor and seeming spaciousness of a unit. Ignore the trappings placed in display models to make them look as attractive as possible; they may divert your attention from noticing a unit's shortcomings. In interiors, livability is the only thing that should be considered when purchasing a trailer or motorhome for full-time use.

BASIC LAYOUTS
▼ ▼ ▼ ▼ ▼ ▼ ▼ ▼ ▼ ▼ ▼ ▼

In a size suitable for comfortable fulltiming, only a few basic floorplans will be found in the four types of RVs discussed in Chapter 6: Class A and Class C motorhomes and conventional and fifth-wheel trailers.

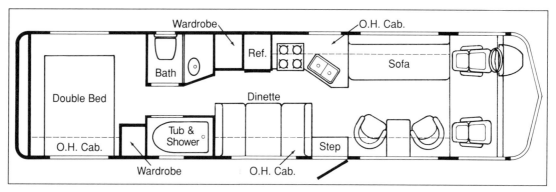

Figure 7.1
A typical layout found in many Class A motorhomes has a rear
bedroom, split bath, and a dinette.

▼ ▼ ▼ Class A Layouts

Class A motorhomes have one basic layout since the cockpit
must necessarily be in the front. The living room is behind the
cockpit because the two swiveling chairs for the driver and the
passenger can become a part of this area when parked. Aft of
the living room is the galley which may have the appliances and
sink on one side and a dinette on the other. The bath is next to
the galley and may be on one side of the unit, or it may be a split
bath with the tub on one side and the toilet and sink on the
other. The bedroom is in the rear on all recent models of Class A
motorhomes (Figure 7.1).

▼ ▼ ▼ Class C Layouts

Many Class C motorhomes have rear baths. Forward of the bath
is the galley. Depending on the size of the unit, a dinette may be
in the galley or opposite the sofa in the living-room area, which
is between the galley and the cab. A bed is over the cab, and this
cabover bed is the only actual bed in a Class C with a full-width
rear bath although usually the sofa and dinette can be converted
into beds (See Figure 7.2).

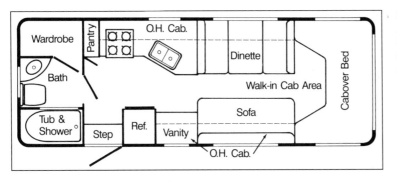

Figure 7.2
A representative layout of a Class C motorhome features a rear bath, split galley, and a dinette.

A mid-size or large Class C with a rear bedroom will have either a side bath or split bath.

Small Class As and Class Cs with a rear bedroom may have a bedside bath: all the usual bath equipment is in the rear on the street side of the unit and tucked in next to the bed, which is located in the rear curb-side corner. Such beds, although called double beds, are usually somewhat narrower than the regular fifty-four-inch-wide double bed, and the baths are not at all spacious. Because of space limitations, they may have only a curtain that can be pulled closed for privacy.

▼ ▼ ▼ Fifth-Wheel Layouts

One of the most popular fifth-wheel layouts includes a split bath located behind the bedroom, which is in the gooseneck (the front section of the trailer that extends over the fifth wheel, or hitch). Behind the bath is the living room, and, in the back, a rear galley, which almost always includes a dining area unless the unit is very small (Figure 7.3).

Another common fifth-wheel layout has a rear living room and center galley (Figure 7.4). A few manufacturers offer fifth-wheel floorplans with the living room in the gooseneck. The galley is adjacent to the living room, and the bath is between the rear bedroom and the galley (Figure 7.5).

It is quite common to find slide-outs as standard equipment on fifth-wheel trailers (less so on conventional trailers and rare

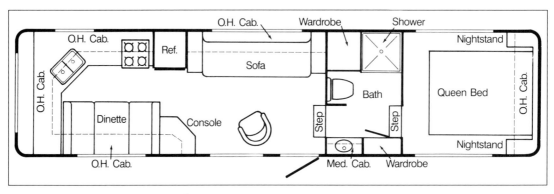

Figure 7.3
This common fifth-wheel trailer floor plan features a rear galley.

on motorhomes). If the slide-outs aren't standard, they are offered as options by most manufacturers. The most common
slide-out holds the living-room sofa (Figure 7.6). The next most
common arrangement is a slide-out for the dinette or free-
standing dining table and chairs. An increasing number of manufacturers are offering a bedroom slide-out. In a fifth-wheel, the
bed usually runs fore and aft with the head of the bed at the
front of the trailer. With a bedroom slide-out, the head of the bed
is in the slide-out, which extends from the street side of the unit
(nearly all manufacturers put all slide-outs on the street side of

Figure 7-4
A fifth-wheel with a rear living room and center galley.

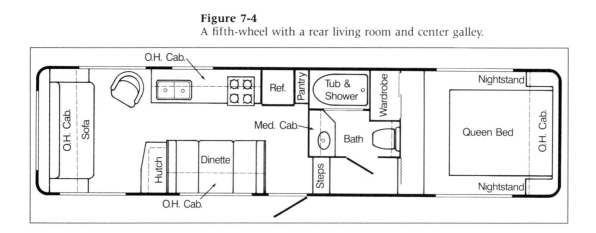

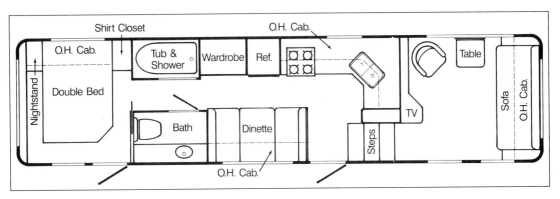

Figure 7.5
The living room is at the front of this fifth-wheel trailer instead of the bedroom.

the unit). When the slide-out is not extended, in order to reach anything forward of the bed in the front of the trailer, you must climb over the bed; there is no room to walk around the foot.

▼ ▼ ▼ Conventional-Trailer Layouts

Conventional trailers do not fit quite so neatly into basic layout patterns, but they have certain aspects to their floorplans that few manufacturers deviate from: the galley or the living room is

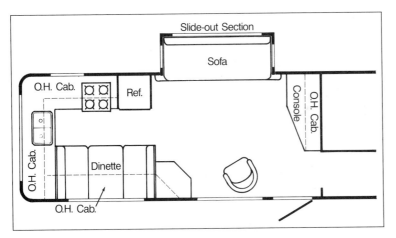

Figure 7.6
A full-size sofa fits in a slide-out room. A love seat and two end tables may be in some slide-outs.

Figure 7.7
A bath dominates the rear of this conventional trailer.

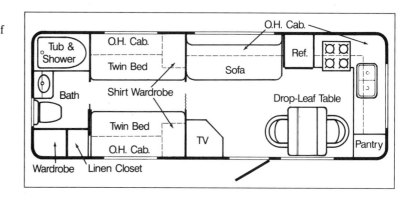

rarely in the rear. The closest the bedroom ever gets to the center of the trailer is when the unit has a rear bath that runs the entire width of the trailer, and the bedroom is in front of the bath (Figure 7.7). In conventional trailers with a front bedroom, the bath remains near or at the rear, and there will be another bedroom, usually with bunk beds, in the rear. Except for a rear bath, be it full width or a bedside bath, the only other bath location is ahead of a rear bedroom (Figure 7.8).

With any floorplan, manufacturers offer certain variations. Slideouts are often an option. Beds can be twin, double, queen, or bunk. Instead of a built-in dinette, a free-standing table and

Figure 7.8
A common arrangement for a conventional trailer is a rear bedroom, side bath, split galley, a dinette, and a front living room.

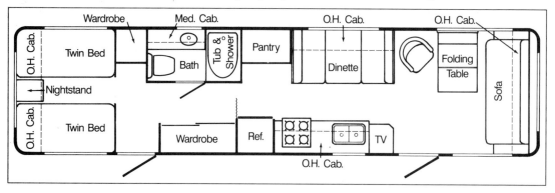

chairs may be an option. Two chairs might be substituted for a sofa. Unless the unit is custom built, the bath and galley locations will be unalterable.

A major concern of fulltimers is the amount of storage space in an RV; they necessarily need to have more items aboard than the average RVer on vacation.

STORAGE
▼ ▼ ▼ ▼ ▼ ▼ ▼ ▼ ▼ ▼ ▼ ▼

The latest trend among builders is to make the interiors of RVs look more like house interiors. To achieve the spacious feeling of house rooms, however, they are sacrificing storage space. A wall that once might have been lined with cabinets is left bare. Deep lockers have been replaced by shallow ones or, worse, open shelves that are virtually worthless for any sort of storage. Free-standing dining tables and chairs replace built-in dinettes, so the storage under the dinette seats is lost. Rarely is the area behind any free-standing furniture devoted to storage, although room often exists for shallow cabinets there.

While all layouts, even those from different manufacturers, are much the same within each type of RV, the storage capabilities incorporated into similar types may be markedly different. Some manufacturers use all the space they can for built-in storage units, whereas others are decidedly unimaginative about where storage compartments could be installed. The quality of the unit seems to have no bearing on this; some luxury models have less storage room than some so-called budget units.

Size is also no indication of the storage facilities. We once compared a 29-foot conventional trailer to the 23-footer we had at the time. The larger trailer had less overall storage space than our smaller one, and the storage space that existed was not well designed for what it was supposed to hold.

Any unit that has a lot of walking-around room—island beds, free-standing furniture—will have much less storage space than units with built-in furniture. Walking-around room is all a slide-out provides—not a bit more storage space. As a matter of fact, storage space is lost with a slide-out since no overhead cabinets can be on the wall above the slide-out.

The RV you select should have enough wardrobes of the right height and width. The galley must have room for all of the appliances and kitchenware you need. Most recently built RVs, even small ones, have a cabinet designed to hold a good-sized microwave oven, which is usually offered as an option. Older units may not have this feature.

Storage space may not be what it seems. When looking at RVs, open every cupboard, cabinet, locker, and wardrobe to see what kind of storage area, if any, is in it. Many will have little or no space in them because the compartment is taken up with plumbing, furnace ducts, fuse panels, or other equipment necessary for some of the RV's systems. Get down on your hands and knees to inspect some of these places if necessary. Also check for usable storage facilities under the dinette seats, bunks, beds, and under the sofas. Many beds lift up, allowing the entire underneath section to be used for storage. This may not always be the case because we have seen units where the water tank was under the lift-up bed, leaving scant room to store anything.

Check outside storage compartments as well. Some of these are so small they are not of much use.

It may be helpful to make notes or mentally picture where you might place your things to see if you will have enough room. If a unit is otherwise suitable but shy of storage space, look for places where storage units could be added later.

Basement-model motorhomes and trailers with their huge storage areas under the floor may have too much storage space. They might hold everything you would ever need, but consider how much weight would be added to the unit if such storage areas were packed full. As shown in the tables in Chapter 6, some units can't be loaded with a lot of cargo even if there is space.

BATHS
▼ ▼ ▼ ▼ ▼ ▼ ▼ ▼ ▼ ▼ ▼ ▼ ▼

Check out a bathroom for size by going through the motions of all your normal bathroom activities. Sit on the toilet. Take off your shoes and stand in the shower. Look in the mirrors. Open medicine cabinets, if you can, while you are standing at the lavatory. Some side bathrooms are so small that a large person could not comfortably use the facilities.

Rear baths are spacious. This is one of the reasons we don't like them. Cleaning bathrooms is not anything either of us likes to do, so the less there is of a bathroom to clean, the better it suits us. What's more, the bath is the room in which we spend the least amount of time, so we prefer to have it as small as practical. The space gained can be used for other purposes.

A feature about a rear bath that appeals to many is that the tub/shower in it is usually considerably larger than that found in a side bath.

The single, small window found in most rear baths will not provide much ventilation and none at all to the rest of the unit if the bathroom door is closed. Many of us like to close off the bathroom even if it is not occupied.

A spacious split bath is found in many fifth-wheel trailers (Figure 7.9). Such baths have a door at each end. One leads to the bedroom, the other to the galley-dining-living-room area. Obviously, no one can go from one room to the other if the bathroom is in use with the doors closed.

Split baths are arranged either with the tub and toilet on one side or with the toilet and lavatory on one side. Sometimes the arrangement is such that the toilet is in a small room by itself that can be closed off from the rest of the bath.

A fifth-wheel's tub/shower can be close to the size of that in a fixed dwelling.

In many small trailers and motorhomes, the only provision for dining is either a dinette or a sofa, chair and fold-up dining table in the living-room area. But space is usually available for both a dinette and a living-room dining area if the model has a bedside bath (Figure 7.10). This bath arrangement makes for cramped quarters, not only in a bathroom, but also in the bed area. This area cannot be rightfully called a bedroom because it is not a room. It is merely a compartment with a bed in it and nothing else except maybe some cabinets.

In a bedside bath, the shower stall is against the rear wall. The toilet is next to it, quite close. There is not much leg room for sitting. The lavatory is opposite the foot of the bed. A solid partition runs between the shower and the bed. A curtain or folding door on a curved track can be pulled around to close off the remainder of the bath. When the curtain or door is in use, the only way out of the bed is though a small opening at the foot which may be no wider than eighteen inches.

Side baths on large motorhomes and trailers may have an

Figure 7.9
A split bath is found in many fifth-wheel trailers. An arrangement such as this allows space for a large tub/shower.

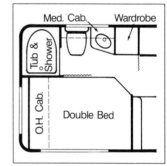

Figure 7.10
Many small trailers and motorhomes have a bedside bath, such as this one, tucked into the sleeping area.

Figure 7.11
This motorhome has access to the bath from the master bedroom and the side aisle.

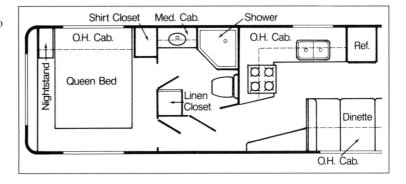

entrance from an aisle or hallway and another from the bedroom (Figure 7.11). Often a wardrobe is accessible from both the bedroom and the bath.

In large units it is not uncommon to find full-size showers with glass doors. This type of residential-size shower is a shower only, not a combination tub/shower.

▼ ▼ ▼

Some fifth-wheel designers should stand back and take a good look at their units with the outside door open. In a great number of them, the toilet is easily visible and the first thing noticed on entering unless the bath door is closed. The bath is less private in fifth-wheels with rear galleys because the living room ends up adjacent to the bath and separated from it by only a thin wall.

One of the aspects of the floorplan we like in our fifth-wheel is that no bathroom equipment is visible when the outside door is open and, even with the bath door open, very little of the bath can be seen from inside; only a sink corner is in view to those seated on the curb side of the unit. This is achieved because all the bath fixures are on one side—the street side. The toilet is between the tub and sink and set well back, next to the outside wall. The tub is behind a wall, and this wall is all that can be seen of the bath from the outside door (Figure 7.12). This is one of the most private bath arrangements we have seen. We feel this ideal (for us anyway) bath was a bonus since we would have purchased this trailer no matter what the bath arrangement was.

Figure 7.12
A fifth-wheel bath arrangement provides privacy without sacrificing spaciousness.

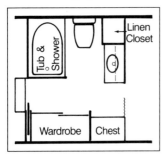

▼ ▼ ▼

A good night's sleep is important to everyone. Most of us are used to getting this sleep on an innerspring mattress. All beds in full-timing RVs should have innerspring mattresses, but although twin, double or larger beds do, other sleeping accommodations have nothing more than a slab or two of foam for a mattress.

Sleeping on foam will not be satisfactory for long. If it is the grade usually used in RVs, after a few months of continual use it will break down, compressing in the sections that support the most weight. When this happens, it provides very little support. Foam is the material used for mattresses in most cabover beds in Class C motorhomes and in bunks, gauchos, and convertible dinettes.

The cabover beds in Class Cs are doubles, but the mattress is in two sections. When not in use, one section is stored on top of the other at the front of the bed. The support for that section of the mattress slides under the two mattress sections, out of the way, so there can be easy access from the cab, with no stooping, to the living area.

Sectioned foam mattresses can be uncomfortable for sleeping. Foam does not have much weight to it so it can easily shift out of place. Someone will end up sleeping, or trying to, on the crack or in the gap that will form between the pieces. This situation occurs with gauchos and convertible dinettes, as well as on cabover beds. The more the foam breaks down, the worse the problem becomes.

If you are considering a Class C for fulltiming in which the only bed is in the cabover section, you will have to somehow climb into the bed every time you go to bed and every time you get up.

Ideally, no bed should have to be specially made up to be used. The best Class C for fulltiming should have a regular bed. A dinette should not have to be converted from a dining to a sleeping unit, a sofa bed should not have to be unfolded into a bed, and a gaucho should not have to be pulled out for sleeping accommodations. Making up a bed from scratch every night and unmaking it every morning is a tiresome chore. We talked with one fulltimer who had just purchased a new trailer. The feature she was most enthusiastic about was, as she put it, "my real

BEDROOMS

▼ ▼ ▼ ▼ ▼ ▼ ▼ ▼ ▼ ▼ ▼ ▼ ▼

bed." She was delighted that she would never again have to go through the morning and evening ritual of converting her sofa into a bed.

▼ ▼ ▼

There are two types of travel—first class and with children.

ROBERT BENCHLEY

▼ ▼ ▼ ▼ ▼ ▼ ▼ ▼ ▼ ▼ ▼ ▼ ▼

Fulltimers with children, however, may have to put up with the inconvenience of making up beds. Most RVs have room for only one bed or a pair of twin beds. Conventional trailers that are two-bedroom models have bunk beds in the rear bedroom. A bed above a front dinette, suitable for two small children, was a standard feature in RVs for years but is no longer common. If a sofa bed is not of top quality, lumps and ridges may develop if it is continually used as a bed.

Bed making on a regular bed in an RV can be difficult unless the bed is accessible from two sides. Many trailers and motorhomes have island beds which makes the chore easier, but the island-bed arrangement cuts down on storage space. No overhead cabinets can be put on either side of the bed since they will project into the walkway. If one side of a bed is against a wall, overhead cabinets can be installed and will be out of the way.

This is a compromise that will have to be lived with: either it will be somewhat difficult to make the bed, or it will be easy and some storage space will be lost.

Our fifth-wheel had an island bed, but we turned it sideways and put it in a corner (see also page 193). Now that we can't walk around the bed to make it, we use a comforter as a bedspread. Its thickness allows it to be easily tossed up over the sheets and blankets and smoothed out, and it covers over any wrinkles that may be in the bedclothes underneath.

The bedroom should have a door or curtain that can be closed for privacy. This is standard on most units.

Some bedside-bath models have storage compartments spanning the rear wall of the unit at the head of the bed. To gain access to this storage one must crawl across the length of the bed. If only little-used items could be stored in this area, it would not be so inconvenient, but in more than one model like this, the only wardrobe in the unit is in this location. Any clothes that needed to be hung on hangers would have to be kept there. Another disadvantage of storage units that fill the entire wall is that they leave no room for a window on that exposure.

On some RV beds, the mattress has one or two corners cut on an angle to provide sufficient walkway space (see the bedroom in Figure 7.5, on page 159). When a mattress such as this needs to be replaced, the only choice is another RV mattress, and often the mattresses used in trailers and motorhomes aren't the best quality. If the mattress hasn't the angled corner and is a standard size, another of better quality could be substituted.

THE LIVING AND DINING AREAS

Most fulltimers do a lot of their living outdoors, but we cannot spend all our time outside any more than we did when we were living in a fixed dwelling. Some fulltimers fail to think about the many rainy or cold days when lawn chairs or a picnic table cannot be used. This is one reason why a table and adequate seating inside the unit are necessary.

Everyone who will be fulltiming in an RV should have a place with comfortable seating for dining. Some dinettes will only seat two adults comfortably. If the only dining table is one that can be pulled out in front of a sofa, try sitting at the table to see if the sofa is high enough in relation to it. Many sofa seats angle downward toward the back. It may be that you have to perch on the edge of the sofa, with your back unsupported, to reach the table easily.

One 36-foot motorhome utilizes a rather makeshift sofa/table arrangement for dining when more than two people must be seated; the only other dining area in the unit is two stools at a galley counter.

Slide-outs with a free-standing dinette can be cramped, since the chairs are limited by the slide-out's walls in the distance they can be pulled out from under the table. If you are considering a four-chair dinette in a slide-out, try out the seating to see if the chairs can be pulled out far enough for easy access, and check for knee room, too; often there isn't much.

All fulltimers living in one unit should have a well-lighted place where they can be comfortable while reading, watching television, engaging in hobby activities, or relaxing. This might be a well-cushioned corner of a bed, a chair, or the sofa if it is comfortable enough for long-term sitting.

If any business work is done in the RV, a comfortable and uncramped place for this purpose should be available.

If you plan to have a television, look for a place where it can be located for convenient viewing. Many units have a special place with an electrical outlet and a coaxial antenna connection for a television. In addition to the TV's 120-volt AC outlet, there may be a 12-volt DC outlet so that an AC/DC television model can be used.

Many televisions in RVs are mounted close to the ceiling or, in some motorhomes, on the floor. For long-term viewing, we would find either of these locations unacceptable. Those with bifocals should check to see if they will have to hold their heads at an uncomfortable angle when viewing.

THE GALLEY

▼ ▼ ▼ ▼ ▼ ▼ ▼ ▼ ▼ ▼ ▼ ▼ ▼

Any RV large enough for comfortable fulltiming will have a galley standard-equipped with a sink, three- or four-burner range with oven, and refrigerator. What a lot of them don't have is an adequate amount of counter space. So counter space, along with enough storage, are the main things to look for when checking out a galley.

▼ ▼ ▼ Counter Space

We have before us many beautiful, full-color brochures from leading motorhome and trailer manufacturers. They cover mid-size and large Class As, Class Cs, conventional trailers, and fifth-wheels. The RVs range from top-of-the-line luxury models to modestly priced units. In every model with a side or a split galley located more or less in the center of the unit, one feature is common to all—little counter space. What could have been additional counter space is taken up by the residential-sized, double sinks that are standard in all the units.

In the galley photograph of one unit, two coffee mugs side by side take up the entire counter space. In another, a loaf of bread fills the counter space. Another has nothing on the counter because, we presume, no item could be found to fit nicely in the three-inch-wide space that constitutes this RV's counter area (we know it measures three inches because it is no wider than the electric outlet on the wall above the counter). Another, with what looks like about the same three-inch counter, is shown with a small dish of candy in the space. With such little counter area where could a toaster, coffee maker, or other appliance be put? Where could cookie or pie dough be rolled out? In the big sink you could easily wash and drain the dishes used for cooking and serving dinner for six or eight, but where would such a meal be prepared if there is no counter space?

A cover for one of the sinks is usually offered as a standard item of equipment. Achieving counter space by this means, however, is awkward and is something we, as fulltimers, would not want to deal with every time we needed to use the sink. Where is the cover placed when using the sink? Certainly not on the counter because the counter is not wide enough. On the floor? This is where one woman we know puts hers. Maybe you could swing around and put it on the dinette table. However it is dealt with, it becomes a matter of "making do" every time a meal is prepared or baking is done. (Perhaps meal preparation could be done in the bathroom; many RV bathrooms have more counter space than do the galleys.) Had RV-sized sinks been used in these units rather than the residential size, from six to ten inches of counter space would have been gained. We should point out, however, that many trailers and motorhomes have little counter space even when RV sinks are used.

Use it up, wear it out;
Make it do or do without.
NEW ENGLAND MAXIM

We realize manufacturers cannot build exclusively for full-timers. Their units must appeal to as broad a group of RV buyers as possible, but we cannot imagine that having little or no counter space would be to anyone's liking.

If counter space is meager, check to see if a folding shelf exists or could be installed at the end of the galley counter. A stove cover (an extra-cost item on most units) will provide additional work space but cannot be used if the stove is needed for cooking.

Although some units have pull-out cutting boards, they cannot double as extra counter space because they are not sturdy enough, and, most of them, when extended to their full length, have a decided downward slant.

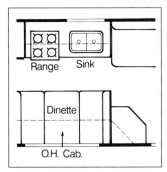

Figure 7.13
A check of this floorplan indicates there is little counter space in the galley.

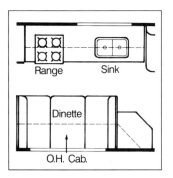

Figure 7.14
This floorplan reveals an adequate amount of counter space between the sink and the stove.

The counter space in a rear or front galley is more spacious than that in a side galley because the counter usually runs along a portion of the side wall as well as the front or rear wall. Even so, in many such units the counter space is surprisingly skimpy. Often the counter extending across the front or rear wall is only about six inches deep—not wide enough to work on. We have seen some models where much of the counter can't be used because it would involve stretching across the range or dinette to reach it.

Again, counter space could be increased if residential-size sinks weren't used. Looking at floorplans in RV brochures usually gives a fairly accurate indication of the amount of counter space (Figure 7.13 and Figure 7.14).

Residential-size sinks add to the weight of a unit since they are made of porcelain-coated heavy steel. This material is much heavier than the stainless steel used for RV-sized sinks.

▼ ▼ ▼ Countertop Materials

Unnecessary weight is also added by many manufacturers who use ceramic tile or Corian for their countertops. At a recent RV show, we were quite surprised to find that a small sink cover couldn't be removed by putting a finger in the hole provided for the purpose. The cover was made of Corian and was very heavy. If sink covers are Corian so is every counter top, and probably every table top, in the unit. Imagine how much weight is added with the use of this material. We're sure Corian is a fine material, but, in an RV, a lightweight plastic laminate is more suitable.

▼ ▼ ▼ Galley Location

We had to look long and hard for our trailer because we did not want a rear-galley model, which is very popular with many other RV buyers. We had to purchase our rear-living-room model without ever seeing one. Dealers just didn't stock them. Our reasons for not wanting a rear galley are many. One of them is the same reason we don't like rear baths; we don't spend a great amount of time in the galley so we don't want this room to take up one of the best locations in the RV. Nearly all rear galleys have windows on three sides. We would rather have this triple exposure in the living room. Often the best view is from the rear of a site, and we want to be able to enjoy it fully. When working in the galley, most people haven't the time to enjoy the view. It's just as well because nothing can be seen from the galley's usual two-louver-high rear window without bending down. With a rear or front galley the living room ends up in the center of the unit, and the view from its windows are often of the RVs parked in the sites on each side of you.

▼ ▼ ▼

Another objection we have to a front or rear galley has to do with traffic through the RV. We don't think we are unusual in that most of what we carry into our RV is food and kitchen supplies, and most of what we carry out is trash, mainly empty containers, and other discarded packaging from food products. Since much of this goes into and comes out of the galley, it must be carried to a rear or front galley through the living room and across the carpet that may be in that area. We avoid this tracking because our galley is immediately inside the outside door.

Although fewer and fewer manufacturers are building trailers with two outside doors, some units have them. But only on fifth-wheels will the rear door open into, or near, the galley if it is in the rear. One builder makes an innovative, two-door, fifth-wheel trailer. One door is in the usual place in the center of the unit on the curb side. The other door is in the center of the rear wall and opens directly into the galley.

The rear of a trailer is the most affected when going over railroad tracks, potholes, or any other types of bumps that may be encountered. The jarring and shaking can cause containers to topple over in cabinets or in the refrigerator, perhaps breaking and spilling the contents. There is usually some slipping and sliding of cabinet contents no matter what precautions are taken. Even though we slow down for bumps, we have had several experiences with items being affected by bumps just because they were in the rear. After one severe jolt, the rear-window shade jumped out of its brackets and fell off, the removable rear table removed itself by itself, and books were bounced out of bookcases. We prefer not to think about what messes we would have had to clean up if our galley had been in the rear.

The galley equipment and supplies, the refrigerator and its contents, range, microwave oven, counters, and many cabinets that may be filled with cooking utensils, appliances, and foods collectively constitute the heaviest "room" in an RV. Weight distribution is supposed to be a key factor in the initial planning of a unit, so any trailer with a rear galley should be designed and constructed to allow for the heavy weight aft. This being said, we still prefer to have a trailer where the area with the heaviest weight is concentrated over, or in front of, the axles.

▼ ▼ ▼ Galley Storage

The Microwave Oven

Many builders now include a specially sized, pre-wired cabinet for a microwave oven. As an option, the builder often offers a microwave oven in a size that takes up all of the space in the cabinet. If you plan to locate a microwave oven in a cabinet, be sure you will have enough remaining storage space for other galley items.

We don't use a microwave oven often enough to warrant having a large one (we didn't want to add the weight either), and we also couldn't do without the storage space that would be lost with a large oven. Since large was the only size the manufacturer of our trailer offered, we decided to purchase and install one ourselves in the size we wanted. With factory-installed microwaves, the oven is visible—not behind a cabinet door. We needed to install ours inside a cabinet (Figure 7.15), so we had to do some careful measuring to be sure the cabinet door would close and there would be enough ventilation space around the oven. (Factory-installed ovens have air vents on the top and bottom of the framework that holds the microwave.) To insure enough air circulation, we constructed a short, pivoting arm that is used to

Figure 7.15
A small microwave oven installed inside a cabinet leaves plenty of room
for storage of other items in the cabinet. Note the foam strip on the
cabinet to the left of the microwave, which prevents possible scratches
to the oven door when wide open.

hold the cabinet door ajar when the oven is in use (Figure 7.16).
We could simply open the cabinet door, but when opened, it
extends into the walkway and is obstructive.

The Refrigerator

A small refrigerator often has storage compartments above and
below it. A large refrigerator may leave no room for other storage
in the wall in which it is mounted.

The two of us managed nicely in our first full-timing trailer
with a refrigerator that had just over a six-cubic-foot capacity.
The small freezer size was adequate for our needs. Admittedly,
on some holidays it became temporarily overloaded. This size
refrigerator had a large cabinet above it and an extra-large
drawer below. In our present trailer, the refrigerator is about two
cubic feet larger. We have no storage below it but have a cabinet

Figure 7.16
To avoid having the cabinet
door open across the walkway and for ventilation when
the microwave oven is operating, a short, pivoting arm was
installed to hold the cabinet
door slightly open.

above only because we have a fifth-wheel trailer and the refrigerator happens to be located where the roof begins its upward slope.

RV buyers don't really have a choice about what size refrigerator is in a unit; it is what it is. We mention size here to show that it is possible to fulltime with a smaller-size refrigerator and to make the point that its size should not be a reason to reject any unit if in other respects it is satisfactory.

Some galleys have a floor-to-ceiling slide-out pantry that offers handy storage for bottles, canned goods, and cereal boxes. A pantry will hold many items in a relatively small area, but remember, when it is full it will add significantly to the weight of a unit. A five-shelf pantry will hold about thirty-five, sixteen ounce cans. If a pantry exists and is not needed for food storage, it might be put to use for storing other things.

WINDOWS

▼ ▼ ▼ ▼ ▼ ▼ ▼ ▼ ▼ ▼ ▼ ▼ ▼

One of the aspects of living in an RV we enjoy is the feeling of being close to the outdoors because of its many windows. We had a four-way exposure in our first full-timing trailer, and we have it in our present fifth-wheel trailer. When we were shopping we found only a couple of manufacturers offered a front window as an option. Since this was high on our list of wants, it figured prominently in our selection of the trailer we bought.

A current practice among many manufacturers is to eliminate windows wherever possible. The fewer the windows in a unit, the easier and less costly it is to build. Front windows, which once were standard on fifth wheels, have almost disappeared on those models with the bedroom in the gooseneck. The fronts of many fifth-wheel trailers are made of fiberglass, and the molds are not designed to incorporate a front window.

When we were looking for a fifth-wheel, the models with living rooms in the gooseneck had just been introduced. Then, nearly every model of this type had a front window. When we inquired about a front-bedroom model with a window, we were repeatedly told that manufacturers didn't put them in because they leaked. Once we received this information when we were standing in a gooseneck-living room model with a window in

▼ ▼ ▼

the front. We asked the salesperson if the type of furniture used in the front room determined whether the window would leak. We sensed he didn't appreciate our attempt at humor.

Front windows are still a standard feature on conventional trailers, so there is no reason they shouldn't be on fifth-wheels too. It is true a front window is more prone to leak than any other window since it receives the full force of the wind as the trailer is being towed and thus tends to work loose.

We had a leak in our conventional trailer's front window, which we fixed, and we have had a minor leak in our fifth-wheel's front window, which we also fixed. We prefer to take our chances with leaks rather than do without a window. Also, so much heat rises into the gooseneck area of a fifth-wheel we want as many windows as possible for ventilation in hot weather. We are not always in campgrounds with an electrical hookup, and we don't have a generator so sometimes we can't use the air conditioner. Besides, we prefer fresh air and only use the air conditioner when it is extremely hot.

Aside from the ventilation provided by opening windows, windows also admit light, which is needed in the relatively small interior of an RV. Without lots of light RVs can appear gloomy and unappealing.

▼ ▼ ▼

Many manufacturers install picture windows in their units in yet another effort to incorporate residential features. We think this is another use that is best left for houses. One of our objections to picture windows is that the opening portion is quite small in relation to the size of the window and provides little ventilation. The other objection we have to such windows has to do with privacy. When a picture window is in a house, which often is set some distance back from the street or side-walk, it is usually difficult for passersby to look in. Not so in a campground, where the sites are almost always close together. In addition to the tall picture window that is generally in the living room, some manufacturers install another one by the dinette. Since the table is visible, the food being eaten, the way the table is set, and the diner's legs are in view of anyone who walks by, or who is looking out from an adjacent unit. Our trailer model had dinette and living-room picture windows, but we persuaded our manufacturer to install regular three-louver opening windows in place of them.

▼▼▼ Window Coverings

Window coverings are often an option on many RVs, and a choice can be made between several types of window shades or miniblinds. Compared to blinds, window shades of any type will do a better job of insulation in both hot and cold weather. Blinds have no insulating effect at all and cannot be closed tightly enough to keep out drafts. Motorhomers also have to put up with the rattling of blinds when they are traveling.

One of the reasons we find fulltiming attractive is that housecleaning is easy and takes little time. We want nothing in our RV home that is difficult to clean and take care of. In our opinion, miniblinds are mainly dust catchers and we want nothing to do with them. When we bought our trailer, we opted to purchase our own window coverings (good quality, room-darkening window shades), but the trailer arrived with a miniblind on the small galley window. We took it off immediately. It's bad enough to have to wipe dust from blinds; we didn't want to contend with cleaning even a small one that would be covered with cooking grease. New, pleated, cloth shades are now widely available in both room-darkening types, as well as those that let in some light and air.

TRY BEFORE BUYING

▼ ▼ ▼ ▼ ▼ ▼ ▼ ▼ ▼ ▼ ▼ ▼ ▼

Before purchasing an RV, try out anything that pulls out, up, or down, or that slides, swivels, or opens. A couple we met found all nine windows in their new fifth-wheel trailer would not open but did not discover this until several weeks after they took delivery of it.

Pay attention to bedroom and, particularly, bath doors that might block passageways if they are left open. On cabinets, see that their doors can be opened fully.

Check all hardware on cabinet doors, especially if you purchase a unit from the dealer's lot. Some units have cabinet hardware that is not very sturdy and that may have been broken by other shoppers checking out cabinets.

Perhaps our outlook on fulltiming is different from other fulltimers, but we are RVers first and fulltimers second. We think an RV that is a home should be outfitted and equipped like a home yet still embody all the desirable qualities of an RV: mobility, ease of maintenance inside and out, and coziness. An RV home should be one in which you can be comfortable and one that will allow you to go about the business of living — cooking, dining, showering or bathing, or relaxing — without any inconvenience, but we do not think it is necessary to achieve this comfort and convenience by incorporating residential features into the RV.

AN OVERVIEW

▼ ▼ ▼ ▼ ▼ ▼ ▼ ▼ ▼ ▼ ▼ ▼ ▼

▼ ▼ ▼

We've already discussed residential-size sinks with their heavy weight and large size. Other residential items turning up in RVs are ceiling fans that don't allow much head clearance under an RV's low ceiling, and washers, dryers, and dishwashers. These are heavy items to haul around, and we have been in many campgrounds where there wasn't enough electricity at the site to run such appliances. Ceiling-high china cabinets as wide as a unit are appearing in many large trailers. Bath skylights, instead of the more practical and, we think, necessary opening vent with an exhaust fan, are being installed in more and more RVs. Often when a skylight has been substituted for the opening vent, it leaves the bath with no form of ventilation to the outside. Only a few of these skylights have a shade to prevent heat loss in the winter and to keep the sun out in the summer.

Wall lamps with glass globes are becoming increasingly common. The screws holding the globes will vibrate loose after some traveling is done, then the globe will topple out and shatter unless the screws are continually checked for tightness.

Chandeliers have been hung in some units. A woman we talked with the other day said she finally took out her chandelier but not before it had dented and scratched a cabinet. She said she could never anchor it securely enough to keep it from swinging while traveling. In a recent motorhome brochure, we noticed ceiling and wall lamps that looked like small, crystal chandeliers. It doesn't take too much imagination to figure out how impractical such lamps would be in a home that was designed to be movable.

If you want these house-type accessories in your RV home, it will be practical only if you do very little traveling or if you intend to park your RV in one place. For traveling RVers, such as ourselves, it would be a nuisance to have them. Some of these items add weight that will cut down on fuel economy; others must have special attention prior to getting under way. No matter how long we have been sitting, we can be ready to go in about a half an hour, and we want to keep it that way. If we saddled ourselves with such items, it would diminish much of the flexibility and freedom that fulltiming affords and that we enjoy so much.

We all have our own fulltiming philosophy; keep yours in mind when shopping for an RV home so you can purchase one that will allow you to pursue the lifestyle as you wish.

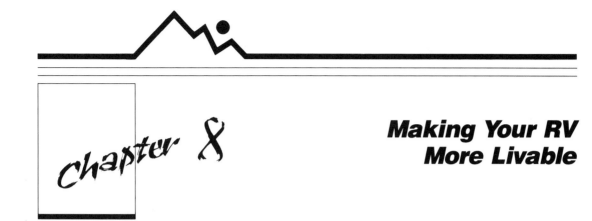

Chapter 8

Making Your RV More Livable

Although RVs are designed and built so everything needed for basic living is in the unit when purchased, alterations and additions can be made to almost any unit so that it is more personalized and better suited for the uses of its occupants.

On new units the livability can be increased and made even more comfortable than it already is. A preowned RV or an RV you may already own that has been used for vacations may need to be refurbished and remodeled somewhat to make it more suitable for fulltiming.

On the following pages, along with general information, we describe some of the ways we modified both our trailers to make them better suited for us and our full-timing lifestyle. Perhaps these ideas, or variations of them, could be applied to your RV home.

COLOR SCHEMES

The colors used in RVs' interiors evolve and change according to what is currently popular in residences because RV manufacturers want their units to look as fashionable and up to date as possible. But something many RV interior designers overlook is the fact they are dealing with an interior that is only eight feet wide. In such a small area, a bold upholstery pattern can be overpowering, and the use of dark woods for the cabinetry and dark colors in the upholstery and carpeting can make the interior seem gloomy and cramped. These impressions are intensified if there are few windows and inadequate interior lighting. We recently attended an RV show where we saw several of these overly dark interiors. One unit had dark teal upholstery, medium-brown carpeting, brown-black walnut cabinetry, and not many interior lights. Because the entire rear wall was taken up by a hutch, there was no rear window to admit any light from that direction. We heard a woman who had been looking at the unit say to her companion, "Let's get out of here; it's depressing." We agreed with her. Dark, dimly lit living areas *can* be depressing whereas bright, light areas can have quite the opposite effect.

If the unit you select has a dark feeling to it because of the color of the cabinetry, you may want to select upholstery, draperies, and carpet colors in the light or medium shades offered. Color choices are very personal, and individual tastes vary widely, but we would never ever opt for a predominantly brown color scheme. Most RV interiors have enough brown with the cabinetry and wall paneling. We would prefer something in the cool blue-and-green spectrum to contrast with the warm wood tones of the cabinets and paneling.

We had no problem with an abundance of wood in our fifth-wheel trailer since all the walls are off-white, so we didn't have to be concerned with selecting a too-dark color scheme. We choose a scheme based on the upholstery we wanted. The only problem was that this scheme included a carpet and draperies in mauve, a very fashionable color when we bought our trailer. Not only do we not like mauve, we didn't want such a trendy color in a unit we intend to keep for many years. We knew in time the mauve would look just as outdated as the chartreuses and oranges that were the fashionable colors in RVs a few years ago.

We were able to persuade the manufacturer to let us combine two color schemes so that a beige carpet and ivory drapes replaced the mauve ones.

If you are refurbishing an old RV, you can decorate with any color you please. But if you intend on keeping your unit for some time, you may want to use neutral or classic colors for upholstered pieces and carpeting and use the current fashionable colors for items that are less expensive to replace, such as decorative pillows, towels, and bedcoverings.

It has long been known that the colors surrounding us can affect our emotions. When only vacations and weekends are spent in an RV, its interior colors aren't as important a factor as they are in a unit in which you live full time.

CARPETING

▼ ▼ ▼ ▼ ▼ ▼ ▼ ▼ ▼ ▼ ▼ ▼

In many RVs, carpeting is standard; where it is not, it is often offered as an option.

The addition of a carpet will add considerably to the hominess of an RV, and it will serve to mute sounds and provide a certain degree of insulation.

Our first trailer, in which most of the walls were wood paneled, came with a carpet option in three colors: dark brown, medium reddish-brown, and light brown, so we decided to install our own in a color more to our liking.

To figure out how much carpeting would be needed, we carefully measured the trailer's floor, scaled down the figures (one foot equaled a half inch), and transferred them to graph paper. We planned to have the carpet pieced in four sections: one each for the bedroom, bath, galley, and living-dining area. Having one long piece would have been difficult to measure accurately, hard to handle when cutting, and very wasteful.

We cut the graph-paper plan into the four sections we wanted so we could try them in various layouts on other sheets of graph paper we had marked to represent the standard 12-foot and 15-foot carpet widths. This way we were able to determine just how much carpet we would need.

Because an RV's interior has many corners, rounded and otherwise, having exact measurements is critical for a perfect fit. Before we began cutting the carpet, we carefully cut templates from newspaper to use as patterns. The templates were placed on the carpet in the same way we had placed our scaled-down sections on the graph paper when we were determining the amount of carpet we would need. Later, when we recarpeted, we used the carpet we replaced as a pattern.

We found we did not need to use double-faced tape or other means to keep the carpeting from shifting; it stayed in place because it was well fitted. Having the carpeting unattached and in sections allowed each section to be lifted or folded back so the floor underneath could be cleaned periodically. It's amazing how much sand and dirt sifts through the carpet no matter how careful you are about wiping your feet before entering. The carpet in our present trailer is securely anchored down, and we are sure we are carrying around a goodly amount of tracked-in sand and dirt we can't clean out because we can't get at it.

We had no hesitation about carpeting the galley area. Today's synthetics are easy to clean, and spots and spills are easily removed with a damp sponge. With carpeting throughout, the entire floor can be cleaned with a vacuum; extra tools for mopping or sponging are not necessary.

In our fifth-wheel trailer, the carpeting was standard (except for the galley area, which was an option we selected). We were somewhat concerned that its light color would be hard to keep looking clean and fresh, but it is a fairly good quality, stain-resistant carpet, and we have found the upkeep to be easy.

Because of easy-care carpeting, fulltimers should not feel that vinyl floor coverings are necessary; carpeting is just as practical, and, for the reasons mentioned above—hominess, sound-deadening qualities, insulation—even desirable.

DRAPERIES AND CURTAINS

▼ ▼ ▼ ▼ ▼ ▼ ▼ ▼ ▼ ▼ ▼ ▼ ▼

Adding new window coverings can go a long way toward giving a new look to an old unit.

If you know how to use a sewing machine, you can make curtains, even pleated draperies, easily. RV-window coverings are short so they are easy to handle, and, being short, they take little fabric and can be quite inexpensive if you make them yourself. Some ready-made curtains and valances will fit RV windows without any alteration, and much of the readily available curtain, drapery, and windowshade hardware can be used in RVs.

Some RV models have a sheer or loose-weave privacy curtain on certain windows, usually in the bedroom, but other units have them throughout. The curtain admits light and air, but, from the outside, the interior is not visible through it unless the inside lights are on. Curtains of this type are useful, easy to make and install, and can enhance an RV's decor if the fabric used is a lighter shade of one of the colors in the upholstery or wallcovering.

Our trailer didn't come with privacy curtains, but we have added them to nearly all our windows. They are useful in the close quarters of some campgrounds. We wanted privacy curtains that could be pulled when we were in a campground site without much privacy but that could be pushed to the side of the window when not needed. The curtains we selected are simply a common, openwork, crocheted-type café curtain. The twenty-four-inch-long standard size fits all but one window without any alteration. The curtains are hung next to the inner edge of the draperies on the same rod. (We don't need to pull the draperies at night because we have window shades.) We bought the curtains at Sears so we could purchase replacements or additional curtains that would match. We first put privacy curtains on only our three bedroom windows. Then we put one on the window by the dinette. Shortly after, we put them on all the remaining windows except for the small galley window. We like the way they look, they afford privacy when it is needed, and when pulled across a sunlit window they provide a pleasant, diffused light instead of the bright glare of the full sun.

PICTURES AND DECORATIVE ACCESSORIES

▼ ▼ ▼ ▼ ▼ ▼ ▼ ▼ ▼ ▼ ▼ ▼

Pictures and displayed mementos do more to make living quarters homey than just about anything else. They can be photos of family, friends, pets, or places you have been that are special to you. They might be paintings and drawings done by artists you admire, or items you, family members, or friends have created.

▼ ▼ ▼ Hanging Framed Accessories

Hanging framed items on RV walls is not as simple as on fixed-dwelling walls. Frames must be firmly attached to a wall so they will not fall off or swing from side to side and mar the wall's finish when the RV is moving.

We have had good luck in attaching framed items by using a small screw in both the top and bottom of the frame. The type of

Travelling in the company of those we love is home in motion.

LEIGH HUNT

▼ ▼ ▼ ▼ ▼ ▼ ▼ ▼ ▼ ▼ ▼ ▼ ▼

frames we use—not always easy to find—are not too thick and are flat, not rounded, or have a flat place through which a screw can be easily inserted. We avoid metal frames because drilling screw holes in them is more difficult than in wood or composition frames.

We use one-inch, number-four brass screws. This length is necessary because even small, thin frames can be a half-inch thick, and enough of the thread must extend through the frame to secure it to the wall. These long, thin screws are rather difficult to find, so we buy plenty of extras when we locate some. Screw heads can be disguised somewhat by coloring them with a permanent marker that matches the frame's color.

We have a set of weather instruments—thermometer, barometer, humidity gauge—set in a wooden panel we wanted to mount in our trailer. The back of each instrument's case projects about three-quarters of an inch beyond the panel. Our problem was to figure out a way to screw it flat against the trailer's wall. Bill finally came up with a practical method: He cut four small wooden triangles, each three-quarters of an inch thick, and glued one in each corner on the back of the panel. The triangles, being the same depth as the projecting backs of the instruments, allow the panel to rest flat against the wall. Bill drilled holes in each corner, through the panel and through each triangle, so the instruments could be mounted to the wall with extra-long screws.

We use double-faced mounting tape to attach some objects to the walls. A picture frame with glass is heavy, so enough tape must be used to hold it securely (directions for the amount to use will be on the package). The quality of mounting tape varies considerably. We have learned that it is best to buy only name brands; the adhesive is better and longer lasting. Still, the holding power of even the best mounting tape is limited; it seems to dry out eventually, so it would be best to not mount valuable breakables exclusively with tape. And it is a good idea to periodically inspect mounted items to see if they are still firmly attached to the wall. Even grasp the item and try to pull it off. Better it should come off in your hands than fall off when no one is around to catch it.

▼▼▼ Other Options for Hanging and Securing Accessories

Mounting tape can be used to hold lightweight, decorative objects on a shelf or counter if they are to remain in one spot. If you want to move the item occasionally, it can be held fairly securely with a small piece of florist's clay. The clay has just enough holding power to keep the item from shifting or sliding; however a little pressure will release it. The clay should not affect the finish of most RV materials, but it might leave a dull area or grease spot on some woods.

Dusting around these semifixed objects can be a bother. Rather than attaching items so they will stay in place when under way, we have found convenient places to stow the few loose breakables we have. Putting them away is a routine part of our getting-ready-to-go procedure.

When a mounted item is removed, pieces or strips of the tape remain on both the mounting surface and the mounted item. It takes a little bit of effort to remove them, but the tape has never marred any finishes on which we have used it.

We wanted a wall clock that was easy to see from our living room, but we didn't want the usual factory-mounted type in the center of a bank of cabinets. We preferred to have a cabinet door there for easier access to the storage space. Because we travel from one time zone to another frequently, we needed to mount the clock securely but in a way that it could be repeatedly removed for easy resetting. If it were hung on a nail or hook, as it was designed to be hung, it would fall off when we were traveling. Our clock, like many wall clocks, isn't flush on the back. The sides of the case are about an inch deep, which means the back of the clock is recessed—the opposite of our weather instrument panel where there are projections on the back—so we mounted it in somewhat the opposite way from the weather instruments. We cut two wooden blocks measuring one inch (the depth of the case's side) by three inches (about two inches less than the width of the clock) and attached them to the wall with mounting tape (screws could be used). The blocks were located so they would be near the top and bottom of the clock inside its case.

Adhesive Velcro strips were put on each wood block and on the back of the clock to correspond with the blocks' locations. For resetting, we simply pull the clock off gently, and firmly press it back on afterwards. We purposely bought a lightweight, inexpensive clock — lightweight so it wouldn't require a great deal of mounting tape and Velcro to hold it, and inexpensive because when we got the idea of hanging it with Velcro we weren't sure it was practical and didn't to risk having an expensive clock fall off the wall when the trailer was moving. This method of mounting has proved to be successful, probably because the clock weighs just a few ounces. It has stayed in place during many thousands of miles of travel.

BATHS
▼ ▼ ▼ ▼ ▼ ▼ ▼ ▼ ▼ ▼ ▼ ▼ ▼

Although most RV baths have plenty of storage space, they often do not have enough practical towel rods for even two people. A couple with children will be hard put to find adequate space for everyone's personal towels.

▼ ▼ ▼ Towel Holders

Our first trailer came with just one towel rod large enough for a bath towel. It was mounted on the bottom of the medicine chest. Being large, a bath towel hung on this rod would have been in the way of anyone using the toilet.

The other towel holder was an impractical contraption built into a center panel on the bathroom door. It had three narrow rods that could hold a bath towel only if it were folded in thirds. We did not want to spend time carefully folding bath towels just to fit the rods, and we needed a place wide enough to spread towels to dry, so we replaced the holder with two brass café curtain rods (Figure 8.1.).

Removing the built-in towel holder exposed raw, unfinished edges in the panel. To finish the edges, we cut pieces of quarter-round molding to fit, mitered the ends, wrapped each piece with adhesive-backed covering in a wood-grain pattern that closely matched that of the door, and nailed them in.

To gain extra space for hanging hand towels and washcloths, we mounted another towel rod on the bottom of the medicine chest just behind the existing rod.

In our new trailer the only provision for towels was the previously mentioned single towel ring in an awkward location. There was wall space adjacent to the shower with sufficient width for only one bath towel rod, so we bought a space-saving double rod, the type where one rod is in front of the other.

Towel rods can be mounted in the shower if care is taken to seal all screw holes so no moisture can enter.

▼▼▼ Shower Curtains

When shower curtains are used in RVs they are usually of standard length, which means they are too long for RV showers. To avoid having a wet, mildewing pile of plastic resting on the floor of the shower, the curtain should be cut off so its bottom edge is about an inch above the bottom of the shower. A standard-size curtain is also too wide for many RV showers, so much of this excess should be cut off. The curtain should be just slightly wider than the shower. In this size, when it is pulled across the shower it will be open to its full width and can dry without mildew forming in damp folds.

▼▼▼ A Convenient Shower-Supply Holder

The contrivances to hold shower supplies—built-in corner units or racks that hang from the shower head—are not suitable for use in an RV. Such holders would very likely spill their contents when the RV was moving and scratch the walls of the shower, unless they were mounted so they couldn't move when under way. We made a more practical holder for shower supplies from excess material cut from the shower curtain. It is nothing more than a series of pockets made from four rectangles of the shower-curtain material. One rectangle is the back panel, and the other three are the pockets. Each pocket was tailored to fit

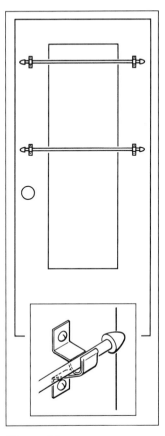

Figure 8.1
Two café curtain rods are used to make a wide towel bar. The rods are attached to the back of the bathroom door. Insert shows closeup of the café rod and how easy it is to install.

the shower supplies we use. The pockets were sewn to the back panel (this can be done by hand or machine) along each side and the bottom. Before attaching the pockets, small holes were punched in the bottom of each so water can drain out. The holder is hung inside the shower curtain on two of the curtain hooks. For the top of the back panel we used a section of the excess material from the top of the shower curtain; it had holes for hanging already there. If we hadn't had a section with holes in it, we could have made four folds about an inch wide, stitched to hold them together, at the top of the back panel to reinforce it before punching the hanging holes.

▼ ▼ ▼ **The Efficient and Usable Bathroom**

The biggest waste of water in the country by far. You spend half a pint and flush two gallons.

DUKE OF EDINBURGH

▼ ▼ ▼ ▼ ▼ ▼ ▼ ▼ ▼ ▼ ▼ ▼ ▼

It is important to us to have a bathroom where everything is convenient for use because we never use an RV park's shower or toilet facilities. Every time we want to shower we do not want to collect the toiletries, towel, shower thongs, clean clothes, and other paraphernalia we might need and troop across the campground to a shower that may not be clean or uncrowded. We don't want the concern about whether the shower will be private or if a bench or stool and plenty of hooks will be provided. We also do not want to be faced with the possibility of running out of hot water or a drain backing up. And we absolutely would not pay an extra fee to use a shower, as must be done in some campgrounds.

But the main reason for using our own bath is because our trailer is our home. When we lived in a fixed dwelling we did not go to the back yard, next door, or across the street to use a bathroom or shower, and we will not do so now. We are constantly amazed, though, at the number of RVers who use campgrounds' showers instead of their own, especially those RVers who have units with suitable baths in them. We know of one full-timing couple who has a large, luxurious trailer with a good-sized bath. They have a washer and dryer in their trailer so they don't have to go out to do their laundry, yet they do go out to use the campground's showers. And last weekend we watched our bathrobe-garbed, campsite neighbors from a brand-new fifth-wheel the same size as ours trek across the campground to the showers on the far side.

Eventually it will be necessary to replace the foam on dinette seats and other foam-filled items that receive heavy use from sitting or sleeping.

The foam in a used RV may need to be replaced to ready it for fulltiming. Age as well as use deteriorates foam.

If the cushion or mattress is rectangular, it will be easy to replace. In most cases the item's cover can be unzipped and a new piece of foam, cut to fit, can be inserted. Sofas or chairs with cushions that are irregular in shape and thickness may need the services of an upholsterer.

If foam is replaced with the kind that is readily available in fabric stores or other retail outlets, it will break down within weeks of regular use. Long-lasting foam can be purchased from foam manufacturers. (They are more common than might be supposed. Check the Yellow Pages under "Foam.") High-density foam is best. Although more expensive initially, it's worth it because it lasts three or four times longer than other types.

In our first trailer, the dinette-seat cushions rested on a series of metal bands that gave them too much springiness for comfortable sitting. To make them firmer, we put a sheet of ½-inch plywood on top of the metal frame the bands were wrapped around. Because the frame had to be lifted for access to the storage area underneath, the plywood had to be anchored so it wouldn't slip out when the seats were lifted. We drilled small holes at the back of the board and, with some thin rope, lashed the board to the metal frame.

Our 23-foot trailer was so small it didn't have a living room. The dinette at the front of the trailer served that function but not very well until we made some modifications. The dinette was designed so it could be converted into a bed, so the table was the length of the seats, four feet long. This made it difficult to get into and out of the seats. Since we did not intend to use the dinette for sleeping, we replaced (at extra cost) the standard

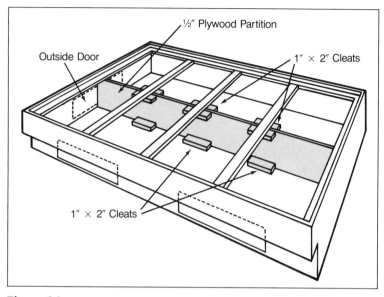

Figure 8.2
A vertical piece of plywood under the mattress support adds extra reinforcement and creates a partitioned storage area.

table with a smaller, extension-type table with a removable leaf.
This table was slightly narrower than the standard dinette table
and, without its leaf, only half the length. We regularly used it
without the extension because it was just the right size for two
to dine on, and it served as a convenient end table when not
being used for meals. Our combination living-dining area was
much more spacious with the big table removed.

In our first trailer, the double-bed mattress supports—three
slats—did not give adequate support to the center of the mattress and consequently did not provide us with the firmness we
wanted, so we added a longitudinal support under the existing
slats (Figure 8.2). A piece of ½-inch plywood, of the correct
height and the length of the bed, was set on edge under the slats
along the center line of the bed. The plywood was screwed to
cleats on the floor and on the slats to hold it in position. This
made the bed much sturdier overall and supported the mattress
suitably.

If you need extra work or seating space in your RV, folding tables and chairs might be used. Most folding furniture collapses into a slim, flat, easily stored unit. Tables are available in many sizes and styles. Perhaps a card table could be used, or one of the many tables designed for outdoor use, or even one or more snack tables. These usually come four to a set with a storage rack; give other RVers the tables you don't need and discard the rack if it presents a storage problem. A custom-made table could be built by anyone who has the necessary tools and a little knowledge of carpentry. In our first trailer, which was short of counter and table space, we added a fold-up table to the end of the bedroom vanity. It was made typing-table height, and much of our paperwork and correspondence was done there. A folding chair fit between the bed and the table. We also often used the folding chair for extra seating. It was stored standing up, folded, against the interior wall of a wardrobe. The clothes in the wardrobe held it in place.

As offered, the living room in our fifth-wheel trailer had no table at all. We wanted a table in the center of the rear wall of the trailer, between the sofa on the street side and the chair on the curb side, that could be used as an end table or extended for use as a dining table when the dinette might be too crowded. We purchased such a table that was a standard feature in one of the other models made by our trailer manufacturer and installed it ourselves. By attaching it to the wall with some unobtrusive hardware we can remove the table if we wish (Figure 8.3). With this hardware, we found the table could slide from side to side as we were traveling or shift out of position if someone leaned against it. In order to prevent this lateral movement, a small block of wood was attached to the back of the table on the underside at a ninety-degree angle to the wall. A barrel bolt was installed on the block. The barrel section fits into a hole drilled in the wall and keeps the table securely in place. The front end of the table is supported by a folding leg.

The dinette table in our fifth-wheel was the typical type set on two pedestals that could be removed if the dinette were converted into a bed. Since we would not need to use the dinette as a bed, we wanted to eliminate the pedestals. We knew from previous experience that in such dinettes the pedestals were always

TABLES AND CHAIRS

▼ ▼ ▼ ▼ ▼ ▼ ▼ ▼ ▼ ▼ ▼ ▼

Figure 8.3
A table attached with this hardware can be easily removed by slightly lifting the free end of the table, which releases the other end from the channel.

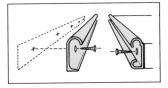

in the way of our knees. When we ordered our trailer, we asked that the dinette table be shipped unmounted and that none of the pedestal hardware be installed. We attached the dinette table using the same type hardware as the rear table, including a barrel bolt to keep it from sliding.

OTHER RV FURNITURE

We noted before that many manufacturers won't do customizing, but nearly all of them will sell individual pieces of furniture or cabinets. The living-room table we put in our small trailer was a standard type in another model from our trailer's manufacturer as was the living-room table in our fifth-wheel. We had seen a console cabinet in the larger models of our fifth-wheel trailer brand, and we were successful in getting the factory to install the same console in ours. We also had a standard bank of cabinets installed in the living room on what was a cabinetless wall on our model.

Extra furniture doesn't necessarily have to come from the builder of your make of trailer or motorhome. If you wanted, for example, an upholstered chair offered in another manufacturer's unit, you might be able to have the dealer for that brand arrange for you to purchase it. For wooden furniture and cabinets to match what you have, though, it would be best to stick with items from your own manufacturer because the woods used vary widely from builder to builder.

▼ ▼ ▼ The Computer Workplace

Many fulltimers are traveling with computers that they use for their work, as we do, or for household and financial recordkeeping, correspondence, or entertainment. If the computer and its peripherals are used frequently, the RV purchased will need to have a place, not only where the computer can be safely stored while traveling, but a place where the equipment can be set up and used conveniently.

RV manufacturers don't include computer workplaces in their units, so most RVers use the dinette table or a living-room extension table when working with their computers or set up a folding table.

Because much of our income comes from the work we do on our computers (we each have a Tandy notebook computer), and because the computers, printer, and the separate disk drive (needed for our type of computers) are often used every day for long periods, a computer workplace was high on the list of what we needed in an RV. A dinette table alone was not suitable since we often work with the computers all day, and we preferred not to have the dining table cluttered with computer equipment that would need to be removed at mealtimes.

We have achieved a spacious computer workplace in the bedroom, but it required a complete rearrangement of the furniture. The major item we moved was the bed. Our bed, like the bed in many fifth-wheels, was an island-type with the head at the front of the trailer. We wanted to turn it so that the head was against the curb-side wall and the one side as far toward the front of the trailer as possible. This, we knew, would be a complete rebuilding job and somewhat complicated because the bed is the type that lifts up for access to the storage area underneath. We had to be certain that when the bed was in its new position it could be lifted without being obstructed by overhead cabinets or the valance on the front window.

We asked if relocating the bed could be done at the factory, but they wanted nothing to do with this bit of customizing. The sales manager, however, did send us a sheet of paneling so the sections of the bed frame we had to reconstruct would match the existing frame.

Once the bed was relocated, we placed one nightstand in the usual way at the side of the bed and parallel to it so the drawers could be pulled out. The second nightstand was turned ninety degrees so its back butted against the side of the other nightstand, making an L-shaped counter. The drawer-side of the second nightstand butts against a chest in our bath/dressing room. This arrangement provided us with nearly five feet of counter space—more than enough to set up all our computer equipment (Figure 8.4).

We cannot use the drawers in the second nightstand without pulling it away from the wall, but we don't need to use them for storage anyway.

The work at the computer counter must be done standing up, but what we do there is mainly printing and disk transferring.

I yield to no one in my admiration for the office as a social centre, but it's no place actually to get any work done.

KATHARINE WHITEHORN

▼ ▼ ▼ ▼ ▼ ▼ ▼ ▼ ▼ ▼ ▼ ▼ ▼

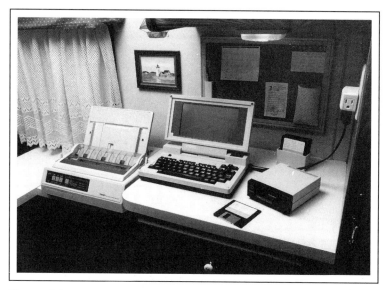

Figure 8.4
The authors' computer workstation. The computer requires a separate
disk drive—the unit on the right. When fanfold paper is used, the
printer is placed on supports and the paper stored beneath. Note the
surge protector in the electrical outlet.

Since our computers are so portable, we can sit wherever we
want when we use them.

The cabinet over the chest is our office-supply storage area. It
contains stationery, pens, pencils, stamps, postage scale, computer disks, the pocketed portfolios we use for filing our paperwork (see also pages 224-225), and other office supplies. The
cabinet is a modified shirt wardrobe and was offered as an
option with our trailer. It was shortened to the height we wanted
at the factory, and we added interior shelves and a light fixture
underneath.

An added advantage of turning the bed was that it provided so
much extra space in the bedroom. We now have room for an
upholstered chair and a bookcase (Figure 8.5). Our "upstairs"
bed/sitting room is a great place for reading, sewing, or doing
computer work because plenty of light comes in the window
next to the chair (we installed a reading light on the wall above
the chair for night-time use), and the bed, in close proximity to
the chair, makes a handy footrest.

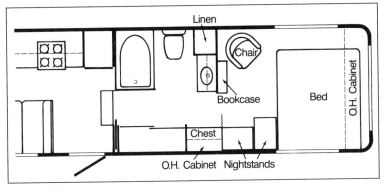

Figure 8.5
Relocating the bed in the authors' fifth-wheel trailer's bedroom provides space for a chair and bookcase. The placement of the nightstands adjacent to the chest makes a spacious computer work station.

aking your RV home more livable may involve changing the way some doors open. If you are ordering an RV, rather than buying a model from the dealer's lot, you might be able to specify how certain doors are to open. This requires some thought because you may not be aware of a problem until you are actually living in the unit.

We had such a problem with the door on our largest galley cupboard on our first trailer. When the door was open it was necessary to stoop to get under it, as it nearly closed off the galley walkway. We always had to be careful about being on the side that gave us access to the interior before we opened it.

We soon decided it was impossible to live with this awkward arrangement. We took off the door and turned it end for end so the hinges were on the opposite side. But the latch, which had been in the right bottom corner, was then in the upper left corner. We lived with it that way (we are both tall enough so we could reach it easily) because removing it would have exposed three screw holes we didn't think we could patch satisfactorily. The previous hinge screw holes were plugged and were not too apparent when the door was closed.

When we ordered our new trailer, we had some extra cabinets installed at the factory, and in our instructions we emphasized the way in which we wanted certain doors to open.

DOORS
▼ ▼ ▼ ▼ ▼ ▼ ▼ ▼ ▼ ▼ ▼ ▼

Fortunately, refrigerator doors are designed so they can be made to open either way. On our first trailer, the refrigerator door opened the wrong way, but it was easily reversed.

Manufacturers should give a little more thought to the door problem, especially since some large RVs now have residential-type, solid doors with doorknobs in places that previously might have had folding or sliding doors. When such residential-type doors are used, they are often on models where access to the bath and the bedroom is from a narrow, curb-side hallway. We looked at some of these units and found, in many, that going from one place to another becomes an exercise in door juggling: one door can't be opened until another door is closed, and both can't be left open at the same time. If your RV has any door complications in its floorplan, perhaps the manufacturer would substitute a different type of door, or you could do it yourself. Residential-type doors may prove to be impractical. Such doors fit into a frame with their hinges recessed into the frame, unlike many RV doors, which have exposed hinges mounted on the wall, and, when closed, the door's edges extend over the door opening similar to cabinet doors. If there is any working of the RV's structural members, the door frame could become distorted, preventing the door from opening and closing properly. In our 23-foot trailer, if we had uneven pressure on the stabilizing jacks, it distorted the frame just enough so that the opening and closing of the entrance door was affected.

We had the factory omit a folding door between our bedroom and bath because it would have interferred with our planned, L-shaped computer counter. For the infrequent times we want to close off the bedroom from the bath, we installed a floor-to-ceiling curtain on a sliding track. We made the curtain ourselves, but we could have used one side of a pair of ready-made drapes. A fabric "door" might be the solution for certain awkward RV-door problems.

If an entrance-door handle is the type shown in Figure 8.6, it is none too sturdy. An ordinary drawer pull can be installed near the handle which will provide something solid and easy to grasp when standing in the doorway and pulling the door shut. And if the door has to be pulled in slightly to secure the deadbolt lock

Figure 8.6
To avoid pulling on the door handle an ordinary drawer pull can be mounted to the left of the handle.

(we make it a habit to engage all locks at night), the drawer pull can be used.

When pulling the entrance door shut from inside, the screen usually pulls away from the door because the magnetic catch holding it to the solid door is not strong enough to hold the weight of both. To keep this from happening, we installed a hook and eye — the hook on the screen door and the eye on the solid door. Now when we pull them shut, they stay together.

In addition to the preceding modifications, we have replaced the two-knob faucets that came on our galley and bath sinks with single-lever types. We dispensed with the tiebacks on our window curtains because they always came undone as we traveled. We removed the reading lights inexplicably installed above a small, open shelf in the middle of a bank of cabinets in both the living room and bedroom. Now, without the utterly useless light hanging from above, we can use the shelf for storing paperback books. We have added four lights in various locations. Our trailer came with knobs for opening the windows. We replaced them with handles, which we find to be easier and quicker to use. We have made other modifications to make our RV home more livable (described in ensuing chapters), adding to our unit's comfort and convenience. It is an ongoing process; we are always finding ways to further improve our trailer.

What makes an RV more livable is up to each individual, but, unless you have an RV custom built to your specifications, there will always be modifications that can be made to a stock RV to make it more suitable for full-time living.

ABOVE ALL, COMFORT AND CONVENIENCE
▼ ▼ ▼ ▼ ▼ ▼ ▼ ▼ ▼ ▼ ▼ ▼

Chapter 9

Storage

We all have more possessions than we need. We continually add to our inventories of "stuff" because of wants, fashions, and fads. We tend to hang onto items that should have been disposed of long ago. Fulltimers should avoid this constant accumulation of possessions, but they do not. Never mind that it is not practical to hang onto rarely used items. Never mind that every pound of weight increases fuel consumption. Never mind that the storage of all these possessions may make for cramped quarters. We must have our things.

Fortunately, an amazing amount can be stored in the average RV. It may require some thorough sorting and evaluation, but you will probably be able to take most of what you want with you—within reason, of course.

Consider what we have in our 29-foot trailer: Because of our work, we have two notebook computers, which are slightly smaller than laptops, and a printer. For works-in-progress and future projects we have files of notes, maps, and reference books, including a large dictionary and an equally large encyclopedia. We have out-of-the-ordinary photo equipment, such as light stands and a slide viewer (used to sort our color slides stored aboard) and a paper cutter, an uncommon amount of office supplies, and files of correspondence, since all our business is conducted from our trailer. If we weren't engaged in the business of writing books, some of which are primarily photographic books, and we didn't have to store so many items relating to our work, we figure we would have fifteen feet of empty cabinet space, three empty drawers, the storage areas under one dinette seat, and those under the sofa and the lift-up bed would have only about a quarter of the area filled.

It's not all work and no play. We enjoy reading and listening to music. We have more than 150 books for pleasure reading (the reference library brings the total up to nearly 200 books) and 288 cassette tapes.

We also have plenty of room for the usual day-to-day living necessities. We can have all these things because we have used existing storage space to its best advantage and constructed additional storage units.

Our experiences in solving storage problems may be of some benefit to you. Even though many of the items you have will be different from ours, all of us have clothing, cookware, toiletries, tools, food, supplies, and paperwork that will be kept in the storage compartments of our RVs.

Some of the storage ideas in this chapter originated with us, but others are variations and adaptations of other people's ideas.

The prime consideration for RV storage is how items will be affected when the RV is moving. All items must be stowed so they will not break, fall, shift, or chafe when the RV is in motion. Also to be considered is the weight of everything stored in the RV and how the weight is distributed (see page 200).

Storage for fulltiming is also different from storing items for vacation use in an RV. More things will be needed — in our case *everything* we own goes with us — and they will have to be kept in some sort of order. You can put up with a mess for a short-term vacation, but facing the inconvenience of disorganized storage every day — not being able to find what you want when you want it, having to continually search through items piled one on top of the other — is something that most of us don't want to live with for long.

FULL-TIMING STORAGE
▼ ▼ ▼ ▼ ▼ ▼ ▼ ▼ ▼ ▼ ▼ ▼ ▼

Don't plan to move into an RV and immediately store everything in its proper place. It isn't possible. It takes some weeks, maybe months, of living with your storage areas to determine exactly where the best and most practical places to keep things will be. Don't be discouraged if you can't fit in everything the way the way you want at first. As you live in your RV, solutions to storage problems will present themselves.

▼ ▼ ▼ The Weight—Again

In loading an RV, the weight added and how it is distributed are important factors. If your RV is designed and furnished so heavyweight items counterbalance each other, this balance should not be disturbed to any great degree. But if you have an RV with many heavy items on one side, try to offset this by using the opposite side for storage of added heavy items.

▼ ▼ ▼ Some General Rules for RV Loading and Weight Distribution

Here are a few general, but not hard-and-fast, rules about RV loading and weight distribution:

1. Heavy items should be stored as close to the floor of the RV as possible.
2. Numerous heavy items should not be located behind the rear axle; the ideal place for extremely heavy objects or an assortment of objects that collectively weigh a lot is over an axle.
3. The weight should be evenly distributed; no RV should be loaded so that it is obviously down in the rear or leaning to one side.
4. If the full-timing RV is a trailer and the tongue weight is too light (see page 148), it can be increased by storing heavy items forward of the axle, as close to the front of the trailer as possible.

▼▼▼ Increasing Existing Storage Space

You can increase the capacity of almost every storage area by adding partitions or shelves or by compartmentalizing the areas with boxes, bins, or other containers. Do this with large cabinets especially, so items stored in them will have little room to move, shift, or fall over when the RV is moving.

On our 23-foot trailer, in the two large lockers that were accessible from both the outside and inside, we installed a partition in each so two separate lockers were formed, one inside and the other outside. In the outside sections of the lockers, we kept items used outside the trailer. The hitch equipment went into one locker. Some of this equipment was likely to have had grease on certain parts of it — the socket ends of the equalizing bars for the weight-distributing hitch, for example, and the hitch itself — so we wanted to keep such items separate. The partition performed this function, as well as reducing the size of the lockers.

The partitions were cut to fit tightly, but we caulked them around the edges so road dust would be confined to the outside sections. The snug partitions also aided in weatherproofing because they cut down on drafts. We noted a marked improvement in our cold-weather comfort after installing these separating partitions.

In our current trailer, the only locker we could use for storing our leveling boards was the outside locker that opened directly to the inside in the rear, under the sofa. We didn't want the sometimes wet, often dirty, leveling boards to be inside the trailer next to the other items we intended to store under the sofa, so we partitioned this area too. Perhaps partition doesn't accurately describe what we did, since we literally constructed a compartment (Figure 9.1). Before we built it, we placed all our leveling boards and jack pads together in various arrangements to find which took up the least space, then built the compartment to that size. To keep out drafts we caulked every seam. This caulking also prevents bugs and spiders, which might be on the leveling boards, from getting inside the trailer.

We also designed and installed the lengthwise reinforcement under the mattress on our 23-foot trailer (see page 190) so it would divide the underbed storage area into two sections.

Figure 9.1
The top of this specially constructed compartment for storing leveling boards slopes downward from the trailer wall and provides a handy, out-of-the-way place for a vinyl pocket in which is kept the handle for the rear stabilizing jacks. The front of the pocket, shown unfastened, is held shut with a turn-button fastener.

▼ ▼ ▼ Improvise for Storage

When a shelf is needed in a cabinet with no wall to which it can be attached, we can sometimes purchase a suitable shelf, often the type made of plastic-coated wire, but if we can't find one that is the right size, we make our own (Figure 9.2). Such a U-shaped shelf can be easily and quickly constructed with a few tools and some ¼-, ⅜-, or ½-inch plywood. The thicker plywood should be used if heavy items will be set on the shelf. The shelves can be movable or fixed in place. Sometimes a box turned on its side with the opening toward the front makes a suitable shelf.

To increase storage capacity in any location, large or small, boxes, bins, or other containers of appropriate size can be used. They can be set on existing shelves, on the floor inside cabinets, or hung on walls or doors (Figure 9.3).

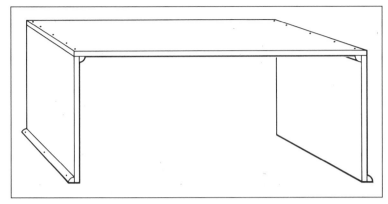

Figure 9.2
A U-shelf, a useful device for adding an extra shelf to a storage cabinet, is made of plywood and ¾-inch, quarter-round molding. It can be movable or installed permanently by putting screws through the molding at the base.

If items are contained and not left loose, there will be more usable space in a given area, items will be easier to find and use, and no damage should result from shifting when the RV is moving.

All sorts of inexpensive plastic, wicker, and cardboard storage containers are on the market. Other items, such as wastebaskets, buckets, and dishpans, also lend themselves to this purpose. Use your imagination when looking for suitable storage containers; they can be found in places other than kitchen and closet departments. Try sporting goods, tool, hardware, baby, and toy departments. It was in a toy department that we found two small, rigid plastic suitcases that are just right for storing some of our power tools and accessories. They take up much less space than the regular cases for such tools.

If we cannot find a container the size we want, which is often the case, we construct one by cutting down or altering an existing cardboard box. If the container will be located where it can be seen, we dress it up with an attractive adhesive-backed, wood-grain covering.

We have certain large items that must be stored but also must be taken in and out of their storage places frequently, such as our

Figure 9.3
Boxes can be installed on cabinet doors for extra storage space; they should be mounted with screws backed up by large washers.

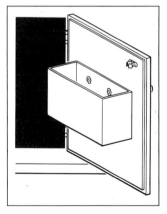

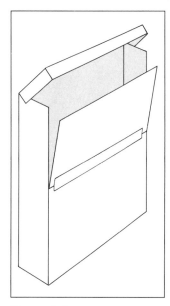

Figure 9.4
A fold-down front allows an item to be easily removed from its storage box.

computer printer and a couple of folding stools we use as foot-stools. Since these items are too large to fit in any storage area on our trailer offering easy accessibility, we constructed a special type of box for the printer and stools, a tall, narrow design with a top lid that folds back and a front that folds down (Figure 9.4). The front, when folded up, is held in place by the lid which fits over the front. We make these boxes just large enough to hold the item, eliminating any extra space so the item cannot shift around inside when we are traveling. The relatively snug fit requires the folding front. When the front is folded down out of the way, a good portion of the stored item is exposed and can be easily grasped to pull out for use. If the front did not fold down, only the end of the stored item would be accessible so, when removing a heavy item like our printer, we would be unable to get our hands far enough around it to pull it out easily, and we would have a problem fitting it back into the narrow opening when we wanted to put it away.

Since our printer and footstool boxes are visible, we covered them with an ivory-color, adhesive-back covering close to the color of our trailer's walls.

The printer, which stands on end in its box, is kept at the foot of the bed in our rearranged bedroom. The ride is smooth in the front of a fifth-wheel, so the printer isn't likely to be bounced around. Once in a while the box becomes tilted, but it can only tilt a few inches because it is so close to the foot of the bed (we've never had a problem with items shifting fore and aft).

The footstools are folded for storage and both kept in one slender box, which fits behind the living room chair against the rear wall and is almost completely concealed by the chair. We didn't have room for the usual footstool or hassock so we bought folding camp stools to use for this purpose. The small, light-weight stools are the type that have tubular aluminum legs and a piece of canvas for the seat. We recovered the seats with an upholstery fabric that harmonizes with our other upholstered pieces.

Various types and sizes of hooks can be used throughout an RV to provide extra storage. The inside of many of our outward-opening cabinet doors has one or more hooks on it. We use them for storing items that would otherwise take up shelf space.

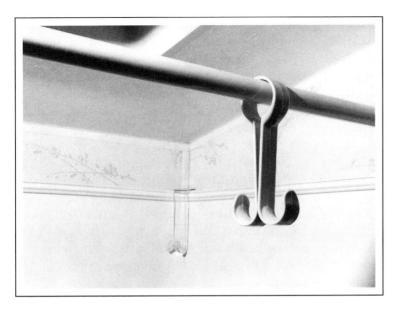

Figure 9.5
Hooks of this type, hung on the shower rod or in the shower itself, are handy for hanging rainwear to dry.

We increased the temporary storage space for rain-wet coats in our shower by adding hooks. We use one sturdy, clear plastic hook—designed to fit over the top of a door—that fits over the shower enclosure in the corner, and another type that fits over the shower rod (Figure 9.5).

Since we have no place wide enough for a conveniently located hand-towel rod in the bath or galley of our present trailer, we hang all hand towels on adhesive-backed hooks.

STORING CLOTHES

Fulltimers' clothing, which consists of casual wear and separates for the most part, only takes up about half the height of a full-length wardrobe, so the bottoms of such wardrobes can be adapted to provide other useful storage space.

In our previous trailer, we had two long, deep wardrobes for clothing storage. We filled up every bit of the space under the hung clothing with bins and shelves (Figure 9.6). We fitted one wardrobe with an L-shaped shelf that extended about halfway across the wardrobe a few inches below the bottoms of the clothes hung above. Its vertical support formed a partitioned

Figure 9.6
This wardrobe holds clothes, a table leaf extension, and a folding chair.

area further partitioned with a bin. These sectioned-off storage areas held wearing apparel that did not need to be hung on hangers: underwear, socks, gloves, nightwear, caps, belts, and some knitted items. The stacking bins we used are found in many retail outlets.

Under one wardrobe was a large, open space that would have held all our shoes and then some—but in a big disorganized pile. The area was in a corner, and deep, making it an inconvenient place for storing shoes that we wore regularly. We added two full-width shelves to the space. When the shoes were lined up on the shelves, they were easy to see and reach. The two doors to the shoe compartment opened outward and downward. On each door we mounted a fabric pocket, which we made specially to fit the doors. Each of these convenient, roomy pockets was used for storing a pair of lightweight shoes or slippers.

The single, double-door wardrobe in our present 29-foot trailer was also adapted to maximize the storage space. Since we have a roomy chest of drawers in this trailer, we need to store only shoes and sweaters in the wardrobe in addition to the hung clothes. It was easy to figure out a shelf configuration for the left half of the wardrobe that would hold our sweaters, but storing all our shoes in the right half presented a problem. As in our smaller trailer, they would all fit in the area if they were just tossed in, but, as before, would end up being separated from their mates, and it would be a nuisance to root out shoes that happened to be on the bottom of the pile.

As we did with the leveling boards before we built the compartment for them, we placed the shoes in various arrangements in the space to see which configuration accommodated the most pairs. We found that if the shoes were placed on end, the greatest number of pairs could be stored in the most accessible way. In order to do this, we had to partition the right half of the wardrobe into four, shoe-width rows so the shoes would stay upright, and put a panel on the front of the rows so they wouldn't spill out. Figure 9.7, which shows the interior of the altered wardrobe, doesn't show the half shelf on the back wall above the shoes. We had room here for a small shelf, so we installed one to hold hats, slippers, and other lightweight items. The top of the sweater

Figure 9.7
This wardrobe features well-utilized space. Sweaters are on the shelves to the left, and shoes, separated by dividers, are placed on end on the right. If needed, another pants hanger could be added under the existing one. An additional shelf above the shoes is not visible.

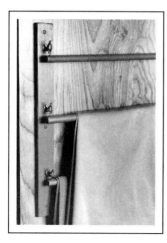

Figure 9.8
An easy-to-make hanger is a good way to store several pairs of pants on a wardrobe door.

compartment forms another shelf. Except for the top and left side, which are plywood, the sweater shelves are made of foam-core board (available at most places where craft supplies are sold) to save on weight; this material is sturdy enough to hold the weight of sweaters without sagging. The center dividers are loose and stay in place simply because we made them to fit snugly. The shelves rest on cleats made of ¾-inch, quarter-round molding. Everything we built into the wardrobe was covered with a wood-grain, adhesive-backed material.

Bill has never liked pants hangers of any kind and does not want to bother with storing pants on a regular hanger under another item of clothing. Long ago we devised a pants hanger that is easy to use and takes up little space; we used it in our house and in both our full-timing trailers (Figure 9.8). Two strips of lath are attached vertically to the outer edges of a wide wardrobe door. A cup hook is screwed into each side for holding the hanger part. Since most RV doors are not solid wood, the lath is necessary to provide a firm mount for the hooks. We used metal hooks because adhesive-backed, plastic hooks are not strong enough for this purpose.

The hanger itself is a half-inch wooden dowel with a screw eye installed about ⅜ of an inch in from each of the ends. To attach the hanger, the eyes are slipped over the corresponding cup hooks. Each hanger can hold up to three pairs of pants but two is better.

The pants hanger is on the inside of one of the wardrobe's doors. On the inside of the other, at both the top and in the middle, are a row of three hooks. The top hooks hold frequently used, long items such as robes, and the middle row is for light-weight windbreakers. And just inside the right door, high up on the wall, is a large hook for holding belts. In this wardrobe, which measures 39 inches wide, 20 inches deep, and 64 inches high on the right side and 71 inches high on the left (the roof slopes upward) we store twenty-two shirts and blouses, seventeen pairs of pants, fourteen pieces of outerwear (rain parkas, sweatshirts, windbreakers, miscellaneous jackets and parkas for cool and cold weather), twelve sweaters, a half-dozen belts, two robes, and sixteen pairs of shoes. We both have hard-to-fit feet and buy shoes when we find some that fit whether we need them or not. If we could just go out and buy a pair when the need arose, we wouldn't have so many pairs to store.

If there is no room in a drawer, on a shelf, or in a storage container to keep items of clothing folded and flat, they might take up less space if they are rolled. Knit polo shirts, for example, can be folded lengthwise down the middle, the sleeves folded in, then rolled up loosely, starting from the hem. If the garment is smoothed out as it is rolled, it will remain almost wrinkle-free. A rolled garment is easy to remove without disturbing other garments, something that cannot be done too easily or neatly with a stack of folded garments. A bin in our old trailer used for storing polo shirts was too narrow to accommodate any folded shirts satisfactorily, but it held six rolled ones conveniently. Garments stored in drawers can sometimes be rolled to create extra space, and some sweaters might be rolled to fit into an odd corner.

Another storage option is to hang a shoe bag on a wardrobe door and use the pockets for small clothing items. Shoe bags could even be used for shoes if they don't put too much weight on the door.

Throw pillows with zippered covers can do double-duty if the stuffing is removed and replaced with clothing or linens: bulky sweaters, light- and medium-weight blankets, afghans, nightwear, swimsuits, or other seasonal items.

When we began fulltiming we used wire clothes hangers. These jumped off the rod in the rear wardrobe as we were traveling. We changed to the thicker, plastic hangers and had no more problems. We have since learned from another fulltimer that if we had hung the wire hangers reversed, they would not have fallen off. She also advised us to reverse rolls of toilet tissue or paper towels if they unwind when the RV is in motion.

DEALING WITH LAUNDRY
▼ ▼ ▼ ▼ ▼ ▼ ▼ ▼ ▼ ▼ ▼ ▼

Where to store soiled clothes until laundry day seems to be a major problem for many fulltimers. Some, who have filled up all other practical storage areas with other items, keep soiled clothes in the shower. A few have doors in their RVs large enough and strong enough to hold a full laundry bag, and some RVs have a built-in hamper, but most of us have no specific or built-in place for laundry.

The general approach to the subject is that all soiled washables should be kept together in one place, usually in a bag. We have long since departed from this common concept and, in so doing, solved the problem of what to do with our laundry.

We keep our laundry in several different places. In our first trailer, resting on the top edges of a bin in each of our wardrobes, was a laundry box. We made these boxes so they fit exactly on top of the bins. They measured 10 inches by 18 inches and were 4 inches deep. One of these laundry boxes can be seen in Figure 9.6 on the right, just under the hung clothing. Most small items of soiled clothing such as underwear and socks were dropped into these boxes. There was plenty of room for soiled hand towels, washcloths, and dish towels as well. When washing time arrived, we dumped the contents of the boxes into a laundry bag that was kept folded and stored in the bottom of one of the boxes.

▼ ▼ ▼

Figure 9.9
An old pillowcase serves as a laundry bag. Velcro strips inside the top of the cabinet and on one edge of the pillowcase hold the bag open for easy access.

In our present trailer, it is necessary to have a slightly different arrangement for the small items. At first we simply put the laundry bag in the cabinet under the bath basin where there was plenty of room for it even when full. To put the soiled items where they belonged, however, the cabinet door had to be opened, the bag lifted out, and opened, then put back in the cabinet. We found we usually ignored the bag and just tossed the laundry into the cabinet. On laundry day we stuffed everything into the bag, hoping we hadn't overlooked items that had landed among the other items stored in the cabinet. We corrected our lackadaisical laundry-collecting habits by hanging the bag, open, inside the cabinet and attaching it inside the top of the door opening with Velcro (Figure 9.9). Now, when we toss laundry into the cabinet, it automatically goes into the maw of the laundry bag. Near the bag is a small drawstring bag into which we put our extra quarters every few days so we will have plenty for the washers and dryers.

When big items such as sheets and bath towels become soiled, we put them directly into the laundry basket which we store in the large compartment under the gooseneck at the front of the trailer. A laundry basket is a difficult item to stow in most RVs unless they are basement models. With our previous conventional trailer, the bed of our pickup truck was covered with a canopy and we kept the laundry basket in the bed. Many motorhomes do not have a large storage area like a pickup bed, but if an auxiliary vehicle is towed, perhaps a laundry basket could be kept in its trunk.

Other items of clothing that need to be washed, such as shirts, blouses, and pants, are kept on their hangers, unless they are very soiled, until laundry day. We don't have so many clothes that we cannot remember which ones need to be laundered.

With this method we found we have no more presorting to do; all the items in the bag and in the laundry basket are washed in hot water, and all the clothing from the hangers goes into machines set for permanent press.

This system of keeping soiled clothes in different places might be worth trying if you have a laundry-storage problem.

GALLEY STORAGE
▼ ▼ ▼ ▼ ▼ ▼ ▼ ▼ ▼ ▼ ▼ ▼

When certain food items are stored improperly for traveling, they can make awful messes if their containers break and the contents spill out. That is one of the reasons why careful attention should be paid to galley storage.

Almost all RVs have a large cabinet under the galley sink that can be made into a more efficient and practical storage area by compartmentalizing it. Most such cabinets have one shelf that, while dividing the area in half, still leaves each half with too large an area to conveniently and safely store items.

On this shelf in our undersink cabinet, we put a large plastic box in which we keep most of the foods that come in glass bottles and don't need refrigeration, such as vinegar, cooking oil, olive oil, various cooking wines, corn syrup, and molasses. In the well-filled box, there is no excess space in which anything could tip over when the trailer is moving. The rest of the shelf is taken up by plastic canisters so the bottle-box can't shift out of its position.

▼ ▼ ▼

If the bottle-box and canisters had not filled up the cabinet, we would have used any extra space for storing rolls of paper towels. These make good fillers in almost any cabinet. The rolls can be stored vertically or horizontally.

Our previous trailer had a U-shelf on the floor of the under-sink cabinet, beneath which we stored an electric skillet. The small space between the top of the U-shelf and the shelf above was just tall enough for storing baking pans. Next to the U-shelf were several small plastic baskets in which we kept potatoes, onions, apples, and the like. We also kept some of our canned goods in this compartment in two separate boxes. In one box, the cans were upright, in the other, on their sides. In this way, we achieved the maximum amount of storage in the existing space in the cabinet and in the boxes.

In our fifth-wheel, the floor of the undersink cabinet was on two levels. The back portion, about six inches above the floor, was the enclosed wheel well. Running along the entire width of the cabinet at the front was an exposed furnace duct. We put in a false floor that rests on the wheel well and extends over the duct to the front of the cabinet. Even though this shortened the height of the bottom of the cabinet by about six inches, the space provides better storage because we can now use the entire depth of the cabinet. On one side, in the back corner, is a high-sided plastic box similar to the bottle-box previously mentioned, where we keep some of the cleaning supplies we use frequently: glass and carpet cleaner, sponges and rags, all-purpose cleaner, and dusting spray. We use a box so the liquid items won't spill and also to keep all the cleaning supplies well separated from the canned goods we store on the other side of the cabinet. Since we don't use many canned goods, we don't need too much storage space for them. In this trailer, we started out using the same boxes for cans we had in our other trailer, but we soon found a more efficient way of can storage. Four one-inch by one-inch wooden cleats were cut in a length to equal the cabinet's depth. These were nailed to the cabinet floor, running front to back, so they formed three rows just as wide as a one-pound can—a little over three inches. The cans are lined up between the cleats, which prevent them from sliding from side to side as we travel, and the height of the cleats is just enough to keep the cans from falling over.

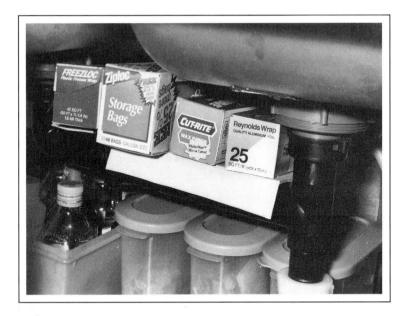

Figure 9.10
This is a space-saving way to store long, slim boxes of foodwraps and bags.

The drainpipe for the double sink extends horizontally for a distance across the cabinet, three-and-a half inches under the sink bottoms. The area above the drainpipe was wasted space until we realized we could put a shelf there that would be just the right size for holding long, slim boxes of kitchen wraps and storage bags. The shelf and its support are nothing more than a length of cardboard folded into an L-shape. The "L" is inverted so the bottom becomes the shelf and the stem of the "L" becomes the support. The front of the shelf rests on the drainpipe, and the support, beginning at the back of the shelf where the fold is, extends down to the cabinet shelf. The support is taped to the cabinet shelf (with clear mailing tape); this is the only attaching needed since the shelf portion was cut to fit snugly between the two vertical pipes coming from the sink drains (Figure 9.10). Not only have we increased our storage space, we have arranged it so the often-used foil, waxed paper, plastic wrap, and top-sealing plastic bags can be easily seen and reached.

The undersink storage space on some RVs comes equipped with roll-out wire baskets. If yours does not have this feature and you want it, you can install your own. Often these types of baskets, which are found in home-improvement stores, are too deep or otherwise too large to fit into RV cabinets. Sometimes they can be made to fit if the track length is shortened. But if these residential-type baskets are unsuitable, a rolling storage container can be custom-made to fit just about any cabinet by using ball-bearing drawer slides, which come in various lengths, for the tracks. For an installation of this type, the drawer slides are mounted on the floor of the cabinet. A sheet of plywood should be attached on top of the slides as a base for the storage container that will be mounted on it. The container might be a wire basket; a plastic, openwork crate; a cardboard or plastic box; or one, two, or maybe three wastebaskets mounted on the same piece of plywood. A barrel bolt or a hook and eye can be used to prevent the container from moving when the RV is under way.

One door of our undersink cabinet holds a plastic wastebasket we use for a garbage container (Figure 9.11). Although we made the container removable—three holes in the wastebasket's back fit over the heads of three screws in the door—it could be screwed directly onto the cabinet door; use washers under the screwheads in this case. Disposable bags are used to line the wastebasket. Sometimes the garbage is heavy, so the wastebasket is supported by a small wooden shelf attached to the door by L-brackets. The positioning of the wastebasket on the door is important since there must be clearance all around in order for the door to close properly.

The dishwashing liquid and sink cleanser are at the top of the other door, in a box similar to that in Figure 9.3. Under it is another box that holds plastic lids for various sizes of storage and mixing bowls. The bowls are in another location and stacked one inside the other to save space.

We rarely store any foods that come in bags or boxes in their original containers. Instead, we have plastic containers in many sizes and shapes into which we transfer these foods. After much trial and error, we finally have plastic containers and canisters that fit into our galley cabinets with no wasted space. By using our own containers, we do not have to contend with such nuisances as cereal boxes too tall to fit on a shelf, rice and pasta packages that, once opened, cannot be resealed properly to avoid spilling, and foods in packages and boxes that would have to be piled helter-skelter on shelves.

Figure 9.11
A shelf was added to the door of an under-sink galley cabinet to support a wastebasket serving as a garbage container. Food scraps can easily be swept off the counter into the container.

Brown sugar, cocoa, baking soda, flour, sugar, rice, pasta, crackers, cereals, and other food items we use regularly each has its own special container. Cooking or mixing instructions, if needed, are cut from the original package and put into the container along with the food. A portion of a cereal's box with the name of the cereal on it is tucked into each cereal container.

The containers use all the cabinet space to the best advantage. The foods are handy and are kept fresher than they would be if the unused portions were stored in their original packages.

In our previous trailer, we had one long cabinet above the sink in which we stored dinnerware and glasses, which would have shifted quite a bit when the trailer was moving. To keep this cabinet's contents in place, we made a shallow cardboard tray that was anchored to the middle of the cabinet with double-faced mounting tape. The tray sectioned off the cabinet and was used to hold some of the items that formerly slid around: salt and pepper shakers, toothpick holder, and juice glasses. When nonskid shelf lining was introduced (available at many RV-supply stores), we began using it on all our shelves and have continued to do so.

The inside of cabinet doors that open outward (instead of upward) can be used for storage. Our largest galley door contains measuring cups and spoons and hot pads (Figure 9.12).

Figure 9.12
A galley cabinet door is utilized for optimum storage space. The white notes (upper right) are commonly used cooking and measuring references.

Figure 9.13
To identify spices stored upright in a drawer, mark the tops of jars and tins with a permanent marker or make labels with a label marker.

The measuring spoons are hung on finishing nails (the holes in the spoon handles won't fit over nails with heads) driven in at a sharp angle. Our graduated set of measuring cups was hung on spring-clip cup hooks until we made a wooden holder for them. It is simply a one-inch by one-inch wooden cleat with recessed cut-outs for the cup handles. A screw on each end holds the holder to the door.

We don't like to keep spice containers on an open shelf because they might fall off when we are traveling. Besides, the containers are hard to keep clean when exposed to cooking spatters. We keep our spices in a galley drawer we have partitioned off so the spices are lined up in rows (Figure 9.13). Since spice containers are not designed to be stored this way, in order to identify the contents of each tin or jar, we had to label the tops of the containers.

When we use up a spice, we look for a replacement in a container that is short enough to fit in the drawer. If we can't find the spice in a suitable container, we transfer the spice to the old container.

Figure 9.14
Baking pans are stored on edge to take advantage of the upward slope of the cabinet so no storage space is wasted.

Most of our pots, pans, and skillets are stacked one on top of the other. We store them with a piece of terry toweling between each to protect their inner and outer finishes. Otherwise, they rub against one another when the trailer is moving. (The finish on nonstick coated items can wear off in spots by this action unless protected.)

Two of our galley cabinets are higher on one end than the other because the high end is where the roof of our fifth-wheel begins its upslope to the bedroom. To utilize one cabinet to the fullest, we store cookie sheets and baking pans on end on a wire shelf (Figure 9.14). The wire construction serves as a rack and helps hold the utensils upright because the handles on the ends of the cookie sheets and some of the baking pans fit between the wires. Mixing bowls are on the other end of the shelf and more baking pans fit beneath it.

We store our small, artificial Christmas tree in this sloping cabinet's counterpart on the other side of the trailer. The tree is at the top of the cabinet, suspended on the back wall, and hanging on a slant to match the slope of the roof. To keep dust off, the tree is kept in a sealed plastic bag. Two slings of webbing cradle the tree. Grommet holes on the ends of the slings fit over hooks on the back wall. There is nothing else we could have stored in such an odd, rather inaccessible place, but with the tree kept there, the entire cabinet area is now utilized for storage.

Appliances that mount under cabinets might work as space savers in some RVs. We saw a trailer with a small microwave oven mounted on the underside of a galley cabinet. Unless the cabinets are solid wood, special care must be taken when anchoring holders for any such appliances. The holder must be attached securely enough so that traveling vibrations, along with the weight of the appliance, wouldn't cause the screws to work out. The appliance should be attached in the holder so it also cannot work out.

▼ ▼ ▼

If your galley storage space is tight, analyze your cookware and appliances to see if you can eliminate some and put others to use in a variety of ways. Cakes can be baked in pans other than the size specified in recipes by increasing or decreasing the amount of baking times. A blender can be used for many food-processor operations, and a hand mixer can serve some of the purposes of a blender. Consider how often you use items as well. If you have a waffle iron, yet rarely make waffles, perhaps it could be dispensed with; when you get a yen for waffles, you might satisfy it with the restaurant variety or toaster waffles.

We knew we would not have space in a trailer for all the recipe books we had in our house. We also realized, like most people, we use only a small number of the recipes in any book. To save space we cut out our favorite recipes from all the books and pasted them on small looseleaf sheets which fit easily in one binder (we don't have convenient space for a card file in the galley). The looseleaf feature makes adding recipes easy. Our binder measures nine-and-a-half inches by six inches; a regular-sized notebook is too large to store conveniently in any of our galley cabinets and takes up too much counter space when open for use. The binders can be found in most office-supply stores.

The refrigerator should be considered as a storage unit and items stored in it accordingly. Pack it well to cut down on open space so items can't slide around or fall over, and so there are plenty of chilled items to hold the cold, if you travel, as we do, with the refrigerator off (see also Chapter Eleven, pages 289–290). When we know we will be traveling regularly in hot weather and don't have the refrigerator full, we fill the empty spaces with cans of soda pop. They can stand upright or lay on their sides to fill up empty spaces, and they retain the cold well.

The microwave oven can also double as a storage compartment if the items stored in it can't slide around. When we have a cake to stow for traveling and it won't fit into the refrigerator, we usually put it into the microwave oven where it rides safely. The range oven might also be used for storing skillets, baking pans, or other suitable kitchen utensils.

One of our galley drawers is partitioned with drawer organizers, and in it we store flatware and cooking utensils, but another galley drawer, fitted with the same type of organizers, is used for an assortment of hand tools, such as screwdrivers with various tips (it seems every other screw on an RV needs a different type of screwdriver), regular and long-nose pliers, diagonal cutters, crescent wrench, hand drill, tack hammer, small pry bar, small socket-wrench set, utility knife, tweezers, string, glue, and other small items we use for minor repairs and simple installations. Even in our smaller trailer we set aside a galley drawer for these tools. It's easy to take care of little repair jobs quickly if the tools are handy.

The other day we tightened a window handle the minute we found it was loose, and many times we have tightened a loose knob on cabinets as soon as it was noticed. The crescent wrench came in handy for unscrewing a clogged water-faucet filter. With the pliers, we bent in a bracket so a window shade with a penchant for falling off would be held more securely. The flat-blade screwdriver is sometimes needed for prying off light-fixture covers when a bulb needs to be replaced. For the innumerable little repairs and minor fix-it jobs that need to be done on any RV, we do not have to go out of our way to pull out our large chest to find the proper tool.

If bread is the first necessity of life, recreation is a close second.

EDWARD BELLAMY

BUILT-IN STORAGE

▼ ▼ ▼ ▼ ▼ ▼ ▼ ▼ ▼ ▼ ▼ ▼ ▼

Figure 9.15
A bookcase for paperbacks is small enough to fit in several locations in many RVs.

Almost every RV has some space where extra storage units could be installed without disturbing or rearranging existing furniture or cabinets. In our previous trailer, we needed more places to store books. Most RVers don't have to carry as many books as we do so they may not need special storage areas for them, but where we located our bookcases might give you ideas for adding extra storage units for items you carry.

To cut down on weight, we buy books in paperback editions whenever we can. Many of the books we read for pleasure are the small-size paperbacks. In our previous trailer, we had room on the end of a galley counter for a bookcase that would hold paperbacks (Figure 9.15). If we had not had enough galley counter space in that trailer, the area would have been used for a foldup counter extension. The bookcase was in the entryway, but it was only 4¾ inches deep and did not project into the walkway far enough to cause any problems. The area on the end of the counter was tall enough to accommodate four shelves, but we chose to make an enclosed bin with a lid instead of a fourth (top) shelf. In it we kept small, frequently used items, such as a flashlight, a ring with keys for the outside lockers, and a level.

The books needed to have something to keep them from falling out of the shelves when we were traveling. A hole was drilled in each side of our plywood bookcase about three-quarters of the way up from the bottom of each shelf. Brass welding rods were bent to fit across the shelf and into the holes. The rod rested against the books and held them in. It was a simple matter to raise the rod to remove a book.

Now, in our fifth-wheel trailer, this bookcase is in our bed/sitting room. In its top bin we keep computer disks and other small computer-related items since it is just an arm's length away from our computer workspace.

▼ ▼ ▼

In our 23-footer, we put another three-shelf bookcase for slightly larger paperbacks on the end of the vanity in the bedroom. This bookcase was movable and typing-table height. When moved to the right it formed the end support for the fold-up typing table mentioned on page 191.

We installed another bookcase behind the dinette in our small trailer. A top-opening storage compartment formed a shelf behind one of the dinette-seat backs. The lid did not run the full length of the compartment; there was just enough space for a small bookcase on the end. In this tight little corner the bookcase height was limited to two shelves; any more would have interfered with the corner of the window valance. Small as it was, the bookcase held twelve books on each shelf, and we eventually added another bookcase on the rear wall under the table.

Our fifth-wheel trailer has plenty of cabinet space for books, but we store as few heavy, hardbound books as possible in overhead cabinets; we prefer to keep heavy items in floor cabinets or other low storage areas. Our overhead cabinets are considerably deeper than a standard bookshelf, and we found no matter how neatly we lined up the books in them, they slid out of place when we traveled. We solved this problem by putting rolls of paper towels along the backs of the cabinets, effectively making the cabinets the right depth for books. Now the books stay in place because they have no space in which to slide around, and they are at the front of the cabinet, making them easy to see.

We have a six-inch-wide shelf along the entire rear wall of our trailer under the window. There are eight inches of wall space from each corner to the edge of the window frame. We built two little boxes with a floor and just two sides to fit on the shelf in each corner (Figure 9.16) and anchored them to the shelf with strips of double-faced mounting tape. These two small bookcases hold nineteen small books we refer to often, mainly reference books for birds, trees, wildflowers, and other nature-related subjects. These books provide an example of the bounce occurring at the rear of a trailer when traveling: twice the books have bounced out with such force it tore off the front of the cases.

We have a large collection of music audiocassettes and have always wanted a bookcase-like place to keep them. Finally, in our fifth-wheel, we have arranged a storage place for them that keeps them aligned so every one of our 288 tapes is visible and accessible (Figure 9.17). Our trailer came with a four-foot-high slide-out pantry in the galley. When we were shopping for a trailer, we hoped we could find one with a pantry of this sort

Figure 9.16
A bookcase for small books is tucked into each corner of a shelf that runs across the rear wall of the authors' trailer.

Figure 9.17
A former galley pantry has been modified into a storage unit for an extensive collection of audiocassettes.

because we had already figured out that a pantry, with considerable modifications, would be the perfect place for our tapes.

First, we built a plywood bookcase with Masonite shelves just wide and high enough for cassettes. Its overall size was determined by the existing pullout frame holding the pantry's four wire baskets (which we removed). Merely mounting this tape case to the frame wouldn't have worked because the frame didn't slide out far enough to see or remove the tapes at the back. Drawer slides were used on the existing pullout frame to make, in effect, a double-distance pullout. Two boards of ½-inch plywood were affixed to the frame, one a few inches down from the top of the frame, the other near where the bottom of the case would be when installed on the frame. The drawer slides were attached to the boards and the case installed on the drawer slides. When pulled out all the way, no part of the case is in the cabinet so every tape is visible. To pull out the frame we put a U-shaped handle on the outside vertical member, and to pull the case out as far as it will go, we put a knob on the side of the case. To prevent sliding while traveling, a hook on the case fastens to an eye on the frame, and the frame is locked, at the bottom, by the bunk latch that came with it. We retained the bottom pantry basket and use it for storing a rewinder, head cleaner, and other cassette accessories. A small broom and flyswatter hang in the narrow area on the inside wall of the compartment just opposite the tape case. Since our tape case is technically in the galley, the inside of the compartment door has several cup hooks for hanging long kitchen utensils, such as spatulas and stirring spoons, that don't conveniently fit in a drawer.

▼ ▼ ▼

On our 23-foot trailer there was a space only 7½ inches wide between the head of the bed and the wardrobe next to the bed. It was wasted space until we built a gun case to fit into it. The case was just wide enough to hold a rifle and shotgun upright. This tall, slim container was similar to the type shown in Figure 9.4 with a fold-down front for quick and easy access.

For both our trailers we have made small wastebaskets that can be tucked into odd corners too small for regular ones. These are nothing more than cardboard boxes that fit exactly into their spaces. We cover the wastebaskets with an adhesive-backed covering that blends with the wall or the furniture next to the wastebasket. Such tiny wastebaskets scattered about are handy and unobtrusive.

You don't need to be a carpenter or have special tools to build some storage units. Often a cardboard box can be found in a suitable size or one can be altered to fit. The bookcase behind the dinette back on our small trailer was made from two heavy corrugated cardboard boxes. We found one box in just the size we needed for the bottom "shelf," and cut down another box to fit on top. The boxes were carefully covered with an adhesive-backed, wood-grain covering that many people thought was actually wood.

After we bought our folding footstools, which didn't come in a box, we happened to be in a store where a salesclerk was unpacking some folding chairs for display. We noticed that with some slight alteration, the box holding the chairs would be just right for the footstools. When we found that the clerk was going to dispose of the box anyway, we asked if we could take it off his hands, and then we put it to use building another piece of cardboard "furniture."

Our gun case was first made from cardboard. It was the first time we used the folding-front design and the cardboard case was to be a prototype to see if it would work satisfactorily. It did. We used the cardboard case, again covered with a wood-grain material, for several years before we replaced it with a wooden case of the same design.

If something is to be made of wood, of course woodworking tools are required, but when using cardboard for the construction material about all that is needed is a utility knife, something with a straight edge to cut against, a ruler or tape for accurate measuring, and a pencil or pen. To assemble the pieces, we use the aforementioned clear mailing tape—which is long lasting and adheres well to almost any surface—on each join. If the storage unit will be visible, we always dress it up with an adhesive-backed covering.

CONSTRUCTING STORAGE UNITS
▼ ▼ ▼ ▼ ▼ ▼ ▼ ▼ ▼ ▼ ▼ ▼

PERSONAL AND BUSINESS PAPERS

▼ ▼ ▼ ▼ ▼ ▼ ▼ ▼ ▼ ▼ ▼ ▼ ▼

Carrying around all the papers for your personal affairs and perhaps your business is something the occasional RVer doesn't have to be concerned with, but fulltimers will need to keep their papers with them in their RV home. Motorhomes and trailers don't have room for file cabinets, and the usual storage areas in an RV don't lend themselves to conventional methods for storing papers. Because of our various writing and photography projects, we have more papers to deal with than any other fulltimer we know of and even more than many of our unmobile friends. It was important to find a way to store the papers relating to our business in an organized, convenient way. After much trial and error we settled on using side-opening, pocket portfolios for storing most of our papers.

These portfolios, manufactured by Mead and Duo-Tang among others, are readily available at office-supply and discount stores. We prefer the Duo-Tang brand because the pocket, which runs across the full, opened width of the portfolio, is stapled in the center, which keeps the contents of each side separate.

The pocket feature keeps everything in the portfolio secure. There's no chance of anything falling out unless the portfolio should be turned upside down. They're large enough to hold a standard, letter-size ($8\frac{1}{2} \times 11$) sheet of paper, yet can be placed vertically in many RV cabinets or laid flat on a shelf. The portfolios come in many colors and two styles, one with just two pockets, the other with pockets and a three-prong strip that will accommodate notebook paper. We use the prong type for an address book and another for expense records. In separate, plain-pocket portfolios we keep bills to be paid, letters to be answered, and stationery. Any correspondence waiting for an answer or any papers pertaining to something unresolved is put in a "pending" portfolio. We have another for storing statements and other documents from each of our bank and investment accounts and yet other separate portfolios for insurance policies and medical records.

It's especially important for fulltimers to keep warranties for all their products and equipment with them in their RV homes. We use two portfolios for storing these papers—warranties, instructions, service-center locations—that come with so many items. One portfolio is for just the trailer and its original equip-ment. The other is devoted to other equipment, household items, and appliances. On each warranty, we note the date the item was purchased, and then periodically weed out any warranties no longer in effect.

Our papers and files were always difficult to work with and keep organized until we started using this type of RV-compatible portfolio system. You, too, might find the portfolios useful as a means of keeping your paper storage under control.

Valuable papers, such as titles, stock certificates and the like, would be safer if stored in a fireproof box.

Computer storage presents no real problem for those full-timers who have a laptop computer. A laptop isn't much larger than a notebook, so a suitable, secure storage place can be found in almost any RV. The storage place for any type of computer should be where there is minimal bounce and vibration and, for safety's sake, in a low spot, so there is no danger of its falling out of a cabinet if the door should accidentally come open when the RV is moving or toppling out when the cabinet door is purposely opened to remove it.

Those who travel with a desktop model will find it difficult to locate a safe place to store it for traveling yet have it easily accessible when it is to be set up for use; few RVs have cabinets large enough to hold a desktop computer.

If no suitable built-in storage place exists, a top-opening chest might be used. It would be fairly easy to lift the computer out of such a chest to set it up. A chest like this, which might be made of wood or even wicker, could be lined with foam to provide cushioning. Being large, the chest would most likely be kept on the floor where it would ride well. Perhaps the chest could also double as an end table in the living room or as a nightstand in the bedroom. The printer must be stored just as carefully as the computer. As we mentioned earlier, we store our printer in one of our folding-front boxes at the foot of the bed. We don't want to risk having the rather heavy printer slip out of our grasp as we take it from its box, so we always lay the box flat before the

COMPUTER STORAGE

▼ ▼ ▼ ▼ ▼ ▼ ▼ ▼ ▼ ▼ ▼ ▼

printer is removed, lifting the box the short distance up onto the bed and onto its back so the folding-front is up. Using the bed as a table and working at bed-height, it is easy to slide the printer out of the box, then turn, and set it in place on the nightstand, which is the same height as the bed.

OUTSIDE STORAGE

▼ ▼ ▼ ▼ ▼ ▼ ▼ ▼ ▼ ▼ ▼ ▼ ▼

Basement-model motorhomes and trailers are becoming increasingly common. A problem we see with some of the cavernous compartments running from one side of the RV to the other is that what is stored in the center of the compartment might be hard to reach. Sliding baskets, similar to those described earlier for use in undersink galley cabinets, might be a solution to this problem. The basket could be kept in the center of the compartment but slid out on the track so it would be adjacent to the compartment door for easy accessibility to its contents.

If a sliding basket or a nonsliding storage container is used, it might end up being stowed far enough into the compartment so it is beyond arm's reach. In this case, something long with a hook on its end could be kept in the compartment so the item wanted can be snagged and pulled into reach. A crowbar, walking cane, or telescoping boat hook (a regular boat hook might be too long to stow easily) might suffice for this. We don't have basement compartments but we have a hooking device for reaching items at the front of our pickup's bed so we don't have to climb into the truck. Our "snagger" is a ski pole (purchased at a Salvation Army store for less than a dollar) with a clothesline hook on its end. Since we don't use it to pull heavy items, we used tape (more of that strong, clear, mailing tape) to secure the hook to the end of the pole. If we required it for more heavy-duty work, we would attach the hook either with hose clamps or bolts. Aside from use in the pickup truck, the snagger has been used to reach items that end up under the truck or trailer—a lug nut, for example, once rolled under the trailer—and for pushing or pulling low-hanging tree branches away from the side of our rig when maneuvering into a campsite.

A large storage area is under the gooseneck on our trailer, as on many fifth-wheels. This compartment is so cavernous that everything would soon be in an awful jumble if the items weren't organized, so nearly everything we keep here is in boxes. Storing odd-shaped items or a collection of related small items in boxes utilizes existing space to good advantage. The boxes can be stacked all the way to the top of the compartment if need be. Locating what is wanted is easy if the boxes are clearly labeled.

CONTAINMENT
▬▬▬▬▬▬
▼ ▼ ▼ ▼ ▼ ▼ ▼ ▼ ▼ ▼ ▼ ▼

The key to workable and convenient storage anywhere is containment, keeping hard-to-store items in boxes or bags and all items of one kind together in one receptacle (if the items are of a size making this feasible). For instance, we keep all our extra 12-volt interior and exterior light bulbs in a box along with all extra flashlight bulbs. When any bulb burns out, we have to look in only one place for a replacement. All fuses are also kept in one box, as are all glues and sealants.

We have two water hoses of different lengths. Each one is kept in a bag so it cannot get loose and spread out in the compartment where both are stored. We find that a flat hose is easier to store and takes up less space than a round one. Battery jumper cables are kept in a bag so they will not snake through their compartment and interfere with other emergency automotive equipment kept in the same compartment.

Containment is especially useful for collections of small items. In the bath, we have a large, counter-to-ceiling cabinet at the side of the sink counter. We use part of this cabinet for holding toiletries and pharmaceutical items. On one of its walls, we put a wire, double-shelf spice rack to hold small items such as eyedrops, nail polish, and pill vials.

On the inside of the cabinet door is a cardboard bin of the type shown in Figure 9.3 in which we keep many of the items we use every day: combs, razor, shaving lotion, toothpaste, hand lotion, and such. Putting like items in boxes and bags makes them easy to find and use and maximizes storage space.

FULLTIMING AND STORAGE
▬▬▬▬▬▬
▼ ▼ ▼ ▼ ▼ ▼ ▼ ▼ ▼ ▼ ▼ ▼

We have tried to arrange our storage so it is just about as easy to stow items where they belong as to leave them unstowed; because of this, our small RV home is never messy. Items are logically stored and easily accessible so we can find what we want when we want it; we are rarely irritated because we can't

▼ ▼ ▼

locate something or because it is too difficult to get out of its storage place. Nothing can make a neatnik out of someone who isn't inclined that way, but if a little time is taken to work out efficient storage, fulltimers won't have to spend much of their time searching for items they need or become annoyed because they can't find them. Proper storage has the added advantage of not having to live amidst a constant mess. "A place for everything and everything in its place" is a good motto for fulltimers.

STORAGE IN PICKUP BEDS

▼ ▼ ▼ ▼ ▼ ▼ ▼ ▼ ▼ ▼ ▼ ▼ ▼ ▼

When we had a canopy on the bed of our pickup truck, we ringed the perimeter of the bed with built-in, top-opening plywood bins. These provided a great amount of storage. The bins on the sides were slightly wider than the wheel wells, and all were no higher than the top of the bed's sides.

We could no longer have a rigid canopy over the bed when we decided on a fifth-wheel trailer, so we purchased a flat, fiberglass bed cover that had a large storage compartment with hinged lids on each side at the front. The rear portion of the cover had two lids that were removed for towing. The front storage compartment, partitioned off from the rear of the bed, was more than large enough for everything we wanted to carry there, but additional items could have been stored in back along each side of the bed. The spare tire was kept in the bed under the hitch.

▼ ▼ ▼

One of the major problems with this type of cover is that the lids over the hitch, which are fairly large, must be stowed someplace while towing the trailer. Even though the lids fit behind the hitch in the remaining open space in the bed, we always had to be careful about how we placed them so they wouldn't become scratched; each lid had sharp-edged, L-shaped, metal clips on the underside (these held the lids in place on the cover). We made protective sleeves from old blankets, but it was always a hassle trying to hold open the sleeve in order to insert the unwieldy lids into them. It wasn't too long before we figured out a way to dispense with the sleeves. We attached small blocks of wood to a plywood floor in the bed. When the lids were removed, their

L-shaped clips fit into routed-out indentations in the blocks. Three blocks were used for the three clips on the smaller lid. The larger lid was stowed over the smaller one in two blocks with indentations for its two metal clips and two more blocks with a groove in each into which the lip on the rear of the lid fit. The blocks for the large lid were made tall enough so this lid rested about an inch above the lid underneath. The blocks were designed so the lids would not touch at any point, preventing chafing against one another as we traveled. Even though we had solved the lid-storage problem to some degree, we sold the cover and replaced it with another type because the front storage compartment proved to be neither waterproof nor dustproof enough for what we carried in there.

At the front of the bed we now have a low-profile, steel storage box with a sliding cover. The back of the bed is covered with a simple vinyl cover held on with snaps all around; the box has an aluminum angle iron on the rear where the snaps are located. When towing, the cover is rolled up against the box and secured with straps. We plan to add a storage box on each side of the bed behind the hitch, similar to the built-in bins we had in the canopy-covered bed. It's not that we really need the extra storage space, but we want to fill in the open area as much as possible to cut down on drag (we prefer a solid tailgate). The vinyl will then be altered to fit into the much-reduced open area between the side boxes. A separate panel will extend from the rear wall of the front tool box and terminate just in front of the hitch in order to close off the open area. This panel will stay in place while towing; the rear panel will, of course, be removed.

If we didn't need an enclosed storage area in the truck's bed, we might have considered an electrically (12-volt-DC) operated rollup bed cover, the type made of aluminum slats that's waterproof. However, a cover such as this rolls into a box about a foot-and-a-half-wide at the front of the bed, taking up space that might otherwise be used for a storage compartment. Another drawback for those with a solid tailgate and drag concerns is that the entire cover must be rolled into its box for towing, leaving most of the bed open.

We have seen a few fifth-wheel rigs with a sliding canopy over the bed. For towing, the flexible, full-size canopy and its rear window in an aluminum frame slide on a track until they rest, accordion-folded, against the rear of the cab. We talked with one fifth-wheel owner who told us he had cracked the canopy's rear window glass after making a sharp turn; even though the folded-up canopy extends only a few inches out from the rear of the cab, there wasn't enough clearance between the canopy and the front of the trailer when making this particular turn, and the trailer brushed against the canopy. In addition, in the towing position this cover does nothing to counteract drag.

The perfect bed cover for fifth-wheel towing (which, to our knowledge, hasn't been invented yet) should incorporate some form of lockable, waterproof storage; cover most of the bed when towing to minimize drag; be easy to prepare for towing (perhaps by incorporating self-stowing, hinged, folding, or sliding lids) and be designed so rain and snow can run off and not collect in pools.

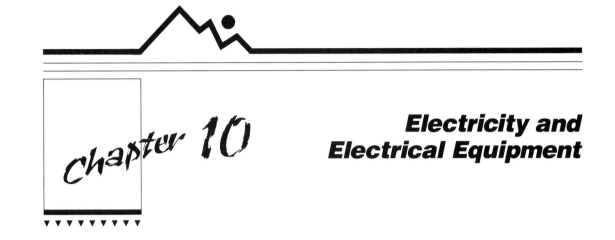

Electricity and Electrical Equipment

chapter 10

▼ ▼ ▼ ▼ ▼ ▼ ▼ ▼ ▼

From the fulltimer's point of view, the single most important aspect of an RV is its electrical systems. Just as in a fixed dwelling, the pleasures, comforts, and conveniences of an RV home would not exist without electricity. In fixed dwellings the power is there when needed, and using it rarely involves anything more complicated than turning on a switch or plugging in an appliance. But the power for an RV home won't exist unless the occupant sees to it that it is operative. And since most RV systems depend on electricity for their operation, fulltimers should have a basic understanding of how an RV's electrical systems work. Often the quality of electric service depends greatly on how fulltimers use their electrical systems, whether in a campground with an electrical hookup or in a primitive campground with no hookups. The safety of your RV home and its occupants is also affected by how electricity is treated.

An RV's electrical systems are not complicated. Merely understanding how they function will enable you to solve many simple problems, should they arise.

All modern RVs have a 120-volt alternating-current (AC) electrical system—the standard type found in fixed dwellings—and a 12-volt direct-current (DC) system. The 120-volt AC system receives its power from a campground hookup or other external source (this is sometimes referred to as shore power). The 12-volt DC system is powered by the RV's batteries.

THE 120-VOLT AC SYSTEM

▼ ▼ ▼ ▼ ▼ ▼ ▼ ▼ ▼ ▼ ▼ ▼ ▼

A modern RV's 120-volt AC system consists of an external power cord, a switch/circuit breaker for each circuit, several 120-volt outlets, and the converter/charger. The converter/charger is so named because of its two functions: It converts 120-volt AC current to 12-volt DC power, and it supplies a charge to the batteries, if needed.

The AC electricity can be used to run most RV refrigerators, and this system is needed for the operation of air conditioners and other 120-volt equipment, such as televisions, toasters, coffee makers, microwave ovens, and electric heaters.

▼ ▼ ▼ 120-Volt Electric Accessories

Extension Cords and Adapters

Some extra accessories, most of which are not expensive, are needed in order to use an RV's 120-volt system with the varied outlets found in campgrounds across the country. Used RVs may already have much of this equipment.

Most RVs are equipped with a three-prong, 30-amp plug on the external 120-volt power cord, but not all campgrounds have outlets to accommodate this plug; some have only 15-amp service. If the dealer does not provide a 15-amp male to 30-amp female adapter, you will need to purchase one (Figure 10.1), as well as a 30-amp male to 15-amp female adapter (Figure 10.2).

Some luxury motorhomes and large fifth-wheel trailers have four-prong, 50-amp plugs. Other adapters would be needed to connect such units to 15- and 30-amp outlets. In Figure 10.3, the three types of the most common campground outlet configurations are shown.

One or two heavy-duty, 10-gauge (10/3) extension cords in twenty-five or fifty-foot lengths should be part of your electrical

Figure 10.1
A 15-amp male to 30-amp female adapter may be necessary in many campgrounds.

Figure 10.2
A 30-amp male to 15-amp female adapter may also be useful in some instances.

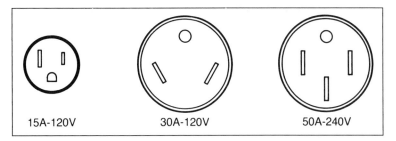

Figure 10.3
From left to right, 15-amp 120-volt, 30-amp 120-volt, and 50-amp
240-volt AC outlet configurations are shown.

equipment. Such cords are available with either 30- or 15-amp
connectors. (A 30-amp male to 15-amp female adapter will be
needed when a 15-amp extension is used in a 30-amp outlet.)
Heavy-duty extension cords are available at well-stocked RV-
supply and hardware stores and electric-supply companies.

A drop or loss in voltage occurs when long extensions are
used, no matter what the wire gauge. The longer the extension,
the greater the drop; however less voltage drop occurs with
heavy-gauge wire than with a light-gauge wire of the same
length. For this reason, never use an extension cord unless
absolutely necessary and, if you have extension cords in various
lengths, use the shortest one possible.

Circuit/Polarity Analyzers

A circuit/polarity analyzer is a device no fulltimer should be
without (Figure 10.4). When plugged in, the analyzer's three
indicator lights are illuminated in various combinations to show
a proper circuit, any of several aberrations that may be in the
circuit, or when no indicators are lit, no power. An explanation
of the light combinations is printed on the analyzer housing.

After plugging the RV's external power cord into a 120-volt
AC outlet, check the electric service with the circuit-polarity
analyzer by plugging it into a 120-volt outlet in the RV. Our
analyzer is plugged into an outlet on the underside of a kitchen

Figure 10.4
A circuit/polarity analyzer is
useful for checking electrical
circuits.

cabinet; we can check on it through the kitchen window without going inside. When we are getting ready to leave a campground, we plug in the analyzer so it will be in place, ready for use, when we arrive at the next campground. The analyzer can be plugged directly into the campground's electrical outlet prior to connecting the shore cable. We sometimes do this if we suspect there is no electricity at a site. Analyzers have the 15-amp male-prong configuration, so adapters will be needed for use in both 30- and 50-amp outlets.

After the analyzer is plugged in, note which of the analyzer's three lights are on. Most times it will indicate that no problem exists.

If the lights show reversed polarity, it should be corrected. Operating electric equipment such as a television, VCR, or computer with this condition can cause damage. You may have noticed that the two-prong plugs on some electrical equipment have one prong with a wide, flared end. This is so the plug can be inserted in only one way thus assuring the proper polarity. This plug affords no protection if reversed polarity exists in the circuit, however.

Reversed polarity usually occurs with incorrectly wired 15-amp outlets. It can be corrected on such outlets simply by turning over a two-prong plug and reinserting it so the prongs are opposite the way they were before. Many 15-amp plugs, however, have a round brass grounding pin in addition to the two prongs and cannot be reversed because, in the upside-down position, there is no hole for the grounding pin.

A two-to-three prong adapter will have to be used to achieve the configuration that allows the pin to be reversed. (If the two-prong side of the adapter is polarized — one of the prongs being wider than the other — it cannot be reversed.) With such an adapter, the plug will have no grounding provision, so a ground wire must be attached to the plug and fastened to something metal that will provide a ground, such as the metal conduit or the box on the outlet. Any ground must be metal and be set into the earth.

We made an easy-to-use grounding adapter (Figure 10.5). One end of a three-foot length of 14-gauge wire is attached to the

Figure 10.5
A two-to-three-prong adapter with grounding wire is used with a three-prong 15-amp connector when polarity must be reversed.

grounding screw on a heavy-duty, two-to-three-prong grounding adapter. An alligator clip on the other end makes it easy to attach to the conduit or box (which, if installed to the electrical code, will be grounded).

Reversed polarity doesn't often occur in a 30-amp outlet, but if it does, using a 30-amp male to 15-amp female adapter in the outlet and the two-to-three-prong grounding adapter (mentioned previously) on the power cord will achieve proper polarity.

Ungrounded 30-amp outlets are also uncommon, but we have encountered this situation often enough to warrant making a 30-amp grounding wire. It, like the 15-amp grounding adapter, has an alligator clip on one end and a crimp-type, ¼-inch ring connector on the other end. The opening in the connector slips over the grounding pin of the 30-amp plug (Figure 10.6). This is not an ideal ground by any means, but it will afford some degree of protection, and it's better than no ground at all.

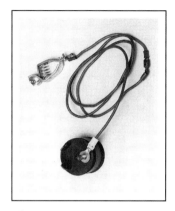

Figure 10.6
A grounding adapter for an ungrounded 30-amp outlet is shown. The crimp-type connector fits over the grounding pin.

If the readout on the circuit-polarity analyzer indicates that the grounding pin is carrying the current—is the "hot" wire—a dangerous situation exists. The outlet should not be used, since there is a risk of fire and severe electrical shock.

When we find such an outlet on a site, we move to another site and check the outlet there with the circuit-polarity analyzer before plugging in to see if it is wired correctly, even though it would be highly unusual to find all sites in a campground wired incorrectly in this manner. This situation usually occurs when an inexperienced person has repaired an existing outlet that was originally correctly wired. Any such condition should be reported to the campground manager.

AC Voltmeters

It is useful to know and monitor how much voltage is received from a campground electrical hookup. This can be easily checked with a simple plug-in 120-volt voltmeter, or a voltmeter can be installed in the RV. A voltmeter can also be used to check voltage from other AC sources such as a generator or inverter.

It is amazing how often campground voltage is less than satisfactory. Low voltage can cause certain electrical equipment to overheat, and it can harm or cause some equipment to malfunction, especially electronic items such as microwave ovens, televisions, and computers, as well as compressors on air conditioners. None of this equipment should be operated on fewer than 100 volts. If some electrical equipment is used in a low-voltage situation, keep in mind that it will lower the voltage even more.

We once noticed the picture on our TV screen shrinking in size. A check of the AC voltage with a voltmeter indicated the trailer was receiving only 90 volts. On many other occasions, we have noticed the lights seemed dimmer than usual. When this happens, a voltage check will usually show the voltage is low. This situation occurs when the converter isn't getting enough voltage to operate properly, and the lights are running off the RV's batteries.

In some campgrounds, low voltage may occur when too many RVers are using too much electric equipment at the same time, especially air conditioners or heaters. The low voltage, in many instances, occurs because the campground is inadequately wired. When a notice is posted at a campground stating that no air conditioners or heaters are allowed, it is usually because the wiring won't stand such loads.

If a campground has old or inadequate wiring, a campsite at the far end of a campground or on the end of a row of sites may have the lowest voltage. It is important to be aware of this if a long-term stay is planned at such a campground.

AC Power Indicator

When we are plugged into shore power, we want to know when we are or are not receiving power. We use a tiny, neon night-light for this—the type with the light incorporated into the plug casing, not the kind that requires a replaceable bulb. The night-light is kept permanently plugged into an outlet visible from all parts of the trailer. A glance lets us know whether the 120-volt power is on or off. Flickering indicates that the voltage is low.

Surge Protectors

Most electronic equipment is very sensitive to voltage surges (spikes), which can originate from the local power plant or be generated by electric storms when lightning strikes power lines. A surge protector guards against spikes. The unit senses a momentary voltage overload in the circuit and either absorbs the extra voltage or burns out, much in the same way as a fuse does. Many surge protectors have one or two lights that indicate the unit is functioning properly and that a good ground is present. Surge protectors won't do the job when used on an ungrounded circuit.

We have installed surge protectors on our microwave and television outlets, and use one on the outlets for our computer equipment. The surge protector we purchased for the television is a special type that not only protects against spikes in the AC power line but grounds the coaxial antenna cable as well. While surge protectors are not lightning arrestors, they do offer some protection. Before we used surge protectors, we had a blown picture tube on our TV from a nearby lightning strike and, on another occasion, an antenna amplifier was burned out during an electrical storm. (See page 316 for more about the effects of lightning.)

Usually the price of a surge protector indicates its quality; the higher-priced units offer the best protection.

Ground Fault Interrupters

A ground fault interrupter (GFI) is a device incorporated into a 120-volt outlet for preventing shock. It senses when an unsafe condition is present and deactivates the outlet so no current flows through it. It is reactivated by a reset button or switch. Most modern RVs have a GFI in a bathroom outlet and may have other GFIs on other circuits. If your unit has no GFI outlets, or you want to install additional GFIs, it is simple to do; the only tool needed is a screwdriver.

GFIs can create some interesting situations. On our 23-foot trailer, the bathroom outlet, which had a GFI, was wired into the same circuit as the outside patio outlet. Bill found he could not use the bathroom outlet with his electric razor as long as it was raining heavily outside.

▼ ▼ ▼ Amperage Ratings and Overloaded Circuits

Many RVers have a cavalier attitude about using a campground electrical hookup; it's there to be used so they plug in and think no more about it unless a problem develops. Many don't realize that, unlike a house, which has many circuits, a campground electrical hookup is just one circuit, and consequently, many RVers' electrical problems stem from overloading this one circuit. Such problems can be avoided if amperage is considered when using an electric hookup.

The ampere rating of an electrical connector (a plug and the wire it is joined to) designates the maximum amount of amps (current) it is designed to carry. For example, no more than a 30-amp load should ever be put on a 30-amp connector, and a 15-amp connector should never carry more than 15 amps. Incidentally, these ratings are for intermittent use; no connector should carry a *constant* load of the full 15 or 30 amps. The full load should be used for short intervals only.

To determine the total number of amps being used, the amperage rating of electrical equipment must be known. The wattage or amperage rating is imprinted on most electric equipment and appliances. If only the wattage is listed, the amperage can be calculated by dividing the wattage by the voltage. For example, a 900-watt toaster would have a rating of 7.5 amps: 900 divided by 120 (volts) equals 7.5.

Using Table 10.1, some quick mental calculation will prove, for example, that a microwave oven, an electric heater, and a hair dryer cannot all be running *at the same time* on one 15-amp circuit. The least that will happen is that the circuit breaker will trip, or if fused, the fuse will blow. The worst circumstance would be that the connector or outlet would char or melt, ruining one or the other or both. For safety's sake, this simple calculation should always be done to avoid overloading your campground outlet.

Table 10.1

Wattage and Amperage of Common AC RV Appliances

Item	Watts	Amps
Color television, 9-inch	60	0.5
Automatic electric/gas refrigerator		
(running on 12 volts)	300	2.5
Converter/charger, 45-amp	620	5.17
Coffee maker	900	7.5
Microwave oven, 450-watt*	960	8.0
Hair dryer	1,200	10.0
Electric heater	1,500	12.5
Air conditioner, 13,500 Btu	1,630	13.6

*Given wattage of a microwave is cooking wattage only; in operation wattage increases to about twice the amount of the given wattage: 450 watts = 960 watts or 8 amps.

One winter, in an Oregon RV park, our neighbor ended up with a cord that was burned through in two places when he used a single, interior-type, 15-amp, 16-gauge, two-wire extension cord to run two 1,500-watt (12.5-amp) electric heaters.

We buy electric heaters that are rated either at a maximum of 1,200 watts (10 amps) or that have a 1,200-watt setting. This wattage provides plenty of heat and allows for the use of a television and other items of low wattage at the same time the heater is being used on a 15-amp circuit.

The 12-volt DC system, the primary electrical system in modern RVs, consists of the batteries, the interior and exterior lights, water pump, furnace, and fuse (or circuit breaker) panel.

Some RVs are equipped with refrigerators that can be operated on 12-volt current and may have certain other items, such as a built-in stereo, that run off the 12-volt system.

With the installation of 12-volt outlets, an AC/DC television and other 12-volt appliances and equipment—videocassette recorders and players, shavers, fans, spotlights, mixers, hair curlers and dryers, vacuum cleaners, sanders, drills, soldering irons, and even certain computers—can be operated off the RV's batteries.

THE 12-VOLT DC SYSTEM

On conventional trailers, the batteries are nearly always mounted on the tongue or in a compartment at the front of the trailer. Fifth-wheel trailers usually have their batteries installed under the gooseneck or in a side compartment near the front of the trailer. Motorhomes generally have one or two batteries for starting the engine and other automotive functions and a separate coach (or house) battery, or a bank of two or more coach batteries.

Familiarize yourself with the fuse panel in your RV. If each circuit is not identified as to what it services, you might want to label them yourself. Pull one fuse (or switch off one circuit breaker), then turn on all lights and try the water pump and other 12-volt accessories. Anything that *does not* work would be on that circuit. Repeat this process for each circuit. Always keep spare fuses on hand.

▼ ▼ ▼ Battery Types

RVers use two basic types of batteries. The deep-cycle battery is for coach use; the other type is for engine starting. Batteries designated as requiring no maintenance are usually for engine-starting. This type of no-maintenance battery is effective only when constantly kept in a fully charged condition. It should not be used in situations where a large percentage of the battery's capacity will be drained before it is recharged, for instance, in an RV without an electrical hookup for a period of time.

A deep-cycle battery is the only type suitable for RV coach use. Before purchasing any battery, check to see that it is specifically labeled for RV use or for RV-marine use. Recently, a no-maintenance, deep-cycle battery was introduced. If you want the convenience of a no-maintenance type for coach use, be sure it is also designated a deep-cycle battery.

If your fulltiming will include boondocking, that is, staying at primitive campgrounds or camping in other places without an electrical hookup, your RV should be equipped with at least two batteries, but if you will always plan to stay in a place with an electrical hookup it would be possible to get by with just one.

Table 10.2
RV Battery Sizes

Group	Cold Cranking Amp Averages	Reserve Capacity Averages	Amp-Hour Averages
24	500-520	120-130 min.	70-85
27	570-635	150-165 min.	90-110

▼▼▼ Battery Sizes

Popular RV battery sizes are shown in Table 10.2. Note the group classification for batteries. Group 22 batteries are available, but this classification has been omitted because they haven't a large enough capacity for practical, full-time boondocking. Higher-rated batteries than the ones shown can be purchased, but their physical size may make them inconvenient or impossible to use in an RV. Six-volt golf-cart batteries are one type of higher-rated, larger-sized batteries that are practical for RV use if space for them exists.

Batteries carry a rating for their cold-cranking amps, the battery's ability to start an engine at a certain ambient temperature. For coach batteries, this is a useless rating. To buy a proper coach battery, some indication of the ampere-hour (AH) rating or the reserve capacity is needed. Each coach battery in a two-battery bank should have a reserve capacity of at least 120 to 130 minutes or 75 ampere hours. If the reserve capacity of a battery is known but the ampere-hour rating is not, the ampere-hour rating can be calculated by multiplying the reserve capacity figure by a factor of 0.6.

Table 10.3 shows how many hours a typical battery will operate under different amp loads. The figures in the table indicate the useful life of a battery under a constant load, but in most normal use, loads are applied intermittently rather than constantly, so both batteries listed would last longer than indicated.

As a battery is discharged, the voltage decreases. When the voltage drops below 11.8 volts, much of the electrical equipment,

Table 10.3
Battery Discharge Rates*

Group	2.5 Amps	5.0 Amps	10.0 Amps	15.0 Amps
24	17 hr	7.25 hr	3.1 hr	1.9 hr
27	21 hr	9.00 hr	3.9 hr	2.4 hr

*Figures represent a 50 percent discharge under a constant load.

will cease to operate. Many batteries, when discharged to below 50 percent of capacity, will reach this voltage.

Ideally, all batteries in a bank should be of the same age and from the same manufacturer.

▼ ▼ ▼ Battery Maintenance

To achieve the best service from batteries, keep the terminals clean and see that the water is at the proper level. A little petroleum jelly or dielectric tune-up grease (available at auto-parts stores) on the terminals helps prevent corrosion. If corrosion should occur, it can be dissolved with a baking-soda solution. We put a teaspoon of baking soda into a 3½-ounce paper cup and fill the cup with water. Bending the edge of the cup forms a V-shaped spout and the solution can be poured directly onto the terminal. Keep the cell caps on while cleaning the terminals so none of the soda solution will get into the cells.

Only distilled water should be used when adding to the fluid level of the cells. We always keep some of this on hand in case we need it when we are far from a source.

▼ ▼ ▼ Battery Discharging and Recharging

Determining the Rate of Battery Discharge

When an RV is operating on its 12-volt DC system, it is useful to know how much 12-volt equipment can be used and how much the batteries will be discharged by using such equipment. This can be calculated by adding together the ampere rating of each

Table 10.4
Typical Hourly Amperage Draw of RV Equipment

Item	Amps
DC color television, 9-inch	4.0
DC black and white television, 9-inch*	1.5 to 2
Incandescent ceiling light	1.2
Single fluorescent light	.7
Furnace, 31,000 Btu	8.2

*Late-model, 5-inch, black and white TVs use only .8 amp.

electrical item used, then multiplying this total by the number of hours each will be run in a given period. Table 10.4 includes some average examples of the hourly amperage draw of certain items. During an evening, an average fulltimer might use two lights continuously for four hours and the color television for three hours. The total ampere-hours for these usages would be 21.6, calculated accordingly:

$$2 \text{ lights @ } 1.2 \text{ amps } = 2.4 \text{ amps } \times 4 \text{ hours } = 9.6 \text{ AH}$$
$$\text{color television @ } 4 \text{ amps } \times 3 \text{ hours } = \underline{12.0 \text{ AH}}$$
$$\text{Total} \quad 21.6 \text{ AH}$$

The water pump, which is used to supply water to the faucets and for toilet flushing, would most likely be used at times during the evening. The water pump would draw 8 amps if it ran continuously for an hour, but it is not used continuously, so the cumulative number of amps used is generally small. Another 2 ampere-hours might be added to allow for the water pump and other lights that might be used intermittently, bringing the evening's total usage to 23.6 ampere-hours.

To carry this example further: If the batteries are discharged by 23.6 amps in an evening's use, 23.6 amps will have to be put back into the batteries to recharge them. The more a battery is discharged, the longer it will take to recharge it. Lengthy recharge times may be impractical for those who camp for extended periods without an electrical hookup, so to avoid a long charging time, it is advantageous to recharge the batteries often and as quickly as possible.

If the battery bank's total capacity is 150 ampere-hours (two 75-ampere-hour batteries wired in parallel), only 15 percent of the batteries' capacity would have been used in the preceding example. If you had one battery of 55-ampere-hour capacity, the usage would have depleted that battery's capacity by 42.9 percent. Having large-capacity batteries allows you to live more comfortably for much longer periods of time before any recharging is needed.

The foregoing recharging rates and amperage-draw calculations are theoretical because many factors—battery age, ambient temperature, and others—make it impossible to calculate the recharging time or discharge level accurately, and also because proper recharging requires 1.1 to 1.2 amps be restored to the battery for each amp used.

To be on the safe side, batteries should be discharged no more than 50 percent of their rated capacity, even though some batteries, in certain circumstances, can be discharged to 60 to 80 percent of their rated capacities.

Phantom Loads

The amperage draw of the so-called "phantom" loads existing in many RVs must be included in any battery discharge calculations. Many RVers are unaware of phantom loads because, as the name indicates, some of them are concealed, or they are simply overlooked as a source of amperage draw. Phantom loads are present in illuminated switches, built-in monitoring meters, clocks, the memory in stereos (which requires power even when the unit is turned off), gas detectors, and the refrigerator if it is an automatic model. The electronic brain of our automatic refrigerator consumes .74 amp per hour, whether it is running on 120 volts or on propane. The clock and memory of our stereo and our gas detector each require amperage of about .025 AH. These phantom loads add up to .79 amp per hour or a whopping 18.96 AH per day. We have known people who left their rigs without an electrical hookup for a day or two and returned to find their batteries dead because of the continual amperage draw of phantom loads.

Battery Charging

As long as coach batteries can be kept charged, fulltimers are free to go anywhere they want and enjoy all the comforts and conveniences of home without having to depend on electrical hookups. Lots of fulltimers want to go off into the wilds and camp but are apprehensive about doing so. What holds them back, usually, is the concern about keeping their units' batteries charged during a period of boondock camping.

Nowadays there are plenty of efficient ways to recharge batteries, and, if an RV is properly equipped, there need be no worries about camping without hookups. We truly enjoy this sort of camping; cutting the umbilical cords of hookups seems to impart a greater sense of full-timing freedom. We find it's wonderful to be miles away from towns, traffic, and crowds in a primitive camping place, yet be able to live with all the modern conveniences.

Principles of Battery Charging   To have a satisfactory battery-charging system, the principles of battery charging should be understood. Some people mistakenly believe amperage is what charges a battery and the higher the amperage, the better. It is true that high amperage will charge a battery more rapidly than low amperage, but amperage determines the *speed* at which the batteries charge; it is *voltage* that actually charges a battery. (All methods of charging have a limit on the amount of amps at which they can charge, hence the reference to amperage in the ratings of chargers.)

When a discharged battery is connected to a voltage source with a voltage higher than the voltage of the battery, current (amperage) will flow from the higher voltage to the lower voltage. The greater the difference in voltage, the faster the current will flow. This can be likened to water flowing downhill from a high container to a lower container: the higher hill, the faster the flow.

Measuring Battery Charge   Table 10.5 shows the different levels of battery charge as measured by two different methods. The old and still reliable method is to use a hydrometer to

Table 10.5
State-of-Charge of Battery By Specific Gravity and Voltage

State-of-Charge (%)	Battery Voltage	Specific Gravity
100	12.7	1.27
75	12.5	1.25
50	12.3	1.19
25	12.1	1.15
Discharged	11.8	1.12

determine the amount of sulfuric acid in the electrolyte liquid in the battery. This provides a reading of the specific gravity of the solution.

The other, easier, method is with a battery-condition meter (discussed on pages 260–261), which indicates the state of charge by reading the voltage of the battery.

A fully charged battery at rest (with no load on it) should give a reading of 12.7 volts and a discharged one, 11.8 volts. The difference between being fully charged and discharged is not much—only about one volt.

Most battery chargers provide between 13.5 and 14.5 volts to effect a charge. This voltage, being higher than the voltage of a partially charged battery, allows current to flow to the battery and thereby recharge it.

As mentioned earlier, the greater the difference in voltage between the charging source and the battery, the faster the current will flow into the battery. But during the charging process, the difference in voltage between the charging source and the battery is constantly decreasing and, as a result, the charging rate continually slows.

▼ ▼ ▼ Alternators and Alternator Charging

When moving on after camping without hookups, the engine alternator in a motorhome or a tow vehicle will act as a battery charger for the coach batteries. The primary function of an engine alternator, however, is to charge the engine battery. This is what it is designed to do, and it performs this operation efficiently. When the engine is started, the alternator quickly replaces the slight discharge that occurs in the engine-starting battery. But with deep-cycle coach batteries, which might be discharged as much as 50 percent after a typical night's usage, it will take some original-equipment alternators as long as five or six hours for recharging, and even that may not be enough to bring the batteries to full strength. As the voltage of the battery increases during charging, the amperage flow from the alternator decreases until it reaches about 5 amps or so. When this occurs, many more hours of charging will be needed to charge the batteries to 100 percent of capacity. The use of 12-volt equipment such as an air conditioner or lights in the tow vehicle or motorhome during travel will increase charging times because some of the current flow, which would otherwise go to batteries, is diverted to the 12-volt equipment.

The charging rate is directly affected by the engine's RPM, so running at a higher speed will charge batteries more quickly than when the engine is at idle speed.

When staying over in a primitive campground, the engine can be used to charge batteries, but with the engine running at idle speed, only about 10 amps will be produced from an alternator rated at 65 amps, hardly enough for rapid battery charging.

Battery charging can be improved considerably if the alternator has a higher output. Many recent motorhomes are factory equipped with adequately sized alternators having outputs that range from 100 amps to as much as 160 amps, but tow vehicles may have only a 30-amp or 65-amp alternator. Aftermarket alternators are available with charging rates as high as 160 amps or more. A high-output unit is best for fast, efficient battery charging (a 120-amp alternator will charge at about 65 amps with the engine idling).

It may be necessary to install a higher-output alternator if your RV has a three-way refrigerator and you intend to operate it on 12-volt power during travel. When the refrigerator is operating on 12-volt DC power, it draws 15 to 35 amps; a low-output alternator may not be able to provide enough current to run it along with other equipment.

*Correct me if I'm wrong —
the gizmo is connected to the
fling flang connected to the
watzis, watsiz connected to
the doo-dad connected to the
ding dong.*

PATRICK B. OLIPHANT

▼ ▼ ▼ ▼ ▼ ▼ ▼ ▼ ▼ ▼ ▼ ▼

Installing Adequate Wiring

Motorhomes are wired at the factory and have the equipment for battery charging built in. With trailers, though, the dealer is often the one who installs the tow vehicle's coach-battery-charging system, except for the alternator. Motorhomes are generally wired to automotive standards so the wiring is adequate, but trailer owners will have to be responsible for seeing to it that suitable wiring is installed on their rig; dealers or service technicians probably won't do it on their own. It will cost a little more to have the proper gauge wire used in battery-charging installations, but it will be worth it.

Wire gauges are designated by number. The higher numbers denote the lightest wire: 8-gauge wire is heavier than 14-gauge wire. The lighter the wire and the longer its run, the more the voltage drops; if voltage drops too much in a charging line, the batteries will not charge at all.

The run from the alternator to the trailer electrical connector cable (our own abbreviation for this is TECC) outlet (at the rear of the truck for conventional trailers and in the middle of the bed for fifth-wheels) is long enough so that wire no lighter than 8 gauge should ever be used. Any lighter gauge wire will not provide adequate battery charging. In Table 10.6, the voltage drop is figured for twenty-five feet, which is about the distance from the alternator in a full-size pickup truck tow vehicle to trailer batteries mounted at the front of a trailer. The wire size should also be determined by the alternator size. For instance, a 120-amp alternator should be wired with a minimum of 4-gauge wire for a run of ten feet or under. Longer runs require 2-gauge wire.

Alternator-to-battery voltage drop is not as critical in motorhomes because most motorhome coach batteries are in the engine compartment close to the alternator.

Service personnel at RV dealers, auto-parts store clerks, and auto mechanics cannot always be relied upon to give good wiring advice. Once when we were trying to purchase some 8-gauge wire, an RV service manager told us we didn't need such heavy wire; any size would charge the battery, he insisted.

Table 10.6
Voltage Drop for Different Wire Sizes and Charging Rates

Alternator Charge Rate in Amperes	Wire Size Gauge (AWG)	Voltage Drop Over 25 Feet	Voltage Loss Effect (Alternator Charge Rate of 14.5 Volts)	
20	14	1.28 Volts	13.21 Volts	*
	12	0.80	13.69	
	10	0.50	13.99	
	8	0.32	14.17	
	6	0.20	14.29	
	4	0.12	14.37	
30	14	1.93	12.56	*
	12	1.21	13.28	*
	10	0.76	13.73	
	8	0.48	14.01	
	6	0.30	14.19	
	4	0.18	14.49	
50	14	3.21	11.28	*
	12	2.02	12.47	*
	10	1.27	13.22	*
	8	0.80	13.70	
	6	0.50	13.99	
	4	0.31	14.18	
75	8	1.20	13.30	*
	6	0.75	13.75	
	4	0.47	14.03	
	2	0.29	14.21	
	1	0.23	14.27	
100	6	1.00	13.50	*
	4	0.63	13.87	
	2	0.39	14.11	
	1	0.31	14.18	
	0	0.25	14.25	
125	4	0.79	13.70	
	2	0.50	14.00	
	1	0.40	14.10	
	0	0.31	14.18	

*Insufficient voltage for fast battery charging.
  The above is a general guide only. Alternator output may vary.

Figure 10.7
The authors' 8-gauge-wire battery-charging extension cord is made from battery jumper cables.

Figure 10.8
This weatherproof receptacle for the battery-charging extension cord shown in Figure 10.7 is mounted on the trailer tongue. Note 8-gauge wire is used from receptacle to battery wires.

When we bought our 23-foot trailer, the dealer installed the necessary wiring. With the engine running and the TECC hooked up, our 65-amp alternator would only deliver 13.5 volts at the trailer batteries, providing a charging rate of a mere 7 to 10 amps. We shortly replaced the dealer-installed inadequate wire with heavier 8-gauge wire and doubled the charging rate.

▼ ▼ ▼

If you boondock as we do, sometimes for several days at a time, you will need to charge your coach batteries daily unless you have a large battery bank. Although we now depend on solar panels for most battery charging (see page 255), we used to charge the batteries every day by using the truck's engine. We did not use the TECC for this because its battery-charging wire was only 14 gauge, which didn't allow enough current flow. Instead, we made a cable using a battery jumper cable of 8-gauge wire (Figure 10.7).

After removing the clips from the ends of the cable, we put a 7-pin male connector, wired to the proper pins, on one end and a 220-volt AC plug, the type used for electric stoves or laundry dryers, on the other end. This was plugged into a corresponding outlet mounted in a weatherproof receptacle on the trailer tongue (Figure 10.8).

In order to have 8-gauge wire throughout the entire charging system, a short length of jumper cable was installed to run from the receptacle to the positive and negative terminals on the battery bank.

To charge the batteries, we connected the six-foot-long cable to the truck and plugged it into the tongue outlet. The engine was started and run long enough to charge the batteries. Our charging rate was 20 amps, so a half-hour's charging in the morning and then again at night enabled us to spend several days without a 120-volt electrical hookup. (We planned our showers to coincide with the times the engine was running, so battery discharge from water pump usage was negligible.) The TECC was short on our 23-footer, but the extension, which was much longer, enabled us to charge the batteries without having to jockey the truck close to the trailer, as we had to do to use the short cable. We were able to use the extension when the truck was parked alongside the trailer, which is often necessary in some campsites.

When we acquired our fifth-wheel trailer, before we installed the solar panels, we used the same sort of charging extension, except we upgraded it to a 6-gauge, 12-foot-long jumper cable. We rewired the truck and the trailer with 6-gauge wire throughout the charging line. The regular connector cable — a 7-pin cable with a 14-gauge charging wire — was bypassed by installing the receptacle with the 220-volt outlet (removed from our old trailer) on the rear of the pin box. This extension provides a charging rate of over 30 amps at the beginning of the charge cycle. Even so, with the 6-gauge wiring and heavy-duty extension, it still takes several hours of engine running to bring the batteries to nearly a 100 percent charge.

Even though we now have solar panels for battery charging, we still use the extension cable if we have had many hours or days of cloud cover, or if we have had a more-than-normal amount of battery consumption after the sun has gone down.

▼ ▼ ▼

Changing over to heavy-gauge wiring will be in vain if the ground connections between the trailer and tow vehicle are poor. They must be the equivalent of the same wiring installed on the positive side of the battery. Often these ground connections are inadequately wired or ignored. On many rigs, the chassis provides the ground or the return negative side of the system; therefore it is important that all connections be clean and make good electrical contact for the system to work properly.

Isolators

Most motorhomes are equipped with an isolator unless they have a dual-output alternator, and an isolator should be installed in any vehicle used as a tow vehicle. Without an isolator, the engine and coach batteries are connected together in a common system. An isolator electrically separates the engine battery from being discharged along with the coach batteries. This eliminates the possibility of not having enough power left to start the engine. An isolator also facilitates proper charging of dissimilar batteries. For instance, the engine and coach batteries are usually dissimilar in size, type, capacity, and each accepts a charge differently.

Isolators are available in different amperage sizes and should be a higher amp rating than the alternator: a 70-amp alternator should be coupled with a 105-amp isolator, for example.

Ammeters

An ammeter is a means of monitoring the rate of charge. Without an ammeter there is no precise way of checking whether the battery is charging when under way.

To monitor the charging rate, we installed a -60-0-$60+$ ammeter in our tow vehicle under the dash (Figure 10.9), in the wire from the isolator to the TECC outlet (at the fifth-wheel hitch). This device also shows the charging rate when we are under way with the regular TECC in use. Ammeters can be installed in motorhomes as well as tow vehicles.

Other Methods of Battery Charging

Without an electrical hookup, aside from the alternator, RV batteries can be charged by a built-in or portable generator or by solar panels. When electricity is available, the converter/charger takes care of keeping the battery charged, and if AC power is available, a portable automotive-type battery charger can also be used.

Converter/Chargers

A converter/charger is a transformer with a rectifier that changes the 120-volt AC power from an electrical hookup into a 12-volt DC power source. When using shore power, all the RV's

Figure 10.9
An ammeter is installed in the tow vehicle for monitoring the charge rate of the trailer's batteries.

12-volt equipment can be used without discharging the batteries. If the batteries are down for any reason, the converter/ charger will recharge them.

Converter/chargers with an output of around 13.5 volts are used primarily for providing 12-volt power; their battery-charging capabilities are limited. They charge at a rate of 5 to 7 amps, which may not be high enough to recharge the batteries in a reasonable length of time if you have been without an electric hookup for two or three days and the batteries are considerably discharged.

Our 23-foot trailer had such a converter/charger. Before we made our heavy-duty charging extension, we spent three days in a primitive campground and went to a campground with hookups on the fourth day. There, with shore power, it took twenty hours for the converter/charger to completely recharge the batteries. During the first few hours, the amperage draw from the converter/charger was so great that it went through many cycles of overheating the circuit breaker, turning itself off to cool down, then resuming charging again.

Figure 10.10
The authors' 45-amp converter/charger is on the left and 600-watt
inverter on the right in this installation. The two, small, white boxes
to the right and directly below the inverter are circuit breakers.

Recent developments in converter/charger design have re-
sulted in units that operate at 14.0 to 14.5 volts and will charge at
a 40- to 75-amp rate (Figure 10.10).

Generators

Many motorhomes are equipped with a built-in generator, and
large trailers often have a place where a generator can be installed. But if no compartment is large enough or otherwise
unsuitable for adding a generator, a portable generator can be
used. Generators have outputs ranging from 400 watts to 6,000
watts and can be powered by either gasoline, diesel fuel, or
propane.

The main purpose of a generator is to provide 120-volt AC
power, but many have a DC outlet that can be used for charging
batteries. The charging rate of most generators is only 7 to 10

amps—not nearly enough for practical charging. But a high-amperage converter/charger allows faster, more efficient charging if such a generator's 120-volt output is utilized so that the converter/charger can take care of restoring the batteries. If a portable charger with a higher amperage rating than the converter/charger is available, it can be employed in the same way. A generator of too-low wattage cannot be used in this manner; it must have a high enough rating to handle the amperage load of the converter/charger or a portable charger on a continuous, not intermittent, basis.

Solar Panels

For a long time, we resisted installing solar panels for battery charging. We knew they would do the job, and do it well; it was a matter of cost effectiveness. We felt that the older solar-charging systems cost too much for the amount of charging they were capable of delivering. Developments in panel design have improved efficiency and costs have come down, making solar panels an attractive alternative to other battery-charging methods. Now this method of charging is no more expensive than other methods and may even be cheaper than some. Certainly the fuel used to power a solar system is the cheapest of all: sunlight is free (see page 258).

The solar panel's photovoltaic cells collect light from the sun and convert it into electrical energy, which charges the batteries.

Solar panels are available in a variety of sizes, ranging from small, one-panel, low-voltage, trickle-charge units that deliver two-tenths of an amp at full power to large 60-watt panels that will charge at 3.5 amps maximum. The small panels usually deliver enough amperage to compensate for the battery drain of phantom loads when the RV is left unattended for any length of time.

While all our efforts to improve our alternator charging paid off, we still didn't have the capability for staying in the boondock camping places we enjoy so much for very many continuous days. We were still plagued with not being able to fully charge the batteries from the alternator without running the engine for four or five hours (which we never did, by the way—we were careful not to discharge the batteries too much and just put up with batteries that were never fully charged).

The problem was solved after we installed a solar system composed of two 48-watt panels and a regulator. Under ideal conditions, the panels will charge 6 amps at a full 14.5-volt rate until the batteries reach full charge. Then the regulator shuts off the current flow until the batteries drop in voltage to 13.4 volts, when it again allows current to flow.

This is the ideal way to charge batteries—at full voltage, but at a reasonable amperage rate, until the batteries are fully charged.

We were surprised to find how little light is needed for the panels to start charging. In the morning, with the sun just barely over the horizon, the panels will begin charging at an amp or so. The charging rate increases as the sun rises toward its zenith. Even on cloudy days the panels will charge at a reasonable rate. A big advantage of solar charging is that during the day, amps drawn from the battery for normal use are replaced almost instantly, so these amps will not have to be replaced later, as would be necessary with other methods of charging.

To travel hopefully is a better thing than to arrive.
ROBERT LOUIS STEVENSON

Our regulator is mounted in the bedroom, and, when camping without an electrical hookup, we awake in the morning to find the regulator's indicator light burning, which lets us know the batteries are being charged. The system works automatically, and best of all, it's quiet. We, and our camping neighbors, if any, are not bothered by the noise of a generator or engine running.

A solar system is also low maintenance. Once the system is installed, absolutely nothing need be done in the way of maintenance except, perhaps, wiping dust from the panels or cleaning them with window cleaner when they are dirty.

Selecting and Installing a Solar System   Selecting a solar system is easy. Simply add together the number of ampere-hours of all 12-volt items that would ordinarily be used in an average twenty-four hours (see Table 10.4, page 243, for the amperage draw of some common 12-volt items). The total of amps used will indicate how many panels will be needed to restore what has been drawn from the batteries. For example, a 33-cell, 47-watt panel will charge about 15 ampere-hours in the winter and

Figure 10.11
Solar panels are situated on the sloping portion of the roof on the
authors' fifth-wheel trailer. Note the wire entry is through the
holding-tank roof vent.

24 ampere-hours in the summer (summers days are longer than
winter days, and temperature affects panel efficiency). A good
rule of thumb is to figure one panel for each battery in the
system: two panels, two batteries, and so on.

Installing the panels is easy, too. Each panel is mounted on
the RV's roof with eight screws (Figure 10.11). Our greatest
concern with the installation was that a hole might need to be
drilled in the roof so the two-conductor wire could be routed to
the regulator. This proved not to be a problem because we were
able to use an existing hole in the roof; the wires were fed down
one of the nearby holding-tank roof vents. Inside the trailer, a
hole was drilled in the vent pipe just below the ceiling. The wire
was pulled though, connected to the previously installed regulator, then routed to the batteries. The complete installation took
about two hours.

Figure 10.12
A solar-panel regulator indicates the panels are charging
just over 4 amps. A remote
inverter switch is under the
regulator.

A holding-tank vent pipe was the best wire access for our installation, but a refrigerator roof vent could also be used as an alternative to drilling a hole in the roof.

On our roof the only space for two 13 × 48-inch panels was on the portion that slopes upward to the gooseneck. If the panels don't receive enough sun, they can be raised to a vertical position facing either forward or aft.

Solar-Panel Regulators We opted for a regulator with a two-scale meter that gives both the battery voltage (its condition) and the amp-charging rate (Figure 10.12). The regulator has a blocking diode to prevent reverse current flow, a phenomenon that occurs when panels draw current from the batteries after dark. Our regulator has adjustable set points for both the high voltage and low voltage, so the panels can be adjusted to turn on or off at any desired voltage level.

As a safety precaution, we installed a 25-amp fuse in the positive wire going to the battery.

Our regulator model has a separate terminal for a trickle charge line that can be used on motorhomes for topping off the engine-starting battery.

A motorhomer we know put his solar panels to use in an unusual way. His alternator broke down while on a trip. He used his solar panels to generate the electricity needed to run his engine, and he was able to drive home for repairs.*

▼ ▼ ▼ Battery Conservation

When relying on an RV's 12-volt DC system for electricity, battery conservation should be paramount. No lights should be on unless they are being used and, if possible, limit usage to one or two lights at a time. Turning off the television unless someone is watching it, giving up long, leisurely showers, and using exterior lights only as long as needed are additional ways to conserve

* For detailed information about solar systems consult *RVer's Guide to Solar Battery Charging* by Noel and Barbara Kirkby. It can be ordered for $12.00, including postage, from RV Solar Electric, 14415 North 73rd St., Scottsdale, Arizona 85260, (602) 443-8520.

battery power. As mentioned before, we often took our showers while the alternator in the truck was charging the batteries. Such extra 12-volt usage could be planned to coincide with the times a generator is being used for charging, too. In such situations, it's a good idea to wait to use the water pump until as much charging as possible is done in order to give the batteries the benefit of the higher initial charging. All such usage is "free" since battery charging keeps up with battery depletion.

One switch on the inside of our trailer controls four outside lights. From the inside, with the shades pulled, we cannot see that they are on. In order to be aware of this, especially when on battery power, we installed a light-emitting diode (LED) in the switch plate (Figure 10.13). When the switch is on, the red light of the LED is a highly visible reminder to turn it off. Before installing the LED, we had forgotten, on several occasions, to turn off the outside lights, and they ended up being on all night. Fortunately, we had an electrical hookup each time; if we had not, the batteries would have been severely drained.

Another way we conserve power is to reduce phantom loads. We installed a switch on our stereo radio to turn off the power to the clock and pre-set button memory. Since our refrigerator will not run either on AC or gas unless 12-volt power is supplied, we have to be content with the .75 amp it continually draws. However, to keep foods cold or frozen, the refrigerator doesn't need to run all the time, so during the times we aren't opening the doors during meal preparation, we might turn it off for a few hours. We have two TVs and use the 12-volt black and white television when on battery power; it draws less than half the amps of the color TV when used in the DC mode.

Figure 10.13
A signal LED on an inside switch warns of outside lights left on.

▾ ▾ ▾ 12-Volt DC Outlets

All the 12-volt appliances and equipment mentioned earlier are equipped with a cigarette-lighter plug and can only be used in an automotive-type cigarette-lighter socket.

Most older RVs are not furnished with cigarette-lighter sockets, but a few models have one such socket incorporated into a television amplifier installed near where the television will be located. Newer RVs might have 12-volt sockets in the living

Figure 10.14
A 12-volt plug and outlet can be installed to replace most cigarette-lighter plugs and sockets. These connectors can be used on most 12-volt equipment.

Figure 10.15
This bathroom installation shows 12-volt outlet next to a 120-volt outlet with a ground-fault interrupter.

room and bedroom for use with TVs, but often the sockets are inside a cabinet. Unless other lighter sockets are installed (some manufacturers offer them as options), any other 12-volt equipment will have to be used in the sockets provided.

We don't like the cigarette-lighter connections for a number of reasons: Often a good connection cannot be made, especially after the plug and socket have received much use, the sockets are unsightly, and the unwieldy plugs are in the way when storing the 12-volt item. We did away with all such connectors and replaced them with DC connectors that look like miniature versions of the standard 120-volt outlet and two-prong plug (Figures 10.14 and 10.15). These connectors are rated at 7.5 amps, which is adequate for most 12-volt items. The plugs have one prong larger than the other for proper polarization, an important feature because many direct-current items will not work unless the polarity is correct. This type of connector is available from most large electronic-supply stores.

▼ ▼ ▼ Electrical Monitoring and Measuring Equipment

Battery-Condition Meters and Monitor Panels

A battery-condition meter, useful for keeping track of the state of charge in batteries, is nothing more than an expanded-scale DC voltmeter reading between 10 and 15 volts. An RV's monitor panel will usually include a battery-condition meter. The level of charge may be indicated by a simple meter or, more commonly, a series of three or four lights representing good, fair, and low battery levels. Lights are not as accurate as analog, needle-type meters or those with a digital readout, which are sensitive enough to show small changes in the battery's charge level.

If you want a more accurate battery-condition meter than the one is installed on your RV, several types are available, and installation is simple for someone who understands wiring. A battery-condition meter can be purchased for about $30.

Figure 10.16
A 12-volt system monitor panel providing digital readouts of amp usage of the RV's 12-volt equipment and the state of charge (voltage) in the batteries also monitors all charging systems. An AC voltmeter is below the monitor panel. The switch on the left selects usage of either the converter/charger or the charging function of the inverter.

Some high-tech monitor panels serve as battery-condition meters since they give accurate digital readouts of battery voltage (state of charge), as well as amps being charged into the battery and amps being used. We installed such a panel next to our AC voltmeter (Figure 10.16). Both are mounted on the side of the lavatory cabinet in the bath where they are unobtrusive, yet easy to see.

In addition to the battery-condition-meter functions, our meter has a provision for two separate current measurements. We wired it so different functions can be monitored individually. We can check on the amperage draw of the inverter and any piece of 12-volt equipment in the RV's system. A readout of the charging rate can be obtained for all charging systems: converter/charger, inverter in its battery-charging mode, solar panels, and the tow vehicle's alternator when the TECC is connected and the engine is running.

Some sophisticated battery meters show the ampere-hours that have been discharged from the battery. This may be a feature of some monitor panels, too. When the battery is fully charged, the meter reads zero. As current is used, the meter registers the total amp-hour accumulation. Then as the battery is charged, the number of amp hours decreases back to zero.

Multimeters

A multimeter is a most versatile instrument for checking and troubleshooting either AC or DC electrical systems and equipment. A simple, analog, needle-type multimeter that incorporates all the functions needed by the average RVer can be purchased for less than $20. Sophisticated, digital multimeters with many functions are more expensive (Figure 10.17).

Multimeters are easy to use but, unfortunately, there seems to be no simple way for the beginner to *learn* to use one. Instructions for multimeters are not usually basic enough for beginners, and many are poorly written and organized.

We use a multimeter as a backup for our other meters on both 12-volt DC and 120-volt AC electrical systems, especially when checking voltage. We made special test leads with 12-volt and 120-volt plugs for convenient, safe use. Using our multimeter, we

Figure 10.17
A multimeter that provides a digital readout.

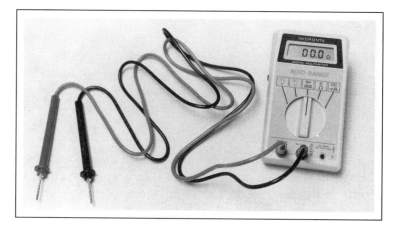

have been able to save time and money by locating and solving electrical problems that otherwise might need the attention of an outside service person.

Analog multimeters are best for checking AC voltage and troubleshooting campground outlets. They can be used to check the presence of DC voltage, but the scale is not expanded enough for accurate battery monitoring.

Digital multimeters provide highly accurate readings of both AC and DC voltages and are especially useful for determining the condition of a battery. The voltage can be read from a DC outlet or directly from the battery.

Devices are available that provide 120-volt AC power without a hookup. In particular, a generator can be used to operate all 120-volt electric items, and an inverter will convert 12-volt DC battery power into 120-volt AC power.

120-VOLT AC POWER WITHOUT A HOOKUP
▼ ▼ ▼ ▼ ▼ ▼ ▼ ▼ ▼ ▼ ▼ ▼

▼ ▼ ▼ Generators

Generators are the most commonly used device to provide RVers with 120-volt AC power when shore power is not available. Aside from charging the batteries as previously discussed, generators of the proper wattage can be used to operate just about any 120-volt electric item independently of shore power, such as microwave ovens, televisions, electric tools and appliances, and air conditioners.

If motorhomers want adequate air conditioning while traveling, they must use a generator to run their roof unit. A dash air conditioner couldn't begin to cool even a small motorhome.

Generators are designed for heavy loads, such as air conditioners. It is not cost effective to use them for light loads, such as a television, or intermittent loads, such as an electric drill. When operating, generators deliver their full wattage rating, and with a light load, little power is used for the fuel expended. The life of the generator will be prolonged if it is used to carry proper loads.

One of the biggest drawbacks of a generator is the noise it creates when it is running. Some campgrounds, even some with no hookups, have regulations prohibiting generator use or restrictions on the times a generator may be used.

A generator can add hundreds of pounds to an RV's weight. If you use a portable gasoline generator and carry extra fuel, store the fuel in an approved container. State laws vary as to the type of containers that can be used, and some states require carrying gasoline containers outside the vehicle. The nuisance of carrying extra fuel for a generator can be eliminated with a propane generator; this type can be connected to the RV's existing propane system.

▼ ▼ ▼ Inverters

An inverter is just the opposite of a converter/charger; it converts 12-volt DC battery power into 120-volt AC power and uses battery power to do so — a great deal of battery power. Even so, with judicious use, inverters can be a valuable accessory for the full-timer. Unlike a generator, an operating inverter is completely silent.

Inverters are best used for short-term, 120-volt convenience loads, such as running appliances or electric tools that are not normally run for long periods. Long-term operation can seriously deplete the batteries. Such loads are more ideally handled by a generator as are high-amperage loads.

A rotary inverter, or motor generator, a small, 12-volt motor with a 120-volt generator mounted on its shaft, is the least efficient type of inverter because it requires a considerable amount of 12-volt power to operate. It is also noisy and can be annoying to neighbors as well as the user.

A simple type of inverter produces unregulated AC voltage and can be used to run motors such as those on electric drills and shavers. The voltage can vary and become excessively high, so they should not be used for electronic equipment, televisions, or VCRs, unless the inverter has a frequency control, which is found on some models. Simple and rotary inverters draw their full-rated amperage load when operating, thus creating considerable drain on the batteries.

Solid-state inverters are the most efficient of all and have many built-in automatic features that protect against overload, overheating, and low-battery voltage, any of which will shut down the unit. Unlike other inverters that operate at maximum amperage power at all times, solid-state inverters have a search mode so the current and voltage are shut down until a load is on line. Then the unit is activated and delivers just enough current to run the item being used. A rough estimate of battery consumption is that for every amp of AC power produced, 10 amps will be drawn from the battery. Solid-state inverters can remain on continuously in their search mode, thus providing constant AC-power availability, because in this mode, they draw only a minuscule .022 to .06 amp (.5 to 1.5 AH in twenty-four hours). Remote-control switches are available so the inverter can be turned on and off from a convenient location.

Some inverter models have a built-in battery charger with ranges from 25 to 100 amps, along with an automatic transfer switch (relay). If AC power fails or is turned off, the inverter switches to battery power automatically. When shore power returns, the inverter switches off and the battery charger begins to recharge the batteries.

Considerable rewiring of the RV's AC system may be necessary for proper transfer-switch utilization. The inverter must be wired into the RV's system between the shore-power line and the main circuit-breaker panel. The air conditioner, the AC water heater, and other high-amperage items should be removed from the system and provided with their own circuit-breaker panel because running such items from an inverter is impractical. Figure 10.18 is a schematic for such an installation according to manufacturers' recommendations.

Because we needed a power source for our computer printer (the computers can be run on internal batteries or a 12-volt source), we purchased a solid-state inverter when we got our solar panels. Since these inverters are available in 200-watt to 3,000-watt models, we had to determine the size we needed. The amperage of the printer is low enough for a 200 watter to easily handle, but we figured as long as we were going to buy and install an inverter, it might as well be a size suitable for running

Figure 10.18
Shown is a wiring diagram for inverter transfer switch utilization as recommended by manufacturers.

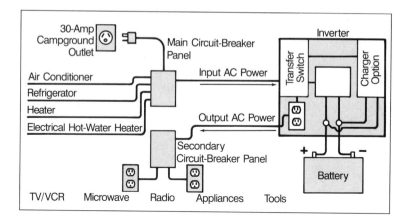

much of our other 120-volt equipment so we could use it while boondocking. We made our selection based on the amperages for the AC equipment we intended to use and purchased a 600-watt model with a built-in 25-amp battery charger. This was an ideal wattage for our battery bank of two, Group 27, 105-AH batteries (higher-wattage inverters require more batteries with higher AH ratings). Being small and lightweight, it was much easier to install than a higher-wattage unit. The installation is shown in the diagram on page 267.

The 600-watt unit has proven to be more than adequate. About the only equipment we have that cannot be run from it is, of course, the air conditioner, and an electric heater. We thought we might have to do without the use of our microwave oven when boondocking, but we found that we can use it for about one minute without any problem.

An Inverter-Wiring Plan

We devised a wiring plan that allowed us to install the inverter so that the built-in transfer switch is not used, but so the inverter still functions automatically (Figure 10.19). A 30-amp, AC, double-pole, double-throw relay is installed in the shore-power line before the circuit-breaker panel. One input comes from the shore-power line and the other from the inverter's AC outlet. The

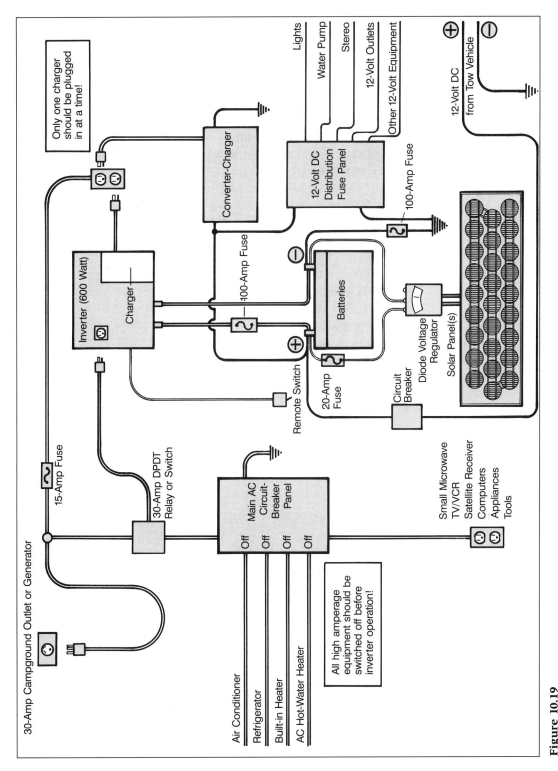

Figure 10.19
The authors' wiring plan bypasses the transfer switch but still allows the inverter to function automatically.

output is connected to the circuit-breaker panel; the exciter coil circuit comes from the shore-power side. With this wiring arrangement, when we want to use the inverter, we make sure the air conditioner is off at the main breaker panel, and we set the refrigerator to operate on propane.

When the shore power is off, the relay automatically switches to the incoming inverter power supply. It is not necessary to physically plug in the inverter.

If an inverter has its battery charger or a converter/charger plugged into an AC outlet when the inverter is in operation, the inverter will burn out. To prevent this from happening by accident, we installed a special AC circuit with an outlet for operating either the converter/charger or the inverter's battery-charger. This circuit is wired into the shore-power cord ahead of the relay. When current comes through the power cord, the current will reach the charging equipment, and when the power is off, the charging equipment is automatically disconnected. The circuit is protected by its own 15-amp circuit breaker.

For safety's sake, it's a good idea to install a fuse in the 12-volt DC positive cable from the inverter to the battery. We use a 100-amp fuse, which is the right size to protect our inverter (Figure 10.20), and another fuse of 100 amps or more on the

Figure 10.20
To protect the authors' inverter, a 100-amp fuse was located in the battery compartment and installed in the 12-volt DC positive cable from the inverter to the battery.

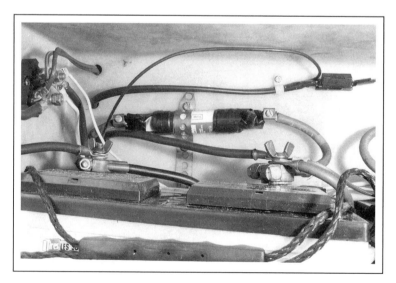

ground side of the 12-volt system where the batteries are connected to the chassis (Figure 10.21).

We use the inverter more than we ever expected. It works efficiently with the computer printer, since, with the search mode, it draws no appreciable amperage except when the printer is actually in use.

Once when we were without an electrical hookup, we discovered a bolt had sheared off on the trailer's front jacks. The only way to repair it was to drill out the broken bolt. It was easy to do using an electric drill powered by the inverter.

An inverter and a solar system are good partners. When we stop traveling to prepare lunch, we often have a sandwich conveniently heated in the microwave. By the time we are ready to get under way again, the solar panels have charged up the batteries.

Some other information about inverters: A surge protector needs a grounded electrical system to operate properly and will not function as it should when using an inverter for AC power. When not plugged into shore power, the RV loses its ground, except for the natural grounding effect of the metal chassis, which is not sufficient for the surge protector to do its job. But protection from power-plant surges is not needed when an inverter provides the AC power.

When an inverter is in use, GFIs will hum because a good ground is not present. If the hum is annoying, pop the test button on the GFI if the outlet is not being used.

We have gone to considerable lengths to insure we have an efficient 12-volt DC and 120-volt AC electrical system in our RV. This has added immeasurably to our full-timing enjoyment, not only when we are in campgrounds with electrical hookups, but especially when boondocking.

Those who do not want, or do not have, a system as elaborate as ours can still have a virtually trouble-free electrical system if these few basics are implemented:

▼ Carry the needed adapters and extensions.
▼ Always check the campground outlet with a circuit analyzer.
▼ Don't operate sensitive equipment on low voltage.

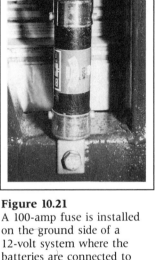

Figure 10.21
A 100-amp fuse is installed on the ground side of a 12-volt system where the batteries are connected to the chassis.

▼ Don't overload circuits.
▼ Have suitable capacity batteries for your needs.
▼ Practice battery conservation when without a hookup.
▼ Be aware of phantom loads.
▼ Use heavy-gauge wire for rapid, efficient battery charging.

With a little knowledge, coupled with common sense, it is possible to have a safe electrical system in your RV that will provide you with all the electrical power needed.

Water, Holding Tanks, and LP Gas

Chapter 11

Water and propane systems are rather simple; either they work or they don't, and most of the time they do. They are relatively trouble and maintenance free. If the water pump is defective, it can be replaced. If the propane regulator does not work, a new one can be installed. Loose connections in either the water or propane system may cause leaks, but these are easily corrected. In our previous trailer, a loose wire made the water pump inoperative; it was fixed in minutes.

There may be more problems in a used RV's gas or water system because of certain unknowns, such as the amount of wear the water pump has received or the condition of the propane-carrying lines or hoses. It may not be possible to determine how long either system has been out of operation, which usually causes more problems than using a system continuously. However, once any problems occurring from disuse or abuse are corrected, fulltimers can use their RVs' systems with confidence.

RVs can receive an unlimited supply of water from taps when hooked up to an outside water connection. Water is also available from the internal water tank.

THE WATER SYSTEM

Both water supplies work on pressure. The internal pressure is provided by the RV's 12-volt water pump; the external pressure will be that of the city water system. (In many older RVs, the pressurization was achieved by building up air pressure in the water tank, either by a hand pump or a 12-volt air compressor. These water tanks were made of heavy metal so they could withstand the pressure. Today's lightweight plastic water tanks would not have served.)

Either system routes water to the water-heater tank. As long as water pressure is available, the water-heater tank will be replenished whenever necessary, and as long as the heater is lit (or operating on electricity, if it is a dual system), there will be hot water.

Water from either the internal tank or the city water connection is used to flush the toilet.

The internal water system starts at the fill pipe, which is connected to the water tank. A 12-volt pump draws water from this tank and maintains pressure in the lines at all times. A check valve stops any backward flow of water. After the check valve, water lines run to the taps, toilet, and water heater.

The external water part of the system is simply a screw-in hose attachment with another check valve. This is coupled to the outside water system with a hose. The external system uses the same piping as the internal system.

Only one system should be in use at a time. Even though the check valves prevent pressure from one system from flowing into the other, the water pump might be damaged with dual usage, although this is rare.

▼ ▼ ▼ Water System Accessories

Every fulltimer will need a hose specifically for drinking water, and it should be so indicated on its label. Any other type of hose might impart an objectionable taste to the water or taint it in other ways. Hoses for potable water are usually white or blue.

The hoses are sold in lengths of twenty-five and fifty feet. Fulltimers should have fifty feet, but for ease in handling, two twenty-five-foot lengths can be used.

A drinking-water hose may be either round or flat, but we prefer flat hoses. When in use, round hoses rarely lie flat; their coils loop along and above the ground and present a tripping hazard to anyone walking in the vicinity. Because of the tendency to coil, they are almost impossible to drain after use, and when coiled for storage, they take up a fair amount of space.

The flat hose we use is not the type that self-stores on its own reel: Before a reel hose can be used, all of its length must be unwound from the reel, which requires more time and effort than readying the other types of hoses; we talked with several RVers who have had problems when rewinding the hose. Kinking is sometimes a problem, and if the reel's built-in squeegee doesn't work properly, all the hose won't fit on the reel. A hose on a reel, however, takes up less storage space than any other type.

We like our type of flat hose so well that after twenty years of use, we have never been tempted to switch to another kind. It's easy to drain and can quickly be folded and unfolded. We have two lengths of hose that total fifty feet, and each length is kept in its own bag. A net bag with a drawstring top, such as the type citrus fruit comes in, makes an ideal storage bag. Before storing, we screw the ends of each hose length together; it makes storage easier and keeps out dirt and insects.

▼ ▼ ▼

A recreational vehicle's water system is designed to operate at a maximum pressure of about 40 to 45 pounds per square inch (psi). The city water pressure in some places may be as high as 125 psi. Too much pressure coming into the RV's system can make the toilet leak around its base and might cause pipes to crack or split. One RVer told us that his shower-head hose once ruptured when he hooked up to a high-pressure water tap.

A water regulator, a simple, inexpensive device, should be used whenever hooking up to a city water supply since there is no way of knowing what the pressure is. The regulator will reduce high pressure to a level safe for the RV's system. Use the regulator at the faucet, not at the RV; this will protect the hose from bursting from pressure that's too high. High-pressure hoses, usually copper colored, should not be affected by high pressure, but because they're made of a very stiff material, they are extremely difficult to handle and store. In spite of the use of water regulators, high pressure will eventually cause problems with hoses and fittings.

It's easy to forget the regulator when leaving the campsite, but it's unlikely the hose would be forgotten. Fasten the regulator to the hose with a wrench so it is tight enough to require some force to remove it, then always attach the regulator to the faucet so it is just finger-tight. This way, the regulator will stay on the end of the hose when it is disconnected.

A "water thief," a handy device with a rubber sleeve on one end and a regular hose fitting on the other, is necessary for filling the water tank from a faucet that does not have a threaded hose connection. The tight-fitting sleeve goes over the faucet, and the other end is connected to the hose.

Unthreaded faucets are often found in public campgrounds where individual sites don't have water hookups. They are un-threaded to discourage people from hooking up to them long term. Don't use a water thief to deprive others of a communal water source; use it just for filling jugs or the RV's tank.

When a hose is connected to the RV's outside water inlet or inserted into a fill pipe, the hose tends to kink at the point where it begins its vertical drop. To eliminate this, thus prolonging hose life, use a connector with a ninety-degree elbow screwed directly to the outside water inlet. For filling the tank, purchase a sepa-rate spout to attach to the elbow. The spout fits easily into the fill pipe, unlike most hose nozzles.

Fulltimers should also have a Y-valve to use when one faucet serves two campsites—in case your neighbor doesn't have one.

Our owner's manual recommends that the water pump be turned off when traveling. To let us know at a glance that the water pump switch is off, we installed an LED on its switch-plate, the type we used on the exterior light switch (page 259).

If the water tank needs to be filled when no water faucet is nearby, it's often a messy, wasteful job when using a water jug. The spout may not be long enough to fit securely into the fill pipe; consequently much of the water may spill. This problem can be solved by using a funnel with a long, flexible nozzle that fits deeply into the fill pipe (Figure 11.1). So it doesn't have to be a two-person job, the funnel can be held upright by means of an

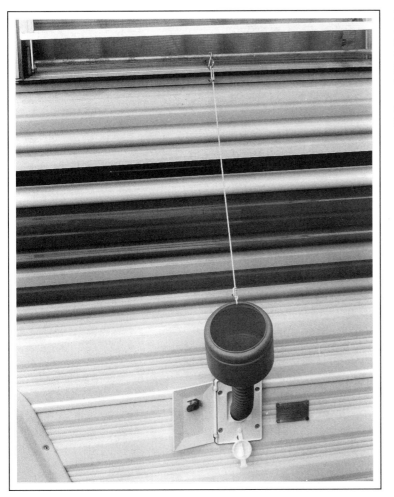

Figure 11.1
An efficient funnel arrangement, as shown, can be used when the water tank cannot be filled with a hose. The window must be open so the S-hook, on the end of the string, can be secured to the rod.

S-hook on a length of string attached to a window above the water intake. The funnel should be used for drinking water only and kept clean by storing it in a plastic bag between uses. Suitable funnels can be found at auto-parts stores.

▾ ▾ ▾ Water Quality

Perhaps the greatest concern for traveling fulltimers is the quality of the water that goes into their RV homes.

Different parts of the country have different kinds of water: hard, soft, sulfur or metallic tasting, cloudy, foamy, or crystal pure. In a few localized areas, the water may be downright unsafe. If so, nothing can be done except to use bottled water or move on to another place. Most other water-quality problems can be taken care of by using a water filter.

Sanitizing a New RV's Water System

Before using water tanks and lines on new RVs, they should be sanitized according to the manufacturer's instructions. If no instructions are available, the following procedure can be used:

1. Half-fill the tank with water.
2. Then, through the fill spout, pour in ¼ of a cup of chlorine bleach for each 15 gallons of tank capacity. Never pour straight chlorine into the fill spout; always dilute it with water.
3. Fill the tank to capacity with more water.
4. Open all faucets until the water flows steadily from them; then close them.
5. Leave the bleach in the tank for three hours.
6. Drain the system and flush it by using the tank drain and faucets. To remove any remaining chlorine taste and odor, dissolve ½ cup of baking soda in one gallon of very hot water. Be sure all the baking soda is dissolved.
7. Pour the solution into the tank and let it stand for eight to ten hours or overnight.
8. Use the faucets and tank drain to drain the tank, then flush the system twice with fresh water.

Sanitizing a Used RV's Water System

With a used RV, there is no way of determining the condition of the tank or how long it has been standing, full or empty. Either might cause the water to have a bad taste or foster bacteria growth. On any RV whose water system is suspect, more will have to be done to make sure the system is clean and safe. The following procedure can be used:

1. Flush the system by putting four teaspoonfuls of dishwashing detergent for each ten gallons of water into the tank.
2. Fill the tank, then open every tap in the RV and run the soapy water through until the tank is empty.
3. Refill the tank with clear water and drain by running the water through all the faucets.
4. Put a strong chlorine mixture in the tank: ⅔ of a cup to ten gallons of water. Again, dilute the chlorine in water before pouring into the fill pipes.
5. Open each faucet individually and allow water to run through it until a chlorine smell is detected. Repeat the running at hourly intervals until the chlorine smell is immediately evident when the faucet is opened; it may take several hours of repeating the procedure for this to happen.
6. When the smell can be immediately detected, empty the tank by running the chlorinated water through the faucets, then flush the system with fresh water until no chlorine taste remains, or use the baking-soda solution mentioned on page 276.

Any cleaning and purifying procedure is time consuming, but must be done when warranted.

Unlike many RVers, we use the water from our tank — our internal system — all the time. Rarely do we hook up to a water faucet for longer than it takes to fill the tank. By using the tank water regularly, the water never sits long enough to become stale or for bacteria or algae to grow.

Because what is in the tank is our sole water supply, we are very careful about the water we put into it. Before filling our tank we run some water through the campground faucet to get rid of rust or other matter that might have accumulated in the pipe. Often we run some water into a glass to see if it is foamy, cloudy, colored, or clear, or if it has an abundance of particles such as sand or those mysterious black flecks that we often encounter. We always taste the water. If it is disagreeable, we don't use it. Sulfur water, which is often found in many southern states, smells awful as it comes from a faucet, but aeration usually removes the odor. Fortunately, movement of the RV provides plenty of aeration.

The Water Filter

No matter how the water checks out, we always use a filter whenever we fill the water tank, and we would use the filter if we were using a water hookup instead of the tank (Figure 11.2). Some RVers use two filters for double filtration.

We install the filter at the campground faucet, which protects the hose as well as the RV's water tank from impurities. A short length of hose is attached to the faucet, then to the filter, so the filter can rest on the ground. For storage, both ends of the short hose are screwed to the filter openings. We started this practice, and that of screwing the hose ends together, after once finding

Figure 11.2
It would be difficult to attach a water filter of this type directly to a faucet, so a short length of hose is used to make the hookup easier.

several earwigs in the inlet side of the filter. Most water filters come with pipe fittings. For use with a hose, hose fittings will have to be added.

Although the type of filter we use can be permanently installed in a water line, we have not done this for two reasons. First, to have filtered water at both the bathroom and kitchen sinks, we would need two separate filters; each would take up valuable storage space. We could get by with one filter installed near the water pump, but changing the filter cartridge would be inconvenient since many items in the water-pump compartment would have to be removed to gain access to the filter. Second, we want the filtering process to take place outside the tank so impurities never enter it.

▼ ▼ ▼

A water filter is not the same as a water purifier. A filter will remove sand and other particles from the water and improve the taste to some degree. Water filters, available in different sizes, can be purchased from RV-supply stores and many other types of outlets. We have a small filter because it is easier to store and the cartridges are inexpensive (larger ones cost about three times as much). We have had to replace filters after just a couple of uses in two different campgrounds that had a high iron content in their water, and, in another place, we got only one use from a filter because it became completely plugged with sand during a single filling of the tank. Normally a filter will last us for several months of tank fillings, however.

Some water purifiers provide the cleanest, purest water since they remove everything the filters do, plus bacteria and disease-causing viruses and micro-organisms. Such units generally cost hundreds of dollars. Other purifiers, which are still pricey, don't treat water quite as thoroughly. For RV use, there are certain drawbacks to using a water purifier: Some require 120-volt AC electricity for their operation; some require high-water pressure, which means that they won't work with the RV's water pump; most are large units that don't lend themselves to convenient placement in an RV; most are slow acting as they process the water; and certain units waste a considerable amount of water because they require several gallons to produce one gallon of purified water. It would be impractical to install two water purifiers in an RV, so only one faucet, probably in the galley, would dispense potable water. Brushing teeth and drinking from the bath faucet would be done with unpurified water. It would also be impractical to install the purifier so it served all faucets and processed shower and dishwashing water. If you are thinking about installing a purifier, it would be wise to do lots of investigating to find one that does what you want because of the considerable cost involved.

Fulltimers who travel a lot should purchase a brand of filter or purifier for which cartridges or supplies are easily obtained.

▼ ▼ ▼ Water Conservation

Water conservation is a way of life with us, not only because we never hook up to outside water and want to avoid having to refill the tank every other day or so, but also because we spend a lot of time in places without hookups and often without any potable water source. When we are being reasonably conservative, the sixty gallons in our tank last about five days. When really conserving, we can push it to seven days—including some showers, albeit skimpy, but certainly better than none at all.

Lots of water is wasted when adjusting a two-knob shower faucet to the right temperature. We predetermined the knob placement for the mixture that provides the temperature we like, and then marked each of the knobs with a thin strip of colored tape at that point. We put two more strips of tape at intervals on each knob to indicate the position where the water flow would be increased. By using these settings we can obtain the right mixture instantly, and there is never any doubt about the direction the knobs must be turned.

For a conservative shower, we adjust the push-button valve on the shower head to just a trickle for wetting down and turn off the water completely while soaping. We allow a little bigger trickle for rinsing. (Jan thinks she may hold the world's record for the least amount of water ever used for a shower.) We use the same method for washing hands and faces. The tap is never left running during the whole operation.

We also conserve water when dishwashing by using a dishpan instead of one side of the double sink to hold the wash water. Our dishpan is usually the largest pan or bowl we have used for preparing the meal. Since a skillet is too shallow to be a satisfactory dishpan and too large to fit inside a bowl or pan for washing, we wash it last by pouring the water from the dishpan into it. For rinsing, we set a washed bowl or pan filled with hot water in the sink, and dip other items into it. To complete the conservation cycle, we reserve this water for rinsing the sink itself after cleaning it. Before washing, we clean off all food residue from the dishes with a spatula or paper towel. Having nearly clean dishes to begin with means less water is needed to wash them. It will keep drains from clogging, too, since food particles and grease aren't flushed down.

In our present trailer, the water heater is located close to both the galley and the bath sink. In many RVs, especially those with rear galleys, the run from the heater to one sink or the other can be quite long. On our previous trailer, the water heater was much closer to the bath than the galley. So when we were making an extra-concentrated effort to save water, we drew hot water for galley use from the bathroom tap. Even though the heater was in close proximity to the bath, at least three cups of water had to be run before it became hot. We didn't waste these three cupfuls; they were collected in a pan or bowl and saved for other uses. Of course, we only resorted to such stringent conservation measures when water was not readily available and when we stayed in the same dry area for some time.

▼ ▼ ▼ Water Heaters

Most water heaters in recreational vehicles have either a six-, eight-, or ten-gallon capacity. The water heater may be a propane-only model or a combination type that operates on either propane or electricity.

The propane model operates on the same principle as a household unit: the pilot light is lit and the thermostat set to the temperature desired. On some propane heaters, the pilot light must be manually lit with an igniting device—a spark gun or flame lighter. This is the type of heater we have and, for convenience, we keep a lighter in the heater compartment.

Another type of propane water heater has a 12-volt DC-powered electronic-ignition unit, controlled by a remote switch inside the RV, for igniting the propane. There is no pilot light; when water temperature drops to a certain level, the propane burner is automatically ignited.

The combination-type heater has both an electric heating element and a burner and may be operated on 120-volt AC power or propane, or for extra fast recovery, the gas and electric modes can be used together. The electric heating element is rated at 1500 watts and draws a considerable amount of amperage, so the water heater could not be used with inadequate campground electrical hookups in combination with other high-amperage equipment. With this type of water heater operating in its electric mode, RVers often overlook it as a source of electrical overload problems.

▼ ▼ ▼

All water-heater compartments have some sort of ventilation to dissipate heat, usually a grillwork area in the compartment cover. Since a high wind can enter through the grill and blow out the pilot light, the flame can be protected from the wind by attaching a shield. A piece of heavy aluminum foil can be taped over the grill, or use one of the manufactured devices sold for this purpose. When using foil, don't seal off the grill entirely. Rather, loosely arch the foil over the grill, and tape down only the top and bottom edges and the edge facing the wind direction. We had a problem with the foil-and-tape method; we tried several brands of tape but each took some of the door paint with it when it was removed. We finally bought a metal deflector, which is easier and quicker to install and remove than the foil. Since it is too large to store in the heater compartment when not in use, we keep it in the nearby refrigerator outside-access compartment.

We almost never use anything but the pilot light for heating the water in our six-gallon tank (the controlling knob is set to the pilot position instead of the on position). When the burner is in operation, even with the thermostat set at its lowest position, the water is hotter than it needs to be. Unless the outside temperature falls below freezing, the pilot light alone keeps the water in the six-gallon tank hot enough for most purposes. If we need scalding hot water, we heat some in the teakettle on the galley stove.

If all the heated water is used at one time, the pilot alone will take quite a while to heat another tankful of water. But when we take our usual conservative showers we find six gallons to be plenty of hot water—even if each of us showers one right after the other.

Those who hook up to outside water may not be as conservative, and a six-gallon-capacity tank probably would not provide enough hot water for two close-together showers. The burner would be needed to quickly heat the tank water.

One of the main reasons we use only the pilot is to spare us, and our neighbors, from the blowtorch noise of the burner. We started this practice early on when we were living in our 23-footer. The water heater was located under the bed, and the noisy burner going on during the night disturbed our sleep.

HOLDING TANKS
▼ ▼ ▼ ▼ ▼ ▼ ▼ ▼ ▼ ▼ ▼ ▼

Just as RVers are responsible for hooking up their electricity, so are they responsible for getting rid of their own sewage. Emptying the holding tanks is something none of us enjoys, but it must be done. Modern RVs are designed so the chore can be done quickly and easily.

Water from the sinks and shower goes into a gray-water holding tank; the black-water holding tank collects the toilet wastes. A recreational vehicle without holding tanks is not practical for fulltiming. That's not to say fulltiming cannot be done in an RV without holding tanks, but it will be very inconvenient to collect all the RV's wastes in a container and trundle it off to a disposal site every day or so.

Holding tanks can be emptied into a sewer hookup at the site in an RV park or at dump stations, which are found in many private parks even if all sites have sewer hookups. Some states have free dump stations in highway rest areas; they are often found at service stations; and some public parks have dump stations, even if the park has no campground.

Often a dump station will have two water sources, one for flushing the dump area; the other, a few feet away, is potable water for filling tanks. Signs generally indicate which is which. Usually there is a hose of some type on the dump section's water source. If a hose is also attached to the drinking-water faucet, we will not use it for filling our tank. We use our own hose, as we have no way of knowing how sanitary the drinking-water hose is. To avoid contamination, we are careful not to let our hose ends touch the ground in any dump station vicinity.

▼ ▼ ▼

Recently we were in a small campground with only one potable water outlet, which was adjacent to the dump station. The manager had provided one long drinking-water hose that reached to all sites, so those who were staying for a few days would not have to move their rigs to fill their water tanks. Our own hose was not long enough to reach our site so we went over to get the campground hose, which happened to be inside a trailer at the dump station. This aroused our suspicions. When we asked the occupant of the trailer about the water hose, she said we could have it as soon as she was finished flushing out her holding tank. We could see the hose in the toilet. "I'll have to wash it off first," she said. We told her not to bother. We would not think of filling our water tanks from a hose that had been in a toilet!

Yesterday we saw our neighbor rinsing the end of his sewer hose by putting the water faucet into it. He didn't seem to be taking any precautions about not touching the faucet with the sewer hose. We rarely rinse our sewer hose at the water faucet, but if we did, we would hold the hose well below the faucet so there would be no danger of them touching each other, and we would avoid splashing water so nothing undesirable would splatter on the faucet end, handle, or on the ground in the vicinity.

We have seen messes at dump stations caused by dimwitted people who haven't the intelligence to figure out that a sewer hose should always be used when dumping. Such people park their RV close to the dump station opening, take the cap off their holding-tank pipe, and open the valves, which allows the sewage to spill over a good portion of the dumping area.

Although most RVers are careful about handling holding-tank disposal, there are too many careless and downright stupid people who are clearly not concerned about cleanliness or sanitation and who have no consideration for others who may come in contact with the filth they have left behind.

Only one of us handles the dumping operation. We have a pair of loose-fitting rubber gloves to wear when handling the sewer hose. If it is necessary to fill the water tank at the dump station, hands are washed with soap and water before touching the water hose.

▼ ▼ ▼

On the few occasions when we want to thoroughly flush out the black-water holding tank, and a dump station hose is not available or not long enough, we use our regular hose. We equip it with a special nozzle for only this purpose, one that is pointed, with a small orifice, and able to deliver a strong, narrow steam of water. We never put the hose into the toilet, but hold the hose above it and direct the water stream into it. If any splashing occurs on the hose end, it should be washed off with water, then wiped with undiluted chlorine bleach, and rinsed again with water.

A special hose attachment for flushing holding tanks, a long wand that can be inserted into the toilet, can be purchased. The wand delivers a jet spray that can be aimed into the corners of the holding tank where waste often collects.

When using a sewer hookup, it's a good idea to open the black-water valve every three or four days. This will allow some liquid to accumulate in the tank so when it is dumped it will wash away paper and solids. Otherwise, the black-water tank may need to be flushed out periodically.

Fulltimers should carry a variety of sewer fittings and adapters. From time to time, we find it necessary to use a coupler that reduces the diameter of the sewer hose or a curved 45-degree hose adapter. We carry twenty feet of sewer hose in two ten-foot sections. To join them together, we like the threaded type of fitting that can be screwed in. We have never felt the need for any device to support the sewer hose so that it runs on a slant into the sewer connection, although if the sewer hose is hooked up and used on a continual basis, such a support might be useful. There are several supports on the market, but the sewer hose affixed to a slanted two-by-four will usually provide the same results.

Some campgrounds have a catchment for gray water at each individual site. These gray-water dumps are not regular sewer hookups, and it may be awkward to use the sewer hose for dumping. For such installations, it is useful to have a cap with a fitting for a regular water hose for the holding-tank drain. A length of hose for gray-water use (never to be used for drinking water) can be attached to the cap and easily directed into the gray-water receptacle. We always use a green hose for this purpose so it won't be mistaken for our white drinking-water hose.

The most flexible sewer hoses are made of fairly thin plastic and do not last long. If this type is used, a new hose will periodically have to be attached to the adapter that fits on the holding-tank drain. Unless the adapter is a screw-in type, this is not easy to do; as soon as one side of the hose is slipped on, the other pops off. Pour some hot water on the end of the hose that is to be attached; this will cause the plastic of the hose to expand and become more flexible.

▼ ▼ ▼ Plumbing and Cold Weather

More and more recreational vehicles are being built with an enclosed underbody and the heating ducts routed near the holding and water tanks and water lines. These RVs rarely have any freezing problems in cold weather. Our previous trailer did not have this feature, so we needed to take certain precautions in below-freezing temperatures.

When we were not hooked up to a sewer, we put some anti-freeze in both holding tanks every other day or so. Depending on the temperature, we used anywhere from a half a cup to one cup for each of the 40-gallon tanks we had. The antifreeze was added, not so much to keep the tanks themselves from freezing (it would have to be very cold for a sustained period of time before this would happen), as it was to keep the drain open and the valves unfrozen.

Once we were caught with our tanks antifreezeless in a sudden cold spell. The drain and valves froze solid. We eventually thawed them by leaving a heating pad tied around the drain for several hours and periodically giving the valves sustained blasts of hot air from a hair dryer.

When it is very cold outside, the water lines inside the RV can freeze if they do not receive enough heat. Keeping cabinet doors ajar on all areas through which the water lines are routed usually will keep them warm enough to prevent freezing.

Another reason we use water from the internal tank rather than hooking up to outside water is to avoid having the water hose freeze in cold weather. In many campgrounds in cold weather areas, each site's water faucet is protected by insulation or wrapped with heat tape that keeps it from freezing, but the hose attached to it, being full of water and exposed to the air, will freeze. The hose itself can be wrapped with heat tape, but this is a nuisance unless you are staying put in one place for some time. We have seen some fulltimers with a special heat-tape-wrapped hose they use only in cold weather. To be effective, a layer of insulating material must cover the heat tape. Use the shortest length hose possible; it should be just long enough to reach from the faucet to the RV's water connection. In extremely cold weather, the hose may still freeze.

Heat tape also could be wrapped around the holding tanks' valve-and-drain assembly to keep it from freezing. (For other cold-weather protection methods, see pages 292–302.)

When driving in cold weather, the vehicle's rate of speed has the effect of lowering the air temperature and can cause drains and valves to freeze if antifreeze is not used in the vehicle's holding tanks.

The three great elemental sounds in nature are the sound of rain, the sound of wind in a primeval wood, and the sound of outer ocean on a beach.

HENRY BESTON

▼ ▼ ▼ ▼ ▼ ▼ ▼ ▼ ▼ ▼ ▼ ▼

LP GAS

▼ ▼ ▼ ▼ ▼ ▼ ▼ ▼ ▼ ▼ ▼ ▼ ▼

Liquid-propane (LP) gas, also known simply as propane, is so easy and convenient to use that many of us tend to forget it is potentially very dangerous. In an unventilated area the fumes can kill. Improperly or carelessly used, it can cause fires and devastating explosions. Although common sense will prevent these disasters, everyone who uses the substance should be aware of the potential.

The most common problem RVers have with propane, if they have any at all, is leaks. Every person living in the RV should know gas leaks must never be investigated with any type of open flame, yet never a year goes by that we do not hear of someone doing it this way, invariably with dire results.

If a leak is suspected, check it by brushing a soapy solution on the questionable joints. Bubbles will appear if a leak exists.

If you smell gas when entering an RV, never turn on or use *anything* that will cause an electrical spark or flame until all the windows and doors have been opened and the gas has dissipated. Propane is heavier than air, so it will settle to the lowest point in the RV. Since the water pump is usually located at a low point, it's especially important not to use the pump if propane odor is detected.

Never sleep with all windows tightly shut when any unvented propane equipment, such as a catalytic heater, is being used. Open a window an inch or two to replenish the oxygen. We habitually sleep with at least one window cracked at the head of the bed, no matter how the trailer is being heated or if it is being heated at all. A gas detector can be installed that will warn of a leak by emitting a high-pitched tone.

▼ ▼ ▼ Filling Propane Cylinders

All propane cylinders are designed to be only 80 percent filled with liquid gas and should never be filled beyond this level. Although a cylinder will hold more gas, it is dangerous to fill it to more than the 80 percent level.

Propane cylinders are filled either by weight or volume, depending on which part of the country you are in. No matter which method is used, the operator should open the cylinder's 80 percent bleeder valve before filling by unscrewing it with a screwdriver. The cylinder should then be filled just until liquid propane vents from the valve, which usually occurs either when the scale indicates the proper weight has been reached or the meter registers the proper gallonage. At that point, the supply of gas to the cylinder should be shut off. The cylinder will then be filled to the right level.

Those responsible for filling propane cylinders should be instructed in the right methods, but when the gas is purchased from other than a bulk dealer there is good chance of encountering operators who know next to nothing about filling propane cylinders. RVers should always oversee the operation so their cylinders will be properly filled. If the operator has never heard of the 80 percent valve (many have not), use your own screwdriver to open it and explain what you are doing.

Cylinders also have a relief valve. Any time excessive pressure builds up in a tank, the relief valve automatically releases the pressure. Pressure increases can occur in hot weather because heat causes expansion within the tank, so especially in hot weather, cylinders should never be overfilled.

A propane cylinder should not be transported in a position other than the one in which it is used: Upright cylinders should be carried upright and horizontal cylinders should be transported in a horizontal position. Empty or full, cylinders should never be allowed to roll around or be tipped over. A plug must be in the valve for cylinder transportation in some states. The preceding applies mainly to those with trailers; most motorhomes have a built-in tank that can only be filled by driving the motorhome to the supplier or having the supplier come to the motorhome. And, of course, a motorhome's unremovable tank cannot be weighed, so it must be filled by volume.

▼ ▼ ▼ Use of Propane While Traveling

Many fulltimers travel with their refrigerators and water heaters operating, but we always turn off the propane when we are under way. The items in our freezer never defrost, even in the hottest weather — not even ice cream. The interior of the refrigerator stays at a safely cold temperature for several hours. Maybe it's because our refrigerator is well insulated and has doors with a good seal (we always give them an extra push to be sure they are firmly shut before we start traveling). But perhaps the main reason we have no problems with retaining cold in the refrigerator when it is off is because of our traveling habits. We almost never travel 200 miles in a day; 100 miles or less a day is more usual for us, so the refrigerator is never off for very many hours. In hot weather, we keep the refrigerator well packed; empty space will not retain cold but chilled items will; soft-drink cans are good space fillers. We try to avoid opening the refrigerator door during the trip, as well.

We also seem to have enough residual hot water in the tank to take care of our needs for the short times we are traveling.

We have heard that in some states it is illegal to travel with the propane cylinders open, yet we have never seen any rules posted to this effect, except for traveling through tunnels or on ferries.

Because propane equipment requires a flame to operate, all such equipment must be turned off when the rig is in a filling station. If we used propane-fueled items while traveling, we would make sure they were off *before* we were anywhere near the pumps. Many RVers, however, find it too much of a bother to turn off and then relight propane equipment, in spite of the great inherent danger.

▼ ▼ ▼ Fulltimers' Propane Usage

Many trailers come standard-equipped with two 5-gallon (20-pound) propane cylinders. For full-time living, these should be replaced with 7½-gallon (30-pound) cylinders, often available as an option.

Those who fulltime in a motorhome do not have a choice of size since most motorhomes have a built-in tank. It fits into a certain area so no larger tank could be installed, but most motorhomes come equipped with sufficiently large tanks anyway.

When we are not using propane for heating, one 7½-gallon cylinder will last a month or more. If the furnace is on when temperatures are in the twenties or lower, one cylinder lasts about a week.

We don't generally refill a tank immediately after it runs out unless we are staying put for a while. Why should we haul around the weight of a full propane cylinder if we won't be using it? So we won't forget to refill it before the other cylinder runs out, we keep a record of the date when the cylinder ran out. Because we know our average usage, it's easy to determine when we need to refill. If we are not aware of how much propane we are using, the distinctive rotten-egg smell when a stove burner is lit reminds us we are about to run out.

Fulltimers will use propane several times a day for one thing or another. This constant use is better for a propane system than the occasional use and extended layup periods a vacation-RV's propane system receives.

When preparing cylinders for a long layup, air may be inadvertently introduced into the cylinders. They will have to be purged before they can be used again. A gas appliance with intake and exhaust ports may require major servicing if insects decide to use the ports as nesting places when the appliance is out of operation. Evidently they are attracted to the odor-causing chemical that is added to the gas.

Chapter 12

Climate Control

Fulltimers can control the climate in which they live simply by moving their RV homes to places where the weather is cooler or warmer. But no matter where they go, they may still experience some hot weather in the summer, and wintering in the South can sometimes be chilly, even cold, so having methods of heating and cooling their RV homes is important.

Climate-control equipment should always be kept in operating condition in case of unseasonable weather. One year, at the end of summer, we had an early cold wave with nighttime temperatures in the low twenties. We did not have to do anything to ready the furnace for use other than turn it on.

INSULATION

Fulltimers who intend to spend any time in cold climates should have an RV suitably insulated for such weather. All RVs are insulated, but the amount and quality vary widely. Carefully reading manufacturers' brochures usually can provide a good indication of how well a unit is insulated. Some brochures don't even mention the subject, some have a cutaway illustration showing insulation but include no other information about it, and some manufacturers boast about how well their units will withstand cold weather. One trailer manufacturer promotes an optional cold-weather package that makes the trailer safe and comfortable to live in at thirty degrees below zero. If a unit is needed for cold-weather living, be suspicious of those manufacturers who ignore or gloss over information about insulation in their brochures.

Block styrofoam and residential-type fiberglass batting are the most prevalent types of insulation used in RVs. Block foam is used in most motorhomes; trailers may have either or a combination of both.

Even if you don't intend to spend time in a climate where insulation would be needed for warmth, remember that good insulation helps keep an RV cool in hot weather, too, and serves to deaden outside noises.

Some units have an enclosed underbody with a heated compartment for the holding tanks and water lines—an excellent arrangement for cold-weather RVing.

For comfort heating, most RVs are equipped with propane-fueled furnaces, with the forced-air, ducted type being the most common. A few luxury motorhomes have a perimeter heating system in which a small electric pump circulates heated water through pipes around the perimeter of the motorhome. RVs can also be heated with electric and catalytic heaters.

HEATING

▼ ▼ ▼ ▼ ▼ ▼ ▼ ▼ ▼ ▼ ▼ ▼

▼ ▼ ▼ Forced-Air and Convection Furnaces

Most newer recreational vehicles have excellent heating systems, consisting of a thermostatically controlled, forced-air propane furnace with a 12-volt blower and heating ducts and outlets throughout the coach. The furnaces in late-model RVs usually are operated automatically and don't have to be manually lighted. In nearly all cases, the Btu (British thermal unit) output of the furnace is sufficient for the size of the RV in which it is installed. Our 31,000-Btu-output furnace can keep our 29-foot trailer shirtsleeve-warm when temperatures are well below freezing, without storm windows and under-trailer skirting.

Some older RVs have a convection-type furnace. Cold air enters from the bottom of the furnace grill and warm air is emitted from the top. An advantage of this type of furnace is that it has no fan that uses 12-volt power, so it can be used where there is no electrical hookup without affecting the battery. A disadvantage is that it has no ductwork, so it does not heat evenly. Both convection and forced-air furnaces are vented to the outside.

Furnaces are relatively trouble free if they are kept clean. Dust should be vacuumed away regularly. A duct register that can be closed completely is useful for keeping dust out of ducts in seasons when the furnace is not being used. Most manufacturers don't install this type of register, which, in addition to closing completely, has dampers that can be adjusted to regulate heat flow, but they can be purchased at RV-supply stores for easy self-installation.

If the furnace blower or thermostat does not operate, a fuse may be blown. When the thermostat is turned up high enough to kick on the burner but does not, the contacts in the thermostat may be pitted. A multimeter can be used to troubleshoot most electrical problems connected with the furnace or thermostat.

Nothing should be stored on top of the furnace ducts if they are made of flexible tubing, and no items that could puncture or tear the ducts should touch them. If they are squashed, the air cannot flow freely through them, and any sort of an opening, even a pinhole, destroys some of the heating efficiency. Sharp angles in the ducts' routing will reduce heat flow. If the duct is not stretched out smoothly when it is installed, this too will affect the amount of air that goes through it.

In our previous trailer, we had one duct that ran across the end of a storage compartment under the bed. To avoid damaging it when items were being removed or replaced in the compartment, we enclosed the duct in its own little compartment by putting up a simple partition.

Forced-air furnace blowers draw between three and eight amps, depending on the size of the furnace and its age; later models are a great deal more efficient. Prolonged use of the furnace on battery power could seriously drain the batteries. The blower operates intermittently, but it will have to run more often to maintain the desired temperature as the outside temperature decreases.

If the RV is stored in one location for quite a while, the furnace intake and exhaust ports should be covered with tape to keep insects, even birds, from nesting there. Wire-grid covers for the ports can be purchased in RV-supply stores, but the grids are too far apart to be effective for keeping out insects.

▼ ▼ ▼ Catalytic Heaters

We use a catalytic heater for those times when we do not want to expend battery power to run the furnace. Our heater's 6,000-Btu maximum output is enough to keep our trailer comfortably warm in below-freezing temperatures. A larger trailer or motorhome might need two heaters to achieve the same results. Several models of catalytic heaters are available: manual or automatic ignition, thermostat-controlled, vented or unvented, with Btu outputs ranging from 3,000 to 8,000. If the heater is not vented, open a window slightly when the heater is in use. Electronic models use about ⅓ or ½ amp of 12-volt DC power.

Catalytic heaters are simple and quiet; they have no fan or other moving parts. Since such a heater has no provision for circulating the air, it should be installed as close to the floor as practical to take advantage of the natural rise of heated air.

When a catalytic heater is put in an RV, it is often installed on the end of a galley counter. In our 23-foot trailer we put ours in a more central location—in the walkway between the galley and the side bath, on the outside wall of the bath—so more of the trailer would benefit from its heat. There is no such location on our present trailer to install a heater, and we did not want to run gas lines to service two heaters. Our solution was make our one heater portable. We purchased optional legs so the heater could be freestanding and had a six-foot extension hose fabricated so the heater could be moved and turned to face the direction we wanted. For the gas supply, a tee was installed in the refrigerator's gas line. In our trailer, this line runs through the storage compartment under the bath floor. A copper tube extends from the tee through the wall to the left of the steps to the bath and terminates in a flared fitting with a plug. Although the plug itself would probably be enough to prevent gas leaking, as an extra safety measure, a petcock was installed in the tubing, out of sight behind the wall. It might seem that with this installation it would be a nuisance to use the heater, but it is not. By opening the trapdoor to the storage compartment, the petcock is easily reachable. The wrench needed to attach the heater to the tubing is kept about an arm's length away in the galley tool drawer described on page 219. The heater is stored with the legs attached so it does not have to be assembled each time we want to use it, and nothing has to be moved out of the way or off the heater to remove it from its storage place in the compartment under the gooseneck.

When the heater is in place, the extension hose allows the heater to be moved so that it can face the living room in the rear of the trailer, or it can be taken up the steps into the bath where it can be turned to face the bedroom.

As with other heaters, keep dust from a catalytic heater by covering it when not in use. Slip-on covers are available from outlets where the heaters are sold. For the wall-installed heater in our previous trailer, we made a three-sided dust cover from brown mat board (Figure 12.1). The cover was reversible and foil-lined so it could also serve as a reflector, which we used when the heater was on to keep heat away from the wall above and also to direct the heat outward.

For use as a dust cover, the top corners were held together with Velcro on the foil side. To keep it tight against the wall — the bottom tended to swing out — another strip of Velcro on the bottom was attached to an adhesive-backed piece of Velcro on the wall.

To use the reflector, the corners were opened, then the cover was reversed and turned upside down. The top of the box then fit down behind the heater. It was held in place with a short length of wire twisted around a small screw in the door frame.

The sides of the reflector could be angled to direct the heat. Used as a reflector, the heater cover was not particularly attractive, but it did the job.

Because of the heater's location opposite the galley, the galley counter received a good deal of heat. To keep the heat off, a dishtowel was hung from the top galley drawer. When the heater

Figure 12.1
This catalytic heater cover is constructed of mat board and serves to protect the heater from dust (*left*). When the heater cover is opened, turned upside down, and reversed, it serves as a heat reflector (*right*).

was on its highest setting (not often), we hung a long sheet of foil from the drawer to reflect the heat away from the galley counter. The foil also was bent slightly to direct the heat.

With our present catalytic heater installation, we no longer need to worry about any close-by surfaces receiving too much heat, but we wanted a way to direct the heat. We came up with the idea of using movable doors for this purpose (Figure 12.2). For just a few dollars, a sheet-metal shop fabricated a door for each side of the heater from heavy-gauge aluminum, bent to conform to the wire-grill front. Each door was attached to a side of the heater with two hinges held on with pop rivets. When closed, the doors cover the grill and self-store by fitting snugly against it. For channeling heat, the doors can be opened to any position desired. They provide some dust protection as well, but for long-term storage we enclose the heater in a plastic bag.

▼ ▼ ▼ Electric Heaters

An electric heater can be used to warm the entire coach in cool weather but will not often do the job alone when the temperature is much below freezing.

Figure 12.2
The doors—designed and installed by the authors—on this catalytic heater, are used to direct heat. The extra-long hose allows the heater to be moved "upstairs" in their fifth-wheel to provide maximum heating in both the bath and the bedroom.

When using an electric heater, not only will the amperage rating of the external power cord and outlet have to be high enough to withstand the wattage of the heater, but so will any extension cord used with the heater inside the RV.

As a safety practice, we are never absent from the trailer with the heater running, even for as little as a half an hour, unless we are within sight of it. In spite of having the proper cords and outlets, fires have been known to occur from a malfunctioning heater. An electric heater should be set well away from any combustibles, making sure that no papers or other flammable materials can fall onto or into it.

It is important to keep electric heaters clean, too. When used regularly in the confines of an RV, dust can accumulate. The dust on the case and grill can be vacuumed off, but the heater will have to be dismantled in order to thoroughly clean the fan blades and motor. A clean heater will operate more quietly and efficiently than one with a heavy dust buildup.

Lots of heaters on the market are small enough for convenient use and storage in RVs, but it may take some looking to find one that has a 1,200-watt setting or a maximum rating of this wattage. Many heaters are rated at 1,500 watts, but this wattage is not safe to use with many campgrounds' electrical hookups. Find a heater that automatically shuts off if it is tipped over.

We recently purchased an efficient heater (the manufacturer calls it a furnace) that produces heat from a ceramic element instead of coils. Its thermostat can be adjusted to settings ranging from 350 to 1,500 watts. It provides plenty of heat at the lower settings and operates more quietly than any other heater we have owned. What's more, it is a tiny, six-inch cube, quite heavy for its size, making it unlikely to tip over.

CONDENSATION
▼ ▼ ▼ ▼ ▼ ▼ ▼ ▼ ▼ ▼ ▼ ▼ ▼

When it's cold outside and an RV is being heated by any means, condensation can form, which is often a nuisance. The cooking, bathing, even breathing of the RV's occupants all create moisture. And since the moisture is relatively confined in an RV, it becomes concentrated and turns into water droplets. These collect on windows and roof vents, walls and ceilings in the galley when cooking, and in the bath when showering. Wall areas adjacent to studs may develop condensation if the unit has an aluminum frame. Larger RVs have fewer condensation problems than smaller units because any moisture generated has more room in which to disperse. For example, much less condensation develops in our 29-footer than in our previous 23-foot trailer.

Condensation can be reduced somewhat by cracking the roof vent in the bath when showering, and by operating the range-hood fan when cooking. Teakettles should not be allowed to boil and steam for any length of time.

Sometimes condensation will form and eventually turn into mildew in enclosed, floor-level, unventilated storage compartments. We had such condensation problems in our 23-footer, especially in locations where the morning sun struck the outside of the trailer. The warmth of the sun would create condensation in the still-cold compartment. We stopped the condensation in the worst problem area, the bottom corner of the rear wardrobe, by lining the corner with half-inch-thick panels of styrofoam. Leaving storage compartment doors open during cold nights so the compartments can receive heat from the furnace or other heaters can prevent condensation from forming.

STORM WINDOWS

▼ ▼ ▼ ▼ ▼ ▼ ▼ ▼ ▼ ▼ ▼ ▼ ▼

For prolonged stays in cold weather, storm windows would be useful accessories for fulltimers. They can cut propane consumption if the furnace is being used, and they will eliminate condensation on windows.

On some RVs with sliding or nonopening, double-paned windows, separate storm windows would not be needed.

A common type of storm window found on trailers is a large piece of glass mounted in a rigid frame that fits into the window frame over the screen. Some are held in place by turn tabs; others fit into a channel on the regular window frame. Unless the storm window is a tight fit, drafts could enter all around the frame. These can be eliminated by putting weatherstripping on the edges of the storm window or by taping it on all sides.

Large, rigid storm windows are difficult to store in the rig when not in use, although they would probably fit in the storage compartments of some basement-model RVs. If stored anywhere in the RV, they will need to be protected so they won't become cracked or broken during travel.

The vinyl storm-window kits for residential use sold in hardware and home-improvement stores usually can be adapted for use on RVs. Read the instructions carefully before purchasing to see if there might be any restrictions preventing use on your RV.

One type of vinyl storm window is simply taped to the window frame. Another type uses a two-section channel to hold the vinyl in place. One section of the channel is tape-mounted to the window frame. The cut-to-fit vinyl is placed over the window and the channel, and the other channel section snapped into the first. Vinyl storm windows affect visibility only slightly. If care is taken with removal and storage, they may be reused.

Storm windows cannot be put over motorhome windshields or on driver and passenger side windows, so there will be considerable heat loss in this area unless the motorhome is equipped with a heavy curtain that can be pulled across the cockpit.

Roof vents and skylights should have their own "storm windows" to reduce the considerable heat loss and to eliminate annoying, dripping condensation. Clear vinyl (it can be found in hardware, fabric, and variety stores), cut to size and taped to the vent frame with clear, waterproof tape, will do the job and not block out light from translucent or transparent vents.

Ready-made vent covers are available as well. One type is made of flexible, opaque vinyl and affixed to the vent frame with snaps. Another type is a thin, rigid, opaque, plastic square held on with a bracket screwed into each corner of the frame. Neither of these covers is held tightly against the frame, so they won't completely stop condensation from forming but they do stop the dripping.

We purchased a rigid type for the bedroom vent, which we use year-round. In cold weather, it prevents condensation from dripping onto the bed or us. It blocks out early morning light and campground lights at night, and, in the summer, it keeps out the sun. The bracket is designed so the cover can be placed on two different levels. When we want the vent open but also want to block the light, we put the cover in the lower position, which holds it slightly away from the vent and allows air to circulate through the vent.

If it is necessary to use tape for any sealing, try to find the type that will leave no residue. Some may not leave a residue when applied for a short time; however, if left in place for several months, they may leave a difficult-to-clean gummy mess. Rubbing alcohol or a spray lubricant such as WD-40 will clean this up, but test the surface in an inconspicuous place first to make sure that the products won't harm it. Sometimes a piece of fresh tape firmly pressed onto the residue, then quickly lifted off, will remove residue, but this may take several pieces of tape and quite a bit of time to finish the job.

COLD-WEATHER SITUATIONS

When staying in cold weather for an extended period of time, the RV should have some type of skirting around it. This will prevent wind from swirling around underneath the RV and provide a certain amount of insulation so the unit, especially the floor, will be warmer, and there will be less chance of anything freezing. Skirts can be flexible vinyl or tarp material attached to the unit, with the bottom edges weighted with brick, stones, or logs to keep them from blowing around. Rigid vinyl and aluminum skirts can also be used. A fellow RVer who planned to spend one winter in Montana cut composition-board panels to fit snugly under and around his trailer and installed a thick layer of insulation under the entire floor.

Insulated drapes and good-quality window shades of heavy-weight vinyl do much to keep out cold and cut down on drafts from windows.

Throw rugs, small carpet pieces, or anything else that will fit along the bottom of the door will prevent drafts from that area.

One winter, when we were living in our 23-footer, we taped an oversize vinyl panel inside each of our exterior compartments, making the interior of the trailer that was nearby warmer and less drafty. One side and the bottom of each panel was left loose so we could get easily get at items stored in the compartment. If we had not needed frequent access, we would have run tape all around the outside of the compartment door to seal it off completely. All exterior doors should be weatherstripped unless you have the rare RV with well-sealed exterior compartment doors.

In winter, you might find yourself sealed into your RV by frozen-over doors, as we did once after an ice storm. We remembered reading about another couple to whom this had happened and tried their trick—using a hair dryer to de-ice the door. It worked. We also discovered that a hair dryer can be used to thaw other frozen equipment and plumbing.

An often-overlooked cold-air entry point is the range-hood vent opening. Since it's a large opening, when facing into a strong wind, it creates a tremendous draft. Some RVs have a panel on the vent that can be secured with turn tabs to close off the opening. It's easy to open when the exhaust fan is needed while cooking. Other vents have louvers over the opening. In order for the vent to be used when needed, don't seal off the louvers from the outside. Instead, cover the filter screen on the range hood itself with a piece of foil. Remove the filter screen, wrap or tape a piece of foil around it, and put it back in place. The foil can be removed to use the exhaust fan. If you use tape, fasten only the opposite ends; then the tape on one end can be loosened and one side dropped down to use the fan.

COOLING
▼ ▼ ▼ ▼ ▼ ▼ ▼ ▼ ▼ ▼ ▼ ▼ ▼

The ability to travel and live comfortably in an RV in hot weather is made possible by fans, opening windows, awnings, and, most important, air conditioning.

▼ ▼ ▼ Air Conditioners

Most fulltimers want an air conditioner for hot-weather use. A roof-mounted air conditioner (or two if the RV is large) is the most common arrangement, but some RVs are equipped with central air-conditioning units located in a compartment inside the RV.

Like furnaces, air conditioners require little maintenance other than cleaning. For cooling efficiency, periodically rinse the filter (located behind the grill) under a water faucet. While the grill is off, remove any visible dust inside the unit. Seasonally remove the outside cover from the evaporator on the roof to clean out road dust, leaves, and insect nests.

It is important to know the amperage rating of your air conditioner; most draw from 11 to 13 amps. It may not be possible to use a large unit on a 15-amp circuit if nothing more than the converter/charger (some models draw 6 amps) and the refrigerator are operating on the same circuit. If you are careful

▼ ▼ ▼

about your amperage load, you can get away with using a smaller air conditioner and certain other electrical equipment at the same time on a 15-amp circuit. When we use our air conditioner on a 15-amp circuit, we operate the refrigerator on gas and resort to our solar panels for our 12-volt needs so the only load on the AC circuit is the air conditioner. Usually in the evening we can dispense with the air conditioner and go back to using the converter/charger.

A common problem with air conditioners is not in the unit itself but in the campground's electrical hookup, which may have voltage too low to operate the air conditioner properly. Air conditioners require a specific amount of voltage for the high momentary surge needed to start the compressor. If the voltage does not meet this requirement, the compressor may not start; it will just hum.

Most newer air conditioners have an overload device that shuts down the compressor when it becomes overheated — usually the result of low voltage. The overload will reset itself in a few minutes, allowing the compressor to run again. If the compressor goes on and off, check the voltage before assuming there is something wrong with the air conditioner.

▼ ▼ ▼

Long-term use of an air conditioner on voltage that is marginal — not quite low enough to trip the overload device — may cause premature compressor failure.

At times there may be enough voltage to start the compressor, but during the several hours the air conditioner may be running, a low-voltage situation will develop, for example, if the campground is not properly wired and your neighbors turn on their air conditioners or use other high-wattage electrical equipment. Monitor the voltage with a voltmeter to be on the safe side.

You can cause a low-voltage situation yourself if you need to use an extension cord to reach the campground hookup, and the extension is of an inadequate wire-gauge size.

As long as air conditioners are regularly operated with the proper voltage, the compressor itself should not be damaged. So many fail-safe devices are built into today's air conditioners that compressor blowout is rare. If a service person diagnoses blow-out as your problem, it would be a good idea to have a second opinion from another professional before authorizing replacement of the compressor, the cost of which is just about half that of a new air conditioner.

If the air conditioner runs normally but does not cool, the problem may be a leak. It will have to be tracked down, fixed, and the air conditioner recharged with refrigerant.

If the circuit breaker trips repeatedly each time the air conditioner is turned on, it is an indication that an electrical or mechanical problem exists.

Many brands of roof air conditioners can be equipped with heating elements, most of which draw 16 amps and should not be used on a 15-amp circuit. Another factor to be weighed when considering this option is that the air conditioner's location is on the ceiling — the worst place for any kind of a heater. Since hot air rises, parts of the floor area will not receive much heat. The air conditioner's blower moves the hot air around, but it cannot direct it to where it is really needed.

▼ ▼ ▼ Fans

If air does not circulate well in an RV home, a fan can help move it along. It does not have to be one that operates on 120 volts AC. Several styles of 12-volt fans are available. Some are designed to be permanently installed, and others are portable and can be used wherever a 12-volt outlet is available. A 12-volt fan draws about the same number of amps as does a 12-volt light bulb, making it practical to use when boondocking.

A small 12-volt fan would be a welcome addition to the cabover bed area on a Class C motorhome. It could be put to good use even when 120-volt power is available, since most 120-volt fans would be too large for that particular area.

A roof-vent fan can move lots of air through an RV — not the tiny 12-volt exhaust fans found in many bath vents, but the type on which the blade area fills nearly the entire opening of the vent. This sort of fan was offered as an option on our trailer, so we had one installed in the bedroom vent. It has proven to be an excellent accessory. We use it on the exhaust setting to remove hot air from the trailer, especially in warm weather when we return to a closed-up trailer after being away. With all other vents and windows closed, only a rear window is opened so air will be pulled through the entire trailer, and in just a few minutes the hot air is sucked out.

We prefer natural ventilation to air conditioning, especially at night when we are sleeping. With the fan on its intake setting on the lowest of its three speeds and the window at the head of the bed open, a gentle, cool breeze wafts over us. The fan has a thermostat so it can be adjusted to shut off or come on at a desired temperature. (Using the intake is not recommended if the roof vents for the holding tanks are closer than four feet to the fan; fumes from the holding tanks might be drawn into the RV.) The brand of fan we have has clear plastic blades that don't block the light from the vent. It takes little amperage to run these vent fans, so they can be used to great advantage when boondocking.

In addition to the vent fan, we have a portable 12-volt fan and a small 120-volt floor fan. When we are using the air conditioner, even though it's ducted to the bedroom, we set the floor fan in the bath, facing toward the bedroom, to better circulate the cooled air to the bedroom's higher level.

▼ ▼ ▼ Windows

The more opening windows an RV has, the better the ventilation will be. Unfortunately, many RVs built today don't have as many windows as their counterparts of previous years. Front windows on fifth-wheel trailers are almost nonexistent, windows are disappearing from baths, and rear windows don't exist on some RVs if the bedroom is in the rear. For years, rear windows have not been installed on certain motorhomes, and now some trailer manufacturers are omitting them too. We visited a couple in a neighboring campsite yesterday who have a brand-new trailer, a rear-bedroom model without a back window, and the bedroom, we thought, was quite gloomy. Aside from the ventilation pro-

▼ ▼ ▼

vided by opening windows, we, like many RVers, enjoy the feeling of being close to the outdoors when we are in our RV, a feeling that can't exist in units with few windows.

For ventilation, louvered windows are better than those that slide because they can be adjusted to admit plenty of air even when it is raining.

Tinted window glass is standard equipment or available as an option on some RVs. The darker windows will definitely keep a unit cooler in the summer, but in the winter, when some warmth from the sun is wanted, tinted glass will block much of it out.

Reflective adhesive-backed sheeting on windows is another way to keep out sun, but unless most of your time is spent where temperatures are around 100°F for long periods, this sheeting should not be needed.

Sheer or open-weave privacy curtains will diffuse sunlight but admit air. When it is hot, heavy window shades will block a good deal of heat from entering, just as they prevent inside heat loss in cold weather. When we are traveling in hot weather, which it is nearly every day in the summer, we pull all the shades, so no matter in which direction we travel, no sun can enter. When we arrive at our destination, we often find the temperature inside the trailer to be five to seven degrees cooler than the outside temperature.

▼ ▼ ▼ Awnings

A full-length awning, another useful RV accessory, will keep the coach cooler inside, with or without the air conditioner operating, and provide shade outside. Some RVs have a full-length awning on the curb side and individual awnings on all side windows. On trailers, rear and front windows may have stone shields—sometimes called rock guards—on them, which serve as awnings when raised.

It is not always possible to park so that one awning will keep the sun off all day. A full-length awning could also be placed on the street side of a unit, but since big awnings are heavy items, the added weight of a second awning might be impractical.

On trailers, one of the supports of a full-length awning might have to be located over a window. When the window doesn't open, it presents no problem, but if it opens outward, it cannot be opened until the awning support is lowered.

▼ ▼ ▼ Hot-Weather Site Selection

Where and how the RV is parked can make a difference in keeping it cool. If the campground has trees, try to park in a place where there will be shade in the afternoon, the hottest part of the day. If shade isn't available, a site where the afternoon sun will not hit the RV broadside—unless you have an awning that can shade it—is desirable. We sometimes try to select a site where the door faces north so it will be in the shade all day, and we can have the door open without the sun streaming in. Other external factors need to be considered: We once received some heat bounceback and unpleasant, glaring reflected light when we were parked close to a white building. If possible, park where there is good air circulation. If buildings block the wind, you may find your site hot because little breeze can reach it.

Incidentally, the refrigerator will function better in hot weather if the RV is parked so that the side the refrigerator is on is shaded, or away from the full intensity of the sun.

A point about RVs that most people, including manufacturers, don't give much thought to: An RV with a dark-colored exterior will absorb more heat and thus be more difficult to cool than white or light-colored RVs.

Chapter 13

Electronic Entertainment and Information

▼ ▼ ▼ ▼ ▼ ▼ ▼ ▼ ▼

Fulltimers in their RV homes should be able to enjoy the same quality of electronic entertainment from television, radio, and tapes, both audio and video, as they did when living in a fixed dwelling.

When some people begin fulltiming they want to divorce themselves from the world and what is going on in it. This is their privilege, but any fulltimer who travels at all needs to have some way of receiving reliable weather reports, at the very least.

The best weather reports, short of those broadcast by the National Oceanographic and Atmospheric Administration (NOAA) on special weather radio stations (see also page 328), are on television. The forecasts usually include detailed state-wide coverage and a brief summary of weather throughout the country. Visuals depicting storm patterns and the direction in which they are moving are often imposed on a map of the lower forty-eight states. Radio reports are usually brief, localized, and of not much use to someone who is passing through an area.

We have often put weather information we received to good use. Once, we selected a certain town for a mail drop, not

WEATHER REPORTS AND TRAVEL INFORMATION

▼ ▼ ▼ ▼ ▼ ▼ ▼ ▼ ▼ ▼ ▼ ▼

knowing the only campground in town was a very expensive one. Our mail had not arrived when we got to the town so we had no choice but to stay at the campground until it came. On the midday television news we heard that a major winter storm was headed our way and was expected to reach us the next day. The forecasters were not sure whether we would receive rain or snow, but warned listeners to prepare for the worst. We did not want to spend any more time than necessary in the high-priced campground, as we would have had to do if several inches of snow fell, and we could not go on since we would be headed into the storm.

We scouted around and found a mobile-home park twenty miles away with much lower rates. Next day, after we picked up our mail, we hitched up early to make our short run before the weather deteriorated. It had already begun to rain lightly as we were getting ready to go. Our neighbor asked us if we knew what the weather was farther north. He could not get any weather on his FM radio and knew nothing of the winter storm watches and warnings in effect until we told him.

We were settled in the mobile-home park just as the rain began to fall heavily. We don't know what happened to our fellow traveler, but we heard that more than a foot of snow fell in the area where he was headed.

▼ ▼ ▼

Another time, we were within hours of a major city when we heard that the portion of the interstate on which we would be traveling was closed because of a construction accident and would not be open until late in the day. Any sort of communications receiver, AM/FM radio, television, or citizen's band radio (CB) is often useful to travelers.

TELEVISION
▼ ▼ ▼ ▼ ▼ ▼ ▼ ▼ ▼ ▼ ▼ ▼

Television has become a vital part of most of our lives, and there is no reason why fulltimers can't enjoy the same sort of television reception they had in a fixed dwelling.

A television for your RV home can be as large as you wish as long as there is a place to keep it for comfortable, convenient viewing, and a safe place to store it while traveling. Large picture screens, however, are not necessary because in an RV you can't get very far away for viewing. This is an advantage in a way: smaller TVs have sharper pictures.

Any color television is larger and heavier than a black and white TV of the same size. And if it is an AC/DC model (one that runs on both 120-volt AC electricity and 12-volt DC power from the RV's batteries), a color television operating on 12-volt DC power will draw nearly twice as many amps as a black and white TV. Small TVs, color or black and white, require less 12-volt power to operate than larger ones. Fulltimers who boondock will benefit from having an AC/DC television. Motorhomes factory equipped with an AC-only television usually have an inverter just for the TV so it can be used when on battery power. We have two televisions: a nine-inch color AC-only model and a five-inch black and white AC/DC TV. We enjoy color television but don't want to use it with its high-amperage draw when on battery power. That's why we opted for an AC-only color TV. We saved some money because a two-mode, nine-inch color television costs about $50 more than an AC-only model. Incidentally, a nine-inch television is the smallest size available with a remote control.

▼ ▼ ▼ Television Antennas

No matter how good the TV, it won't receive an acceptable picture without a proper antenna. Rarely will the built-in antenna on the television itself be satisfactory.

Television antennas come in several different styles, all of which are one of two types: directional or omnidirectional.

Directional antennas receive stations from only one direction and must be rotated and aimed at each station's antenna. Omni-directional antennas receive stations from all directions at the same time.

The reception from both is good; however, the omnidirec-tional antenna's range is between 30 and 40 miles, whereas the directional antenna can bring in stations up to 100 miles away.

Televisions can receive two types of signals; those that are broadcast on the VHF frequencies (channels 2 though 13) and those on the UHF frequencies (channels 14 through 83). Some

The impact of television on our culture is . . . indescribable. There's a certain sense in which it is nearly as important as the invention of printing.

CARL SANDBURG

▼ ▼ ▼ ▼ ▼ ▼ ▼ ▼ ▼ ▼ ▼ ▼ ▼

antennas will receive the stations broadcasting on UHF frequencies better than other antennas, and some won't pick up UHF signals at all.

Select an antenna that will receive both frequency ranges since many small-town stations either broadcast in the UHF range or use UHF translator relay stations that rebroadcast larger cities' stations in their area.

Some antennas mount on the side of the RV, others on the roof. All roof antennas are controlled from inside the coach and are raised for use and lowered for traveling.

The higher a television antenna, the longer its range, so roof antennas have a better chance of bringing in distant stations.

The most common styles of roof antennas are either those that are V-shaped with a succession of rods or those resembling a long, thin bar with a raised, slightly thicker, midsection. A less-frequently-seen style looks like a flying saucer. Most roof antennas are directional.

Side-mounted antennas aren't as expensive as roof antennas, and they can be easily and quickly installed simply by attaching a couple of brackets. A hole in the roof must be made to accomodate a roof-mounted antenna, and then, when the antenna is in place, its mount must be well caulked so it won't leak.

One type of side-mounted antenna fits into a bracket. The antenna itself, which is simply two whip antennas, is pulled from its bracket for use, then pushed back in, where it self-stores when under way. It often requires much adjusting and positioning to get the best reception.

Another side-mounted, omnidirectional antenna has four separate arms that unfold like an umbrella and store inside a permanently mounted tube.

Traveling fulltimers, who will be in many different areas where television reception will range from excellent to marginal, will be most satisfied with a directional, roof-mounted antenna.

One roof antenna is designed to be used while the vehicle is in motion, so passengers in a motorhome can watch television while traveling.

Some RVs may have a provision for the television in only one place, and the antenna wiring will be routed to the antenna outlet there. If this is not where you want your TV located, or you want to use it in other locations, proper antenna wiring will have to be routed to each different location for decent reception.

There are two types of antenna wire: a flat, wide ribbon called twin lead, with an impedance of 300 ohms; and round, coaxial cable, with an impedance of 75 ohms.

The coaxial cable is better for long runs for several reasons. Most important, there is less signal loss. In addition, it needs only a tiny hole for routing through walls or cabinets, is easier to handle and bend, and makes for a neater-looking installation than the ribbon type, especially if any of the antenna wire is visible. Only the best quality 300-ohm or 75-ohm wire should be used for any installation. Most recent-model trailers and motor-homes will have the 75-ohm wire.

The impedance of an antenna wire should be the same throughout the installation or significant signal loss will occur. The impedance of an antenna is 300 ohms; the antenna input terminals on the back of a television set are also 300 ohms. A matching transformer can be used to connect wires of different impedance (Figure 13.1). For example, if 75-ohm cable is used for an installation, a matching transformer will have to be attached at the antenna connection and another at the television. Matching transformers are small, inexpensive, and available from many stores, including Radio Shack.

If the television has separate terminals for VHF and UHF channels, a signal splitter will be needed in order to have the antenna wire feed both sets of terminals at the same time, no

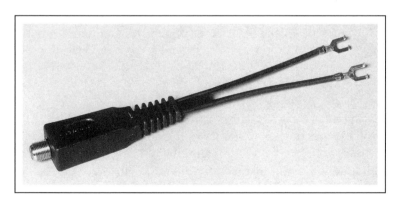

Figure 13.1
A matching transformer is used to connect television antenna wires of different impedence.

Figure 13.2
Some television sets have separate antenna terminals for UHF and VHF channels. To connect the different terminals to the antenna, a transformer-splitter is used.

matter what type of antenna wire is used. For most installations, a transformer-splitter, which incorporates both a matching transformer and a signal splitter in one unit, will be needed. (Figure 13.2).

A coupler-splitter is a device that allows one antenna to feed two televisions or two signal sources (such as cable service and an antenna) to feed one television (Figure 13.3).

Since many fulltimers have to store their television in a different place than where it is located for viewing while traveling, some simple wire connectors can be used for quick attaching and detaching of the antenna wire; it is a nuisance to have to use a screwdriver for this operation. For 300-ohm wire, a clothespin-like device called an antenna clip can be used for disconnecting. Attach the antenna wire to the clip and the jaws of the clip to the antenna terminals on the back of the TV. Either screw-on or push-on F-connectors can be used with coaxial cable (Figure 13.4). The push-on connector is the easiest to handle and can be put to good use on a television that is moved frequently. The screw-on type should be used for more permanent connections.

Figure 13.3
One antenna can feed two televisions with a coupler-splitter.

▼ ▼ ▼ Television Amplifiers

Having a high-quality antenna may not be enough in itself for good long-distance reception. Adding an antenna amplifier will improve the picture quality (Figure 13.5). The television antenna and antenna outlet installation on an RV, whether done by the manufacturer or the dealer, usually include an amplifier.

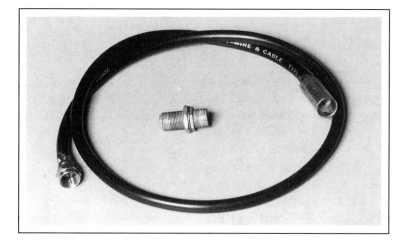

Figure 13.4
A length of coaxial cable is shown with a screw-on F-connector on one end and a push-on F-connector on the other.

The signal strength of an antenna is called *gain*. An amplifier can greatly increase the gain of an antenna in receiving the weak signals that exist in fringe areas.

Amplifiers are either 120-volt AC or 12-volt DC models. Full-timers should purchase an amplifier, if needed, from an RV-supply store; they sell only 12-volt models, which are the most practical for use in an RV.

Amplifiers, which cost around $50, can be the type shown in Figure 13.5, or the type with a cigarette-lighter socket and amplifier incorporated into a single unit. They are available with a 300-ohm input and output, a 75-ohm input and output, and mixed versions: 300-ohm input with 75-ohm output or vice versa. Here again it is important to have the right impedance match on the input and output for your particular installation.

It is best to have an amplifier with an on-off switch since the amplifier may not be needed when close to a local station; in fact, using an amplifier in this situation may overload the signal and result in poor picture quality.

Some amplifiers have an LED pilot light to let you know when they are on. Since the 12-volt amperage draw of these amplifiers is measured in milliamps, it would not have much effect on the batteries if the amplifier were left on all the time; but a current flows through the amplifier which, like anything electric, can short out, so the amplifier should be turned off when not in use.

Figure 13.5
A television amplifier often improves picture quality.

An amplifier we installed in our previous trailer had neither a switch nor an LED, so we added both. The saucer-shaped antennas mentioned earlier and some of the bar-type antennas have built-in amplifiers.

Amplifiers of all kinds are susceptible to static charges from lightning during electrical storms. In order to avoid damage from lightning, lower the antenna and turn off the television and amplifier in severe electrical storms.

An antenna with a built-in amplifier can be protected by installing a switch on the 12-volt wires that run to the amplifier so it can be turned off. If the built-in amplifier were blown, it would probably be necessary to replace the entire antenna.

Damage from lightning is quite a common occurrence. It does not have to be a direct hit; the static present in the air from a distant electrical storm is sometimes enough to cause damage.

▼ ▼ ▼ Cable Television

Many RV parks now have cable-television hookups for their guests, often at an extra charge of a dollar or two above the site fee. In most parks, what you get for your money is real cable television with its many channels. In some other parks located where television reception is poor or nonexistent unless a high antenna is used, the cable may be nothing more than a hookup with the park's master antenna. This provides only the few stations that the park's antenna is capable of picking up. We stayed at one park that furnished satellite TV, but since only one channel can be viewed at a time with a satellite system, if we wanted to watch TV, we had to be content with the channel the campground owner selected.

It is important to have the right television to use with cable hookups. Many color and all black and white TVs will not pick up UHF cable channels (14 through 83) without a special converter—usually supplied by the cable company. It would be impractical to try to get a converter from the cable company for a short-term stay at a campground. So, if you want the full range of cable channels, buy a television equipped to receive them.

Such TVs are designated cable ready or cable compatible and usually have a switch for changing from the antenna mode to the cable mode. Many of these TVs have a 155-channel tuner as well as a wireless remote control.

All cable television connections are 75 ohm. Often the campground will furnish a length of coaxial cable for the hookup. For older TVs with 300-ohm terminals, a transformer will be needed to connect the coaxial cable. If the campground provides the coaxial cable, a transformer will probably be included.

Unless you have a new recreational vehicle with a built-in exterior cable connection, the cable will have to be routed through a window or door. On our 23-foot trailer, we made our own permanent cable installation. We did not want to route anything through the screened windows, which would have necessitated poking a hole in the screen, or through the door opening, preventing the door from closing properly. A length of 75-ohm cable was routed inside the trailer through several compartments to the exterior compartment that contained the shore-power cord. One end of the cable terminated there; the other end was attached at the place where we kept the television for viewing.

Sometimes a deposit is required for the use of the campground's cable extension. We made up two cable extensions, a twenty-five footer and a forty-five footer, which can be connected to each other if necessary.

▼ ▼ ▼ Satellite Television

Nowadays RVers can have television wherever they are. Imagine being camped in an isolated place, miles from the nearest town or TV tower, and being able to watch a football game in which your favorite team is playing, or pick up an opera performance, or just keep up on what is going on in the outside world. This is now not only possible but practical when a satellite dish is installed on the RV.

This is not to say there aren't some drawbacks to using satellite dishes with RVs, but future developments will certainly improve on, or eliminate, existing problems. Besides, the problems aren't serious enough to dissuade anyone from having satellite TV if it is wanted.

Many of those shopping for a satellite system are assaulted with unfamiliar terminology and may not be aware of the equipment needed for a complete system. Exhibit 13.1 gives, in a nutshell, a not-too-technical explanation of the components of a satellite system. They are the same for residences and RVs.

All satellite television broadcasts originate by beaming a strong transmission signal from the ground to a small satellite transponder located over the equator at an altitude of 22,300 miles above the earth. The satellite is moving in the same direction as the earth's rotation and at a synchronous speed with the rotation so the satellite remains fixed over one precise location on the earth's surface. This is called a stationary orbit. The satellite receives the signal from an earth station and rebroadcasts the transmission back to earth where it is picked up by satellite dishes. Today there are over thirty of these satellites in orbit sending more than 150 channels of television programming back to earth.

A satellite antenna is usually a parabolic-shaped dish that gathers the video and audio signals from the satellite trans-

---

▼ ▼ ▼ ▼ ▼ ▼ ▼ ▼ ▼ ▼ ▼ ▼ ▼

Exhibit 13.1
The Components of a Satellite TV System

1. A **dish** made of aluminum, fiberglass, or metal mesh. Large dishes, eight to twelve feet in diameter, are for residential use; RV dishes are only five or six feet across. The dish, sometimes referred to as a dish antenna or a satellite antenna, is the antenna (see Figure 13.6).

2. A **feedhorn** (or feed). This device is positioned precisely at the dish's focal point by an arm, or arms, mounted either at the center or at the edge of the dish.

3. An **LNB** (Low-Noise Block) **downconverter.** The LNB is incorporated into or attached to the feedhorn. Both the feedhorn and LNB are included when a dish is purchased, but they are components that can be changed or modified.

4. A **receiver/tuner.** Mounted inside the RV, it may or may not have a built-in descrambler. When a descrambler is built in, it is called an integrated receiver decoder or IRD.

5. A **television,** of course.

PHOTO: WINEGARD

Figure 13.6
This motorhome features a typical RV satellite antenna system.

ponder and reflects, or focuses, them onto the feedhorn in much the same way a reflecting telescope focuses light rays onto its eyepiece. This signal is sent to the receiver/tuner where it is amplified and processed by the decoder/descrambler before it reaches the television.

Television signals are being transmitted in two different groups of frequencies: C-band and Ku-band. A different size dish is needed to pick up each of the different bands. The C-band signals are received on the larger residential-size and RV-size antennas previously mentioned. Because Ku-band satellite transponders have higher-powered transmitters and operate on higher frequencies than C-band, Ku-band transmissions can be received on a much smaller dish—eighteen to thirty-six inches in diameter. This would be ideal for RVs but, at the present time, C-band carries most of the popular channels—Home Box Office and other movie channels, Disney, Cable Network News, ABC, CBS, NBC, Fox, and a variety of other entertainment and information channels. Ku-band carries a rather limited selection: some network programming, unedited news feeds, and lots of sports broadcasting. As more Ku-band satellites are put into orbit, the programming will increase and, in time, C-band may even become obsolete.

Eventually, dishes for Ku-band reception will be even smaller than they are now, and the prices for them should be well under the cost of C-band dishes, making satellite television available to nearly anyone who wants it and very practical for RVs. The technology exists for these downsized dishes. In fact, the Ku-band system is currently used extensively in Japan and England where two-foot-square dishes are common.

It is possible to receive Ku-band transmissions on C-band dishes if the dish is equipped with a C/Ku type of LNB, but it is not possible to pick up C-band signals on a Ku-band dish.

▼ ▼ ▼ Selecting a Satellite TV System

The most elaborate and expensive RV roof-mounted satellite antennas have 12-volt DC motor drives for raising, lowering, and aiming the dishes. All this is accomplished with a controller or positioner—a computerized unit that can be programmed for locating up to ten satellites and which will automatically raise the dish for viewing and lower it for traveling.

The other type of dish mount is a manually controlled unit that works in much the same way a regular roof-mounted television antenna does: An elevating crank on the ceiling of the RV is turned to raise the dish (it takes from about seventy-five to ninety turns), and then the whole mount is rotated until the satellite is found. This is easier to do than it might seem. A compass (which may be included with the system) is used to locate north, and then a rotation plate on the inside control is adjusted to align with north. A chart, included with the antenna, provides the azimuth angle and elevation (or declination angle) of the satellite from your particular geographic location. Azimuth angle is measured in degrees (indicated on the rotation plate) clockwise from north. Elevation is determined by the number of turns of the elevating crank. Once the mechanics of locating the satellite are learned, it is a simple matter to position the antenna. We have seen dish owners raise their antennas and position them in just a few minutes.

Some fulltimers, mainly those who stay in one location for a length of time, might use portable satellite antenna systems that can be set up on the ground outside the RV and manually adjusted for use.

A C-band satellite dish and a receiver/tuner without a descrambler will provide reception of the unscrambled C-band channels only — and there are very few of these. Programmers, understandably, want viewers to pay for everything they receive by satellite. The programming that local stations broadcast at no charge from the major networks — ABC, CBS, and NBC — when picked up from a satellite is scrambled.

To receive the channels commonly offered on cable, which are scrambled from the satellite, a descrambler is needed. It can be purchased separately, or it may be built in to the receiver/tuner. At present, Ku-band transmissions are not scrambled.

To receive programming unscrambled, the descrambler user must subscribe to a program service and pay a monthly or annual fee. Programming can be customized to individual tastes either by selecting a package that includes many channels — a package similar to that provided by local cable TV companies — or by selecting desired individual channels. Once you have signed up with a program service, you provide them with the special identification number marked on your descrambler, and the service will broadcast a micro-burst control signal containing an authorization code — called a hit — which will program your decoder with the channels you have paid for.

The cost of a satellite system can run from around $1,500 to $4,000 including receiver/tuner and descrambler. A programming service's basic package subscription of about seventeen channels costs about $130 a year; the annual cost for all channels is over $400. On a monthly basis, the basic charge begins at about $12.

You own anything which comes down in your yard, and you have a right to use it.

TOM WALTERS
On selling satellite dishes

Problems with RV Satellite Television

Many RV televisions will run on both 120-volt AC or 12-volt DC power, which allows the users to operate them on either shore or battery power. Receiver/tuners operate only on 120-volt AC, as

*[T]elevision] should be our
Lyceum, our Chautauqua,
our Minsky's, and our
Camelot.*

E. B. WHITE

▼ ▼ ▼ ▼ ▼ ▼ ▼ ▼ ▼ ▼ ▼ ▼ ▼

does the descrambler if it is a separate unit. So for RV use, either a generator or inverter will be needed to operate the satellite system when the RV is in a place without an electrical hookup.

When subscribing to a programming service, the dish must be pointed at a satellite at the beginning of each month in order for your descrambler to receive the special authorization code that is broadcast to it by the programmer. These "hits" reprogram your decoder each month so it will receive the programming on the channels that you have subscribed to for that particular month. (The services believe it is necessary to change the individual authorization codes each month to prevent piracy of their programming.) The descrambler's authorization code is broadcast over and over, randomly, at many different times and days at the beginning of each month. To receive the hit, the descrambler must be on. If your descrambler doesn't happen to be on and misses the hit (you'll know because everything will be scrambled), you will have to phone the programmer and have them initiate a special hit for your system.

The design of the descramblers creates another problem for RVers. When the descrambler is turned off, a small battery maintains the memory should there be a temporary power outage or for the short time a unit might be off in the course of a move to a different location. The memory-battery has a shelf life of ten years, but the continual and sometimes lengthy absence of shore power that fulltimers have when traveling a great deal will deplete such a battery rather quickly; it might fail after only a year or so. The descrambler will have to be taken to a repair center for battery replacement.

The physical size of most receiver/tuners, particularly those with the built-in descrambler, are too large to fit inside the typical RV cabinet, and mounting such a unit under a cabinet is not attractive because the receiver/tuner will protrude from under the average cabinet by several inches. It might take a lot of shopping to locate one, but a couple of manufacturers have receiver/tuners in a suitable size for RV installation. These receiver/tuners have no built-in descramblers, which makes for much smaller-sized units. The descrambler can be purchased separately, and when it is separate from the receiver/tuner, it will usually fit into an RV cabinet.

High winds can degrade the reception of the signal from a satellite when the feedhorn vibrates or shakes. To avoid damage, a roof-mounted antenna may need to be lowered in windy conditions and a portable dish stowed away. Ku-band antennas, because of their smaller size, are not as susceptible to the wind as the C-band units.

If the RV is in the path of microwave transmissions from telephone or television towers or near motors or electrical equipment that can cause interference, a poor picture may result.

The manufacturers of RV-size satellite dishes have long been aware of the widespread interest and growing use of satellite television by RVers; there are many different brands of dishes available that are designed just for RV use. This awareness has not reached the receiver/tuner manufacturers, however. They haven't begun to address the needs of the RV market: receiver/tuners are too large and should be equipped with a rechargable memory battery or operate on 12-volt power.

In spite of the problems with satellite television, it is worth having, particularly if you enjoy the medium to the extent that you would miss it if you are in areas of poor or no reception or want to have the equivalent of cable TV no matter where you are.

A welcome adjunct to an RV's television system might be a videocassette recorder (VCR) or a unit without the recording capability, a videocassette player (VCP).

VCRs AND VCPs
▼ ▼ ▼ ▼ ▼ ▼ ▼ ▼ ▼ ▼ ▼ ▼ ▼

VCRs are only available in 120-volt AC models, but VCPs will operate on both AC and 12-volt DC power. On 12-volt operation, a VCP draws little amperage.

Installing either type of videocassette unit could be a problem; like satellite receiver/tuners, they are designed for residential use and may be too large to fit in RV storage compartments. VCRs are usually larger than VCPs. Our VCP sits snugly on a shelf inside the console on which we keep the TV; it would not have fit at all into any convenient overhead cabinet. In our installation, the VCP is wired to a coaxial switch installed in the cable between the antenna and the television so we can either switch to the antenna for TV use or the VCP. Most VCRs have a coaxial jack on the back for connecting the antenna to the recorder, thereby routing the signal from the antenna though the VCR and eliminating the need for a switch. A word of warning: If the antenna is connected to the VCR, it can be damaged along with the television in electrical storms.

On some RVs, mostly motorhomes, a VCR is offered as a built-in option. It is usually placed in a cabinet on either side of a built-in TV or in the same cabinet as the TV. Having a VCR built in and factory installed eliminates any concerns about where to install one yourself.

Several television manufacturers have a nine-inch AC/DC TV model that incorporates a VCP. These compact combination units are about the same size as a regular nine-inch TV except that they're about two or three inches taller and not too much heavier. They can be easily lifted from a counter for storage on the floor during travel.

We have had a VCP for several years and use it often to watch movies we have missed in theaters or that we want to see again. Being eternal transients and having no permanent local address, we wondered if we would have problems renting tapes, but we haven't. We always explain our situation and use the address and phone number of the campground where we are staying. A large supermarket chain in the West and Midwest, however, will not rent tapes to persons who do not have their names listed in the local telephone directory. Tapes can also be rented at some campgrounds.

AM/FM Stereos and CD and Cassette Players

Automotive stereos, or small stereos specifically designed for RV use and usually installed by the manufacturer, are the type most commonly found in RVs. They often include a cassette or compact disc player. The stereo itself may be an option, but many RVs are standard equipped with the wiring for a stereo, an external antenna, and maybe two or four speakers.

If good sound reproduction is important to you, particular attention should be paid to the brand of stereo offered by the manufacturer; sometimes they are not top-quality units and, if offered as optional equipment, it might be better to purchase your own. If speakers are included as standard items, they too may be unsuitable for good reproduction. We replaced all four of our standard speakers with better ones.

An RV's metal outer skin or metal frame acts as a shield against radio waves, so an external antenna is needed for optimum radio reception. An external antenna will provide good local reception on AM and FM and some distance reception on FM, particularly if the radio has a built-in distance amplifier. The television antenna can sometimes be used as an FM antenna if wires are run from a signal splitter to the FM radio.

Automotive stereos, which are small and operate on 12-volt power, are ideal for RV use. Unless the RV has a solid-state converter/charger with a built-in electromagnetic interference (EMI) or hum filter, the 12-volt connections should be made directly to the battery, bypassing the converter/charger. Many converter/chargers lack a filtering system and cause a hum in the radio, especially on the AM frequencies. A separate filter can be installed, but whether it will eliminate or reduce the hum depends on the filter: some do, some don't. (Even the filters on some of the newer converter/chargers don't do as good a job as they should in counteracting the hum problem.)

Portable AM/FM stereo cassette players with speakers attached (commonly called boom boxes), can be run on batteries, 120-volt AC, or 12-volt power if a DC cigarette-lighter plug adapter is used. But this type of stereo has a built-in antenna, which gives poor reception inside the coach in fringe areas. You can get better reception by running a wire from an external antenna to the stereo and attaching it to the built-in antenna with an alligator clip.

The amperage used by 12-volt automotive stereo cassette players ranges from about $\frac{1}{2}$ amp to as much as 8 amps on some of the high-wattage units. The amperage draw increases in proportion to the volume increase. An equalizer with a booster can add as much as 6 more amps. Without shore power, merely listening to the radio or playing cassettes can cause quite a drain on the battery. Many motorhomes have the stereo wired to the starting battery instead of the coach batteries. We have met several motorhomers who hadn't considered this and found themselves without engine starting power.

A record is a concert without halls and a museum whose curator is the owner.

GLENN GOULD
Paraphrasing André Malraux

▼ ▼ ▼ ▼ ▼ ▼ ▼ ▼ ▼ ▼ ▼ ▼

A small AC/DC black and white television usually includes an AM/FM radio that operates through the TV antenna. Radio reception is generally quite good, if one is not too fussy about the quality of the sound, particularly with distant stations.

The traveling fulltimer probably will not want to bother with a 120-volt AC electric clock radio since it will have to be reset each time the RV is moved.

A useful publication for travelers, the *North American Radio Guide,* lists all the radio stations in the country by location and includes the type of programming — news, talk, type of music — offered on each station. It has other listings of specialized broadcasting, such as sports and weather. All television stations are also included. The guide, issued annually, can be purchased at some RV or electronic-supply stores, and some newsstands.

RADIOS
▼ ▼ ▼ ▼ ▼ ▼ ▼ ▼ ▼ ▼ ▼ ▼ ▼

There are several types of radios, aside from the stereo units most common to RVs that add to fulltimers' enjoyment, convenience, and safety.

▼ ▼ ▼ Shortwave Radios

In addition to the automotive-type AM/FM stereo cassette player we installed in our trailer, we have a shortwave radio we enjoy listening to when we are in isolated areas where other radio and television stations are out of range. For the best reception, we needed a shortwave antenna, so we installed a small, telescoping type on the roof near the AM/FM antenna and also added a switch in the radio compartment, enabling us to use either antenna with either radio. The shortwave antenna doubles the AM reception of the stereo. A long antenna provides the best reception for a shortwave receiver, so, thanks to an idea from a ham radio operator, before we got a special shortwave antenna, we used to extend the AM/FM antenna's length by using a Slinky. This popular child's toy contains many feet of wire in its coil, yet compresses down to a small size for storage. The Slinky was attached to the antenna with a large alligator clip and allowed to hang down towards the ground. It was strange looking, but it worked.

▼ ▼ ▼ Ham Radios

Many fulltimers are ham radio operators, sharing a fascinating, worthwhile hobby that allows them to communicate with each other over long distances and sometimes provide invaluable help to people in distress.

Most ham radio equipment operates from either built-in batteries or a 12-volt power supply and takes up little space, so full-timing hams can easily use and store their equipment in a recreational vehicle. The necessary special antennas can be installed on their rigs permanently, or the extremely long antennas can be set up for use, dismantled quickly, and stored on the roof of the RV or in the tow vehicle during travel.

Hams can communicate with each other over vast distances with their equipment—even around the world by using special amateur radio satellites, and ham radios can be linked to computers and other sophisticated equipment.

To become a ham radio operator requires special training and licensing, but acquiring the skills and knowledge needed are within the capabilities of nearly everyone. Knowledge of Morse code used to be a requirement for all classes of ham licenses, but now a license class exists that does not require code.

If you are interested in learning more about ham radio, contact any ham operator or the American Radio Relay League Incorporated, 225 Main Street, Newington, Connecticut 06111. It is also possible to buy books on the subject at Radio Shack and other electronic-supply stores.

After Bill received his amateur radio license, he began communicating on the two-meter band with other hams as we traveled around the country. We recently spent some time in a remote campground in the Blue Mountains of Oregon, and, with a small 2½-watt hand-held transceiver, he was able to talk to a ham operator located north of Spokane, Washington, over two hundred miles away, using a network of two-meter-wavelength repeaters. Networks of these repeater stations are linked together across the country. For instance, in the Northwest, one such network allows a ham operator in Medford, Oregon, to talk to another operator in Vancouver, British Columbia. This repeater linkage gives us a great feeling of security. If we encounter a problem as we travel, we can usually reach a repeater almost anywhere we happen to be.

Ham radio operators can also enjoy long-range, direct communications with other operators who have similar interests by participating in various networks. On these networks, or nets, roundtable discussions of topics of interest to its members are conducted.

The Good Sam Network, which boasts a membership of over 350 Good Sam Club members, "meets" every weeknight on a frequency of 7.292 MHz (40 meters) at 9:00 P.M. Central Standard Time and on Sundays on 14.240 MHz (20 meters) at 2:00 P.M. CST. The group keeps tabs on the comings and goings of its various members, exchanges travel information with each other, holds rallies, and provides help if a member has rig trouble or a health problem when traveling. Since the members are located all over the country, chances are someone will always be nearby if needed. Ham operators need a General Class License to participate in this network. For information, write Ken Ness, 130 Windsor Road, Red Lion, Pennsylvania 17356, and enclose a self-addressed stamped envelope.

▼ ▼ ▼ Weather Scanners and CB Radios

A weather radio that receives nothing but the before-mentioned NOAA broadcasts is useful, but it will only pick up the signal from the transmitter when the station is fifty miles away or less. Reception is better in nonmountainous areas because of the nature of the VHF radio waves, which are line of sight.

NOAA broadcasts also can be received on scanner radios that receive a variety of other broadcasts, such as police, fire, marine, and aircraft communications. A scanner requires a special external antenna.

A citizen's band (CB) radio can be a convenience for traveling fulltimers. With it you can ask for and receive information about road conditions. When traveling, other CBers can let you know if something is wrong with your rig that you may not be aware of: perhaps a tire going flat or a raised television antenna. Maybe someone behind will spot smoke or water coming from under your coach and alert you to the problem.

One of a CB's most important uses is to obtain help in an emergency. The highway patrol monitors Channel 9 for this purpose.

It is often interesting and entertaining to listen to or talk with truckers or other RVers as you are rolling down the highways. Most RVers use Channel 13 for communicating from rig to rig. A CB is also handy when traveling in a group or caravan.

An entire portable CB outfit, including the special antenna it requires, can be purchased for about $50. Many portable CBs simply plug into a cigarette-lighter socket; an antenna with a magnetic base can be set on the roof of a vehicle's cab and removed for safekeeping, or both the antenna and the CB can be permanently mounted. No special license is needed to operate a CB radio.

Chapter 14

Rig Maintenance – Inside and Out

Low maintenance is one of the real joys of fulltiming. If you are used to keeping up a house and yard, you might actually feel somewhat guilty about how little maintenance you will have with your RV home. It's almost as if you are getting away with something. Enjoy. The guilt will soon go away with the realization that low maintenance is just another of the benefits of this way of life. After a while, when you see some poor individuals mowing their lawns, you may chortle smugly to yourself and wonder why they haven't seen the light and taken up your free and easy lifestyle.

Except for jobs requiring specialized equipment, fulltimers can perform nearly all general maintenance and many repairs if they want to. Some fulltimers have enough money, so they do not have to become do-it-yourselfers, but if you are on a limited budget, doing your own maintenance and repairs can save you a great deal.

There is another advantage to doing your own work: You will make sure things are done right because it will be in your best interest to do so. You will care because what you will be working on is your property.

Of course, not all mechanics or service people are careless or incompetent, but often you never know until the work is done. They might leave out a part. They might not tighten all fastenings properly or be careful about keeping dirt or foreign objects from items on which they are working. If they cannot fix what needs to be repaired, they might not admit it but charge for the "work" done anyway.

Whether or not you do your work yourself, you should understand how all the systems in your RV function. None are complicated. The benefit of knowing about your RV is that you can make an intelligent judgment about what work needs to be done or if it needs to done at all. Informative articles about RV systems appear regularly in *Trailer Life* and *Motorhome* magazines. More detailed information about maintenance and care can be found in Trailer Life Books' *RV Repair & Maintenance Manual* by Bob Livingston. Instruction booklets are also a good source of information.

For your own protection, don't be like the motorhomer we met who said he didn't want to know how anything worked (after we had just helped him with his electrical hookup). "I just want to push a button or flick a switch and have it work," he said. Don't we all wish it were as simple as that?

If a problem crops up with a piece of equipment on our trailer, we often call the manufacturer for advice. They usually can tell us what is causing the problem and how we can fix it. A telephone call is cheap compared with any repair bill. The number to call is often found on the equipment's warranty or in its instruction booklet, and many manufacturers have a toll-free number as well.

▼ ▼ ▼

On one occasion, our refrigerator cooled only intermittently when operating on electricity. We called the manufacturer, and their consumer-service representative described two possible causes of the problem and how to correct each. Both were easy to do, and with this information, we were able to fix the refrigerator ourselves.

If a service person tells us we need an expensive repair, we will usually call the manufacturer for a second opinion.

It is a good idea to periodically inspect all areas that may need maintenance. This will help you to stay on top of potential repairs before they become major problems.

HOUSECLEANING TOOLS

▼ ▼ ▼ ▼ ▼ ▼ ▼ ▼ ▼ ▼ ▼ ▼ ▼ ▼

Most fulltimers find that a vacuum cleaner is their main interior cleaning tool. Some RV manufacturers offer their units with a built-in vacuum system. When we inquired about having this option on our trailer, the salesman advised against it. He said a satisfactory amount of suction would not be available in the outlets farthest away from the vacuum motor. We decided against the built-in vacuum, but not for that reason. We found the hoses and accessories for a built-in vacuum took up more space than a portable vacuum would.

A vacuum cleaner with the usual attachments can be put to good use even if the RV doesn't have carpeting; it will pick up grit and dirt from a vinyl floor. Upholstery, dusting, and crevice tools are particularly useful for cleaning a recreational vehicle's small areas, odd corners, and storage compartments.

We use a 120-volt AC vacuum cleaner because the 12-volt models we tried take longer to clean and are not powerful enough to do a good job. What's more, most of them do not have many, or any, attachments.

Small canister-type vacuums will fit into storage compartments on some RVs, but it should be an inside compartment. We've noticed that some RVers store their vacuum in an outside compartment. If we kept ours outside, we are sure we wouldn't use it as often as we should.

For many years we used a canister vacuum, but a few years ago we purchased a Bissell 3-Way Vac. It can be used as an upright, a hand vacuum, or with the extension hose. We don't have space for storing an upright, but the Bissell's handle folds down, making the vacuum about two feet long. We have several places where we can store such a short, slender item.

A carpet sweeper can replace the vacuum cleaner when 120-volt power is not available. Small, RV-sized carpet sweepers are easily found, not only at RV-supply stores, but often at other outlets where sweepers are sold. On a close-out table in an RV-supply store, we once found two little hand sweepers, which we purchased. We keep one in the bath and the other in the galley for quick cleanups of such things as dusting powder, food crumbs, or tracked-in dirt. A broom is also a handy item. If there is no room for one with a handle, a whisk broom can be used instead.

In addition to the normal cleaning tools and supplies, we save old toothbrushes to use for jobs such as cleaning stove knobs, stubborn spots on our textured window shades and walls, and sink faucets and along counter edgings.

When living full time in a recreational vehicle, dust will collect quickly. It's always in the air and has to settle somewhere. In an RV, it does not have much area in which to dissipate, and a certain amount of road dust will enter even the best-sealed coach. Even though dusting will have to be done frequently, there is much less of it to do in an RV. A vacuum dusting tool will take care of this chore quickly.

Since window and door screens are on the inside of most RV windows, they will collect their share of dust. Whenever we dust with the vacuum instead of a dustcloth, we always go over all the screens with the dusting tool, including those in the roof vents. As long as we are at it, we dust all grillwork: the furnace compartment covering, furnace duct registers, the air-conditioner grill, and the back, sides, and top of the television. We would dust miniblinds this way if we had them (or purchase a special tool just for miniblinds). A vacuum dusting tool is the only way to clean such items easily and thoroughly.

DUSTING

As a result of heavy, concentrated use, carpeting will become soiled more quickly in an RV than it would in a larger area. Eventually, vacuuming alone will not remove the soil; the carpeting will need to be cleaned by another method. The carpeting we have throughout the trailer, even in the galley, is fairly good quality and stain resistant. Most spills and other soil can be wiped off with a damp sponge. When more thorough cleaning is

CARPETING, DRAPERIES, AND UPHOLSTERY

needed, we don't use a detergent carpet cleaner since this type leaves a soapy residue that will attract dirt. We use either Woolite or Scotchguard carpet cleaner instead.

In some large coaches, there is room enough to maneuver a steam cleaner or shampooer, which could be used for a badly soiled or dingy-looking carpet.

Carpet will need to be replaced when it becomes so soiled that no method of cleaning restores its brightness. In smaller RVs this might be every few years. In larger units, where the traffic is not as concentrated, carpeting will last longer.

Much dirt, mud, and sand can be kept from the floor by having a doormat inside and outside the door. Throw rugs can be used for this purpose, but we use carpet samples that cost a dollar or two, and when they are soiled beyond the stage where cleaning with a damp sponge is not enough, we throw them away and buy new ones.

To give us another foot-wiping place, we have carpeted the fold-down doorsteps. After some experimenting, we found the best way to attach the carpeting is with wire. The ends of a length of wire are pushed down through the carpet and through the perforations in the metal step, pulled tightly so the wire is semi-buried in the carpet nap and the ends twisted firmly together under the step.

We don't use ready-made vinyl-loop mats (the kind that are attached with an adhesive strip) because they are too thick to allow our steps to fold.

When we travel, we might stop several times along the way to ' shop, refuel, or have lunch. We usually enter the trailer during these stops. The trailer is often parked in a place where oil or grease is on the ground, such as in service stations or highway rest areas, or where the ground is wet, so before traveling, we always put a vinyl runner over the carpet in the entryway to avoid tracking in the dirt and wet (Figure 14.1). The runner is cut to fit the entryway and extends from the door across the trailer. We keep it handy in the entryway, rolled up and stored in one of our special fold-down-front boxes. On this box, the entire front drops down when the lid is raised, so the rolled-up vinyl can easily be removed and replaced. The box fits tidily into a space next to the door. So the box would be unobtrusive, we covered it

Figure 14.1
This unobtrusive box, with a front that drops down when the lid is lifted, is used to store a vinyl runner.

with adhesive-backed vinyl in a color close to that of the wall. We roll the vinyl with the ribbed side out, so when it is unrolled and in place, the ends don't curl up.

Upholstery and draperies should be cleaned according to the instructions in your owner's manual—maybe. The owner's manual for our previous trailer said the draperies should be dry cleaned. When we took them to the cleaners we were told dry cleaning would ruin them; they should be washed. A second opinion agreed with the first. We crossed our fingers and washed the draperies. They cleaned up beautifully. Most owners' manuals are written to cover all RV models of a particular manufacturer, so the manual might not deal specifically with a variation you have in your particular RV. Check with professionals when in doubt.

We often give the draperies a light going-over with the vacuum dusting tool, and we use the vacuum upholstery tool for regular cleaning of upholstered items (and sometimes for the carpet in places where the rug tool won't fit). Our upholstery is stain resistant like the carpet and needs only be wiped down with a damp sponge to remove most spots. However, we clean the seats of the sofa and chairs about every other month. This furniture receives so much concentrated use that if we didn't clean it regularly, the seats would eventually become slightly grayer than the rest of the upholstery. As with the carpeting, we use Woolite or Scotchguard cleaner.

To remove stains and stubborn grime from just about any surface, we often spot clean with Simple Green liquid cleaner diluted or undiluted according to the intensity and type of the stain or soil.

BATHS

▼ ▼ ▼ ▼ ▼ ▼ ▼ ▼ ▼ ▼ ▼ ▼

Most RV bath fixtures are plastic or fiberglass, which means they cannot be scrubbed with a harsh, abrasive cleanser. Repeated scouring with even mild cleansers can roughen the surfaces of plastic fixtures. A liquid cleanser such as Soft Scrub works well when some abrasiveness is needed. Window cleaner makes fixture surfaces sparkle. We especially like it for cleaning the shower walls; it easily removes dried water spots and leaves the walls streak-free.

Always wipe the walls dry in the tub-shower after use, and also thoroughly dry any molding around the edges of the tub-shower basin. If the molding is not sealed tightly all around, water can seep down behind it and cause mildew to form or wooden structural members to rot.

Rather than use a special holding-tank deodorizer, which is expensive and may contain hazardous chemicals, we prefer to use pine oil. Any one of the pine-oil cleaners on the market will do a satisfactory job; however, the greater the product's concentration of pine oil, the more effective its deodorizing properties will be.

If the sewer holding tank is not allowed to become too full, a deodorizer may not be necessary. Holding tanks are their most odoriferous in hot weather.

WOODWORK AND WALL COVERINGS

▼ ▼ ▼ ▼ ▼ ▼ ▼ ▼ ▼ ▼ ▼ ▼

Most cabinets in recreational vehicles are wood or imitation wood paneling. Both have an easy-care finish that can be wiped with a damp cloth to remove soil. A spray dusting/cleaning product will remove finger smudges.

Because some of our galley cabinets pick up a film of cooking grease, we clean them every couple of months or when needed with a grease-removing, liquid spray cleaner. The solution should be used sparingly and the cleaned surface wiped with a damp cloth or sponge, then dried with a soft cloth. Never use large amounts of water or liquid cleaner when cleaning wood or imitation wood finishes. Consult your owner's manual for recommendations about cleaning genuine wood surfaces.

Vinyl wall coverings also can be cleaned with a liquid spray cleaner. Sometimes where the edging on a countertop meets a textured wall covering, a dingy, gray buildup occurs in the textured finish because of repeated counter wipings. We use liquid cleaner on a toothbrush to scrub out the buildup from the little indentations in the texture. The toothbrush bristles are tiny enough to clean between the bumps and ridges of the texture. If liquid cleaner doesn't do the job, we resort to Soft Scrub on a toothbrush. Rub gently to avoid removing any of the wall covering's finish. Any cleaner should be thoroughly rinsed from the wall covering.

Coach ceilings will stay clean for a long time if the RV's occupants do not smoke and if the range-hood fan is used regularly when cooking. Dishwashing detergent or a liquid cleaner will remove soil or film from most ceiling finishes. When using any liquid above your head, take care to shield your eyes from any drops or mist. Fabric ceilings, found in some RVs, can be cleaned with a vacuum upholstery tool, or if badly soiled, use a rug or upholstery shampoo.

ROOF VENTS
▼ ▼ ▼ ▼ ▼ ▼ ▼ ▼ ▼ ▼ ▼ ▼ ▼

Roof-vent covers and their screens collect a lot of dirt and dust. Bathroom-vent covers may accumulate mildew. Most screens can be removed for cleaning by undoing a few screws in the frame (and unscrewing the fan switch on the bathroom vent.) Squirt the screen with liquid cleaner, then go over the entire screen with a brush (a toothbrush is good for this) to loosen dirt. Rinse under a faucet and shake dry. The cleaning and rinsing is better done outside so spatters when using the brush won't make another mess to be cleaned up; rinsing is easier under an outside faucet than in a sink.

The vent covers can be cleaned with a window or liquid cleaner. A toothbrush is useful for cleaning around the vent support and in corners. While cleaning the vents, check the weatherstrip gasket. Reattach it if it has come loose. Sometimes the gasket can be pressed back into place, or it may need to be reglued.

CLEANING SUPPLIES

▼ ▼ ▼ ▼ ▼ ▼ ▼ ▼ ▼ ▼ ▼ ▼ ▼

We rarely do a major housecleaning of the entire trailer at one time. Instead we do little jobs every now and then as necessary so we don't have to devote a lot of time just to cleaning (this is high on our list of least-liked chores). To make this spot- and area-cleaning easy, we have all the cleaning supplies we use regularly in places where they are readily accessible. We keep a box of supplies at the front of both a galley cabinet and a bath cabinet. It might seem redundant to have two sets of cleaning supplies only twelve feet away from each other, but we find we get jobs done more quickly if supplies are right at hand.

We don't have room for a roll of paper towels in the bath, but paper towels are needed for some bath-cleaning jobs. We made a small, narrow, cardboard box to hold a stack of paper towels on end and affixed it to the inside of the cabinet door where the cleaning supplies are kept. It's a small box because the towels are cut in quarters, just the right size for most cleaning jobs in the bath where paper towels would be used.

ODORS

▼ ▼ ▼ ▼ ▼ ▼ ▼ ▼ ▼ ▼ ▼ ▼ ▼

Cooking odors don't have room to disperse in an RV as they do in a house and tend to linger. Almost all of us have entered an RV at some time or other and had our nostrils assailed with stale cooking odors. We don't want a smelly trailer, so we use a room deodorizer all the time. It is a small, solid type that we keep under the dinette seat where it is out of sight but centrally located to take care of the entire trailer. If we cook bacon or some other food that leaves a strong odor, we give the trailer a spritz with a spray deodorizer in the same fragrance as the solid. We also use a powder-type rug deodorizer on the carpeting every now and then.

Some RVs without an enclosed underbody may have gaps around plumbing pipes where the pipes enter the coach through the floor. Any such opening can be the entryway for all sorts of pests, large and small, from roaches to rats (Figure 14.2).

In our 23-footer, we had a charming little field mouse as a house guest for a couple of days. It came in through a small gap next to the shower drainpipe. We sealed the hole by packing steel wool around the pipe and wrapping duct tape over the area to hold in the steel wool.

If screens have holes, flies and mosquitoes will find their way in through them. You can place a piece of tape over the hole

PESTS
▼ ▼ ▼ ▼ ▼ ▼ ▼ ▼ ▼ ▼ ▼ ▼

Figure 14.2
A device to keep mice from entering the coach can be installed easily.

or stuff a wad of tissue in it temporarily, but the screen should be patched with another piece of screen or replaced as soon as possible.

Most people who have traveled in the South know about the precautions that must be taken to keep from being overrun by roaches. For those who have not spent time in the southern states or Mexico, here are a few facts: The cleanliness of your coach has nothing to do with keeping roaches away; they are just as happy living in a clean place as a dirty one. Any roach that gets in might deposit eggs somewhere, or eggs might be brought in from outside, often in the folds of paper bags or under the labels on cans and jars. Any carton that is glued should be suspect as a roach hideout or egg depository; roaches like to eat glue. Groceries should be thoroughly inspected before they are taken inside.

Kill any roach the moment you see it, if you can. Some southern roaches are nearly two inches long—easy to see but difficult to kill unless whacked with a heavy object. We found a hammer to be a good weapon for dispatching these monster pests. If a roach is too fleet-footed for you and runs into a confined area where it cannot be reached with a roach bludgeon, use a spray insecticide to kill it. Do not let it get away or you may have scores of roaches to deal with soon. When spraying, be sure there is adequate ventilation.

As careful as we were, we were not entirely successful in keeping roaches out of our RV when we were in the South. Luckily, we never had a severe infestation—only one or two at a time. A severe roach infestation may require the services of a professional exterminator.

When we were not using a hammer for roach killing, we used an insecticide called Sla, a Reefer and Galler product. This excellent product may be difficult to find; it is sold in closet shops of large department stores and some hardware stores. Sla is promoted primarily as a moth killer—it can be sprayed directly onto most fabrics without damaging or staining—but the label recommends it for getting rid of flies, mosquitos, gnats, wasps, hornets, spiders, crickets, ants, bedbugs, roaches, and waterbugs. We have never needed it for bedbugs or waterbugs, but we can attest that it works quickly and effectively on all the other pests.

it wont be long now it wont be long
man is making deserts of the earth
it won't be long now
before man will have it used up
so that nothing but ants and centipedes and scorpions can find a living on it

DON MARQUIS
archie and mehitabel

▼ ▼ ▼ ▼ ▼ ▼ ▼ ▼ ▼ ▼ ▼ ▼ ▼

Unpleasant as it is, keep roaches in mind when buying a used RV in the South. One of our friends acquired a bumper crop of roaches along with the used trailer he purchased.

We often see bug zappers in use at campsites. They are somewhat effective for keeping insects away from people when they are sitting outside, but we do wish those using the zappers would turn them off when they go inside to bed. Listening to bugs frying all night long is not our idea of pleasant camping. As far as we are concerned, we wouldn't use a bug zapper often enough to warrant the storage space it would occupy. A citronella candle or a spray-on or rub-on insect repellent works well enough for us.

Close all outside compartments when they cannot be observed. We once saw a stray cat jump into an open one. Crawly things could enter the coach this way too.

EXTERIOR CLEANING

The exterior finish on motorhomes and trailers will stay bright and shiny for years with little care other than an occasional cleaning. Most RVers want to clean their units with water, but washing is not allowed at many campgrounds—for good reasons:

1. Water is scarce and must be conserved in many arid areas of the country.
2. Many people use much more water than they need, so their site ends up covered with unsightly piles of suds and puddles of water.
3. Water may be plentiful but expensive; the campground operator may not be able to afford having campers use water for vehicle washing.
4. The operators of luxury vacation and resort RV parks, or the operators of any campgrounds for that matter, may simply not want to have any sort of maintenance work done on their premises.

Some towns have do-it-yourself recreational vehicle washes, similar to car washes. They have bays tall enough to accommodate trailers and motorhomes and a catwalk so the top and roof of an RV can be reached. Truck washes are also large enough to hold a trailer or motorhome.

We used to clean our trailer with water (when there were no campground regulations forbidding it), usually by working from a bucket for the washing, using the hose adjusted to a trickle for rinsing, and cleaning only a small section at a time. But now we rarely use water for exterior cleaning. When we were cleaning the windows one day some of the window cleaner was accidentally sprayed on the painted finish of the trailer and as we wiped it off, found it cleaned superbly. We experimented with more and more of the trailer and in very little time, one entire side, including the windows, which were what we had set out to clean, was spick and span.

▼ ▼ ▼

Now we clean the trailer almost exclusively with this waterless method. And because it's so simple and easy to do, we don't put off what used to be a dreary chore. We don't need to string hoses around the campsite and collect buckets and brushes and cleaner. Taking the time to assemble all the equipment needed for washing often caused us to delay the job. Once all the equipment was out, we felt we had to do the whole trailer; with our tall 29-footer, that is a tiring job, even with both of us working at it. We always put on old clothes and shoes because we got so wet and messy. And then when finished, all the stuff had to be put away.

Using window cleaner is so easy. To do the job, all that is needed is a spray bottle of window cleaner, and a handful of paper towels (we tear them in half). A plastic grocery bag for holding the towels hangs from one wrist. When a towel becomes soiled, it is wadded up and dropped into the bag where it finds its way to the bottom underneath the clean towels. It's easy to work out of the wide mouth of the bag and it keeps the towels from blowing if it is windy.

If the exterior surface is dusty, as much dust as possible is gently wiped off with dry paper towels; if a liquid is applied to dust, the muddy streaking it creates is a mess that requires extra effort and materials to clean.

We like this method of cleaning because we can start or stop the job whenever we want. We never allow the trailer to become really dirty, so a cleaned area doesn't contrast too noticeably with the uncleaned sections. Once at a truck stop Bill went in to make some phone calls; Jan whipped out the window cleaner—a container of which is stored in both the galley and the bath—and a few towels and cleaned a portion of the trailer while she was waiting. We finshed the job later when we arrived at our destination.

The trailer above the window level doesn't usually get very dirty, so it doesn't need cleaning as much as the lower part. If we do clean the upper reaches, we need to use a three-foot stepladder. The highest point on the trailer sides and the top front are cleaned from the roof, since we can't reach these areas from the ladder.

Window cleaner will remove black streaks if they haven't been neglected for too long a time. On our trailer we sometimes get short, black streaks emanating from the lower corners of the windows that window cleaner will not remove. For these a damp sponge with a minuscule drop of Soft Scrub (from an unshaken bottle, so less of the abrasive material is present) is gently rubbed on the streak, which removes it instantly. We wipe the area with a clean, damp sponge (the other end of the same sponge the Soft Scrub is on can be used) so no residue remains.

About eight ounces of window cleaner is all that is needed to clean our trailer and its windows and maybe forty paper towel halves. The cost is probably about the same or less than using a special RV cleaner.

When lots of bugs have met their doom on the front of the trailer, we sometimes use water from a bucket to soften the carcasses, then rub with a net-covered sponge to remove them. Or we might use the type of tar and bug remover that requires no water rinse.

Most manufacturers recommend waxing the RV's exterior finish at least every year. We have never waxed either of our trailers, and the finish on our 23-footer, which was painted aluminum, after five years, was as shiny as the day we bought it.

The lower front of a trailer, usually a pebbled surface, will need more cleaning than any other section because it is the area that picks up road tar and is hit by rocks and gravel thrown up by the rear wheels of the tow vehicle (mud flaps will eliminate some

A peril of the night road is that flecks of dust and streaks of bug blood on the windshield look to me like old admirals in uniform, or crippled apple women, or the front end of barges, and I whirl out of their way, thus going into ditches and fields and up on front lawns, endangering the life of authentic admirals and apple women, who may be out on the road for a breath of air before retiring.

JAMES THURBER

of the flying debris). Since just about everything that hits the trailer will take the paint off, unless the unit is unpainted aluminum, the area may need to be repainted eventually to keep the trailer from looking shabby. A toothbrush is often useful for spot-cleaning a pebbled surface.

Because we have a diesel truck, the lower curb side and about a third of the lower front get repeated doses of diesel soot. We use an almost waterless method for most of this cleaning too. Window cleaner won't do the job on a heavy concentration of soot, and neither will any other liquid cleaner we tried, but Soft Scrub will. Again, as with a dusty surface, very gently wipe off as much of the diesel soot as possible with a dry paper towel, then apply the cleanser, rub gently, and rinse with a clean, damp sponge until no cleanser residue remains. If we have been lax about cleaning and there is a buildup of soot, it may take two treatments to get it all off. When rinsing a pebbled surface, it is necessary to use a well-saturated sponge to flush away the grime. Our site neighbor recommends using a pine-oil cleaner mixed to a stronger strength than for general cleaning to remove diesel soot.

We imagine many of our readers are appalled at our using an abrasive cleanser on an RV's exterior. It will not harm or scratch the surface as long as any rubbing is done very gently and a mild abrasive is used.

Whenever we have a problem with rust (as we do now on the kingpin jack), or are taking measures to prevent rusting, we use a prime coat of Rust Lock, a superior marine product we discovered many years ago. Unlike other products, Rust Lock does not require the removal of all rust before application. It provides a tough undercoat as well as stopping rust. Rust Lock is made by the Pettit Paint Company and can be found in many stores that sell marine paints.

LEAKPROOFING

▼ ▼ ▼ ▼ ▼ ▼ ▼ ▼ ▼ ▼ ▼ ▼ ▼

Leaks inside the coach most likely will come from a roof seam or from around a window. All potential leak sources should be checked regularly and sealed if needed. Look for cracks in roof seams and voids in the window sealant, or, harder to see, hairline-width places along the edges of the sealant where it has come loose. Inspect these areas carefully for tiny holes where water could seep into the walls. Leaks such as these might not be apparent until much damage has been done.

Putting on new roof seam-sealing compound is easy because the old does not have to be removed first. Another coat can be simply brushed on over the existing compound.

On many trailer windows, leakproofing can be achieved with a putty strip (available in rolls at RV-supply stores). After removing the window frame, a strip of putty is laid around the window opening. Then the window frame is set back in place and screwed down.

Putty will shrink eventually. If you find shrinkage or voids when checking around the edges of a window, replace the putty. Before going to the trouble of removing and rebedding a window, make doubly sure the sealant is the problem; check the screws in the window frame to see if any are loose. If so, tightening them might stop the leak. When we removed the trim on our windows to see if dirt had collected behind it and was the cause of the black streaks at the corners we mentioned earlier, we found many loose screws in each window frame. If the screws are removed and coated with caulking before being reinserted, they will be leakproof.

Silicone caulking is often used for sealing on RVs. It must be removed before new caulking can be applied — often a difficult job. Sometimes the bulk of it can be sliced off with a sharp knife, any remaining bits scraped off with a knife or flat screwdriver blade, or rubbed off using a lot of pressure. Silicone caulk seems to attract road grime and turn black. A swipe or two with some tar remover on a rag removes such grime or diesel soot.

VEHICLE AND ENGINE MAINTENANCE

▼ ▼ ▼ ▼ ▼ ▼ ▼ ▼ ▼ ▼ ▼ ▼

Automotive engines are becoming more and more sophisticated and complex. Special equipment is often needed for diagnosing and fixing problems. Unless working on engines is your hobby, most engine troubles are best taken care of by a qualified mechanic. You can do most routine servicing if you want to do it, and if you are in a place that allows such jobs to be done.

Any engine or transmission that has to pull a heavy load, whether in a motorhome or trailer tow vehicle, needs to have basic servicing done more frequently. The owner's manual contains a service maintenance schedule. Tow vehicles have two servicing schedules: one for use when towing, the other for regular use. Follow the schedules for oil changes, transmission fluid changes, filter replacement, brake servicing, and the like; otherwise, serious mechanical problems may result, making the vehicle unsafe to drive. Proper maintenance makes any vehicle last longer.

On trailers have the wheel bearings cleaned, inspected, and repacked according to manufacturer's instructions and the brakes checked at regular intervals.

▼ ▼ ▼

Changing oil and transmission fluid are two of the most important maintenance procedures for fulltimers who put a lot of miles on their rigs. We remind ourselves when to do these jobs by putting two small pressure-sensitive labels on the inside back wall of the glove box where they are easily seen every time it is opened. One is labeled "oil," the other, "transmission." Each has the date of the last servicing and the mileage at which the next servicing is due. (Because we have a diesel and a clean fuel filter is necessary for optimum performance, we have a fuel-filter change-reminder label also.)

In a steno notebook, we keep a record of all fluid changes, when oil is added between oil changes, and servicing of any type that is done.

Unless engine batteries are no-maintenance, add water as needed. Coach batteries should be checked regularly as well. While under the hood, inspect the fan belts for cracks and for tightness.

Any trailer hitch ball, whether on a trailer or on a tow dolly, as well as the area where the pin box fits on a fifth-wheel hitch, should be well greased. On a conventional trailer hitch, lubricate any part of the hitch equipment that works against a metal surface, *except* for the sway control's slide bar, which must never be lubricated.

Electrical connections between a tow vehicle and trailer or between a motorhome and the lights on a tow dolly or an auxiliary vehicle should be sprayed regularly with a moisture-removing compound such as WD-40.

It's a good idea to check out running lights each time before the RV is moved. If one light does not work and the bulb is not burned out or improperly seated, the bulb may not be making proper contact. Remove the bulb and spray some WD-40 in the socket. If that does not solve the problem, try cleaning all the contact points with emery cloth.

▼ ▼ ▼ Tires

An often-overlooked basic maintenance item is proper tire inflation. Check tire pressure frequently, but for accurate readings, do so when the tires are cold.

When a trailer or motorhome is parked for some time in one place, the tires should be covered to protect them from the sun, which can cause deterioration. Anything can be used that will keep the sun off. Some RVers merely stand a piece of plywood next to the tires, or ready-made snap-on or slip-on tire covers can be purchased.

We have never stayed in one place long enough to bother with covers, but we assume that if tires can deteriorate from sitting in the sun, the sun will have the same effect on them when they are rolling along the highway. To help preserve trailer tires, we apply a protectant to them that blocks out ultraviolet rays. We probably don't need to take this precaution because, like many full-timers, we wear out tires from traveling long before they have a chance to break down from exposure to the weather.

A trailer tire that blows out can cause a lot of damage to the trailer. Trailer tires, like all tires, should be replaced before they become dangerously worn. All RV tires, including trailer tires, should be balanced.

It is becoming difficult to find trailer tires in the older sizes. If they cannot be located, other sizes can be substituted as long as there is plenty of clearance between the tires and also enough clearance in the wheel wells. If the space is not sufficient, the tires may hit the wheel wells when going over bumps. Be sure that any tires used have the proper load rating for the RV.

MAINTENANCE AND REPAIR EQUIPMENT

▼ ▼ ▼ ▼ ▼ ▼ ▼ ▼ ▼ ▼ ▼ ▼ ▼ ▼

Earlier we mentioned keeping an assortment of tools handy in the coach for doing simple maintenance and fix-it jobs. No tools should be so buried that it is a problem getting to them; jobs might be left undone or let go too long if tools are not accessible.

The tools and spare equipment needed will depend on the amount of work you do yourself and where you travel. A trip along the Alaska Highway will require more items than travel over interstate highways in populated areas.

A complete set of fan belts should be carried for travel in most areas. Keep extra oil, transmission and brake fluids on hand. Don't store opened containers of brake fluid; moisture from the atmosphere can enter the container and might cause brake problems if used. Buy the smallest size containers of brake fluid and don't open until needed.

We have used a small hydraulic jack many times for various purposes. We also carry an air compressor that runs on 12-volt DC power.

If a water filter is used, keep extra cartridges on hand. The more flexible type of sewer hose never lasts long, and it cannot be used if there is a rip in it. An additional length of sewer hose should be carried as a spare and for use when an extension is needed to reach a sewer connection.

Chapter 15

Campgrounds

▼ ▼ ▼ ▼ ▼ ▼ ▼ ▼ ▼

Surprisingly, finding a place to park the rig seems to be one of the most worrisome aspects of fulltiming for many of those about to embark on the lifestyle. But this shouldn't be a concern for anyone; not only are there plenty of campgrounds throughout the country open in all seasons, there are numerous publications to aid in finding those to suit your needs and pocketbook.

Locating campgrounds is easy. Several different campground directories can be purchased at bookstores, newsstands, and RV-supply stores, or the *Trailer Life Campground & RV Services Directory,* published annually, can be ordered by mail from TL Enterprises, 3601 Calle Tecate, Camarillo, California 93012. The American Automobile Association (AAA) has several regional campground directories available to members. Many states issue their own camping guides as well.

Directories list all types of campgrounds, from those that are primitive with no hookups to resorts with every type of facility any RVer could want. Nearly all contain specific travel directions for reaching each campground, along with information about the number of sites, what hookups are available, and whether the campground is open all year or seasonally (Figure 15.1).

HOW TO FIND A CAMPGROUND

▼ ▼ ▼ ▼ ▼ ▼ ▼ ▼ ▼ ▼ ▼ ▼ ▼

How to Read a Campground Listing

Each listing gives you information in advance such as the exact location of the campground, its rates, and the completeness of its facilities. The following example is from the *Trailer Life Campground & RV Services Directory,* which carries a full explanation of all its symbols and details.

Location on map. Check for the proximity of the campground. Is another one closer?

Elevation. High elevation may mean a long, steep (gas-burning) climb.

Good Sam Club. The Good Sampark symbol means that Good Sam Club members save 10 percent on camping fees if they pay cash.

Season. Avoid an unnecessary drive; be sure the campground is open. Rates may be lower during "shoulder" seasons, in this case, April and October.

Access. Good access roads mean saving wear and tear in getting there.

Directions. Precise directions save you a telephone call and searching time. If the campground is just off an interstate, it might be more expensive than another farther from the highway. If it's a remote campground, save backtracking by picking up supplies in advance.

Regulations. In this case, if you have a pet, you know not to waste a trip to this campground.

Site description. You can save an unnecessary trip if the sites are unsuitable for your needs. The availability of shaded sites may mean less air-conditioning time (note the extra charge for running an air conditioner, indicated by the dollar sign). Note also the availability of hookups If you don't need them; compare the number of available sites to the number of hookup sites. If some sites do not have hookups, you can probably save money by requesting such a site. Note also extra charges for cable TV and running an electric heater.

Facilities. Evaluate your needs of the moment; if you need some simple groceries, or need to fill your LP tanks, the availability of such services can save you a side trip.

Recreation. If the campground seems to have enough to interest every member of the family, you'll undoubtedly save on day trips away from the campground. If there's a boat ramp, you'll save the launch fees you'd pay elsewhere.

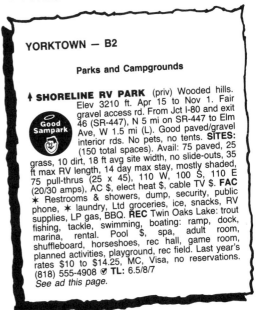

YORKTOWN — B2

Parks and Campgrounds

↟ **SHORELINE RV PARK** (priv) Wooded hills. Elev 3210 ft. Apr 15 to Nov 1. Fair gravel access rd. From Jct I-80 and exit 46 (SR-447), N 5 mi on SR-447 to Elm Ave, W 1.5 mi (L). Good paved/gravel interior rds. No pets, no tents. **SITES:** (150 total spaces). Avail: 75 paved, 25 grass, 10 dirt, 18 ft avg site width, no slide-outs, 35 ft max RV length, 14 day max stay, mostly shaded, 75 pull-thrus (25 x 45), 110 W, 100 S, 110 E (20/30 amps), AC $, elect heat $, cable TV $. **FAC** ✳ Restrooms & showers, dump, security, public phone, ✳ laundry, Ltd groceries, ice, snacks, RV supplies, LP gas, BBQ. **REC** Twin Oaks Lake: trout fishing, tackle, swimming, boating: ramp, dock, marina, rental. Pool $, spa, adult room, shuffleboard, horseshoes, rec field. Last year's planned activities, playground, rec field. Last year's rates $10 to $14.25, MC, Visa, no reservations. (818) 555-4908 Ⓥ **TL:** 6.5/8/7 *See ad this page.*

Rate guidelines. Rates listed in the *Trailer Life Directory* are for two adults, exclusive of additional fees. These are always just guidelines, but useful for comparisons with other campgrounds. If you like, enjoy the "float" period that charging allows; note that charge cards are accepted.

Ratings. These are just as important as the rates. They tell you what you're getting for your money: the completeness of facilities, the condition of the restrooms, and also the campground's scenic and environmental quality.

Advertising. The presence of an advertisement can be useful; an ad may supply additional information, such as a map that just might determine your choice of campground.

Figure 15.1
A campground directory provides RVers with valuable information: location, travel directions, and specific services and facilities offered.

Most list the time limit, if one exists, that an RV can occupy the site, maximum size of RV that can be accommodated, and services available at the campground: laundry, pay phone, propane, groceries, and the like. Some include the altitude and fee charged, if any (a few places still exist where it costs nothing to camp). The *Trailer Life Campground & RV Services Directory* is unique in that it has three ratings for each campground. Two of the ratings are generally for the same criteria as found in some other directories: completeness and quality of facilities and cleanliness and physical characteristcs of the restrooms and showers. Trailer Life's third rating is for the scenic and environmental quality. When this rating was introduced, we didn't think it would be of much use to us, but we have found it to be helpful; it often influences us when we are trying to choose between several campgrounds in an area. The TL directory is also the only one that lets campers know whether a campground's sites can accommodate slide-outs and rates a campground's laundry facilities for cleanliness.

Some directories contain a map of each state on which all the towns where campgrounds are located are indicated. State directories generally arrange their listings by county or area.

The Trailer Life directory is the one we refer to the most. All the countrywide directories are big, thick books, and we do not have space to keep more than one of these in a place where it would be handy for quick reference. Most directories list almost the same campgrounds, except for the AAA directories, which include only those that meet AAA standards.

Campgrounds are eager to have your business, and several sources lead you to them: advertisements along highways, brochures, and state campground directories that can be obtained from tourist information centers and chambers of commerce.

The familiar blue signs with a white trailer, seen on all interstates and many other highways, have arrows beneath them indicating the way to campgrounds (Figure 15.2). On a few occasions, we have seen one of these signs where no campground was listed in our directory. If we have the time, we check it out in case we might want to stay there at some future date.

Many road maps indicate public campgrounds, but few provide any more information than just a symbol designating the

Figure 15.2
These familiar signs, directing RVers to campgrounds and dump station locations, are found on all interstates and many other highways.

location. Relying on a map alone for finding a campground isn't practical. Locations are sometimes imprecise, and there is no way of knowing in advance whether the campground will be suitable for the length or type of your RV.

If you must stay in an area where no campgrounds are listed in your sources, perhaps one can be found in the Yellow Pages of the local telephone directory. Look under the headings Mobile Home Parks, Trailer Parks, Campgrounds, or Recreational Vehicle Parks.

If you are a member of the Good Sam Club (all fulltimers should be) the *Trailer Life Campground & RV Services Directory* is the one to have. It is the only directory that indicates whether a campground is a Good Sampark. At these parks, members receive a 10 percent discount on the daily rate, a benefit that greatly influences our selection of a campground.

TYPES OF CAMPGROUNDS
▼ ▼ ▼ ▼ ▼ ▼ ▼ ▼ ▼ ▼ ▼ ▼ ▼

All types of campgrounds are available, from those in the heart of cities to those off the beaten path in the backcountry. They may be private or public. Some are under the administration of the federal government: those in national parks and national forests, on Bureau of Land Management (BLM) lands, and at Corps of Engineers (COE) projects. Nearly every state has a park system, and many of the parks have campgrounds. Some county parks have camping areas. All across the country, from the smallest hamlet to good-size towns, are city parks with camping facilities. Campgrounds are maintained by some paper, lumber, and power companies, and there may be camping available at fairgrounds.

Even though the contiguous forty-eight states have an abundance of campgrounds, there are areas in certain states where camping facilities are some distance apart.

Membership campgrounds may not always be conveniently located for fulltimers. All too often they are heavily clustered in vacation areas and almost nonexistent in other places. Some membership campground associations do not have facilities in all states.

The highest campground rates will be found in resort towns, vacation areas, and at RV parks in and around large cities. Rates will be higher in campgrounds with such amenities as swimming pools — heated or not — saunas, tennis courts, golf courses, and good security.

▼ ▼ ▼ Private Campgrounds

Some private campgrounds have a flat fee that includes all hookups while some have one base fee and an additional, separate charge for each hookup: electricity, water, or sewer. If you elect to have no sewer hookup in one of these places, there may or may not be a charge if you use the campground's dump station. We have stayed at some campgrounds where the base fee plus the dumping fee was higher than the charge for a full hookup.

In some campgrounds, the rate with or without hookups does not include the use of the showers; there may be an extra charge for shower usage, or the showers may have a coin-operated meter on them. Many campgrounds impose a charge of $1.00, $1.50, or $2.00 per day if an electric heater or air conditioner is used. If the campground offers cable television, it may cost an extra dollar or two if you wish to use it.

One fact about private campgrounds has few exceptions: Any campground adjacent to an interstate highway will cost more than a comparable one that is not as conveniently located for the traveler. If you want to save money, find a campground a distance away from the interstate. Rates at many campgrounds on old highways that have been bypassed by the interstates are some of the best camping bargains.

Many of the times we have stayed at campgrounds on interstate highways we have observed that the people running the campgrounds seem to be rather cold and impersonal and give the impression they are only interested in taking our money. We'll give them the benefit of the doubt and assume this attitude occurs because so many of their customers are transients who pull off the highway late in the day and are gone early next morning, and those registering the campers are so busy that they have no time to establish any personal rapport with their customers. Nevertheless, we do not feel welcome or at home in many such campgrounds, and we rarely return to them a second time. Aside from the high rates, a campground next to an interstate highway is noisy. This is a fact with no exceptions.

Off-season rates are rarely found at any campgrounds unless they are located in a resort area.

We are of the opinion that any time the cost for a campsite approaches that of a motel room — any motel room — it is overpriced. After all, maid service is not provided with any campsite as it is in a motel. What's more, a motel never charges extra for using heat or air conditioning as is the practice in many campgrounds, regardless of how high the base rate is. And most motels have a phone in the room for their guests' use and impose no extra charge for cable TV, which often includes some extra-cost channels not in the basic cable package.

No matter where you stay, you should get what you pay for. With electricity, often you do not. Any time we are charged $10 or more for a campsite that does not have 30-amp service, we feel we are being ripped off.

Some misguided campground operators will fuse a 15-amp circuit with a 30-amp fuse and claim you are getting 30-amp service. All you are getting is cheated. In such a situation, electrical equipment drawing the full load of 30 amps can be used for only a short time, perhaps only half an hour, before your plug and the site's outlet will begin to burn. If you have to use a 15-amp plug in any outlet without an adapter, it's not 30-amp service no matter what amperage fuse is used in the circuit.

Cable television is another item that may not be what you think you are paying for. As we explained on page 316, if the cable outlet is merely a connection to the campground's antenna providing the usual local programming, you may not want to spend any extra for it.

Facilities may not always be as listed in a directory. Once we stayed in a campground that had a notice posted stating that after October 15 the main bathhouse, which contained the showers, would be closed for the season. After that date, not only would there be no place for showers, but the only toilet facilities would be two unheated portable toilets. The rates, which were high, would remain the same. This did not affect us because we do not use campground bathrooms or showers, but if we did, we would have been angry, after pulling in in mid-October, to find the campground's facilities were far short of what were listed in our directory.

We have noticed, too, that rates are rarely lowered when the swimming pool or other recreational facilities are closed for the season. It is wishful thinking, but we would like to receive lower rates if we did not use the campground's bathhouse, pool, or any other convenience or recreational facility provided.

Inquire about weekly rates, even if you plan to stay in a campground for as little as four days, and check the monthly rate if you will be staying only two weeks.

We have stayed in numerous campgrounds where the rate for a few days equalled or exceeded the weekly rate, and the monthly rate was just a little more than that for two weeks. Since we have a loose schedule and don't usually have to be any place at a certain time, we have often stayed over to take advantage of these types of rates. And if, for some reason, we want to leave before the period we have paid for expires, we may still be money ahead, or at least break even on what we would have paid with a daily rate.

▼ ▼ ▼

Aside from saving money, another advantage of paying for a longer period than you plan on staying is that if the weather is bad when you intend to leave, you can stay over without any extra charge. This has worked to our advantage several times.

When we are undecided about whether we want to stay longer than overnight, we sometimes ask if the overnight rate can be applied to a weekly rate; many places will allow this, but some won't. Before staying long-term, we sometimes prefer to spend at least one night in the site to see if we have noisy neighbors and to determine if the campground might otherwise be unsatisfactory.

Often the lowest weekly or monthly rates are found in mobile home parks.

▼ ▼ ▼

We try to avoid campgrounds with rates for each individual hookup. Almost without exception, they seem to be the most expensive campgrounds. We prefer to seek out small, out-of-the-way places with a reasonable, flat rate. We found such a campground on the Oregon coast. The owner is an RVer himself. He told us that nothing irritates him more than to pull into a campground and find he has to pay extra for everything. So he charges one flat and very reasonable rate that includes cable TV. The campground rate is low because no recreation or bath facilities are provided—all RVs must be self-contained—and, unlike many others in the area, it is not on the oceanfront. When we stay at this campground, an ocean view is not important to us. As fulltimers, we know we will be parked in many other places with an ocean view. Every single place we stay does not need to have a glorious panorama we can view from our windows. In this campground we are satisfied, for the time we spend there, with a grassy site surrounded by tall conifers and the ocean less than a quarter of a mile away.

In the same section of the Oregon coast, we once stayed in another campground across the road from the ocean. It was years ago, and then we paid the high rate of $10 for electricity only. Our assigned site had the laundry on one side and another RV, quite close, on the other. Our view from the front was a metal storage shed; from the back we saw the rear of a restaurant. (Interestingly, as we write this, we are in a campground in Montana at which the daily rate is also $10, but this includes full hookups, a wide site, use of the pool, and a breaktaking view of mountains in every direction.)

▼ ▼ ▼ Public Campgrounds

Many state parks have a day-use charge in addition to the camping fee. In some states, the day-use charge need not be paid if the user has purchased an annual permit. One year we saved quite a bit by buying annual permits for three different states' parks. In a few states, residents of the state pay one rate for using the state facilities; nonresidents pay more.

If you frequent national parks or any other places under the auspices of the National Park Service, a Golden Eagle Pass might be worthwhile. The cost for camping in the parks will be the same, but you will not have to pay to enter any places where a fee is charged during the calendar year for which the pass is issued.

Most campgrounds in national parks have no hookups of any kind. State parks' facilities range from primitive to full hookups. If a city or county park has any facilities, it is usually just electricity. Sometimes water will be available on each site; if not, a central water supply is nearly always accessible. The most primitive campgrounds usually have toilets of some sort and may have a drinking water source as well.

Camping in national parks and forests used to be one of the best bargains around, but the rates for these campgrounds without hookups have increased to the point where you can stay in a private campground with hookups for almost the same amount of money. What you will have to decide is whether you want the beauty, quiet, and away-from-it-all ambience found in many of these campgrounds. Such features are certainly worth some consideration.

Camping in some state parks is not a bargain either. A few years ago, when all rates were lower than they are today, we entered a state park and found the cost was nine dollars. Only electricity was included at the site. Except for being well maintained, the park was not appealing. It was neither beautiful, nor quiet, nor away by itself; it was a large, treeless, grassy area next to a highway just outside a town.

CAMPGROUND SITE SELECTION
▼ ▼ ▼ ▼ ▼ ▼ ▼ ▼ ▼ ▼ ▼ ▼

We prefer to select our own campsite, but often this isn't possible. Sites are assigned in many private campgrounds and in some public parks during peak seasons. Sometimes we are allowed to select a site from a chart. When this happens, we try to take a look at the site before signing up for it.

The features we look for first are whether the site will be long enough for our rig, if there is enough room for maneuvering into the site, and whether there are any low overhanging tree branches. We have been in many well-maintained private campgrounds in which the operators overlook trimming back tree branches that might interfere with parking, or might not clear the roof of tall RVs, or obstruct the TV antenna when it is raised.

We look at how level the site is. We have to use leveling boards in about two-thirds of the sites in which we stay. This is no problem because we have several leveling boards we can use singly or together for different leveling situations. (Unless the RV is equipped with automatic levelers, all fulltimers should carry leveling equipment; see also pages 378–380.) In a few sites we have come across, leveling the trailer as much as necessary would be impossible.

We check to see if the site slopes upward or downward. If the back of a site inclines downward, it may not be possible to raise a trailer, conventional or fifth-wheel, high enough to release it from the hitch, or, if it can be unhitched, lower it enough to level the unit. If a site is higher in back than in front, a trailer or motorhome may not be able to be raised high enough for leveling. In either situation, if the unit can be leveled, one end may be so low there is not enough room under it for stabilizing jacks.

▼ ▼ ▼ Campground Hazards

When selecting a site or a campground, consider how rain, snow, or ice might affect getting in and getting out. Once we had to be pulled out of a muddy site; another time our campsite was over a tiny, grassy knoll that had become so wet and slippery from rain we could not climb out over it. Grass, for all its desirable qualities, can be a nuisance to RVers. We have had so many problems with slick grass that we look askance at any grassy site that isn't perfectly level.

Sometimes an uphill or downhill campground entrance will present a problem in wet weather. A steep, loosely graveled incline can sometimes cause slipping.

We are careful about staying too near streams or rivers when flooding may be a danger. We once intended to stay in a small Nebraska town's municipal park for a few days. We parked in a site about 100 feet away from the river that curved around the campground area. A ten-foot-high bank was behind our trailer, and atop the bank, on another level, was a large, roofed pavilion. While we were registering, the manager volunteered the information that flood waters once reached the roof of the pavilion.

During the night it rained heavily in our area and farther west. By morning the river had risen about a foot to bank level; by nightfall it was creeping toward the campsites. Next morning, water was only about twenty feet from our trailer so we figured it was time to get out of there. We later read in the newspaper that the water in the park rose enough so that about half the trailer would have been submerged had we remained there.

Another time, in Georgia, we pulled into a county park and took a site overlooking the river about twenty feet above the water. The area had been receiving rain for several days, so when we registered we asked if there was any chance that the campground could be flooded. We were assured this had never happened. After setting, up we left to run some errands. When we came back the river had risen considerably. We kept picking markers — branches or rocks — to gauge the rise. All night long we checked periodically as one marker after another disappeared under water. Late the next day the river finally stopped rising when its level was about six feet below our site, so we didn't have to leave.

Since the waters in both these campgrounds were rising slowly, there was no danger of flash flooding. Had there been, we wouldn't have stayed at either place. We greatly respect what the forces of nature can do, and many of the campsites we select are chosen on the basis of what nature might have in store for us.

Before we were fully accustomed to the capriciousness of Mother Nature, we were once given a site immediately in front of a steep hill on which several trees of various sizes were growing. One of them, about eight inches in diameter, was right behind and slightly above the trailer. When we arrived at the campground, it was misting. Soon it was raining heavily, and the wind began to blow. By next morning the ground was saturated. The wind was gusting so strongly we could see the ground over the roots of "our" tree heaving as the tree swayed back and forth. It

▼ ▼ ▼

Some of them seemed possessed of an incorrigible inner urge simply to take off and explore, to use whatever excuse was necessary to travel into country where no one else had been, to see where the rivers went, to find a pass through a mountain range that no one else had crossed.

DAVID THOMPSON

▼ ▼ ▼ ▼ ▼ ▼ ▼ ▼ ▼ ▼ ▼ ▼ ▼

looked as if it could topple onto the trailer at any minute, so we moved to a safer site. The tree stayed where it belonged, but we slept better knowing it wasn't above us.

We are careful about parking under trees with dead branches that could blow down in high winds. But once we were in a campground where tall cottonwoods arched over every site. The wind was blowing strongly one morning as we were having coffee. We were startled by a loud report as if a gun had been fired. The noise brought us and our neighbors outside to see what had happened. A branch about three inches in diameter and two feet long had hurtled down and, spearlike, pierced the top of a fiberglass cover on a pickup truck in the adjoining site.

We cast a wary eye at overhead electrical lines. They, too, have been known to blow down, and nearby electric wires often create interference, which affects televison reception. (Trees around a site can also cause "ghosts" in TV pictures.)

In hot weather we like to have some shade (being careful about the trees we park under, of course), but in cool weather we would rather not be under trees in order to receive some warmth from the sun. Once we were parked in a beautiful site in a dense forest with the trees so thick that the sun never shone on the campsite. They made the trailer so dark that we had to use the interior lights during the day—a concern because we had no electrical hookup.

You may want to avoid parking directly under campground lights if you don't have a way of blocking out light from your sleeping quarters.

If you use campground shower facilities, it's a good idea to inspect them before registering, especially if you intend to stay for a few days or weeks.

▼ ▼ ▼ Other Limitations

Heed the RV-size limitations for sites in national forest and BLM campgrounds, (the limitations are included in most campground directories). It might be that one or two sites in such campgrounds would be suitable for a larger-than-specified RV, but it might not; or someone else might already have occupied the larger sites if they exist.

Whenever possible, we try to scout out unfamiliar national forest or BLM campgrounds before taking our trailer into them. On many occasions we have found campsites that would have been suitable for the trailer, but the roads leading to them were so poor that we didn't want to risk taking the trailer over them.

When we choose a campground, one of the primary factors affecting where we will stay is the rate. But if we find a low-rate campground some distance from a town we want to visit, we might stay, instead, at a higher-priced campground in town. We do some simple calculating to figure how much extra we would spend for fuel to travel to town from the distant campground. This amount, added to the campground rate, sometimes makes the in-town campground the more economical place to stay.

If you are buying a site in a condominium campground, you may not be able to have the site you want unless you select it from a plan before the campground is built. Usually the desirable sites, those with the best view or those located directly on a body of water, are the most costly.

RESERVATIONS
▼ ▼ ▼ ▼ ▼ ▼ ▼ ▼ ▼ ▼ ▼ ▼

We have never reserved a campsite. We don't travel many miles in a day, so we always arrive in early afternoon and would not normally travel in tourist seasons to crowded campgrounds where reservations might be necessary, but if your habits are different from ours, you may need to smooth your way with advance reservations to be sure you have a place to stay.

Know the reservation policy of any campground at which you reserve a site: How long will the site be held? How much of a deposit is needed to hold a space? Will the deposit be fully refunded if you have to cancel? Many disputes have arisen because of the lack of understanding about reservation policies.

UNCROWDED CAMPGROUNDS
▼ ▼ ▼ ▼ ▼ ▼ ▼ ▼ ▼ ▼ ▼ ▼

We always prefer to stay in uncrowded campgrounds. We are never found in popular vacation areas such as Yellowstone Park during the busy season. When we visit Yellowstone we do so in June or October. Yes, there is a chance of encountering bad weather—ten inches of snow in June once and six inches in October last year—but, since our trailer is suited for camping in all climates, we were comfortable, and we enjoyed seeing the white-mantled park unhindered by throngs of people.

On long holiday weekends, and often on any weekend, especially in the summer, we hole up in a private campground in a town and stay out of public parks and recreation areas. Aside from the admittedly selfish reason of wanting to have places all to ourselves as much as possible, we have another reason for traveling, or not traveling, as we do: Since we are free to come and go as we choose, it is fairer to let time-limited vacationers have the sites we might otherwise occupy. Parks are overcrowded as it is in peak vacation periods. Why should we add to the overcrowding—and the long lines at the dump station?

In the northern states in April through June and in September and October travelers will unlikely encounter blizzards or extremely cold temperatures. Any snow that falls usually disappears quickly in these months, as long as you are not at too high an elevation.

We cherish experiences we have had during the off-season: The campground at Monument Valley, Arizona, is on a high bluff. The valley, with its incredible rock formations, falls away at the very edge of some of the campsites. Once, in March, we were the only ones in the campground. We watched the shadows lengthen across the valley as the sun set. That night the stars sparkled with a not-often-seen brilliance; there were no intruding, artificial lights for miles. At dawn the huge, orange sun rose through a purple mist. All the grandeur of Monument Valley was ours alone.

A public park near a small town in Alabama is about a mile outside the city limits. The campground is nestled among wooded, grassy hills, and our campsite was just a few yards from a small lake. During our week's stay one January we discovered that visitors to the park were few and far between. Most days and nights we had the place to ourselves. The attendant came to unlock the park gate at seven o'clock in the morning and locked up at eight o'clock in the evening. No one could get in to disturb us in "our" park. The trees were still bare, the better to see the birds: a pileated woodpecker, brown creepers, Carolina chickadees, and purple finches, among others. We saw twenty-three different kinds of birds without moving from the campsite.

[Rain] hangs about the place, like a friendly ghost. . . . if it's not coming down in delicate droplets, then it's in buckets; and if neither, it tends to lurk suspiciously in the atmosphere.

BARBARA ACTON-BOND

▼ ▼ ▼ ▼ ▼ ▼ ▼ ▼ ▼ ▼ ▼ ▼ ▼

Regularly, midmorning and late afternoon, a large flock of blue-birds came to feed around our trailer.

One October, our trailer was parked in a private campground located on a secluded cove on the Maine coast. A broad sweep of lawn sprinkled with tall pines led to the rocky shore. No one else came into the campground during our stay. We did not have to share the lovely Indian summer days with anyone but the friendly couple who ran the campground. Not being pressured with the rush of business, they were relaxed and free to chat.

We could go on and on, but these experiences illustrate some of the reasons why we prefer camping in popular tourist areas off-season. You could become hooked on it too. It's fascinating to be in a place where no noises other than the sounds of nature surround you, and it's delightful to be off by yourself now and then in a world that is becoming ever more crowded.

CAMPING IN NONCAMPGROUNDS
▼ ▼ ▼ ▼ ▼ ▼ ▼ ▼ ▼ ▼ ▼ ▼ ▼

RVers can park in a variety of places that are not campgrounds, although in many of them stays of only a few hours or overnight are allowed.

▼ ▼ ▼ Rest Areas

Overnight camping without restrictions is permitted in only a few states' highway rest areas. Many have limitations on the time you can park in the rest area—eight, twelve, or eighteen hours, usually—so overnighting could be done. Some have signs posted that warn NO CAMPING ALLOWED, or NO OVERNIGHT CAMPING ALLOWED. Officials don't seem to have a common definition of camping, but it often means that no tents are to be set up in the area. Those sleeping in their RVs are no different than truck drivers who use rest areas when they sleep. If truck drivers can do it, RVers should be able to do the same thing in the same place. Don't take our word for it, though. What is allowed or not allowed as far as RVers are concerned depends in large part on how the law enforcement officers on duty interpret the regulations and how lenient they are.

In years past, we have overnighted at rest areas, but now we would think twice about doing so. These days, some rest areas, especially at night, can be hangouts for those who are up to no good. If it were necessary for us to spend the night in a rest area, we would never step outside the trailer at night.

▼ ▼ ▼ Truck Stops

Sometimes recreational vehicle parking is allowed in truck stops but there may be a charge. A few truck stops have electrical hookups but not much else in the way of amenities for RVers. Truck stops are not pleasant places for overnighting what with the comings and goings of the noisy rigs at all hours and the nonstop roaring of the collective cooling engines on refrigerator trucks. A few truck-stop operators have realized they can cash in on the RV business and have added campsites with hookups to their facility. Usually the campground portion is far enough away from the trucks to diminish their noises, but highway noise and high rates, common to most campgrounds on interstates, prevail.

▼ ▼ ▼ Other Overnight Camping Sites

At restaurants or service stations with large parking areas, overnighting is sometimes allowed. Always ask permission of the manager before doing so. Of course, it would be cricket to patronize the establishment, eat a meal in the restaurant, or buy fuel from the service station. An overnight stay also might be arranged in a church parking lot. Most likely nothing would be charged, but an offer of payment should be made.

We once needed to take a sunset photograph of a certain location. The only campgrounds in the area were many miles from where we would take our shot, and we did not relish a long drive back to one of them after dark. In a nearby town we were allowed to stay overnight in the large parking lot of an auto-parts store.

An elderly lady loner we know prefers not to unhitch her trailer for overnight stays when she is just traveling through an area. Being on a tight budget, she has to watch what she spends. She frequently stays overnight in a small-town shopping center parking lot. If the shopping center has one main store, she will ask the manager of the store if she can stay in the parking lot. If it has many stores, she might check with the manager of the shopping center or the police department to find if any regulations prohibit overnight parking. In any event, she always lets the police know what she is doing. More often than not, they regularly patrol the area and keep an eye on her.

If we intended to overnight in a shopping center, we would try to park in a well-lighted section of the lot, and, as in a highway rest area, we would not leave the RV at night. We, too, would inform the police about what we were doing.

As we travel around the country, we have noticed more and more shopping centers with signs posted prohibiting overnight parking. But we have also seen RVs obviously parked for an overnight stay in such places. We would not park where it was specifically forbidden. We want a good night's sleep; we don't want to risk being rousted out of bed by someone ordering us to move on, writing out a citation, or both.

During your travels, if you plan on living in your RV while parking in the driveway or on the grounds of a friend's or relative's house, ask your host to find out if any local ordinances prohibit this. Some localities will not allow RVs to be parked anyplace where they are visible. Some permit RV parking, but the unit cannot be lived in. These local regulations vary widely, so if you are preparing for an extended visit, know the facts before you make firm plans.

> *I hate small towns because once you've seen the cannon in the park there's nothing else to do.*
>
> LENNY BRUCE

▼ ▼ ▼ ▼ ▼ ▼ ▼ ▼ ▼ ▼ ▼ ▼

COLD-WEATHER CAMPING
▼ ▼ ▼ ▼ ▼ ▼ ▼ ▼ ▼ ▼ ▼ ▼

Cold-weather camping without hookups should not be attempted unless your rig is suited for it, which means more than just having proper insulation. The RV should be equipped with a dependable, adequate source of heat, reliable batteries with enough amperage for your needs and a way of charging them, full propane tanks, an extra food supply in case you become snowed in, plenty of warm clothing, and some way of receiving weather reports.

▼ ▼ ▼ Some Cold-Weather Camping Hints

For comfortable and safe cold-weather camping, the following hints will be useful:

▼ Remember that batteries become more difficult to recharge as the temperature drops.

▼ Keep snow cleared from the refrigerator roof vent as well as the furnace intake and exhaust ports should it accumulate to such a depth.

▼ The campsite should be sheltered from all winds as much as possible, but especially northerly winds. Keep in mind that sheltering trees can blow over in heavy winter winds, and branches can break off when weighted with snow or ice.

▼ Carry chains or have suitable tires on any engine-driven vehicles.

▼ Keep antifreeze in holding tanks so drains won't freeze.

▼ Connect the water hose to the outside faucet only if it is well insulated. Otherwise, use water from the internal tank and fill it as needed.

▼ A blow dryer is useful for thawing frozen drains and iced-over doors. If no electricity is available, keep a can of de-icer handy for use on outside compartments and vehicle doors.

▼ Make sure all outside compartment doors are weathertight.

▼ If an electric heater is used, there must be adequate amperage and wiring for its use.

▼ Crack a window when heating the RV with any type of propane or solid-fuel heater.

▼ Keep lower cabinet doors ajar so water lines will not freeze.

▼ Use storm windows, insulated draperies, and heavy window shades to keep the coach warmer.

▼ For long-term stays in cold weather, the unit should have some sort of skirting around it. Perhaps snow could be piled up around the coach to prevent wind from blowing under it.

▼ If cold-weather camping is done regularly, select an RV with the holding tanks in a heated compartment.

▼ Before leaving to winter-camp in an isolated place, let a relative or friend know where you will be and when you plan to return.

Wintertime camping is becoming a popular pastime. Many campgrounds in the Snowbelt are open year-round, catering to cold-weather campers. They have heated swimming pools, saunas, ice skating, snowmobiling, skiing, ice fishing, and just about any other wintertime recreation you can think of.

No matter where you camp, observe not only the campground's rules but general good manners as well:

CAMPING ETIQUETTE
▼ ▼ ▼ ▼ ▼ ▼ ▼ ▼ ▼ ▼ ▼ ▼ ▼

▼ Keep your site clean and free of clutter. The people who pile all sorts of paraphernalia under their units don't have to look at the unsightly mess, but others do.

▼ Clean up after pets and do not let them run loose no matter how well behaved they are. If your dog barks or whines when left alone, do not leave it alone.

▼ Do not make any extra work for the campground operators; they have their hands full with normal maintenance.

▼ Turn off exterior lights when they are not needed, especially at night, so your neighbor's sleep won't be disturbed.

▼ Do not leave a mess in the shower, laundry room, or at the dump station.

▼ Always leave a good impression, especially if you are a fulltimer, so all of us pursuing this lifestyle will be welcome wherever we go.

Chapter 16

RV Procedures: Setting Up and Breaking Camp

If you have been primarily a vacation RVer before becoming a fulltimer, you will not have had much opportunity to develop systems for getting under way easily, for setting up a campsite quickly and efficiently, or for making sure that nothing is overlooked. As you begin fulltiming and traveling, you will develop certain operational procedures that will soon become second nature to you.

Usually procedures involved with getting ready to travel, hitching, unhitching, and securing the RV in a campsite are a mutual effort with us, but we seem to be in the minority. With many couples, all too often these tasks are left to the man. We think fulltiming is much more satisfying if there is complete cooperation between partners. One person should not always perform certain duties exclusively.

Look at it this way: What if your partner were out of commission or unavailable? Whom could you call on to do his or her work? If you both know how to do everything, you could do it all on your own if need be. A lot of satisfaction and self-confidence comes from knowing you are capable of handling any RV procedure by yourself.

With each type of recreational vehicle, certain procedures will be handled differently. Setting up and breaking camp, for example, are somewhat different when you have a trailer instead of a motorhome, but some procedures are common to all RVs.

Only on rare occasions can RVers leave a campsite without readying the RV to travel. Certain preparations are necessary both inside and outside the RV. So we will never forget any of these, we use a checklist (Figure 16-1). Actually, we have two lists: one for things that must be done inside, the other for outside preparations. Each item on each list appears more or less in the order in which it should be done. On the outside list, we include every step of the hitching procedure no matter how basic. After the hitching is done, we glance at the list to be sure nothing has been forgotten.

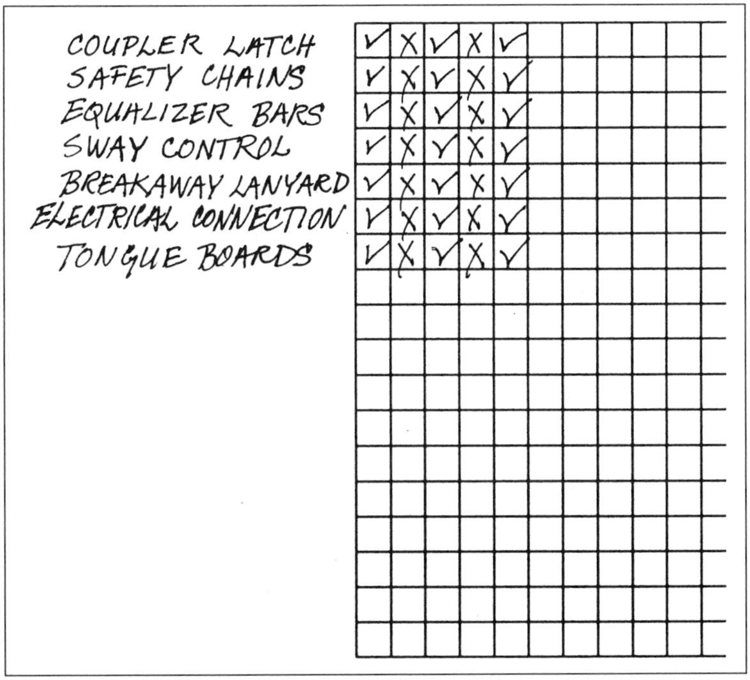

CHECKLISTS
▼ ▼ ▼ ▼ ▼ ▼ ▼ ▼ ▼ ▼ ▼ ▼

COUPLER LATCH
SAFETY CHAINS
EQUALIZER BARS
SWAY CONTROL
BREAKAWAY LANYARD
ELECTRICAL CONNECTION
TONGUE BOARDS

Figure 16.1
A portion of the authors' inside and outside checklist. The complete list includes many more items so that absolutely everything needing to be done will be taken care of before getting under way.

A general inside and outside checklist is shown in Exhibit 16.1. Using this as a basis, it can be expanded to include preparations peculiar to your RV; some preparations are different for motorhomes and trailers.

Once the trailer is hitched, before pulling out of the site, we make sure that all equipment we have used in the hitching process is put away and all outside compartments are locked. We both take a final walkaround, making a visual check to see if everything has been done.

Next, one of us goes to the rear of the trailer to check out the lights as the other one activates — in the same order each time — left- and right-turn indicators, the truck brakes, the trailer brakes (by using the manual override lever on the controller), the running lights, and the emergency blinkers.

If we have used leveling boards, we remove any wheel chocks still in place, then pull the trailer forward, remove the boards, and put them and the chocks in their storage compartment.

Before we leave the campground, we check the trailer brakes to see that they are working properly.

An outside doormat is the only item we keep outside the trailer, and, since it is included on our checklist, there isn't much chance of it being left behind. If we did habitually keep such items as folding chairs or a barbecue grill outside, we would include them on our checklists.

All fulltimers should have some sort of a checklist. No matter how good your memory, there will be times when other things will be on your mind and something may be overlooked. We often see RVs on the highway with the television antenna up or the doorsteps down. On two occasions we have noticed rigs about to pull away from their campsite with the water hose still attached.

Graph paper can be used for checklists — the kind with one-quarter-inch squares is best — or notebook paper will suffice if a few vertical lines are ruled to form the checkoff boxes.

We now produce our checklists on the computer and can print out copies whenever we need them. Traveling as much as we do, we use up the squares on a list quickly. When we began fulltiming, before we had the computer and were doing the lists by hand, we found we were making new lists every month or so. We

▼ ▼ ▼ ▼ ▼ ▼ ▼ ▼ ▼ ▼ ▼ ▼ ▼ ▼

Exhibit 16.1
Pre-Travel Checklist

Interior Checklist

☐ All **windows** and **roof vents** should be closed, unless you prefer to have some air enter the coach as you are moving. (We don't leave vents open when we are under way because too much road dust comes in.)

☐ The **television antenna** must be lowered and the **television** secured so it won't fall or be bounced around. If it is set on the floor in the center or at the front of the RV, not in the rear, it should ride well.

☐ Unless the **refrigerator** is to be run while under way, turn it off. Lock the door if it has a lock; if not, be sure the door (or doors) are shut tightly.

☐ If the **furnace** has been running, turn it off and turn the thermostat down. If any **electric heaters** have been used, they should be unplugged and stowed.

☐ Put all **loose items** away. Anything that could slide off should not be left on any counter or table. (We have a **fruit bowl** that is stowed in one side of the double sink when we are traveling; two small **house plants** go in the other side. A **teakettle** that usually sits on the stove could be put in the sink for traveling; we have space for ours in an overhead cabinet. A few loose items that we keep on a shelf at the back of the trailer are put away in a cabinet above the shelf. The **bedroom clock** is removed from its counter and put into an overhead cabinet.)

☐ Be sure the **water-pump switch** is off. Most manufacturers recommend turning it off while the coach is in motion.

☐ Turn off the **water heater** if you have an inside-controlled electric ignition type.

☐ If the RV has two **doors**, make sure you lock the one not being used.

☐ Secure any **sliding** or **hinged doors** on wardrobes as well as any other inside doors.

Many of the following outside getting-ready-to-go procedures are the same for both motorhomes and trailers.

Exterior Checklist

☐ If items are stored under the rig, put them away before leaving.

☐ Disconnect the **television cable** if used.

☐ Roll up **awnings**.

☐ Depending on the hookups at the site, fill the **water tank**, and empty the **holding tanks** if necessary. (If we know we will be climbing up grades during a day's travel, we often have the water tank nearly empty to lessen weight.) Check to see that all **hoses** and other equipment are put away after each operation.

☐ Turn off the **water heater** if it is not controlled from inside.

☐ If the RV is connected to an electric hookup, disconnect and store the **power cable** and **adapters** if used.

☐ Turn off **propane tanks** unless needed for the refrigerator.

☐ On a trailer, lower any **stone shields** on the front or back windows.

☐ Retract or remove all **stabilizing jacks** and **wheel chocks** or **blocks**, unless you have a trailer and want the chocks to remain in place until hitched.

☐ When there is no longer need to go inside the coach, secure the **steps** and lock the **door.**

Trailers will have to be hitched up at this point. Motorhomes may have to be moved from some site before an auxiliary vehicle can be hitched.

soon developed a method for using one list four times over: We checked off all the squares for the first go-round in pencil, then reused the squares by making an X in ink over the pencil check. After that, a diagonal line was drawn in each square with a colored felt-tip marker. For the fourth check-off, another diagonal line was drawn from the corners opposite the first, with a marker of another color. Writing out the lists was still a chore, so eventually we made several photocopies from a master copy. We followed this procedure until we began using the computer for the lists.

Since we often stop to have lunch in the trailer, we found we needed a lunch checklist. This short list reminds us to close the propane cylinders, shut any windows or roof vents that may have been opened, secure the refrigerator door, turn off the radio, put the plants back in the sink, turn off the lights and the water-pump switch, and remove the wheel chock (if used).

This may seem like pretty basic stuff, but using the list takes only seconds, and we never have to worry about forgetting anything.

HITCHING AND UNHITCHING
▼ ▼ ▼ ▼ ▼ ▼ ▼ ▼ ▼ ▼ ▼ ▼ ▼

Many fulltimers look upon hitching and unhitching as a distasteful chore. It shouldn't be. Establishing a routine for the procedure will make the job easier, and you will soon find shortcuts to make the work go quickly.

A conventional trailer, a fifth-wheel, or an auxiliary vehicle towed on a dolly behind a motorhome all require different hitching routines. A fifth-wheel trailer is much easier to hitch than a conventional trailer. A tow dolly can be maneuvered by hand somewhat, so if it is lined up properly, it isn't too difficult to attach to the motorhome.

▼ ▼ ▼ Conventional Trailer Hitching

Hitching a conventional trailer is somewhat more complicated than the others because of the weight-distributing hitch, which should be used on all but the smallest trailers.

We devised a system for hitching our conventional trailer that worked well for us. After we secured the inside of the trailer and took care of everything outside, including placing all the hitch paraphernalia—equalizer bars and sway control—under the tongue, we were ready to hitch up. The hitch itself was removed from its compartment (we stored it in a trailer compartment so we did not have to carry its considerable weight around with us in the truck when the trailer was parked) and inserted it in the receiver. The trailer tongue was raised, if needed.

One of us backed up the truck while the other, standing at the tongue, gave hand signals and verbal directions for positioning the hitch correctly under the coupler.

We developed a simple technique for positioning the ball exactly under the coupler: One person was stationed to the left of the tongue so he or she would be visible in the driver-side mirror. The other maneuvered the tow vehicle. The driver lined up the tow vehicle as straight as possible with the trailer. The person at the tongue imagined that the hitch bar, on which the ball is mounted, was an arrow that must be pointed directly at the coupler. If the "arrow" pointed to the right of the coupler, the driver was instructed to turn the wheels about halfway to the left. (If it pointed to the left of the coupler, the wheels would be turned to the right.) The driver was signaled to come back slowly until the "arrow" pointed at the coupler, then to stop.

At this point, the driver was told to straighten out the wheels, then slowly back the vehicle. If the wheels were straight, and the driver backed straight, the proper alignment would be made. If not, the driver was again directed to stop, before backing all the way, and make a minor correction of the wheels in the needed direction. Again, the driver backed the tow vehicle until the "arrow" pointed at the coupler, straightened out the wheels once more, and continued the backing. Sometimes we had to go through this routine several times. Even so, it takes longer to read about it than it does to execute the maneuvers.

During this procedure the person at the tongue gives indications, as necessary, with hands or fingers as to the distance remaining between the ball and the coupler. The driver should not try to second-guess the direction-giver by looking in the rearview mirror or the passenger-side mirror. Instead, the

Don't lose
Your head
To gain a minute
You need your head
Your brains are in it.
Burma Shave.

ANONYMOUS

▼ ▼ ▼ ▼ ▼ ▼ ▼ ▼ ▼ ▼ ▼ ▼

▼ ▼ ▼

driver's attention should be focused solely on the driver-side mirror and the person visible therein and nowhere else.

If one person miscalculates, the other just does what is necessary to correct without creating a scene. No doubt we have all witnessed some of the dreadful arguing that goes on between some couples during hitching up. There really is no excuse for such behavior. Keep calm and take your time. Fulltimers do not have to be in a hurry.

(Bill miscalculated once. He signaled with his thumb and forefinger that Jan was to come back a quarter of an inch when in fact the distance was only three-sixteenths of an inch. We are just funnin', but in truth, we perfected this system to such a degree that we could understand how much to move back when the distance was a mere fraction of an inch.)

Once the ball is under the coupler, but too far to one side or the other, it can be shifted slightly sideways while the tow vehicle is stationary: Turn the wheels of the tow vehicle to the right or left, and the ball will move one way or the other. With the truck we had then, the position of the ball could be shifted as much as an inch either way with this maneuver. The amount of lateral shift will vary from vehicle to vehicle, depending on the distance from the rear axle to the ball: the greater the distance, the more the shift.

Sometimes the coupler will slide over the ball, but it cannot be latched. Merely shifting the stationary tow vehicle into neutral (from reverse where it has been since backing up) will often create enough of a movement to permit latching. If it does not, then shift into drive. That almost always does the trick.

After the hitch was connected to the coupler, we stationed ourselves on each side of the tongue, each attaching the safety chain and the equalizer bar on his or her side. One person put on the sway control; the other attached the breakaway lanyard and electrical connection. One cranked up the tongue jack; the other removed the boards from beneath it. Unhitching was done in reverse order.

A trailer tongue jack should always rest on something solid so it will not sink into the ground. In a level site we used two blocks of wood under the jack, with a combined height of about five inches. Each was about a foot long, so when used together they would not teeter or shift. If the back of the site is higher than the front, more boards might be needed to raise the tongue high enough for fore-and-aft leveling. When more than two boards are used, they should be crossed, with the bottom board running fore and aft, to eliminate the tendency for the stack to roll. If the back of the site is lower than the front, only one board might be needed.

If you have to hitch up by yourself all or most of the time, you might want to have one of the several types of hitching aids available. These can be found in RV-supply stores, or they may be advertised in *Trailer Life* magazine.

▼ ▼ ▼

Without a hitching aid, perhaps a method we used on occasion might be helpful: Put a piece of 4-inch long, ¾-inch wide tape (use a dark color so it will be easy to see) vertically in the center of the trailer (just above the propane cylinders on most conventional trailers). The tape should be aligned directly behind the coupler. Put an identical piece of tape on the rear window of the tow vehicle (or rear canopy window) above and directly in line with the hitch ball.

Position the tow vehicle squarely in front of the trailer. (This procedure will not work if the tow vehicle must be brought in at an angle.) Back up, using the rearview mirror to keep the two pieces of tape lined up, until the hitch is about two feet from the coupler. Get out of the tow vehicle and note the distance remaining between the ball and the coupler. Get back behind the wheel, leaving the door partially open. Find a spot on the ground that is in line with your eye and the back edge of the door. From this spot, locate another spot on the ground that is approximately the same distance as from the ball to the coupler. (Both spots can be marked with a twig or stone.) Back up until the door edge is even with the second spot. The ball should then be in position. If it is off laterally, move it by turning the steering wheel in the tow vehicle, as previously described.

When it's difficult to hook or unhook equalizer bars, it's probably because the tongue, coupled with the hitch, is not high enough. Raise it with the tongue jack to avoid back strain.

To help remember how many links of the equalizer bar chain to take up, put a ring of tape or paint on the link immediately before the positioning link (the one that goes over the hook or into the slot on the tongue bracket). Any marking on the positioning link itself will soon wear off. If any great amount of weight is shifted in the coach at some future time, the positioning link may be a different one.

With a weight-distributing hitch, it is necessary that the tension on the equalizer bars be such that both the tow vehicle and trailer are parallel to the ground when hitched. The coupled hitch should neither sag nor be elevated.

On occasions when the tow vehicle is tilted sideways in relation to the trailer after the trailer has been leveled in the site, the hitch ball may not release easily from the coupler. Having someone stand on the hitch or rear bumper of the tow vehicle usually adds enough weight to pop it loose. Once, though, we had to use a crowbar to pry the two apart.

In the same circumstances, it can be difficult to snap up the equalizer bars when hitching. It may be necessary to pull the trailer a few feet ahead, off its leveling boards, so it will be on the same plane as the tow vehicle, before the equalizer bars can be engaged.

Hitching with the tow vehicle angled should present no problem, although, in this situation, we found something that may have been peculiar to our rig: When the trailer was hitched and ready to go with the truck on an angle, we could not latch the canopy door until the truck was straightened out. Evidently, the equalizer bars distorted the truck frame just enough so the door would not close properly.

▼ ▼ ▼ Fifth-wheel Hitching

Hitching a fifth-wheel trailer is much easier than hitching a conventional trailer, and if you can drive, you should be able to do it by yourself with ease. Everything you need to see—the hitch assembly and the kingpin on the trailer that must engage it—are visible through the rear window of the truck.

With our fifth-wheel we still work together while hitching only because it's quicker and it saves the driver from having to get in and out of the cab so much. One person is at the front of the trailer and takes care of raising or lowering the front, while the other opens the jaws of the hitch on the way to the cab of the truck. As the driver is backing, the person at the trailer makes any needed height adjustment so the kingpin will engage the jaws. The driver usually can tell when the hitch is latched because there is a loud clunk. When this is heard, the driver shifts into a forward gear and applies just enough throttle to put forward pressure on the hitch. This will securely latch the kingpin into the hitch, and the action pushes the lever to the position where the safety pin can be easily inserted. After the driver does this and applies the truck brakes, the person at the trailer front ducks under the gooseneck to double-check that the jaws are closed, shuts the tailgate, and begins to raise the front jacks. Meanwhile the driver leaves the truck to put the safety pin in the hitch lever and attach the breakaway lanyard and the trailer electrical connector cable. We don't actually use the regular safety pin in the hitch lever; we use a padlock instead. When the hitch lever is held in the latched position with a padlock instead of a pin (which can be easily pulled out), no malicious prankster can remove the pin and open the jaws. It may seem as if we are overly cautious, but we see many fifth-wheel rigs where a padlock is used in place of the pin.

▼ ▼ ▼

Not all hitches will function exactly like ours, but the basic principles of hitching are the same with all fifth-wheel hitches.

We are always extra careful about checking to see that the jaws are closed. We have seen many fifth-wheels whose owners evidently weren't so particular. Their trailers are those with dents in the underside of the gooseneck. Such dents usually occur when the kingpin pulls free of the jaws when the truck is moved, and the trailer drops onto the sides of the pickup's bed.

Once we found ourselves in a site where the level was such that the truck was so low on one side that it was impossible to engage the hitch of our fifth-wheel. We got out of the predicament by putting some leveling boards under the truck's rear wheel on the low side.

It's not necessary to unhitch a trailer every time you stop for the night if the rig is parked on a level surface. With conventional trailers, it is a good idea to lower the tongue jack, release the equalizer bars, and chock the wheels. When staying hitched with the fifth-wheel, we lower the front jacks so we can slightly ease the weight on the truck. If the trailer should need some fore-and-aft leveling, the front can be raised just a little by using the front jacks. If the front needs to be lowered, this can be effected by putting leveling boards under the trailer wheels on both sides.

LEVELING
▼ ▼ ▼ ▼ ▼ ▼ ▼ ▼ ▼ ▼ ▼ ▼ ▼

After moving the trailer into a site, the first thing to do before unhitching is to check its level.

The primary reason for leveling any RV is to insure that the absorption-type refrigerator will work properly, although recent refrigerator models are much more tolerant of off-level conditions than older ones.

The secondary reason for being on the level, as far as we are concerned, is that we do not want to live on an angle or have cabinet doors constantly swinging shut when we want them to remain open.

Leveling doesn't have to be a chore. It will be simple if the level is easy to see and use, if you carry an assortment of leveling boards so the RV can be set straight in any of the variety of site configurations and if you develop a leveling routine.

As with other RV procedures, the more times you level a unit, the more adept you will become at judging just how much it needs to be propped up, and the process will go quickly.

Since an RV's level should be determined by the refrigerator, to establish a norm, we set the level in the freezer and leveled the trailer from side to side and fore and aft. Once it was as level as we could make it, a one-by-two board was nailed to the back of the dinette, which is just inside the door, aligned so that when the level was set on it, its bubble was exactly centered (Figure 16.2). The doorsill agrees with the fore and aft level of the

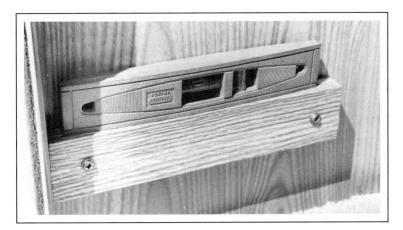

Figure 16.2
For side-to-side leveling, the authors' level is set on a block, attached to the back of the dinette, just inside the door. For fore and aft leveling, the level is placed on the doorsill.

refrigerator, so the level is placed on the sill for the fore-and-aft leveling. The level is stored immediately inside the door in the box we use for the vinyl runner described on page 335.

▼▼▼ Types of Levels and Leveling Equipment

A dependable level is needed. We tried several types that mounted on the outside of the RV but found none that were satisfactory. Two levels must be mounted on the unit so it can be leveled both from side to side and fore and aft. The levels that are stuck on with adhesive can shift in hot weather. We eventually went back to using a nine-inch torpedo level, the same level we always used to double-check the other levels. We find the torpedo level easier to see and interpret, and its bubble movement is quick; it doesn't have the inertia of some of the other levels we experimented with.

Unless a motorhome is equipped with an electric, hydraulic-, or automatic-leveling system, it will have to be leveled with boards. Side leveling is no more difficult than with a trailer, except that boards will have to be placed on the low side under both the front and back wheels. Fore-and-aft leveling, though, presents more of a problem because there is no way of simply adjusting a jack to achieve the proper level.

If a motorhome needs longitudinal leveling, boards will have to be put under both wheels, in the front or back, once the side leveling is taken care of. It may be that boards of different heights will be under three wheels of a motorhome. Boards used for leveling a motorhome from the front or back should be in combinations that will total six inches of height. In some sites the front or rear wheels on a motorhome will have to be propped up this high to make it level. Motorhomers probably will develop a knack for estimating the height needed to achieve level, but doing the actual leveling always takes some time to accomplish.

We carry several leveling boards in different heights: six ½-inch boards (plywood) and four 1½-inch boards (two-by-eights). All are wide enough and long enough to fit comfortably under one tire, yet short enough so they can be inserted between the wheels. Any leveling board an inch or more in thickness should have a 45-degree bevel on one end so a tire will not have to roll over a sharp edge as it moves up onto the board; a bevel on both ends is convenient. We are used to working with the blocks and can level our trailer quickly with them, but some fulltimers might want to purchase levelers. A set of the tapered-ramp type would eliminate the need for carrying boards of different sizes. One simply drives the RV onto the ramp and stops when it has gone far enough up the incline to make it level. Such levels often come with a set of wheel chocks, which are necessary because the wheels are on an incline.

Often we have been able to level the trailer just by backing up or moving forward slightly in the site. This too is something you will be able to judge after a little practice. With a trailer, it is a simple matter to level it fore and aft by raising or lowering the tongue jack on a conventional trailer or the front jacks on a fifth-wheel trailer.

We haven't arranged our level placement for the driver's convenience. The leveling procedure goes faster if the driver stays put while another person checks the side-to-side level and either signals that the level is okay or places leveling boards where needed, then motions the driver to move onto the boards and signals that the tires are situated properly. This way the driver doesn't have to get in and out; the person who is out can do the running around.

We use jacks for the same reason we level the coach: comfort. We don't want a bouncy, unstable, springy home. Many RVers, however, don't bother with jacks.

When jacks are used, don't make the mistake of using stabilizing jacks—the common aluminum stacker jacks—for leveling; they are not designed for this purpose. It would be extremely difficult and dangerous to try to raise the weight of the coach with the jack's tiny handle since it would not provide nearly enough leverage.

Certain jacks are designed to level as well as stabilize. Some coaches may be equipped with this type of jack, or they might be offered as optional equipment. Permanently mounted to the coach frame, they are hinged and fold up under the bottom of the coach when not in use.

Some portable jacks can be used for both leveling and stabilizing; they will be clearly identified as being suitable for both functions.

Jacks should always be placed under chassis-frame members. In some instances, one end of a conventional trailer will be so low that a stacker jack with its threaded screw stem inserted will not fit, even if the stem is at its lowest point. Here's how we used to handle such situations:

1. Remove the stem (the jack can be used without it).
2. Place the base of the jack under the trailer.
3. Slide the jack along the desired frame member until it becomes snug. If there is no point where the jack is snug against the frame member, put the jack base on a board to raise it up.
4. If inserting a back jack, lower the tongue two turns; this will raise the rear of the trailer. (Give a short burst to an electric jack.)
5. Push the jack back until it is again snug.
6. Raise the tongue the same number of turns it was lowered to maintain the fore and aft level already established.
7. Check the jack to see that it is tight. If not, lower the tongue two turns again.
8. Move the jack farther back or prop it up a little more. Then raise the tongue again.

STABILIZING THE COACH
▼ ▼ ▼ ▼ ▼ ▼ ▼ ▼ ▼ ▼ ▼ ▼ ▼

To place a jack base under the front, raise the tongue first, then lower it.

Some permanently installed crank-down jacks cannot be used when the coach is too low to the ground. To be effective, the jack should be at least at a 45-degree angle. If the coach is high off the ground, blocks should be put under the jacks to achieve this angle.

Large motorhomes do not need stabilizing as much as trailers and small motorhomes because they have stiffer springs; they are less affected by people moving around in them.

Although it is not really needed, we use a kingpin jack for extra stability. If nothing else, it cuts down on shake at the front of the trailer in high winds.

CHOCKING

▼ ▼ ▼ ▼ ▼ ▼ ▼ ▼ ▼ ▼ ▼ ▼ ▼

Chocking the wheels is something we always do. It isn't absolutely necessary to chock the coach wheels if the site is perfectly level, but in an off-level site an RV could roll if the wheels are not chocked. We always feel more secure when we follow this procedure, and it is such an easy part of our setting-up routine that we do it regularly. That way, we never have to remember to chock the wheels if the site is off level.

We once used the triangular type of chock that rests on the ground next to the wheel, but some years ago we switched to the type that fits vertically between the tandem wheels (Figure 16.3). Enroute, when we have to park the trailer on a slope, perhaps when we stop for lunch or park in a lot to do some shopping, we use the chock.

A wheel chock can be anything that has enough height to prevent the tires from rolling up over it: a block of wood, a brick, a boulder, a tree branch, a log, or any one of the manufactured chocks.

AIDS FOR OUTSIDE WORK

▼ ▼ ▼ ▼ ▼ ▼ ▼ ▼ ▼ ▼ ▼ ▼ ▼

For most outside work and hitching or unhitching, we wear work gloves. Sometimes the leveling boards are muddy and unpleasant to handle without gloves, and when it is cold, gloves make it easier to work with cold metal.

Figure 16.3
A handy wheel chock that fits vertically between tandem wheels can be secured with a bicycle lock.

UTILITY HOOKUPS
▼ ▼ ▼ ▼ ▼ ▼ ▼ ▼ ▼ ▼ ▼ ▼

The first utility we check at a campsite, using a circuit-polarity analyzer, is the electricity. Each time we break camp, one of the things we do (it is on our checklist) is plug the analyzer in the outlet over the galley counter. It is visible through the window, which is on the street side, as is the shore-power cord and usually a site's electric hookup. After we arrive at the next campground and plug in the shore power, a glance in the window lets us know the state of the circuit.

We keep another analyzer in the compartment with the shore-power cord in case we need to check the electricity before pulling into a site. We often do this in places where the campground manager or attendant is not on duty to inform us about sites where there might be a problem with electrical service, or where the electric outlet looks old, burned, or otherwise suspect. Before we started this practice, there were a few times when we had parked in a site that was difficult to maneuver into, then found no electricity was available.

When we have a sewer hookup, we do not leave the drains on the holding tanks open (except in cold weather when they might freeze in the closed position). Some liquid should be allowed to accumulate along with the solids in the black-water holding tank so it will drain better. If we are spending some time in one campground, we empty the tanks only every three or four days. When we dump, the black-water tank is emptied first. After it is drained, the accumulated gray water is run through the hose to flush it out.

As we mentioned in Chapter 11, there are a number of reasons why we never hook up to outside water, but here's another one: We want to eliminate the possibility of the trailer being flooded with water. We have heard from other RVers about pipes rupturing when the owners were away from their RVs, causing the water to flow into their units until it was turned off at the outside faucet. We have been parked next to several trailers and noticed water dripping from the underbody—a sure sign that water is leaking inside the unit where it shouldn't be. If the owners were at home, we called it to their attention. If they were absent, we took it upon ourselves to turn off the water and either left a note on the door or informed the park manager about what we had done. If we did hook up to city water, we would make it a habit to turn off the water at the outside faucet before leaving the trailer for any extended period.

KEYS

▼ ▼ ▼ ▼ ▼ ▼ ▼ ▼ ▼ ▼ ▼ ▼

Every adult occupant of an RV should have a complete set of keys for everything connected with the RV. We go a step further and have a third complete set of keys that we keep in the trailer. If one of us should lose his or her set, the third set could be used until duplicates were made. If we happen to go outside without our keys and need them, the spare set is kept in a handy place so we can get to them.

Chapter 17

RV Driving and Handling Practices

M any people approach RVing as they do airplane travel, that is, trying to reach their destination as quickly as possible. But this is not what fulltiming is about. Traveling itself constitutes much of the fun in this vagabond lifestyle.

For full-timing couples, traveling should be a partnership. Truly rewarding and successful fulltiming comes from each partner knowing every aspect of operating and handling the rig.

M ost people would probably agree that driving on crowded highways for long periods of time is not fun. No one would choose to take up highway driving as a recreational pursuit, and we are sure no one becomes a fulltimer with the idea of spending most of the time behind the wheel of his or her rig.

Nothing will turn off people to traveling more than too much traveling. Driving back and forth across the country as fast as one can will quickly become boring.

Of course, driving is a large part of RV traveling, but there are ways to make it more fun and less of a drudgery—and at the same time safer: Simply do not go too far in a day's travel, or too fast. There is no reason to be in a hurry. For fulltimers one cliché

TAKE IT EASY
▼ ▼ ▼ ▼ ▼ ▼ ▼ ▼ ▼ ▼ ▼ ▼ ▼

Mileage craziness is a serious condition that exists in many forms. It can hit unsuspecting travelers while driving cars, motorcycles, riding in planes, crossing the country on bicycles, or on foot. The symptoms may lead to obsessively placing more importance on how many miles are traveled than on the real reason for traveling.

PETER JENKINS

▼ ▼ ▼ ▼ ▼ ▼ ▼ ▼ ▼ ▼ ▼ ▼

is especially true: Today is the first day of the rest of your life. Why speed through it on succeeding days? We don't think any occasions exist, save a life-or-death emergency, that would require a fulltimer to drive 500-mile days, or 400-mile days, or 300-mile days, or even 200-mile days. If you feel you must drive many miles to reach your destination, either allow more time for the trip or choose a closer destination. Our attitude is, if we have to drive long distances day after day, we might as well get a job driving an 18-wheeler and make some money at it.

Our day's runs are usually under 100 miles; if they exceed that amount, they rarely reach 150 miles. Many have been only 20 or 30 miles. Once we went just 3 miles — to another more appealing campground on the shore of a large lake.

▼ ▼ ▼

Short trips are easier on both people and equipment. After a long spell at the wheel, your reactions may not be as quick as they should be; you may become drowsy and find it difficult to be as attentive as necessary. Even if you and your partner share the driving chore equally, long driving days are tiring and often boring. A bonus of making the day's run short is that it will enable you to avoid night driving and night arrivals.

Our short runs allow us to leave late in the morning, after the rush-hour traffic, and to arrive at campgrounds before they fill up. We have plenty of time to stop along the way for sightseeing, shopping, and lunch. We can even delay our departure until after lunch if we desire. One of the greatest benefits of short trips is not having to drive fast to make miles.

Fulltimers who live in motorhomes may tend to drive for longer hours than those with trailers, because during travel, even though it's an unsafe practice, some motorhomers may prepare and eat simple meals and use the toilet facilities. Trailerists must stop every now and then for these purposes. But we find it refreshing to get out, stretch, walk around, and relax by concentrating on something other than the highway or traffic.

Tires will last longer if they are given a chance to cool down occasionally. Stopping provides an opportunity for visually checking the tires and hitch to see that everything is in order.

The speed at which you drive your rig affects its safety and your physical well-being. If you want the stress of battling for your space on the highways at fifty-five or sixty-five miles an hour, go ahead. We would ask you to wave at us as you go by, but you won't have time for any such pleasantries; you will be concentrating too much on the road.

Our experience has taught us that on interstate and four-lane highways with a top speed limit of fifty-five miles an hour, forty-five miles an hour is a good speed for us when towing the trailer. On interstates with a top speed of sixty-five miles per hour, we travel at either fifty or fifty-five miles per hour. These speeds have many advantages. They allow everyone who wants to travel at the speed limit to pass us without any problem. Since we do not keep up with the pack, we are never dangerously boxed in with other vehicles close ahead, behind, and beside us. All the traffic disperses around us, leaving plenty of space. We rarely have to switch lanes for passing because everyone is passing us.

When traveling at the lower speeds, it takes less time to slow down or come to a complete stop—something that must always be considered when driving a heavy rig. It allows a little more time to react in critical situations. When moving slower than the rest of the pack, there is even time enough to enjoy the scenery.

Not the least of the benefits of slowing down is that it will increase the amount of miles you get from each gallon of fuel. Cutting speed by as little as ten miles an hour can result in significant reduction in fuel consumption.

When we are on a two-lane highway, we will travel at our usual under-the-speed-limit rate if we are not holding up others behind us. When those behind have no opportunity for passing, we will travel at the posted speed limit if we cannot pull off onto the shoulder or other safe place to let them pass. Usually we cut our speed when another vehicle is passing us on a two-lane highway to enable the passing vehicle to get around us more quickly.

We do not like drivers who follow too closely behind, so we give them every opportunity to pass by signaling our intentions by tapping the brakes, edging over to the right as far as we can, then slowing down so they will not have to speed around us.

TAKE IT SLOW
━━━━━━━━━━━━━━━
▼ ▼ ▼ ▼ ▼ ▼ ▼ ▼ ▼ ▼ ▼ ▼

*T*hanks to the interstate highway system, it is now possible to travel from coast to coast without seeing anything.

CHARLES KURALT
━━━━━━━━━━━━━━━
▼ ▼ ▼ ▼ ▼ ▼ ▼ ▼ ▼ ▼ ▼ ▼

NO SCHEDULE IS THE BEST SCHEDULE

▼ ▼ ▼ ▼ ▼ ▼ ▼ ▼ ▼ ▼ ▼ ▼ ▼

The hazards of too-rigid preplanning are many. No one can know in advance what lies ahead each day. A schedule may be upset by traffic jams, bad weather, or detours. When this happens, most schedule makers feel they have to make up for time lost. The result may be that they drive too fast or too long, creating a great deal of stress for themselves in the process. Those that set tight schedules for themselves are not in the best humor when they are not on schedule.

Our preplanning involves nothing more than deciding to be out of the cold weather in the winter and the hot weather in the summer. Even such loose planning does not always work out for us. We often end up spending time in places where the climate is less than ideal because we have found something we think is worth staying around for, regardless of the weather.

▼ ▼ ▼

When people ask us where we will be next month or next week, we can never give them a definite answer; we simply don't know. If we think we know where we will be at some future date, we still won't tell anyone about it—not anymore, that is; we might change our minds.

A few years ago we decided to go quite far south for the winter months. We met a friendly couple in a campground as we were on our way and found we were bound for the same area. The other couple was planning to stay in that area for several months; we didn't know how long we would end up staying once we got there. We agreed to look up the couple when we arrived. Our newfound friends were traveling much faster than we were (it seems as if everybody travels faster than we do) and left early next morning. As we were heading south late in the morning, we changed our minds about where we wanted to spend the winter, and went back to the campground where we had been the night before. The rate was reasonable, it was in an area we liked, and far enough south so that any winter storms would not be too severe. It would also be a base from which we could explore the interesting, surrounding countryside.

We eventually moved a little farther south—we don't like to spend months at a time in one place—but we never got as far

I think there is a fatality in it—I seldom go to the place I set out for.

L. STERNE

▼ ▼ ▼ ▼ ▼ ▼ ▼ ▼ ▼ ▼ ▼ ▼ ▼

into the Sunbelt as we had "planned," and, of course, we never rendezvoused with the friendly couple either.

Leaving a campground and then returning within hours was somewhat unusual for us. Normally, we would decide to stay over before we were on the road. We are more likely to change our plans about where we are going in the middle of our driving day. We might stop sooner or go on for a few more miles than we planned. Then again, we might take off onto a beckoning route in a different direction.

Once, we stopped for lunch in a remote rest area on a little-used highway. It was on a high hill overlooking a beautiful valley. We decided to spend the night there, since we found no restrictions on camping overnight.

Our loose scheduling doesn't mean we are irresponsible or undependable. We are just taking advantage of one of the greatest features of fulltiming: the ability to go where and when we please. After years of having nothing but time-restricted vacations, it's a wonderful feeling to know we do not have to be in a certain place on a specified date, a freedom we enjoy immensely.

AVOIDING CROWDED HIGHWAYS

▼ ▼ ▼ ▼ ▼ ▼ ▼ ▼ ▼ ▼ ▼ ▼

When we have a choice, we much prefer any road that is not an interstate or a main highway because most such roads are never crowded. If we must use an interstate to get to where we are going, we will rarely be found on it late on a Friday afternoon and never on a Friday afternoon before a long holiday weekend. As we mentioned earlier, we generally do not travel on weekends at all, especially in the summer. We don't need to be on the roads at these times, so why add to the crowding and why put ourselves in the situation of driving on traffic-clogged roads?

In July and August, we avoid roads that are the only routes to popular vacation areas. If we want to visit these areas, some of which are only open or accessible in the summer, and have to use such a route, we park the trailer somewhere else and do our visiting in the truck.

Limited-access, high-speed highways such as expressways, freeways, and interstates are the best and quickest ways to travel through big cities, but they often have heavy traffic. To avoid the traffic as much as possible, we avoid entering or leaving a large city during the rush hours in the morning and evening, especially if we have never been there before. We have found that the noon hour is one of the least crowded times on these highways; most of the truckers are stopped for lunch, eliminating much of the traffic.

DEALING WITH INCLEMENT WEATHER
▼ ▼ ▼ ▼ ▼ ▼ ▼ ▼ ▼ ▼ ▼ ▼ ▼

If the weather is very bad, don't travel unless you have to. Fulltimers can wait out blizzards, cloudbursts, high winds, dust storms, and fog. By the same token, we can move our rigs out of the path of hurricanes and flooding.

If you are caught in a bad storm while traveling, try to find a place where you can safely pull off the road and wait it out. The shoulder is *not* a safe place. If you are having trouble with visibility, so is every other driver on the road. Someone may decide to pull off onto the shoulder just where you are parked. Try to find a turnout, rest area, or parking lot where you will be well off the road.

When weather conditions deteriorate, always reduce speed. In heavy rain or blowing snow, the windshield wipers may not be able to remove the rain or snow fast enough to provide good forward visibility at fast speeds.

Note instructional road signs and slow down for curves more than you normally would. Pay attention to warning signs about wind-gust areas, blowing dust, and the like. Be mentally prepared for anything that could happen.

Even light rain or mist can make highways slippery. In slippery conditions, reduce speed so there will be no problem with stopping if it should be necessary.

HANDLING LONG, HEAVY RIGS
▼ ▼ ▼ ▼ ▼ ▼ ▼ ▼ ▼ ▼ ▼ ▼ ▼

Both the length and weight of a rig affect its performance and handling. The length necessitates wider turns at corners. The weight will affect slowing and stopping, requiring more braking and stopping distance for both. Heavy head winds will increase fuel consumption markedly, while tail winds will provide a boost. Strong winds hitting a rig broadside require that the person at the wheel pay strict attention to his or her driving.

Long trailers are more affected than shorter ones by pull or sway from passing trucks. Those who are caught off guard and who are not prepared for the suction that may ensue encounter the most problems from passing trucks. When a truck is seen in the mirror in the passing lane and well behind the rig, it's time for *both* the driver's hands to be on the wheel in order to hold it as steady as possible as the truck passes. The speed at which we habitually drive, usually less than that of passing trucks, helped cut down on our conventional trailer's tendency to yaw. (Passing trucks don't have much effect on fifth-wheels.) Regular monitoring of the mirrors lets us know when we are about to be passed by a truck.

▼ ▼ ▼

If your trailer starts to yaw, don't panic; the yawing can be corrected. Keep a firm grip on the wheel and try to steer as straight as possible. Don't try to correct for the yaw. The idea is to keep the trailer and the tow vehicle in the normal configuration—in a straight line. Sometimes increasing speed will help to straighten out the rig. If you feel you must brake, use only the trailer brakes (by using the manual override lever on the controller) and brake for just a second or two at a time.

Constant problems with suction caused by passing trucks call for an assessment of hitch equipment to determine if it is adequate, if it is installed correctly, or if the hitch weight is heavy enough. If all are satisfactory and problems still exist when trucks pass, you are probably traveling too fast. Certain wind speeds and directions can also increase truck suction. Be extra cautious on windy days.

Some who have trailers find towing them to be a chore because they do not track well. Such problems can usually be traced to the hitch area: its size, its installation, how much tension is on the equalizer bars or the hitch weight. Towing should be easy and effortless if the trailer and tow vehicle are properly hitched with the right equipment.

When driving through cities on six- or eight-lane expressways, freeways, or interstate highways, we stay out of the far right lane so we will not be affected by entering and exiting traffic. When driving in the far right lane, traffic might prevent you from moving to the to the left to make room for entering vehicles so you might have to slow down. Slowing and stopping cause most chain-reaction accidents on high-speed, multi-lane highways. An added concern about driving in the far right lane is that nearly all lanes marked "exit only" are far right lanes. You might be shunted off the highway at a place you didn't intend to go because it was impossible to move over into another lane.

The middle lane on a six-lane highway or the lane second from the right on an eight-lane highway is best for traveling through; however, using these lanes means you will have to travel at the speed of the rest of the traffic. Going slower than the maximum posted speed limit is only feasible in the far right lane.

▼ ▼ ▼

Forget about fast getaways from a standing stop with any kind of full-timing rig; it can't be done. But the rig should be accelerated as rapidly as possible when entering an interstate or other high-speed thoroughfare, whether in urban or rural areas. The safest way to merge into the traffic on such highways is to move at the same speed as the traffic. Then the rig can be inserted into a smaller hole and the other vehicles on the road will be spared having to dodge around a slow-moving entering vehicle. It's dangerous to be pokey or indecisive when entering a high-speed highway. When making lane changes or proceeding onto a highway, use turn signals and make sure they are turned off after the maneuver.

Rig drivers don't like to make U-turns on highways, but often it is the easiest or only method for correcting a navigating mistake (if the law allows). A long motorhome towing an auxiliary vehicle will need many lanes in order to execute the maneuver. We read about one motorhome/auxiliary vehicle combination that required seven lanes to make a U-turn. We could negotiate U-turns with our 23-footer on a two-lane highway as long as there were wide shoulders on both sides, so in effect we used about four lanes for the turn. Longer trailers would need more room. U-turns with a fifth-wheel trailer are a snap. The fifth-wheel driver can start from a narrow shoulder on a two-lane highway and turn into the far lane without swinging wide. Fifth-wheels can be turned with the truck at a ninety-degree angle to the trailer, but it must be done very slowly to avoid actually rolling the tires from the rims since the fifth-wheel trailer pivots on the tires.

Long trailers and motorhomes have a good deal of overhang on the rear, and when they are turned, the rear end makes a wide arc. Caution will have to be exercised so the rear end doesn't wipe out such things as mailboxes that may be positioned close to the road.

Rigs that carry heavy weights on the rear bumper may yaw even when traveling on a straightaway with no other vehicles creating suction, and the rig will be hard to control when turns are made at too high a speed.

Too much weight too high in the RV, or in roof pods, will raise the already high center of gravity that RVs have and may create handling instability. When cornering, the sensation may be one of toppling over because of the top-heaviness. High winds can affect the stability of top-heavy rigs, especially winds that hit the rig broadside. Distributing some of the weight to places lower in the rig will help to alleviate the problem.

The front of fifth-wheel trailers may kiss the side walls or tailgate of the pickup on a short, steep incline such as those found at entrances to some parking lots, and the rear of any rig can drag on such an incline.

When driving a motorhome or towing a trailer, you may not be able to go up and down hills as quickly as you might like. Be patient, especially on long, steep grades. Because of the weight of the rig, when going uphill you may be practically crawling before reaching the top, but so what? No hill in the country suitable for taking a full-timing rig on is so long or so steep that it would cause any significant amount of lost time because it could not be climbed at top speed.

UP AND DOWN HILLS
▼ ▼ ▼ ▼ ▼ ▼ ▼ ▼ ▼ ▼ ▼ ▼ ▼

If you are one of those who is disturbed by being passed by nearly everyone else, you had better change your attitude, stick to the flatlands, or give up driving an RV rig.

This continent, an open palm spread frank before the sky.

JAMES AGEE

▼ ▼ ▼ ▼ ▼ ▼ ▼ ▼ ▼ ▼ ▼ ▼

Any combination of steepness, high altitude, and hot weather can cause problems for some vehicles. We try to pick routes that do not go over the highest passes. If a steep grade is on our route, we might stop at a campground nearby and scout it out before taking the trailer over it. Mainly we check the steepness of the grade, and look for places where we could pull off the road if we needed to.

We made one such scouting expedition at Townes Pass, leading into Death Valley from the west. The pass reaches an elevation of only about 5,000 feet, but the grade is thirteen percent. One of our maps noted that it was not recommended for trailers. To reach Death Valley from our location via the only other existing route would have meant an extra 100 miles of driving on a mundane highway that did not interest us.

Other business took us to the vicinity of the pass, so we only went a few miles out of our way to check it out. Scouting in the truck, we found the uphill grade was not thirteen percent all the way; in several places it leveled out to a much more moderate incline. Quite a few spots were available where we could pull off and park well off the highway. We had no worries about overheating because of hot weather since it was December.

We decided to chance it. We made it, albeit very slowly, with no problems whatsoever. No overheating occurred because almost immediately after we started the uphill climb we had to shift into second gear, then soon afterward into first gear. Every downshift we made lowered the temperature, which had begun to rise slowly.

▼ ▼ ▼

Downshifting is a good method for preventing overheating when climbing hills. Never mind that using the lower gears sometimes makes it necessary to crawl up the grades — we were down to eighteen miles an hour at one point on Townes Pass — if you are a fulltimer you don't need to be in a hurry. If traffic behind you cannot pass because the grade hasn't a slow-vehicle lane (major highways with steep grades usually have this extra lane) or a shoulder wide enough for safe travel, it is not really your problem. You can only proceed according to the capabilities of your vehicle. Those behind will have to put up with your slowness for the few minutes it takes.

When going downhill, downshifting will allow the engine's compression to help in slowing without using the brakes constantly. All rigs perform differently when going downhill depending on the steepness of the grade and the weight of the rig. On certain grades, the weight of the trailer seems to hold us back; on others we need to do considerable braking.

▼ ▼ ▼

Brakes should never be applied constantly or they will overheat. (Aside from avoiding heat buildup, the less brakes are used, the longer they can go before having to be relined.) When too much heat builds up, brakes may fade or fail. It works this way: As brakes begin to heat up, more pedal pressure must be applied. Eventually, no more pedal pressure can be exerted. When this happens, no reserve braking power is left, and it may be impossible to slow down. Trailerists can use the trailer brakes to aid in slowing, but these brakes should only be activated intermittently for a second or two at a time. Those driving a motorhome and towing an auxiliary vehicle must be extremely cautious; the considerable extra weight of the car puts that much more load on the brakes of the motorhome. Motorhomes can be equipped with a device called a retarder, which will keep the rig from picking up speed on a downgrade.

Heed grade-warning signs. Check brakes before beginning a long downgrade. We make it a practice to start down steep grades at a very slow speed. If there is a place where we can pull off at the top of the grade, we often do so to allow all traffic to get around us so we can negotiate the grade at our own speed.

Everyone knows that backing a motorhome is much easier than backing a trailer because it is one unit, and it is not necessary to contend with another unit hitched to it that often seems to have a mind of its own. However, if the motorhome is towing an auxiliary vehicle, either with a tow bar or tow dolly, it will have to be unhitched before any backing is done; it is almost

BACKING A MOTORHOME
▼ ▼ ▼ ▼ ▼ ▼ ▼ ▼ ▼ ▼ ▼ ▼

impossible to control the movements of a hitched auxiliary vehicle when backing.

Some sites are laid out so that a motorhomer backing in might wish his or her unit did bend in the middle like a trailer. In such sites, where the ability to jackknife would be an advantage, motorhomers, especially those who have units with considerable rear overhang, will have to pay particular attention to the rear of the unit. It may swing beyond the side perimeters of the site into trees or shrubbery or something else that could cause damage to the motorhome.

Most drivers will have to back by using the side mirrors, since many motorhomes don't have rear windows, or if they do, they are too far from the cockpit to provide the driver with much visibility. Some motorhome owners might want the additional aid of a rearview TV monitor.

BACKING A CONVENTIONAL TRAILER

▼ ▼ ▼ ▼ ▼ ▼ ▼ ▼ ▼ ▼ ▼ ▼ ▼ ▼

When it comes to backing a conventional trailer, here's the oft-cited way of determining wheel-turning and direction when backing: Put your hand at the bottom of the steering wheel; whichever direction you move your hand is the way the rear of the trailer will go. This is good advice as far as it goes and the simple instruction is easy to remember, but once into the maneuvering, it is no longer relevant. Backing requires both hands on the wheel to control it during the several turns needed during the operation. Furthermore, the interaction between the tow vehicle and trailer is not immediate; some distance may be covered before the steering wheel transmits its movement to the trailer (See Figure 17.1).

We would suggest placing your hands on the wheel in a normal fashion and keeping your eyes glued to the driver's side mirror so that every movement of the trailer can be seen. When the back of the trailer moves in a direction you don't want, turn the wheel in the other direction. Of course, when the trailer is lined up straight and you want to back straight, you will need to glance at the steering wheel to see if it is in the position where the tow vehicle's wheels are straight.

Understanding the different pivot points involved in backing a conventional trailer may shed some light on the seemingly

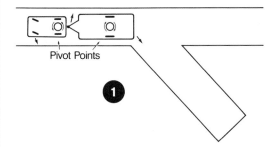

Pivot Points

1

When beginning to back a trailer to the left, turn the wheels of the tow vehicle to the right. Note position of trailer wheels in relation to campsite.

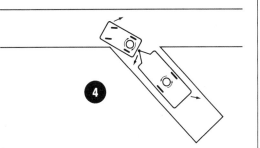

4

When the trailer is at the desired angle, a movement must be started to bring the tow vehicle and trailer into line. This is accomplished by turning the tow vehicle's wheels again to the left.

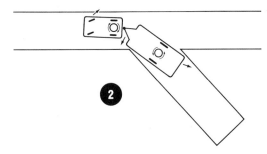

2

When the trailer starts to turn, the wheels of the tow vehicle should be turned to the left for a short time to prevent the trailer from turning too sharply.

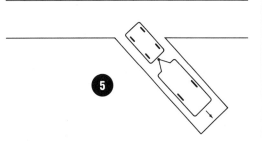

5

As soon as the trailer and tow vehicle are aligned, straighten the tow vehicle's wheels and complete backing into the site.

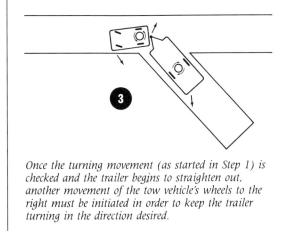

3

Once the turning movement (as started in Step 1) is checked and the trailer begins to straighten out, another movement of the tow vehicle's wheels to the right must be initiated in order to keep the trailer turning in the direction desired.

Figure 17.1
Five steps to successful trailer backing.

mysterious subject. The tow vehicle pivots on its rear wheels. Several feet away from the rear wheels is another pivot point: the hitch. The trailer itself pivots on its wheels.

When backing, as the front wheels of the tow vehicle are turned to the *right*, the front of the tow vehicle moves to the *left*. As the tow vehicle is pivoting on its rear wheels, it forces the pivot point of the hitch (the ball and coupler) to the *right*. As a result, the rear of the trailer will begin to turn to the *left*. Therefore, turn the wheels of the tow vehicle in the opposite direction you want the trailer to go (See Step 1, Figure 17.1).

Once the trailer is in its turning mode, things will not remain status quo. The trailer will not continue turning in a constant circle. It will describe more of a spiral movement, which will become progressively tighter as the turning continues, and will eventually cause the trailer to jackknife. If the tow vehicle's wheels are straightened out after the initial turning effort, the trailer still will jackknife eventually. A countermovement must be started because, once into the turn, the only control the driver has is to either increase or decrease the rate of turn.

Decreasing the rate of turn is achieved by turning the wheels in the same direction as the direction of turn (See Step 2, Figure 17.1). The rate of turn is increased by turning the wheels in the opposite direction to the direction of the turn, just as is done in the initial turning movement (See Step 3, Figure 17.1). It requires considerably more distance to decrease the rate of turn than it does to increase it.

If the trailer turns too much, it can be straightened out quickly by turning the tow vehicle's wheels in the direction opposite the way the trailer is turning and pulling forward a few feet. It may be necessary to increase and decrease the rate of turn several times before the trailer is maneuvered into position (See Steps 4 and 5, Figure 17.1).

BACKING A FIFTH-WHEEL TRAILER

▼ ▼ ▼ ▼ ▼ ▼ ▼ ▼ ▼ ▼ ▼ ▼ ▼

Backing a fifth-wheel trailer is, in theory, the same as backing a conventional trailer: the wheels of the tow vehicle are turned in the opposite direction from the way the rear of the trailer is to go. But because the hitch pivot point on a fifth-wheel is just about over the rear wheels of the tow vehicle, all turning actions are much quicker and all correcting actions take longer. Given the same attitude of the tow vehicle's wheels, a fifth-wheel trailer will jackknife more rapidly than a conventional trailer. Turning the tow vehicle's wheels in the opposite direction cannot unjackknife the trailer unless the trailer has many, many feet in which it can be maneuvered while backing — certainly not the situation with most campsites. The only practical way to unjackknife a fifth-wheel is by pulling forward. The jackknifing tendency is an advantage when maneuvering into some tight sites, once you get the hang of how to control it. In fact, a fifth-wheel trailer can be more easily maneuvered into some sites than can a conventional trailer (See Exhibit 17.1 for backing-up tips).

When a fifth-wheel is backed up, any adjustment of the tow vehicle's wheels is transmitted to the trailer much more rapidly than with a conventional trailer, consequently just a slight turn of the tow vehicle's wheels will result in a quick, sharper turn of the trailer. Such movements can be avoided by making turns as shallow as possible. Some general safe-backing tips are listed in Exhibit 17.1.

▼ ▼ ▼ ▼ ▼ ▼ ▼ ▼ ▼ ▼ ▼ ▼ ▼ ▼ ▼

Exhibit 17.1
Backing-up Tips

The following list will aid in backing your rig:

▼ If you are unsure of what is happening when backing, stop, get out, and take a look.
▼ When backing, take it slow, stop, and analyze what movement is needed before proceeding. It isn't necessary to keep the rig moving all the time.
▼ A slightly angled site is easier to maneuver into than a site at a right angle to the road.
▼ The shorter the trailer, the more quickly it will turn.
▼ A backing turn to the left is easier to execute than backing and turning to the right because it affords the driver better visibility.

▼ If the campsite is edged with a curb, remember that a trailer is wider than the tow vehicle. Keep the tow vehicle's wheels well away from the curb to avoid scraping the trailer tires against it. If the trailer wheels are too close to the curb, neither backing nor going forward may move them away. To move out, it may be necessary to ride up on the curb or go over it, neither of which will do the tires any good. When parallel parking next to a curb, follow the same practice; keep the trailer wheels well away from the curb.

When backing any trailer, don't hesitate to pull forward as often as needed if the trailer starts to turn too much or if you have misjudged any distance or maneuver. Anyone who backs a trailer should realize that pulling forward is one of the best maneuvers for successful backing. It is the rare back-in site that doesn't require us to pull forward at least three or four times before we can maneuver easily into it.

When learning, stop the rig each time the wheels are turned and think about what is happening instead of moving constantly. Whenever possible, avoid extremes in turning the wheel. Overcorrecting causes more difficult situations than undercorrecting does.

PRACTICE, PRACTICE, PRACTICE

▼ ▼ ▼ ▼ ▼ ▼ ▼ ▼ ▼ ▼ ▼ ▼

Practice makes perfect. The only way to learn is to practice, practice, practice. To perfect your backing technique, try practicing in a large shopping-center parking lot when there is not much traffic in the area.

Back up with the wheel turned in either direction just to see how it affects the trailer's movement. Learn to achieve the movement desired by turning the wheel as little as possible.

Practice backing straight by looking in the left-side mirror. This will give you a good feel for how to turn the wheel to make the trailer behave the way you want. You will find that the wheel must be constantly turned — a little this way, a little that way — in order to back straight.

Try to put the trailer between the lines marking one of the parking spaces. The width of the parking space will be narrower than the average campsite, so if the trailer can be put neatly into it, campsites should present no problems. Approach the space from ahead and from each side. Learn how far to pull past the parking space to allow enough room for turning into it. Notice the position of the trailer's wheels and how they track when turning into the site.

In all backing situations with a trailer or motorhome, take your time. Stop frequently and get out to assess the situation. Develop a parking routine with your partner (if you travel with one), then rely on your partner when parking the rig. Strangers, even campground personnel, who want to be helpful can lead you astray or give you confusing directions or signals.

An economy of direction signals is better than a series of gestures. When we want the trailer to go in a certain direction, we merely extend our arm and point in that direction. The direction-giver is often stationed on the edge of the site so the driver knows that the trailer must be positioned beyond the stationed person.

Your partner should give only three basic instructions:

1. Come back (or ahead)
2. The direction to turn to correct a situation
3. Stop

The direction-giver should always be in view of the driver in one of the side mirrors so hand signals can be seen, or be walking alongside the vehicle in a position where verbal instructions can be given (which we usually do when the site is to the right of the truck). Those with long rigs who need someone at the rear to keep a check on what is going on back there might use two-way radios to communicate with one another.

The best direction-givers are those who have had experience in backing the rig themselves. They better understand what the driver needs to know. If your partner gives you the wrong directions, do not make a fuss about it; everyone makes mistakes. Discuss only what is necessary to get the job done. Spare others any denouncements of your partner's abilities. If necessary, talk over the problem later, in private, to achieve a mutual understanding so the situation won't happen again.

Perhaps this will be encouraging if you have any trepidations about backing: Every tight spot we have encountered in backing and parking the trailer has been the result of our own bad judgment in assessing the situation. Most of the problems occurred when we were novice trailerists. We have profited from our experiences—as you will profit from yours—and we rarely have any backing and parking problems any more.

Although many campgrounds will have sites for large RVs, these same campgrounds may have roads that are unsuitable for the RV to reach the site. They may be narrow, curving, have trees or other obstacles close to the edge of the road, ditches may exist

DRIVING THROUGH CAMPGROUNDS
▼ ▼ ▼ ▼ ▼ ▼ ▼ ▼ ▼ ▼ ▼ ▼

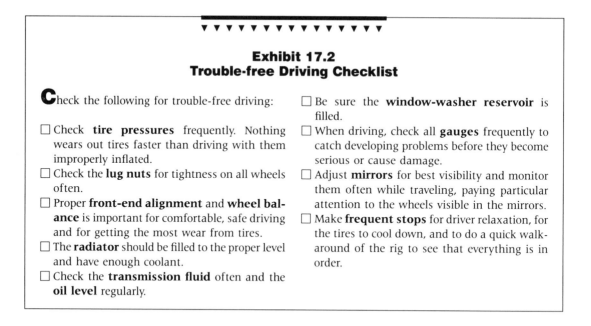

▼ ▼ ▼ ▼ ▼ ▼ ▼ ▼ ▼ ▼ ▼ ▼ ▼ ▼

Exhibit 17.2
Trouble-free Driving Checklist

Check the following for trouble-free driving:

☐ Check **tire pressures** frequently. Nothing wears out tires faster than driving with them improperly inflated.

☐ Check the **lug nuts** for tightness on all wheels often.

☐ Proper **front-end alignment** and **wheel balance** is important for comfortable, safe driving and for getting the most wear from tires.

☐ The **radiator** should be filled to the proper level and have enough coolant.

☐ Check the **transmission fluid** often and the **oil level** regularly.

☐ Be sure the **window-washer reservoir** is filled.

☐ When driving, check all **gauges** frequently to catch developing problems before they become serious or cause damage.

☐ Adjust **mirrors** for best visibility and monitor them often while traveling, paying particular attention to the wheels visible in the mirrors.

☐ Make **frequent stops** for driver relaxation, for the tires to cool down, and to do a quick walk-around of the rig to see that everything is in order.

on either side of the road, or there may be any combination of these factors. If you have a large rig, it might be prudent to walk through such a campground to judge if you can make it through. If you venture onto such a road unawares, you may find yourself at an impasse, with the only way out being the way you came in, except that getting out will have to be done by backing. For trouble-free and enjoyable RVing, general safe-driving tips are listed in Exhibit 17.2.

Chapter 18

Customizing the Cockpit

▼ ▼ ▼ ▼ ▼ ▼ ▼ ▼ ▼

Since many fulltimers spend a fair amount of their time driving, the driver-passenger area, or the cockpit as it is usually called, should be outfitted to make it efficient and comfortable. Whether you drive a motorhome or tow vehicle, you will want certain items near at hand. Maps and directories should be easy to consult; if fuel or service records or a trip log are kept, they should be conveniently at hand for making entries; other items, such as a beverage holder or a litter bag, should be handy for use.

Many motorhomes have a spacious cockpit area that can be adapted for storage of items needed while traveling. We say *adapted* because many of the motorhome builders don't take advantage of the cockpit space available, and it is often devoid of storage compartments. On many models, there is plenty of room between the driver and passenger seats for a built-in cabinet or chest. Only a few manufacturers actually install such storage compartments in their units. It is entirely possible that a ready-made piece of furniture would fit into such an area: a night table or end table with drawers only, or with a couple of drawers and a

EXTRA STORAGE

▼ ▼ ▼ ▼ ▼ ▼ ▼ ▼ ▼ ▼ ▼ ▼ ▼

enclosed cabinet in the bottom, for example. Perhaps a top-opening chest might be used.

Our tow vehicle, a regular-cab pickup truck, does not have a lot of storage space in the cab. As on most vehicles, the glove box is small and, as on most similar trucks, the space behind the seat is not ideal or convenient for storage. Through the years, though, by trial and error, we have managed to arrange for quite a bit of in-the-cab storage space.

If you have a standard pickup truck as a tow vehicle, you might want to adapt some of our ideas for your own driver-passenger area. Those who drive motorhomes or more spacious tow vehicles also may find some helpful ideas.

▼ ▼ ▼ A Custom-made Container

The first thing we did to gain storage space was to put a large container in the middle of the bench seat (Figure 18.1). It's nothing more than a 14 × 14 × 7-inch plastic container that fits nicely between the driver and the passenger seats.

The container would not stay put without something to hold it in place, so we engineered a holder into which the container fits. The holder was originally made of fabric, but when it became faded and old we made another one from more sturdy, fade-resistant, vinyl upholstery material.

Three sides of this boxlike holder are no higher than the container. The fourth side is an extended back, a fourteen-inch-wide strip of fabric that reaches up and over the seat back.

Four Velcro/elastic tabs are attached to the holder to keep it in place. To make the tabs, a one-inch-long piece of Velcro was sewn onto one end of a three-inch length of one-inch-wide elastic. One tab is attached to each corner of the extended back and another to each of the back lower corners of the box section. The holder is secured by passing the box-section's tabs through the seat back and joining them to the extended back's tabs with the Velcro.

The elastic's stretchiness allows the seat back to be pushed forward without straining the holder. The Velcro makes it easy to remove the holder for cleaning.

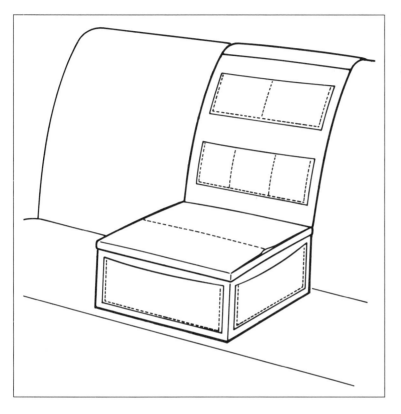

Figure 18.1
A rigid container fits into the specially made fabric "box." The container is covered with a hinged lid made of plywood.

Three sides of the holder have pockets running nearly the full width and depth of the sides; the back has two rows of small pockets sewn on another pocket that is the full width of the back and almost its height; this pocket was sized to hold a large road atlas.

We fashioned a lid of ½-inch plywood for the container. It rests on the top edge of the container and is kept from shifting by cleats on the underside. The lid is hinged across the middle (with a piano hinge so the top is as smooth as possible) and covered with the vinyl. The vinyl is attached with contact cement except in the hinge area where it was left loose so it can flex when the lid is raised. The edges were finished with a cemented-on strip of the vinyl.

The sides and bottom of the container itself are gridwork. To keep small items from falling through the openings in the grid, we put a thin piece of foam in the bottom; cardboard would do just as well.

The container is at a convenient height for an armrest, and the covering on the lid keeps clothes from snagging on raw wood. When we are traveling, the container serves as a storage place for items we do not like to leave in view when we are away from the truck.

We keep maps in the side pockets, and pencils, pens, markers, magnifying glass, penlight, and scratch paper in the smaller pockets.

We mounted a small suction cup with a hook on the windshield above and to the right of the rear-view mirror, on which we hang a spring clip. When we must remember to do something, we jot it on a piece of the scrap paper and put the paper in the clip. It is located directly in front of us and can't be overlooked, but it's high enough so it doesn't interfere with visibility. When we have been away from civilization for a while and plan on spending a few days in a town, we make a list of everything we want to do in town. A typical list might remind us to go to the bank, pick up mail at the post office, do laundry, take care of servicing or maintenance on the truck or the trailer, and purchase specialized items.

▼ ▼ ▼ Beverages

Our truck has no built-in beverage holder, so we bought a ready-made one and attached it to the carpeting over the floor hump.

Unlike those with motorhomes, we do not have access to drinking water unless we stop and go back to the trailer, so we installed a small, pump-type vacuum jug on the floor of the passenger side. A loop of one-inch-wide webbing with Velcro tabs, attached to the sidewall with a screw, holds the jug in place and upright. Using the cups kept in the beverage holder makes it convenient to get a drink. Such a jug can also be used for coffee or soft drinks.

▼ ▼ ▼ Other Cockpit Items

For a while, we had a gun rack mounted on the rear cab window, but did not use it for guns. At times we hung items from its lower hooks, as long as the items were not so large that they interfered with our visibility. Fabric hats were folded into a small package and secured in the upper hooks.

If we did a significant amount of night driving, we would have some sort of map light if the vehicle weren't already equipped with one.

We have compartmentalized the area behind the seat by installing a length of fabric with various sizes of pockets sewn on it. The fabric runs the full distance across the back of the cab and is attached along its upper edge by screws through grommeted holes. Underneath, resting on the shelf behind the seat, are several boxes we custom-made to fit the items we store there.

▼ ▼ ▼ Directories, Maps, and Books

Our campground directories are kept under the passenger seat. Along with the large Trailer Life campground directory, we have various smaller directories. We keep all this material together in a bag made of sturdy fabric. The large directory slips easily into the bag while a deep pocket on one side of the bag holds most of the smaller publications. It's easy to grasp the bag, and when we pull it out, we have all the reference material about campgrounds together in one place.

For quick reference, we keep two markers in the Trailer Life directory. One is on the page with the map for the relevant state, the other is on the page listing the town where we intend to stay. When nearing our destination, we can easily locate the page we need for directions to the selected campground. The directory also comes with a set of tabs that allow the user to customize the book as he or she wishes.

Maps are, of course, essential items for travel, and most of us refer to them frequently when we are under way. The technology for folding most maps conveniently still has not been perfected,

▼ ▼ ▼

I have an existential map. It has "You are here" written all over it.

STEVEN WRIGHT

▼ ▼ ▼ ▼ ▼ ▼ ▼ ▼ ▼ ▼ ▼ ▼

so we do not bother folding and unfolding them. Instead, we open them to the general area in which we are traveling and put them on a clipboard. So the driver and the passenger (who is always chief navigator on our rig) can see and use the maps easily, the clipboard is kept on the lid of the storage container between us.

Since we do not cover several states in a day's travel, or even much of one state on most days, we do not have to keep changing maps. Once a map is opened to a certain area, it usually stays in that position for several days or even weeks.

We like to have as many maps of a state or area as we can lay our hands on. Our basic maps are the ones we receive as members of the American Automobile Association. We still have many state maps collected from service stations when they gave them away free of charge. Sometimes we will purchase a state or area map, and we always try to obtain a state's official map. In addition to other maps, we often have a U.S. Forest Service or Bureau of Land Management map, which we use for exploring backwoods roads.

Each publisher's map is different from another's. On some maps, the historic sites are well marked and include famous and not-so-famous sites. Others may have more secondary roads indicated. Some have more general informative details, such as the altitudes of cities, and often official state maps have more information than any other for that particular state.

When we are in big cities, we use a large-scale map of the city with all streets indicated, and another map of the metroplitan area. This is often found on the map of the state. A less-detailed map of the cities in the state may also be found on the official map. These maps are handy for determining the major routes in and around the city.

We also carry a sectional map for the part of the country in which we are traveling. Our penchant for maps does not stop there. We also have the large road atlas, mentioned earlier, to which we frequently refer when, as we are driving, we discuss places we might visit in the future. The atlas comes in handy for answering questions that may arise about routes, distances, and other things we need to know.

Many RVers carry a few books, specific to the area they will be traversing or related to their particular interests: birding, archaeology, history, or others. Local bookstores have the best selection on areas you are traveling through.

▼ ▼ ▼ Instruments

Aside from the instruments and gauges necessary for operating the vehicle, you might want to add some others for your own pleasure and to satisfy your curiosity.

We have a compass and an altimeter, a clock that gives the time and date, and a thermometer. We are looking for a very small thermometer that can be put on a window outside and be visible from inside.

For a compass to be worthwhile it must be the type that can be corrected (or adjusted). Although correcting is relatively easy (detailed instructions come with the compass), it may be difficult to locate streets or roads that run exactly north and south and east and west, which are necessary for proper correction. Expect to pay upwards of $15 for such an instrument.

▼ ▼ ▼ The Log Book

We keep a log because we like to have a record of where we have been, the campgrounds at which we have stayed, and the people we have met.

The preprinted logs on the market don't have enough pages for extensive travel and never seem to have spaces for all the things we want to enter, so we use a spiral-bound stenographer's notebook as a log (Figure 18.2). The entries are written horizontally instead of vertically. Two different entries are made on one page using the center line to separate them.

Every time we move the trailer, we make a log entry consisting of the day, date, town, or place from which we are leaving; starting mileage; and time of departure. When we arrive at our destination, we enter the mileage on the speedometer, as well as

Figure 18.2
A stenographer's notebook makes an easy-to-use log to record trip information.

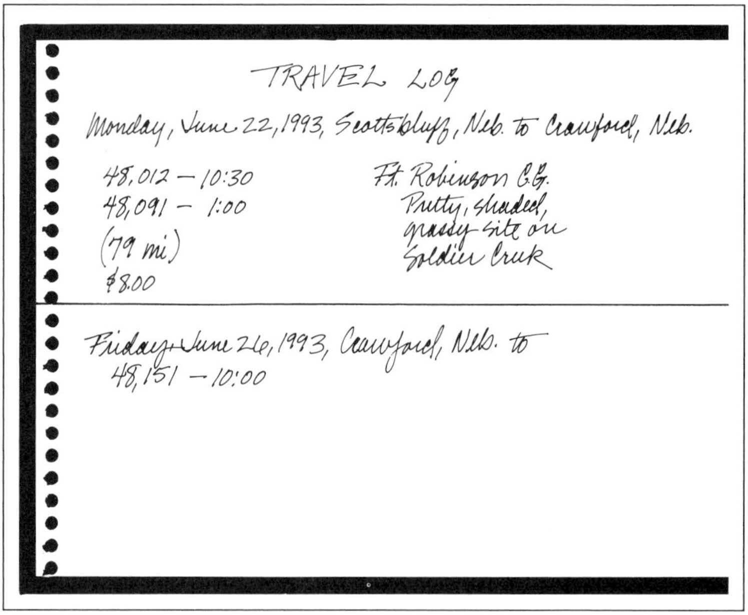

the actual miles driven, time of arrival, the town we are in or near, name of the campground where we are staying, a brief description of the campground or our site, and the rate.

Because we enjoy eating out, we enter the names of restaurants we have sampled in the area with our own rating of one to five stars. Rather than having a separate guest log, we put the names of people with whom we become acquainted and the type of rig they have in our notebook log. Addresses, if needed, are put in a separate address book. We tend to remember casual acquaintances by where we meet them. Their names in the log on that location's sheet makes it easy to look them up later on.

Most of our log entries are merely items we might want to recall at a later date, but some entries are more valuable. By entering the mileage every time the trailer is moved, we have a complete record of the number of miles on the trailer alone. Since we tally up the trailer miles frequently, we know when it is time to have the wheel bearings checked and lubricated.

The campground fee is an indicator of how much we might expect to pay if we should return to that campground. Often we will rent a site for a week or a month. Directories list only daily rates, so our records are helpful in this way too. By adding all the amounts spent for campgrounds, we can determine our average daily costs.

The campground or site description often reminds us that we would not want to go back to a particular campground or, if we did, we might want to arrange to have another site. In the descriptions, we might list such facts as bad TV reception, availability of cable, or any hookup aberrations. For example, we might write: "Sewer in center of site under trailer," " electricity with reverse polarity," or " bad-tasting water." You could also note the positive aspects of a campground, particularly if you've found an exceptionally pleasant site.

A number of pages in the back of the notebook are reserved for fuel and servicing logs (Figure 18.3). These pages are used vertically. Every time we fuel up, the date, mileage, cost per gallon, number of gallons purchased, and the total price are noted. The brand of fuel and the location of the service station are also entered. If we ever revisit the area, we will know where the lowest-priced fuel can be found. When oil is added, the quantity—usually one quart—is entered on a line of its own in the fuel log. We know how often we are adding oil, and we have a complete record of our fuel expenditures.

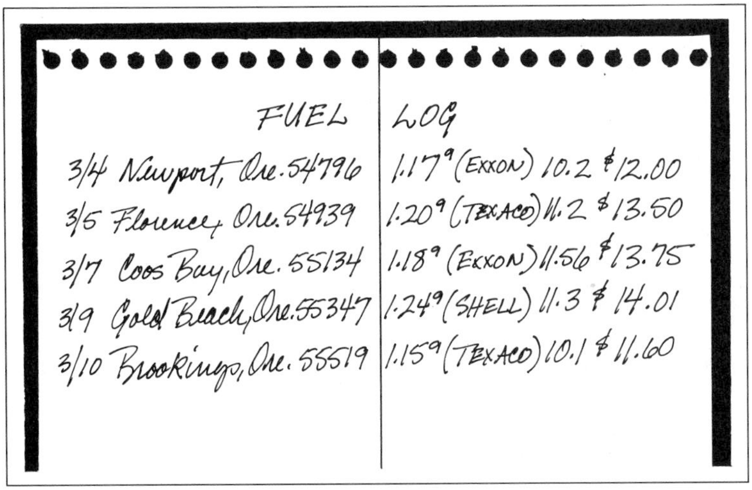

Figure 18.3
Useful information is provided by a fuel log. A few of the back pages of the travel log are convenient to use for fuel entries.

Some other back pages hold the servicing records for both the truck and the trailer (see page 346).

A supply of the pressure-sensitive labels we use to remind us about when to change oil, transmission fluid, and fuel filters is clipped to the back cover of the notebook.

If it is convenient to enter information, the logkeeper will be more likely to keep the records up to date, so we keep a pen tucked into the spiral of the notebook and never have an excuse for not making entries.

SUN SHADES

One of the most bothersome conditions while driving is having sun streaming in. It may be blinding to the driver or cause the cockpit area to heat up, even with adequate air conditioning. A device or two for blocking the sun can be a welcome addition to the cockpit.

The huge windshields found on many motorhomes need something more than the usual visor to keep the sun out of the driver's eyes. An oversize, transparent, tinted visor that covers the center of the windshield will do the job. These are available in models that swing away when not in use or clip on to the regular visor and are folded up for storage. If such a visor is to be used while driving, be sure it is not so dark that it affects visibility; some are not recommended for the driver's use.

Smaller visors that attach to the regular visor can be used on pickup trucks and Class C motorhomes. These tinted, transparent visors can be lowered below the regular visor; some models may have an opaque slider that, in effect, extends the width of the regular visor.

A sheet of tinted vinyl that adheres by static electricity can be used on side windows. The sheet can be trimmed with scissors to fit any size and shape window. It is attached simply by pressing it on and removed by pulling it off. It can be stored rolled up. The material is available in various-sized sheets or sold by the foot.

A tinted window shade is what we use on the side windows, although shade-type sun shields are also made of material with tiny perforations. Visibility is good through both types but they should only be used on side windows.

The shades can be attached in various ways: by hooking over the top of the side window or by inserting clips or the shade case itself in the headliner molding. The unrolled shades will roll right back up if they are not secured at the bottom. One type is fastened with a suction cup, another uses a hook-and-loop fastener. Our shades came with this type, but we didn't want to use them because the part of the hook-and-loop to be attached to the door was adhesive-backed. From past experience we know this adhesive is affected by high temperatures; the attached item may shift or gummy residue ooze out from beneath it lessening its holding ability, and if it is ever to be removed, it leaves a sticky mess that is very difficult to clean off.

We use a small S-hook attached to a short length of sturdy string to hold the shade down, but this might not work on all vehicles. On our truck, the door armrests have an indentation in the top. A screw in the bottom of the indentation is used to secure the end of the string without the hook. When attached, the S-hook fits into a hole in the pull tab on the bottom of the shade. The string and hook lie in the indentation when not in use.

With any window shade that is not attached directly to the window, the shade will have to be rolled up before the door can be opened.

We had to remove the canopy over the pickup bed when we bought a fifth-wheel trailer; the shade the canopy provided for the cab's rear window no longer existed. To keep the sun from reaching us from that quarter, a louvered sunshade was installed, the type that fits into the molding of the window. The sunshade we selected has an unlouvered section at the top center portion of the window so rearward visibility is not hampered. Sunshades with metal louvers usually cover the entire rear of the cab. The louvers are set in a large-diameter tubular frame mounted either in the bed of the pickup or on the bed's sides. Since the frame is normally installed an inch or two away from the rear wall of the cab, it could interfere with a fifth-wheel turning at a sharp angle.

Chapter 19

Recreational Transportation

In addition to a motorhome, auxiliary car, or tow vehicle, many fulltimers want other forms of transportation for recreation, sport, or exercise. These might be boats, bicycles, mopeds, motorcycles, or scooters.

Unless any of these is towed on its own trailer, its weight will have to be considered in the cargo-carrying capacity of the rig, as well as its storage location, especially if it is to be kept on the rear bumper of a motorhome or trailer.

Recreational transportation items of all types should be accessible. If they are not stored in a convenient, easy-to-get-at location, you may find you will not use them.

BOATS

Water-oriented recreation, especially fishing, is very popular with fulltimers, many of whom transport boats with them to fish or explore the recreational possibilities of rivers, streams, lakes, and other bodies of water that abound in locations where a full-timing rig can be taken.

A boat as long as eighteen feet can be carried atop the canopy of a pickup truck, but a twelve- to fourteen-footer is a more practical size from the standpoint of weight and ease in handling (and the size of the outboard motor needed to push it). The motor and other equipment needed for the operation of the boat can often be kept inside the canopy. One fulltimer we know claims that carrying his boat on the top of his truck when he is towing his conventional trailer is as good as having a wind deflector. He notices a distinct difference in handling when the boat is not in position.

Those who have fifth-wheel trailers cannot carry boats this way because the pickup trucks needed to tow them must have open beds. But cab-top racks are available that project out over the truck's hood (and sometimes slightly beyond) for fifth-wheelers who want to take their boats with them.

Canoes and kayaks can be carried on nearly every type of tow vehicle, including autos, and on the roof of motorhomes.

A large boat could be stored on site at a favorite boating area, but if you prefer to take it with you, a sizable boat can be towed behind a motorhome on its own trailer. We have seen small cabin cruisers, open-console fishing boats, and cruising sailboats towed in this manner. The interiors of some of these boats can be used for storing all sorts of items—even bicycles.

In some states it is legal to tow boats on trailers behind conventional and fifth-wheel trailers, but this would not be practical for fulltimers who travel extensively in many different states. A rig like this is almost impossible to maneuver unless you can keep moving straight ahead and park where backing up is never needed. Even though the boat trailer can be unhitched and moved out of the way before backing into a site, it could be much more trouble than it is worth.

If a boat is carried on the roof of a tow vehicle or motorhome, an easy way of lifting and lowering it will be needed. A boat loader will do the job mechanically. The manual types that employ a crank for raising and lowering operations require little effort or muscle power, or an electrically-operated boat loader will do it all.

A boat carried on its own trailer can be launched from the trailer. A boat carried atop a vehicle, once unloaded, can be transported a short distance from the vehicle to the water on a set of launching wheels.

As long as I live, I'll hear waterfalls and birds and winds sing. I'll interpret the rocks, learn the language of flood, storm, and the avalanche. I'll acquaint myself with the glaciers and wild gardens, and get as near the heart of the world as I can.

JOHN MUIR

▼ ▼ ▼ ▼ ▼ ▼ ▼ ▼ ▼ ▼ ▼

Rigid boats are not the only types that can be taken along. Folding and inflatable boats are exceptionally practical and take up less storage room than rigid boats. Lifting or storing them is easier because, when folded or deflated, the boat is a relatively small, easily maneuverable package.

The only folding boat suitable for use as a fishing boat is the Porta-Bote, available at some large RV-supply stores, marine, or sporting-goods stores. For the location of the nearest dealer, write or call the manufacturer:

Porta-Bote International
1074 Independence Avenue
Mountain View, California 94043
(800) 227-8882

The Porta-Bote, which can be assembled in about two minutes, is suitable for rowing or use with a motor; it also becomes a sailboat with the addition of the sailing package. It's available in three sizes, which, when assembled, are eight, ten, or twelve feet long, with corresponding weights of thirty-nine, forty-nine, and fifty-nine pounds, respectively. The weight is less than half that of a comparable aluminum boat because the Porta-Bote is constructed of polypropylene. A special mount allows the boat to be carried flat on the side of an RV (Figure 19.1).

Figure 19.1
The Porta-Bote can be assembled in minutes. Suitable for rowing or use with a motor, it also becomes a sailboat with the addition of a sailing package.

Numerous brands of inflatable boats are available in many sizes and a wide range of prices. When deflated, they will take up very little storage space. Inflatables can be propelled by a motor or by oars, although the rowing characteristics of some designs are not very good. Not having any sort of keel and sometimes having a blunt bow, none of them steer really well, but they are ideal for float trips and whitewater rafting.

Sailing can also be part of fulltimers' recreation. Anything from a sailing dinghy to a sophisticated racing sailboat lends itself to rooftop storage. A sailboard is extremely practical because it's portable, lightweight, and not bulky.

Any boat used with a motor will embroil you in the red tape of registration, which, depending on the state, might be a problem.

Bicycles seem to be as popular as boats among fulltimers. They are often carried on the rear bumpers of motorhomes and trailers, where they may have to be removed for access to a rear storage compartment, but some carriers mount on the front bumper of a tow vehicle or motorhome. Numerous types of bike carriers are on the market. Depending on the type, the bike wheels might fit into channels, or the bike may be hung by its frame on a rack with hooks. A rear deck that is suitable for storing bicycles along with other items might be added to either a trailer or a motorhome.

BICYCLES
▼ ▼ ▼ ▼ ▼ ▼ ▼ ▼ ▼ ▼ ▼ ▼

A bicycle can be carried upright in a roof mount on some tow vehicles. If it is light enough to carry up a ladder, it can be laid flat on the roof of a motorhome or trailer. We saw a motorhomer who used a simple pulley arrangement attached to the roof rack as an aid in lifting up his bikes.

Bicycles and tricycles can be rigid or folding, and both are available in three-speed models. Most folding bicycles have 16- or 20-inch wheels, making them unsuitable for riding long distances or over rough or hilly terrain.

Bicycles and tricycles are ideal for use in large campgrounds where the office, recreation facilities, or even friends may be a considerable distance from your site, or for use anywhere if you are riding for the exercise.

Those who want a rigid bicycle can choose from among a wide variety of multi-speed models and a more limited selection of three-speed models.

▼ ▼ ▼ Mountain Bikes

Mountain bikes are popular because they are easy to ride and as well adapted to rugged, hilly mountain trails as to flat, level pavement. Although mountain bikes are sophisticated—they can have up to twenty-one gears—they hark back to the bikes many of us rode as children in their solidity, feel, and comfort. It is not necessary to hunch over dropped handlebars when riding a mountain bike; the rider sits in an almost upright position, and as a consequence it is easy to see where you are going. Mountain bikes' fat, knobby tires provide good traction on almost any surface, absorbing bumps and rolling over small rocks and branches smoothly. Even though they have many gears, they are easy to operate. Most have double brakes for sure stopping power. A mountain bike weighs from twenty-seven to thirty pounds compared to a touring bike that might weigh twenty to twenty-one pounds.

For those who don't intend to bicycle the backcountry, a modified mountain bike offers all the comfort and ease of a regular mountain bike but has features that make it more suitable for street riding than traversing rugged terrain.

A touring bike is best for those who engage in long-distance trips on paved roads.

Some municipalities require the licensing of bicycles or tricycles if they are used on public streets.

MOPEDS, SMALL MOTORCYCLES, SCOOTERS, AND SPECIAL-PURPOSE VEHICLES

▼ ▼ ▼ ▼ ▼ ▼ ▼ ▼ ▼ ▼ ▼ ▼

Fulltimers can have low-cost auxiliary transportation with either a moped, a small motorcycle, or a scooter. Some of those who fulltime in a motorhome find that one of these is more desirable auxiliary transportation than a small car, which must be towed. Being lightweight, it can be stored in a bumper rack. The only practical way to take a heavier, full-size motorcycle with you is to tow it on its own trailer.

Although these vehicles do not provide the comfort and convenience of a car—it is not pleasant to be out in the open on rainy days, for instance—they are cheaper to buy and maintain. They provide a much greater range than bicycles and could be auxiliary transportation alternatives for those on tight budgets.

Unlike larger units, mopeds, scooters, and lightweight motorcycles do not have the speed and handling characteristics that might be needed to avoid accidents. When ridden in traffic, caution must be exercised and full safety gear—helmet, boots, gloves, jacket—should be worn.

Again, with a vehicle with an engine, the registration will have to be considered, as well as insurance. All states require registration of motorcycles and some require that certain insurance coverage be maintained. Regulations covering mopeds and scooters vary by state.

Carriers designed just for motorcycles and mopeds with a ramp for easy loading and unloading can be purchased. One type is mounted by using a standard hitch receiver.

Some fulltimers enjoy snowmobiling or driving an all-terrain vehicle (ATV). Vehicles of these types will need to be transported on their own trailers. Neither a snowmobile nor ATV requires registration. Fulltimers who regularly spend time in the same location where these vehicles can be used could store them there from season to season to avoid hauling them around.

Any of the boats or vehicles we have mentioned can be rented in many locations. Just about any type and size boat desired—sport-fishing boats, houseboats, cruising sailboats—can be chartered for a day, a week, a month, or longer. Renting has many advantages, the primary one being that it may be less costly than owning, especially if you do not use the equipment regularly year round. Another advantage, particularly applicable to fulltimers who may not reside in one place, is that being a renter frees you from any registration and insurance obligations. There will be no worries about how your property will survive storms if stored someplace where you might not be able to take care of it. Renting or chartering also frees you from maintenance chores and expenses.

HOW ABOUT RENTING?
▼ ▼ ▼ ▼ ▼ ▼ ▼ ▼ ▼ ▼ ▼ ▼

PROTECTING YOUR EQUIPMENT

▼ ▼ ▼ ▼ ▼ ▼ ▼ ▼ ▼ ▼ ▼ ▼

Boats, bicycles, mopeds, motorcycles, scooters, snowmobiles, and ATVs are all expensive items, attractive to thieves because of their cost and portability. If you own any such equipment, you will need a way to protect it from being stolen while it is being transported and when you are at your destination.

Heavy chains with sturdy locks should be used to secure any vehicle carried in a rack, unless the rack itself has a locking device. Although stealing a boat from the roof of a vehicle is more trouble than most thieves would bother with, if we carried a boat on our truck roof, you can bet we would somehow chain and lock it to its rack or the truck.

If equipment is transported on its own trailer, it is not enough to secure it to the trailer. A lock should be affixed to the trailer itself so it cannot be unhitched from the tow vehicle or taken when it is unhitched. An ordinary padlock with a shank thin enough to pass through the holes in the coupler latch or one of the locks specially made for this purpose could be used.

Chapter 20

Safety, Security, and Protection

Fulltiming is not different from other lifestyles when it comes to the precautions you need to take to protect yourself and safeguard your belongings. Unfortunately, you cannot be as trusting as you might like with your neighbors or casual acquaintances or too open about your plans in the presence of strangers. Be especially aware of circumstances that could adversely affect your safety and security and take the necessary precautions.

LOCKS

No lock is burglar-proof. Burglars can get into anything that is locked if they are allowed enough time. Since nothing can be made truly burglar-proof, secure any item of value so that stealing it cannot be done easily or quickly. If your property is protected this way, thieves may give up on burgling it and move on to some other property that is not as well secured.

Interior Locks

Fulltimers who do not have dead bolts on their coach doors in addition to the latches are asking for trouble. Breaking in is easy when the only thing to contend with is a latch that is locked by turning a button or pushing a lever; a screwdriver and a few seconds may be all that is needed to gain entry. A dead bolt can be locked and unlocked from the outside only with a key. A crowbar will dispatch an RV door with a dead bolt, but it might take a little time, and someone attacking a door with a crowbar might arouse the suspicions of passersby.

It is a good idea to have a locksmith change the tumblers on any dead-bolt locks. Many master keys exist for these locks, and, unfortunately, some are in the hands of people who will use them for unlawful entry.

If you are napping or sleeping with the doors open, or when you are alone in the coach, lock the screen doors from the inside. A simple hook and eye will be enough to stop someone from just walking in. For the same reason, we make it habit to lock the outside door when we are inside. We started this practice after we became acquainted with a man in a campground who, when he wanted to see us, would rap on the side of the trailer, then just walk in. He was a friendly, well-meaning individual, but we couldn't count on any real privacy as long as he could enter our trailer at will. And we realized that if he could gain entry just by walking in, so could someone else who was not as friendly and well-meaning. Any type of screen-door lock should be located high or low on the door so that no one can push back the slider and reach in to unlock it.

▼ ▼ ▼ Exterior Locks

The locks on most outside compartments are virtually worthless as far as security goes. Not only are they flimsy but they also have common keys. On occasion, when we have been on a dealer's lot looking at RVs unaccompanied by a salesman, we have been able to use our keys to open compartments on other RVs when we wanted to check them out for size and accessibility. Kits for changing the tumblers on outside compartment locks are available at RV-supply stores.

Valuables in outside compartments could be protected by installing a hasp and padlock (bolt on the hasp; never use screws). This is, of course, a signal that something of value is stored in the compartment. A bolted-on hasp will eventually yield to a well-applied crowbar, but again, time and trouble may deter the thief.

On our conventional trailer, we had two locks that would have delayed — not stopped — anyone who wanted to steal the trailer itself. One was a padlock that was put through the holes in the coupler latch. The hitch could not be attached until the padlock was removed (this method will work on tow dollies too). The other was a bicycle lock that fit on the wheel chock, which we continue to use (see Figure 16.3, page 383). The locking feature was one of the reasons we chose this type of chock. To protect our fifth-wheel trailer from theft, we use a metal collar that fits over the kingpin. The collar is held on with a padlock.

Our batteries were on the hitch on our conventional trailer. To secure them, we put a small eye in one end of a length of stainless-steel cable (we happen to have a tool for this) and passed the other end of the cable around the angle iron of one of the battery supports and made another eye, which secured the cable to the angle iron. We made an identical length of cable and installed it on the angle-iron support for the other battery. The cables were just long enough to fit tightly across the top of both battery boxes, meeting in the middle. The ends were fastened together with a padlock that went through both eyes (Figure 20.1). Instead of purchasing a special tool for making eyes, they

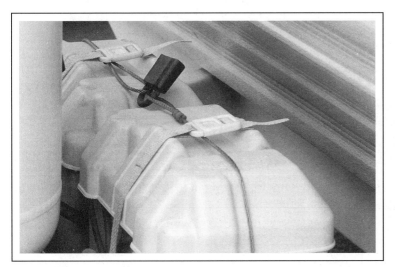

Figure 20.1
A padlock can be inserted in eye ends of two lengths of cable to protect batteries from being stolen.

can be fashioned with wire-rope clamps. The clamps can be removed with a wrench, but that takes time, and if the clamps were positioned so they were difficult to get at, a thief might not bother.

Most canopies on pickup trucks can be broken into easily. Their locks also have many common keys, but thieves rarely bother with keys when the canopy is made of aluminum. Instead, they use a pry bar of some sort, or perhaps an old-fashioned, blade-type can opener. Fiberglass or steel canopies are sturdier than those made of aluminum but how burglar-proof they are depends on the size of the windows. On some it is easy to pop out a window and crawl through the opening. If anything valuable is kept in a canopy, it should not be in view. A hasp and padlock also could be used on a canopy door, but this advertises that there is something inside worth extra protection.

WINDOWS
▼ ▼ ▼ ▼ ▼ ▼ ▼ ▼ ▼ ▼ ▼ ▼ ▼

Whenever we leave our trailer, we never leave the dinette window open, even though other windows might be open. The dinette window is the closest one to the outside door. If it were open, it would be relatively simple for someone to rip the screen, reach in, and unlock the door; no sound of breaking glass would attract attention. Keeping the opening portion of escape windows closed when the RV is unoccupied is a good practice too. The spring-loaded latches that release the part of the window that can be lifted out can be easily manipulated by reaching around through the window from the outside.

If someone were bent on gaining access to our trailer through another open window, it would take some time to bend the louver frame out of the way to make a wide enough space to crawl through. This activity, and the glass that would have to be broken, might attract someone's attention.

Sliding windows or those that open from the bottom do not provide the security of louvered windows. We once saw some trailers on a dealer's lot that had been broken into. The thieves had not bothered with any models that had louvered windows. On trailers without louvered windows they had simply pried out windows with a screwdriver and crawled in. On some, the frames were barely damaged.

RVers, being a friendly bunch, often display their names on the outside of their coaches. If you are one of those who does this, have you considered that someone unfriendly could come to your door and call you by name? "Hey Jim, its Fred." Most of us would assume Fred was a fellow RVer. If we could not quite remember who Fred was, perhaps seeing his face would remind us. Anyway, it would be unfriendly not to acknowledge Fred's presence by opening the door. We heard of one couple who found themselves looking into a gun barrel when they opened their door to a "Fred."

We are cautious when anyone comes to our door, day or night. At night we turn on the outside lights, then ask any callers to identify themselves. If we were suspicious of anyone, we would ask the person to show some identification through the window before we opened the door, although we have never had to resort to this — yet.

▼ ▼ ▼ Security Lights

Some RVs are equipped with motion-activated, exterior security lights. When you leave the RV, it is not necessary to keep an exterior light on so you can see to unlock the door when you return after dark. The lights remain off until movement is sensed and then automatically turn themselves on.

We would never leave exterior lights on when we are away from the trailer. When an exterior light is left on, with no other lights visible in the RV, it is usually an indication that the unit is unoccupied.

If you don't want to have things stolen, don't leave them around your campsite unless they are secured. Trusting people go off and leave expensive coolers, barbecue grills, lawn chairs, and lanterns at their campsites. Bicycles are often left where they can be simply ridden off or carried away.

We even have heard of RVers who had their water hoses stolen. This has never happened to us, and we have never been in a campground where others have had theft problems that we were aware of, but this is one of the lesser reasons we do not have our water hose hooked up all the time.

After unhitching, some trailerists leave their hitch dangling from the coupler instead of removing it and storing it somewhere else. This costly piece of equipment can easily be removed unless the coupler is locked.

If you have an expensive item that might attract thieves, such as a camera, binoculars, or a radio, do not leave it outside unless you are using it and be careful of displaying it needlessly. Even if you put it inside the coach, observant people will take note that you have such equipment and perhaps think it worthwhile to relieve you of it when you are away from your campsite.

If you have such items inside your coach, either keep them out of view or pull the draperies or blinds whenever you leave. Perhaps we are overcautious, but a few times we have even lowered the television antenna before leaving the trailer so it would not be quite so obvious there was a television inside.

It is especially prudent to keep valuables out of public view in crowded public campgrounds, such as in national parks in the busy seasons, because there isn't much security provided by rangers anymore; they have their hands full just managing the crowds. A few years back there was a gang of thieves operating in some of the coastal southeastern states' parks. Members of the gang would watch to see who left their RVs and alert others who would break in by various methods. This professional, well-organized group had master keys for many brands of RVs; if they couldn't simply unlock the door and walk in, a small child was often used to gain entry by way of a roof vent. Most such incidents we have heard about occurred in crowded parks in the summer when RVers might be inclined to leave windows and vents open. Even though we don't normally frequent such places when they are crowded, preferring to visit them in the off-season, any time we are in a public campground we are extra careful about protecting ourselves and our belongings.

▼ ▼ ▼ Be Alert for Suspicious Characters

Sometimes people in a campground will arouse our suspicions. On more than one occasion we have taken down the license plate numbers and a description of the vehicles such people were driving. One time a carload of teenagers pulled into the site next to ours in a city park just as we were leaving for a dental appointment. The young men had no camping gear but they did have some beer. We figured if anything happened to the trailer while we were gone, they would be prime suspects. Fortunately, nothing did happen, but we had the information that would have allowed us to identify their car. Another time, in a state park, two young men in a car kept cruising around the camping area. They too had no visible camping equipment. We were leaving to pick up our mail in a nearby town, but first we recorded their license number and vehicle description just as a precaution.

Where you camp sometimes has a bearing on how safe you are. If your RV is the only one parked in a place, you may be considered an easy mark since there would be no one around to come to your aid. At any designated campground someone will come around to check it out sooner or later, so there is always a chance that thieves might be deterred by this. But if you were spending the night in a little-used rest area or at the side of a road, there might not be any protection at all. If there was, locals who were up to no good might know how frequently the location was patrolled by law enforcement officers.

Although we like to be off by ourselves, we are much more cautious when we are alone anywhere. We watch anyone who comes into our area and keep a check on them until they leave. If they do not leave, we stay alert and thoroughly investigate any suspicious noises.

FIREARMS OR NOT?

▼ ▼ ▼ ▼ ▼ ▼ ▼ ▼ ▼ ▼ ▼ ▼

Those who use firearms for sport of any kind will not have to decide whether to keep a gun aboard for protection; they will already have a firearm that could be used defensively. Others often find themselves in a quandary about whether they want to have a gun solely for this reason. Many people doubt they could use a gun against another person, even in a "them-or-me" situation. Still, gun ownership may be practical because the odds are against your ever being in a situation that would turn into a shoot-out. A gun can be an effective deterrent even if it isn't loaded. Merely pointing a gun at a person might change someone's mind about what he or she intended to do. A rifle or shotgun can also be used effectively as a club.

If you think you might ever shoot a firearm, you should learn how to do so from the experts. In the hands of the untrained, a loaded gun can be just as dangerous to the user as it would be to the aggressor.

Laws governing gun ownership vary from state to state. Full-timers who do extensive traveling might find themselves in technical violation of some of these laws. Border crossings between the United States and Canada and Mexico might present problems if certain types of guns are carried, worse problems if they are concealed and discovered by customs agents.

A firearm for protection will not be of much use if it isn't readily accessible at all times. The gun case we used in our 23-footer was designed so that when the top was lifted, the front dropped down. There was nothing to undo or move out of the way to reach the guns. Although we have no space for the gun case in our fifth-wheel, the guns are just as accessible.

It's a good safety practice to keep a gun's chamber empty but with ammunition loaded in a clip or magazine and stored where it is handy. It is especially important to keep guns and ammunition separate if children are living in the RV.

SAFETY FOR THE RV

To protect the RV and its occupants, certain safety routines should be practiced along with the installation of certain safety equipment.

▼ ▼ ▼ Smoke Alarms and Fire Extinguishers

Smoke alarms have proven their value over and over in houses; they are just as valuable in RVs. Each RV should have at least one smoke alarm. It should be installed some distance away from the immediate galley area, however, because range-top cooking can trigger it.

Even the smallest RV suitable for fulltiming needs two fire extinguishers—one in the front and one in the back, and they should be even more accessible than a gun. Recharge them when needed or replace them when the test device so indicates, and regularly inspect them to see that they are in working order. Don't wait for a fire to figure out how to use a fire extingusher.

Read the instructions, and reread them each time you give the extinguisher its routine inspection.

Plan how you would exit your RV if a fire broke out in any location. Chances are you would be able to get out of the door or the escape window (required on all one-door RVs), but have another plan in case neither could be reached.

A fire would be bad enough if you were in the RV, but it could be disastrous if it occurred when you were not around to take care of it. Do everything possible so that the RV will be safe before you leave it. When we go away, we never leave an electric heater running, and, again perhaps being overcautious, we never leave the air conditioner operating. Even though the air conditioner has a circuit breaker that should trip in case of a problem, the circuit breaker itself could malfunction.

When the gas furnace is in use, we turn the thermostat quite low before we leave so the furnace will not run too often, or at all, while we are gone.

▼ ▼ ▼ Other RV-Safety Tips

We feel more comfortable if all electronic equipment—the stereo, the television, even the television amplifier, and the microwave—is off when we leave the trailer because anything electrical has the potential for causing a fire. If an electrical storm occurs while we are away, there is less chance of damage to such equipment if it is turned off.

Whenever we leave, we turn off the water pump too. If a leak developed somewhere in the line after the pump, and the pump switch was left on, it would pump water out onto the floor until the tank was empty. The pump itself could become wet, short out, and cause a fire. There is no danger of the pump shorting out if you are hooked up to outside water, but a leak from this system would cause a lot of flooding since the leak would be fed by an unlimited source. As mentioned earlier, if we hooked up to outside water and had to be away from the trailer for several hours, we would turn off the water at the outside faucet.

Trailerists who have a CB radio in their tow vehicle might feel more secure if there were another CB in the trailer (or the CB could be removed from the tow vehicle and taken into the trailer). In an emergency situation when an outside telephone is not accessible, the CB might be used for communication. For this application, a CB antenna must be installed on the trailer; a CB won't work with a regular radio antenna. If a motorhome is equipped with a CB, in certain situations it might be more practical to use the CB instead of leaving the coach to use a telephone.

A tip: When using Channel 9, the emergency channel, broadcast details of your situation and location over and over and don't be concerned about a reply. Often police and REACT monitors can hear the broadcaster but the broadcaster can't hear them, and they will be powerless to come to your aid unless they know where you are.

BURGLAR ALARMS

▼ ▼ ▼ ▼ ▼ ▼ ▼ ▼ ▼ ▼ ▼ ▼ ▼

The attitude of many people these days is one of noninvolvement, so you can't count on anyone to take action upon hearing your burglar alarm go off. Nevertheless, a burglar alarm is valuable as a deterrent; thieves do not want to call attention to themselves.

Sometimes a decal on a window indicating that an RV is equipped with a alarm system might cause a thief to think twice about burgling that RV (Figure 20.2).

Figure 20.2
A decal on the window of an RV indicating that it is equipped with an alarm system is a deterrent to thieves.

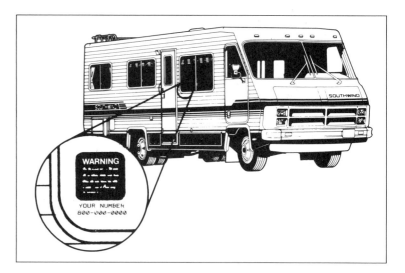

It makes sense to have sources of light available other than the 12-volt interior and exterior lights. For one thing, in an emergency situation, light might not be available where it was needed. In any lighting conditions, we needed a flashlight to identify the fuses on the fuse panel on our 23-foot trailer, and a flashlight is useful when walking in a poorly lit campground at night. Included among the various flashlights we own are two lantern types that have exceptionally bright, long beams. One is kept in the trailer and the other in the truck. If circumstances called for it, we could use these flashlights to temporarily blind someone. The beam could also be used for signaling since it can be seen from quite a distance. We also have a 12-volt, portable spotlight.

We keep a couple of fat candles — the kind that will sit on their own base and do not need a holder — to use sometimes when we want to conserve electricity. Candles can also be used in an emergency when no other lights are available. When keeping candles for emergency use, be sure matches or some other means of lighting them are available. And be sure to take normal safety precautions when an open flame is in use.

We carry cards with information about who to notify in case we have an accident. Our cards are somewhat different from those of people who live in a fixed dwelling. For example, Bill's card reads:

In case of accident notify:
Jan Moeller
in a (brand name) 29′ fifth-wheel trailer at a local campground
or notify:
(Relative's name)
(Relative's address)
(Relative's telephone number)

There aren't too many places where campgrounds are so numerous that they couldn't all be checked out quickly.

PORTABLE LIGHTS

▼ ▼ ▼ ▼ ▼ ▼ ▼ ▼ ▼ ▼ ▼ ▼

NOTIFICATION CARDS

▼ ▼ ▼ ▼ ▼ ▼ ▼ ▼ ▼ ▼ ▼ ▼

When we register at a campground we pick up one of the campground's business cards and keep it in the truck in an obvious place, or one of us might keep the receipt with the campground's name and address in our wallet and the other carry a business card.

**IMPORTANT
NUMBERS**

▼ ▼ ▼ ▼ ▼ ▼ ▼ ▼ ▼ ▼ ▼ ▼ ▼

With us at all times is a list of all our important numbers. It contains serial numbers of our truck, trailer, and every piece of equipment we have that might be the target of a burglar. It also has telephone numbers and addresses for reporting lost or stolen credit cards. We each carry a copy of the list and keep another copy in the trailer in a place where a thief might overlook it.

Chapter 21

Fulltiming with Children and Pets

▼ ▼ ▼ ▼ ▼ ▼ ▼ ▼

Fulltiming with children and pets may be somewhat more restrictive than fulltiming without them, but most people willingly sacrifice some of their freedom in exchange for the joy they bring into their lives.

Even though children and pets can enrich fulltiming, they can also bring their share of problems. Often children are accepted in RV parks where pets are not. On the other hand, some parks — especially those advertised as adult parks — will accept pets but won't allow children below a certain age at all, or will have limitations on the amount of time children can spend visiting those staying in the park. Other parks, however, do not welcome or allow either children or pets, while some places impose an extra charge for each child or pet.

An RV will have to be proportionately larger for fulltiming with children. Each child will need to have a place to sleep, study, and relax, and space to store clothing and other possessions. Bigger children will need more physical space than small ones. Two or more children when beyond the toddler stage should have equal accommodations.

RV ACCOMMODATIONS FOR CHILDREN

▼ ▼ ▼ ▼ ▼ ▼ ▼ ▼ ▼ ▼ ▼ ▼

Few manufacturers have RVs suitable for fulltiming with children. They regularly build units that will sleep up to six, but it is evidently assumed that the six won't be sleeping in the RV for longer than an occasional vacation, so two of the six, if they are small, have to use the dinette for a bed, not an ideal situation when fulltiming. Even if the children don't mind sleeping on the dinette, an adult must make it up each night and disassemble it each morning, and the dinette is out of use for any other activities when it is made into a bed. The only RV models that are truly ideal for fulltiming with children are two-bedroom, conventional trailers with a front bedroom and another bedroom in the rear, usually containing bunk beds. Only a few trailer manufacturers, though, make two-bedroom models. With most RVs, it would take considerable alteration of an existing floorplan to achieve anything close to a two-bedroom layout. And, as mentioned earlier, it would be the rare manufacturer that would do this sort of customizing.

Bunk beds are ideal for children because they take up little space. The addition of a shelf or two and perhaps a curtain to close off the entire compartment can turn a bunk into a personalized, private space. A bed in the cabover portion of a Class C motorhome could have the same treatment. The beds over the cockpit that are a feature in some Class A motorhomes are the least suited for turning into a bedroom. When in use, many of the beds of this type extend beyond the cockpit area and drop down from the ceiling where they are stored, creating a nuisance for those moving about in the motorhome.

A dining area should be large enough to seat all the occupants of the RV at one time. As far as we know, there are no RVs with two baths, so some of those living in the RV might have to use campground facilities at times.

The physical space of even a large coach may be too confining when children are living in it; room to spread out is needed. Extra space can be gained in several ways: a screened "room" can be attached to the side of the RV where children can play or sleep, children can sleep outside in a tent, and a canopy-covered pickup-truck bed can be used for sleeping or playing. If a van is a tow vehicle, it might serve as a children's room.

When traveling with children, campgrounds should be selected with an eye toward activities and recreational possibilites, not only in the campground, but also in the locality. Most children are not happy being cooped up in one place all the time. They want to get out and do things. Campgrounds whose busy season is during the winter months have activities targeted mainly at those who are middle-aged or older. For children living in such a campground, the community should offer recreational opportunities for them.

Children like the excitement of going somewhere—up to a point. That point is just before they whiningly ask, "Are we there yet?" If children travel too many miles in a day they become bored, restless, and irritable. When traveling with children it is especially important to keep trips short and not travel every day; lay over often for a day or two.

Whether traveling in a motorhome or a trailer, make frequent stops so children can work off pent-up energy. A standard pickup truck may not be roomy enough to use as a family tow vehicle. The extra seating capacity of a super or crew cab truck, a van, or a vehicle like a Suburban may be needed. Seat belts will be needed for everyone traveling in the motorhome.

TRAVELING WITH CHILDREN

▼ ▼ ▼ ▼ ▼ ▼ ▼ ▼ ▼ ▼ ▼ ▼ ▼

▼ ▼ ▼ How Adaptable Are Children?

If children are very young, there is little to worry about as far as their adapting to fulltiming. They have little previous experience in the non-full-timing world to color their opinions about it one way or the other.

When children have spent all their years in the full-timing lifestyle, they may accept it as their way of life, but children between the ages of about eight to twelve, to whom fulltiming will be a new experience, may not look upon it with nearly the same enthusiasm as their parents. Fulltiming means their world will be disrupted, they will be thrust into an unfamiliar environment, and their friends will no longer be around. Nevertheless,

The car trip can draw the family together, as it was in the days before television when parents and children actually talked to each other.

ANDREW H. MALCOLM

▼ ▼ ▼ ▼ ▼ ▼ ▼ ▼ ▼ ▼ ▼ ▼ ▼

most children of these ages can adapt to fulltiming and benefit from it.

Children of full-timing parents who travel considerably are usually more self-assured than others of their age. They deal with a host of different situations that stay-put children would never encounter. Their experience is broader in all areas than that of children who grow up in one place. Traveling gives a child an awareness of history, nature, geography, and regional customs that no school could ever provide. Children should be encouraged to participate in travel planning.

A problem with children's adaptability arises when they enter the teen years, especially if their schooling comes from home-study correspondence courses. Children who do not attend a regular high school have no opportunity to participate in the sports, activities, or social life high school provides. They never experience belonging to clubs, playing in the band or on the football team, going to proms, and being publicly recognized for good grades. The all-important graduation ceremony does not take place for them. Such teenagers can become resentful and intractable because of what they have been denied, creating discord that, in a relatively small RV, is not pleasant for anyone. Yet it would be an exceptional teenager who could get through this period without being somewhat dissatisfied with his or her lot.

The value of marriage is not that adults produce children but that children produce adults.

PETER DE VRIES

▼ ▼ ▼ Education

One of the major concerns of full-timing parents is how their children can be educated within the framework of a mobile lifestyle. This can be accomplished in two ways: Either plan on staying in one place during the school year so the children can enroll in school, or use home-study correspondence courses.

With home study, parents are not tied down; they can travel as they wish. This is why many parents who fulltime opt for the home-study method.

Although it may seem desirable to be able to educate your children as you travel wherever and whenever you wish, doing so is not without its problems. The child must devote several hours a day to studying. The parents must oversee the work and function not only as supervisors and disciplinarians but also as teachers. If the child does not follow a regular study routine, this system will not work, and, what's more, such a routine is difficult to maintain when much traveling is done.

Traveling or not, home study requires much discipline on the part of the child and the parents. Children usually handle the disciplinary restrictions more easily than the parents. Many children have spent some time in a regular school before they begin fulltiming, and lessons, homework, and studying have been a regular part of their lives. Parents, though, have been away from school for many years so adapting to a study-teaching regimen may be a lot more difficult for them.

▼ ▼ ▼

Correspondence courses can give children as good an education, or a better one, than regular schools if the parents do their part and see that the children do theirs.

The Calvert School (105 Tuscany Road, Baltimore, Maryland 21210) and the American School (850 East 58th Street, Chicago, Illinois 60637) offer home-study courses for the elementary grades. Certain church-affiliated correspondence courses are also available. For over sixty years, high school curricula have been available from the University of Nebraska, Division of Continuing Studies, 33rd and Holdrege Streets, Room 269, Lincoln, Nebraska 68583-0900.

All home-study courses will cost hundreds of dollars a year. This may seem expensive, but it might be less than what it would cost to send a child to school. Children who study at home do not need a wardrobe of special school clothes or money for meals and snacks eaten outside the home. There are no transportation costs or expenses for school-related activities.

A real plus of home education is that parents have more control over their children's social environment and what they are exposed to, especially drug, alcohol, and tobacco use, and the sexual mores of their peers.

In some states, home education is frowned upon. If the child is being taught through a recognized correspondence school

A man can't stay relaxed too long, not under the best of circumstances, and there's nothing like a trip with your family to prove my point.

MARRIJANE AND
JOSEPH HAYES

▼ ▼ ▼ ▼ ▼ ▼ ▼ ▼ ▼ ▼ ▼ ▼

there will be less resistance to it than if the parents, be they qualified educators or not, draw up the courses of study. Whether this will be a problem depends on your mobility and on others who know what you are doing. There are always trouble-makers who make someone else's business their business. Imagine the following situation: Your child becomes acquainted with another child in the same RV park who is attending a regular school. Your child's friend will certainly have told his or her parents, probably enviously, about how your child does not have to go to school. If the friend's parents are busybodies, you can be sure they will investigate the circumstances of your child's education and may report you to the authorities.

▼ ▼ ▼

Some years ago, something like this happened to a family we know about, when home schooling was an out-of-the-ordinary circumstance. The parents had to appear in court several times to defend their right to tutor their child at home. The court did not see it their way. The court's final decision was that the child had to be enrolled in a regular school as long as the parents were residing in that state.

Other full-timing friends of ours enrolled their son, Kevin, in a public school during the several months the family was staying in one location. Kevin's friends knew he would be moving on after the school term was over, and they, of course, told their parents about the itinerant lifestyle of Kevin and his family. This aroused the ire of one child's parents. When this couple met Kevin's parents at a school function, they openly charged them with getting a free ride in the school system because they did not pay their fair share of taxes.

What these unthinking people did not realize was that Kevin's parents were paying their own way. Taxes were incorporated into the rent they paid at the RV park just as any real estate or property taxes are included in the rent apartment dwellers pay. It is unfortunate that many people do not consider those who live in an RV home in the same light as they might apartment dwellers.

▼ ▼ ▼ Fulltiming with Children — or Not?

Is it really sensible or practical to fulltime with children? The answer is yes and no.

There are happy full-timing families with children of all ages, but there are also former full-timing families who could not make the lifestyle work for them. The success or failure of fulltiming with children depends on several factors.

The personalities, temperaments, and attitudes of everyone involved in the venture are important. If there is not a harmonious family relationship in a fixed dwelling, it will probably change for the worse in an RV home.

The ages of the children and their feelings are other factors. Small children are amenable to just about anything as long as the family unit remains the same. They are used to having their lives organized and controlled by their parents. They are also too young to have any real input about such things as a change in lifestyle. As children advance in age, however, they have definite opinions and feelings that should be taken into account. As with a dissatisfied partner, it will not be pleasant to live day after day with a child who is not happy with the full-timing lifestyle. Forcing children into fulltiming against their will or continuing in the lifestyle when they are terribly unhappy with it can cause long-term resentment. Never mind any benefits of the lifestyle; the child may end up feeling cheated simply because his or her life is different from that of other children.

Deciding whether or not to fulltime with children requires extensive soul searching, but there is no way of knowing for sure how it will turn out. For some families, the togetherness of living in an RV is more than their relationship can stand and it becomes a disaster. For others, this same way of living brings them closer together and is a rich, rewarding experience.

Some Good Sam Club members have organized special Kids 'n Us chapters for families with children so they can participate in camping outings together. Children are the focus of the chapters. At get-togethers there will be other children to play with. The adults have the common bond of being parents of young children and tailor activities to suit the group.

Come, dear children, let us away . . .

MATTHEW ARNOLD

▼ ▼ ▼ ▼ ▼ ▼ ▼ ▼ ▼ ▼ ▼ ▼

TRAVELING WITH PETS

▼ ▼ ▼ ▼ ▼ ▼ ▼ ▼ ▼ ▼ ▼ ▼ ▼

Fulltimers who wish to take family pets along should be aware of the many pet restrictions and regulations they will encounter. In spite of these, having a loving pet along can be comforting and rewarding.

▼ ▼ ▼ "No Pets Allowed"

The sign prohibiting pets is appearing more and more frequently in private RV parks, state parks, and other public campgrounds. Because of this, fulltiming with a pet can put limitations on where pet owners can stay. Very few people could bear to give up a pet they already own just for the sake of being able to stay in the places that do not allow pets. But if you are thinking of acquiring a pet, perhaps this aspect should enter into your decision making.

Pet owners have only themselves to blame for the ever-increasing campground restrictions on pets. Too many dogs and cats have been allowed to run loose, make messes, bother other campers, and make noise at all hours of the day and night. As usual, the owners of well-behaved pets must suffer because of a minority that has soured many campground operators about accepting pets.

This, however, is a large minority, if we can judge from our own experiences. Most of the campgrounds where we have stayed have regulations posted regarding pets, but many pet owners ignore them. The most flagrant violation relates to the leashing rule. Most campgrounds require pets to be leashed so they cannot intrude on other campers' space. We have been jumped on, growled at, licked, and nuzzled by unleashed dogs whose owners were nowhere in sight. We have owned dogs, aren't frightened of them, and know how to handle them, but think how others, who are not used to dogs, would feel in these situations. Very few people hate dogs; most of us like them—if they are under control.

But even if pets are leashed they can be a nuisance. In a state park recently we had a site next to the owners of two large dogs. The dogs were kept outside, tied to the trailer, day and night. The owners left early each morning and did not return until evening.

The trouble with a kitten is THAT
Eventually it becomes a CAT.

OGDEN NASH

▼ ▼ ▼ ▼ ▼ ▼ ▼ ▼ ▼ ▼ ▼ ▼ ▼

Those who ventured past their trailer, or in our case, when we came out the door, were barked at and lunged at by the dogs. Their leashes were just long enough to reach our site, which meant there were many dog droppings around our utility hookups. We did not complain about the situation, but evidently someone else did. A park ranger appeared at our neighbor's door early one day, and they hitched up and left within the hour.

Unleashed cats have been more of an annoyance than a problem for us. They seem to like bounding about under the trailer and doorstep, creating strange noises. Many of these same cats want to take up residence with us, it seems, since we have difficulty keeping them out when we open the door.

While pet owners can control where their pets do their business, they cannot control the barking, whining, or meowing of animals when they go off and leave them behind. If an animal is allowed to befoul the grounds or bother others with its noise, its owner may be asked to leave a campground. Pet owners should be considerate of their animals, but at the same time they should be considerate of other campers.

We have heard about some campgrounds that have a separate registration form for pets. On the form is all the pertinent information about the pet—breed, color, name, and such—along with a clause acknowledging that the owner understands and agrees to abide by all the campground's rules concerning pets. A deposit may be imposed as well, which would be refunded if the pet, and its owner, didn't violate any of the rules.

Cat: One Hell of a nice animal, frequently mistaken for a meatloaf.

B. KLIBAN

▼ ▼ ▼ ▼ ▼ ▼ ▼ ▼ ▼ ▼ ▼ ▼ ▼

▼ ▼ ▼ Pet Safety

Pets should be leashed for their own safety. If they cannot run loose, they will not be run over on a highway or wander away and get lost. It is tragic when a beloved pet becomes lost, but especially so when you are traveling and your pet disappears. RVers on vacation often have no choice but to leave the area and continue on. Fulltimers might be able to stay until they had exhausted all possibilities in tracking down the missing pet. If the animal had wandered away and were lost, there might be a chance of recovering it if they were able to post notices and run

The better I get to know men, the more I find myself loving dogs.

CHARLES DE GAULLE

I loathe people who keep dogs. They are cowards who haven't got the guts to bite people themselves.

AUGUST STRINDBERG

▼ ▼ ▼ ▼ ▼ ▼ ▼ ▼ ▼ ▼ ▼ ▼ ▼

ads. If it had been stolen, however, there is probably nothing that could be done.

Pet thievery is on the increase, so take every precaution against someone stealing yours. Most animals are stolen for the money they bring when sold. No animals are safe. Purebreds can be sold as pets; less desirable animals are often sold to research facilities.

Never leave your pet unattended in any public place. Mark it with some form of permanent identification, such as an ear tattoo, in addition to the identification it should have on its collar. A nose print is just as individualistic as a human finger-print, so it can be used for positive identification of an animal.

Good Sam Club members can obtain identification tags for each of their pets. The tags contain the individual's Good Sam membership number and the toll-free number of the Good Sam Club. When a lost pet is reported to the Good Sam Club, the owner is notified.

A pet should be protected by having a veterinarian give it the necessary shots. Aside from the health benefits, pets cannot enter Canada or Mexico unless they have the proper inoculation certificates.

If a pet should accidentally ingest a poisonous substance or be deliberately poisoned, a twenty-four-hour hotline operated by the National Animal Poison Control Center in Urbana, Illinois, can be used for assistance. The toll-free number is (800) 548-2423. The fee is $25 and can be charged with a credit card.

▼ ▼ ▼ Pet Accommodations

Any pet should be given time to adjust to its new RV environment. Immediately establish a place for it to sleep. If in a motorhome, the sleeping place should be safe and secure when the motorhome is moving. Whether in a motorhome or riding in a tow vehicle, pets must be disciplined so they know the driver's area is off limits. An animal crawling around the driver's feet can be hazardous.

Some RVers have installed pet doors in their units. A ramp from the door usually leads to a fenced-in enclosure so the pet can come and go as it pleases yet not be able to wander away when the owners are absent. To prevent a pet from climbing over the fence and other animals from getting in, a roof of chicken-wire could be put over the enclosure.

▼ ▼ ▼ Costs of Pet Ownership

Those on tight budgets should consider the cost of owning a pet. The initial cost may be nothing, or it may be hundreds of dollars, but the upkeep and feeding will run into thousands. For example, a few years ago the estimated cost of owning a small dog for an average ten-year life span was $3,500. A medium-sized dog would require $6,000, and a large dog $8,350. A cat's upkeep was found to be slightly more than that of a small dog.

Yellow cat, black cat, as long as it catches mice, it is a good cat.

AUGUST STRINDBERG

Chapter 22

Seniors make up 55 percent of RVers, and although no figures are available as to how many fulltimers there are or
what their age breakdown is, we would venture to guess that
seniors comprise over 90 percent of fulltimers.

Those whose ages have passed the half-century mark are in
the best position, financial or otherwise, for fulltiming. Their
children are usually out on their own or in college. They may
have retired from jobs that provide them with incomes from
retirement plans. They have had many years to save for their
retirement years, during which they may have built up equity in
their RVs and paid off the mortgages on their houses.

HEALTH

Nothing, barring a severe health problem, should prevent seniors from pursuing the full-timing lifestyle. And even health
problems would have to be serious indeed to keep determined
seniors from being fulltimers. Remember those mentioned in
Chapter 1—disabled, paralyzed, suffering with debilitating diseases, wheelchair-bound, even one requiring kidney dialysis—
who have overcome their difficulties so they can fulltime as
completely as any able-bodied person.

Fulltiming, while not a cure-all, can benefit those with certain conditions. With an RV for a home, those with respiratory problems never need to live in areas where smog is a factor. They can park their homes in places with clean air or in dry or humid atmospheres as their conditions warrant. If pool therapy is needed for an ailment, they can select campgrounds with pools. As we mentioned before, those who have trouble getting around will have an easier time of it in a recreational vehicle; RV rooms are small compared to any room in a fixed dwelling, so there is not as much area to negotiate, and handholds are plentiful throughout.

Should it be required, medical help is available just about anywhere a fulltimer might go. People in campgrounds are often sources for medical referrals, and so are the people at local senior citizens' centers, found just about everywhere nowadays, even in very small towns.

Living in an RV is a definite advantage when a person must travel to a place where specialized treatment is given. Fulltimers are at home anywhere, and campground rates are much lower than those charged at motels or hotels. Many hospitals have a place with hookups where RVs can be parked, and often campgrounds will be found near major medical centers.

Most private health insurance and Medicare can be used anywhere in the United States.

O time arrest your flight and you, propitious hours, arrest your course! Let us savor the fleeting delight of our most beautiful days!

ALPHONSE DE LAMARTINE

FINANCES

Some seniors have enough of a retirement income to fulltime without the concern of earning money. But for those who need to augment their income or simply want to continue working, there are plenty of opportunities for seniors to put their skills to use for pay.

After a period of some resistance to older workers, employers have come to realize they are a valuable resource. Young people entering the work force today are not nearly as well educated as those who are of retirement age, and because of the baby-boomer period, each year brings a reduction in the number of new people in their late teens and early twenties entering the work force. Older people have a better work ethic than most young people, and they already have on-the-job experience.

This is not to say that older people will be welcomed into the work force and be given full-time jobs with a full range of benefits. They won't. But many opportunities exist for seniors in part-time or temporary work in just about any field.

Seniors can work for a while, earn enough to travel for some time, then go to work in another place when it's necessary to feed the kitty again.

With the direct-deposit feature offered by many financial institutions, it is easy for traveling seniors to take care of their money. Any checks from a retirement plan or Social Security can be sent by the issuers directly to the bank or investment institution of their choice.

▼ ▼ ▼

Federal taxes must be paid if income is above a certain level, as must state income taxes in those states that have such taxes. After retirement, some seniors are shocked to find that they will forever owe state taxes to a state in which they no longer reside. For example, if you worked for a company in California and a portion of your wages went into a retirement account, you will be taxed by the state of California on all amounts paid from the retirement account, even if you no longer live in California and have no ties whatsoever to it. It doesn't matter if you worked for a company or were self-employed. If you contributed to any sort of a retirement account while employed in the state, taxes will be due to California each year that funds are drawn from the retirement account.

What happens if you have moved from California and you are "residing" in another state that has a state income tax? Do you have to pay twice? Or do you somehow apportion a percentage of retirement income to each state? Tax advisors, CPAs, financial consultants, and personnel in state tax offices can't give anything close to definitive answers. States might give credit for taxes paid to another state, but they might not. It is another system set up for nonmobile people, those who live, work, and retire in the same state, and therefore becomes an even more confusing issue than it already is for full-timing seniors, whether they travel or stay put in a retirement spot of their choice.

At this writing, twelve states require state taxes to be paid on withdrawals from a retirement account to which contributions were made while working in that state: California, Indiana, Iowa, Kansas, Kentucky, Louisiana, Michigan, Mississippi, Montana, New York, Oregon, and Utah. More states will undoubtedly follow suit in years to come.

SENIOR DISCOUNTS
▼ ▼ ▼ ▼ ▼ ▼ ▼ ▼ ▼ ▼ ▼ ▼

Seniors can take adavantage of discounts offered by restaurants and other business establishments. In our travels we have come across a supermarket chain that offers a 10 percent senior discount on purchases made on Wednesdays, and we have found discounts for haircuts and auto repairs, among others.

Those who are sixty-two years of age who plan to visit national parks should avail themselves of a Golden Age Passport (See Exhibit 22.1). It is free and can be obtained from any location administered by the National Park Service, Forest Service, U.S. Army Corps of Engineers, or Bureau of Land Management. The holder is admitted free of charge to any federal installation where an entrance fee is charged, and when camping in federal campgrounds the rate is half that of the regular fee. A 50 percent discount is also given on parking or boat-launching fees at any federal recreational facility. Discounts do not apply to privately operated concessions on federal lands.

Some states have passes for seniors entitling them to reduced rates in state-park campgrounds.

ELDERHOSTELS
▼ ▼ ▼ ▼ ▼ ▼ ▼ ▼ ▼ ▼ ▼ ▼

The Elderhostel program is ideal for senior RVers. Educational courses in a wide range of subjects are offered at colleges and universities in many states and in Canada. Previous education is not a requirement for taking any of the courses; no degrees or diplomas are needed. Those who enroll will only have the enjoyment of a pure learning experience; they won't be graded, tested, or have homework to do.

A person must be sixty years old to participate in the program, although when a couple enrolls, one can be as young as fifty.

So popular has the Elderhostel program become with RVers that some places have campgrounds on campus. If such on-site accommodations are not available, there is usually a commercial campground nearby.

Many full-timing seniors travel to different locations to participate in several Elderhostel programs each year.

Elderhostel information and catalogs listing courses can be obtained by writing to: Elderhostel, 80 Boylston Street, Suite 400, Boston, Massachusetts.

▼ ▼ ▼ ▼ ▼ ▼ ▼ ▼ ▼ ▼ ▼ ▼ ▼ ▼

Exhibit 22.1
Federal Park Passports

GOLDEN AGE PASSPORT

If you're sixty-two or older, you're eligible for the federal government's free Golden Age Passport, a lifetime entrance pass to any national park, national monument, recreation area, or wildlife refuge that charges an entrance fee. It also provides a 50 percent discount on charges such as camping fees, parking, and boat-launching at any federal recreational facility, including those administered by the National Park Service (NPS), the Bureau of Land Management, U.S. Army Corps of Engineers, and the U.S. Forest Service (USFS). The card does not cover fees charged by private concessioners. The Golden Age Passport must be obtained in person and the applicant must have proof of age. It is available at most federally operated facilities where entrance fees are charged, as well as at NPS and USFS regional offices.

GOLDEN ACCESS PASSPORT

Blind or permanently disabled persons of any age are eligible for the Golden Access Passport, which provides the same benefits as the Golden Age Passport. You must obtain it in person, with proof of being medically diagnosed as blind or permanently disabled.

GOLDEN EAGLE PASSPORT

If you're between seventeen and sixty-one, you're eligible for the Golden Eagle Passport, which costs $25 a year and entitles a family or carload free admission to any national park, monument, or recreation area. Good for the calendar year, it may be obtained by mail from U.S. Forest Service and National Park Service headquarters and regional offices, and at national parks and wildlife refuges where entrance fees are charged.

NATIONAL PARK PASS

If you frequent one particular National Park Service unit that charges entrance fees, you might prefer to obtain a Park Pass, available for $10 or $15, which is good for unlimited free admission to the park for the calendar year.

DUCK STAMP

If you frequent units of the National Wildlife Refuge system, you can buy a Duck Stamp for $12.50; it's required of waterfowl hunters, but serves as an entrance permit for nonhunters as well. It's available at most post offices, national wildlife refuges, and many sporting goods stores.

Source: *The Rver's Money Book*, Agoura, CA, 1990

No doubt you have noticed, as we have, that some seniors seem older than others of the same age. It is our opinion that this generally occurs when older people get into a retirement rut. All too often these people not only retire from a job, they retire from life by sitting around doing nothing. We've heard such people say, "I've worked hard all my life, now I'm going to take it easy."

A campground owner told us the sad story of a retired man who had this attitude. He and his wife started fulltiming in their trailer after he retired from his job in an eastern state. Once they got to their first destination, Montana, they stopped traveling and the man started drinking heavily. The campground owner sensed that the man was bored and offered him a job that would occupy him for a few hours each week. His duties would include registering RVers when the owner wasn't there and some light maintenance around the campground. "I'm retired," he said, "I don't have to work." A few months later the man was dead. The campground owner claimed he drank himself to death.

Retired fulltimers, by the very nature of their existence, should never be bored. There is always something new and interesting to see around the next bend in the road or over the next horizon. When the means for traveling is there, as it is with all who choose fulltiming for their retirement lifestyle, bogging down or getting into a rut should not be allowed to happen. We're not advocating our lifestyle of constant travel for every fulltimer, but just a change in perspective every few months for those who tend to settle into one spot and stay there. Use the mobility fulltiming affords to see new things, meet new people, and experience living in different locales. Fulltimers' golden years can truly be golden if they take advantage of all the lifestyle offers.

RETIREMENT PITFALLS

It is better to wear out one's shoes that one's sheets.

GENOESE PROVERB

Chapter 23

The Fun and Rewards of Fulltiming

By now we should have convinced you that fulltiming is easy, and, if you thought that problems were inherent in the lifestyle, we hope we proved that they are not problems at all, or that they can be overcome or solved one way or another by anyone who really wants to be a fulltimer. So if you want to join the ranks of fulltimers, don't delay. None of us knows how many tomorrows we have, so make the most of today and take advantage of all the benefits fulltiming offers.

The lifestyle can expand horizons, increase knowledge, and provide opportunities to make new friends every step of the way. It can prevent you from falling into a rut and living in the same never-varying patterns day after day. Fulltimers, unlike most people, can have a constantly changing environment if they wish. Those who are adaptable and aren't afraid of change, who want to see and do new things, will be in no danger of growing old—at least mentally.

CLUBS AND CAMARADERIE

Fulltiming offers the chance to make a host of new friends. Pull into a campground in the off-season or in the South in the winter months. Many, maybe all, of the others in that particular campground will be fulltimers. It shouldn't take long to become acquainted. Maybe your neighbors will even let you get settled before they introduce themselves.

All during the year you are likely to encounter vacationing RVers with whom you will have much in common. If you do not meet again in a vacation spot, you may end up visiting them where they live. Among our non-full-timing friends, many have offered us a place to park our trailer when we come to see them.

When you purchase a recreational vehicle, you may find that a club exists for owners of your particular brand of RV. Club activities often include rallies and get-togethers on the national, regional, state, and local levels, caravans, and many benefits other than the social. All Winnebago or Itasca owners, for example, are eligible for membership in Winnebago-Itasca Travelers, which has a special division for fulltimers called the 365 Club. Fulltimers might also want to join certain other clubs not affiliated with any particular RV manufacturer.

▼ ▼ ▼ The Good Sam Club

Being members of the Good Sam Club (owned and operated by TL Enterprises, Inc.) adds to our full-timing enjoyment. We recommend that fulltimers, as well as other RVers, join the Good Sam Club no matter what other RV-oriented organizations they belong to. The benefits of membership, other than 10 percent discounts at Good Sam campgrounds, are many and constantly expanding: The monthly magazine *Highways,* sent to all members, always contains valuable information not often available elsewhere. The reasonable annual dues provide a wide selection of services for members. Among these are: discounts at more than 3,000 campgrounds and RV-service centers; sizable savings on all Trailer Life publications; a mail-forwarding service; traveler's checks; message service (especially useful for traveling fulltimers); lost credit-card, pet, and key services; various types of medical and health insurance; a plan for Canadians who travel in the United States; a Good Sam Visa card that can be used for interest-free cash advances; a golf card entitling the cardholder to discounts and other benefits at 1,700 golf courses throughout the country; and the use of Good SamTours—

a full-service travel agency. In addition, Samborees and Caraventures go on year-round; members can participate in any of them. (Samborees are gatherings of regional Good Sam members for socialization, good works, and fellowship, and often include seminars on various RV-related subjects. Caraventures are guided tours to world-wide locations. On some tours in the United States and Canada, members travel in their own RVs. Other tours in foreign countries include RV rentals. Sometimes the means of transportation is a cruise ship.)

Available to Good Sam members is a directory of the Standby Sams—Good Samers located throughout the country who provide advice and assistance in emergencies. The Good Sam Club also provides a voice on local, state, and national levels when legislation affecting RVers is proposed. All Good Sam members can sign up for Good Sam Emergency Road Service for an additional fee. This service, unlike others of its type, is geared to RV rigs and provides assistance and towing for motorhomes, trailers, and tow vehicles.

Within the ever-growing 2,000-plus chapters worldwide, the Good Sam Club has many special chapters. Some are service oriented; others are just for fun. Ham radio and CB groups, for instance, are numerous. People from the same profession often form their own groups. The LEOs (Law Enforcement Officers) in Minnesota are an example. Both working and retired officers can join. The Semper Fi Sams is a chapter for retired Marines. Foster and adoptive parents can join the Caring Sams.

As mentioned in Chapter 21, some Good Sam members belong to Kids 'n Us chapters. These chapters are composed of families with children and were established with the focus on children. At get-togethers the children can count on having playmates of their own age, and all activities are family oriented.

Many chapters have been organized by single Good Samers, and another club, Loners on Wheels (P.O. Box 1355, Poplar Bluff, Missouri 63901), is a nationwide club for those who RV by themselves. Not a camping singles club—you cannot remain a member if you have a partner—it is another group of those who have a common interest and get together for the fun and social aspects that clubs provide.

Fulltimers Kay and Joe Peterson formed the Escapees (or SKPs) Club (Route 5, Box 310, Livingston, Texas 77351), with national headquarters and a members' campground in east Texas plus other campgrounds in many other states. Members can use the parks as they would any other campground for overnighting or short-term stays, or they can stay permanently in a site purchased on a renewable ninety-nine-year lease.

▼ ▼ ▼

You may already belong to a club or association because of an interest of your own that has nothing to do with RVing. Being a fulltimer may enable you to attend national and regional meetings and conventions you might otherwise have to miss because of lack of time. If the cost of expensive accommodations has limited your attendance at such functions, as a fulltimer, you will be able to attend economically without ever leaving home.

A rewarding aspect of fulltiming is that those in the lifestyle automatically participate in conserving natural resources just because they live in an RV. Heating and cooling an RV uses little energy when compared to that required for a house or an apartment. Less electricity is used for lighting an RV, too.

FULLTIMERS AS CONSERVATIONISTS
▼ ▼ ▼ ▼ ▼ ▼ ▼ ▼ ▼ ▼ ▼ ▼

No one living in an RV uses much water to flush the RV's toilet. Many residential toilets require five gallons of water for each flush, although some newer water-saving models use two gallons or less. RVers would have to make a concentrated effort to use so much as a gallon for each flush.

Water is conserved in another way when RVers operate from their unit's water tank. When a known quantity of water exists, even though it can be readily replenished, most RVers will normally conserve it make the supply last longer.

Those with an RV home don't have wood-burning stoves and so do not contribute to the polluting pall caused by the burning wood that hangs over some towns in the winter.

Fulltimers who live exclusively in their RVs don't have lawns to water, nor do they use fertilizers, many of which are environmentally objectionable.

Those fulltimers interested in recycling can practice it just as easily when living in an RV home as can those living in a fixed dwelling.

FULL-TIMING ACTIVITIES

▼ ▼ ▼ ▼ ▼ ▼ ▼ ▼ ▼ ▼ ▼ ▼ ▼ ▼

If you think fulltiming isn't interesting or that traveling will be boring, you haven't thought the matter through. Driving long days nearly every day *is* boring, so traveling should not be done all the time. Stop often for a few days, a week, a month, or more to explore and get to know the places in which you stay. No matter how small or isolated the place, you will find interesting people to talk to. Let them in on your lifestyle, and you may be the one doing most of the talking—answering the barrage of questions they will subject you to.

It is fun to participate in regional festivals: ethnic, patriotic, religious, wine, food, harvest, and music—from opera to hoedowns. New Orleans is not the only town with a Mardi Gras, and places other than Nashville have country music festivals.

Experiencing the diversity of our country, learning how others live—their customs, dress, habits, even differences in language—is enriching and educational.

If getting to know people doesn't interest you or is not enough to fill all your time, pick a subject and explore it thoroughly or establish a goal and set about reaching it. As a fulltimer you are always packed and ready to go.

▼ ▼ ▼ A List of Ideas for Recreational RVing

A rather common goal among fulltimers is to visit every one of the contiguous United States. Should you want something more challenging than just ticking off states, you might combine some of the following suggestions with that activity.

▼ Take your own covered wagon and follow some of the trails used by the pioneers—the Oregon, the Santa Fe, the Bozeman, the Abilene, the California, the Mormon—or walk

sections of the great hiking trails such as the Appalachian Trail or the Pacific Crest Trail.

▼ Select a war, for example, the American Revolution or the Civil War, and visit all its battlefields and historic sites.

▼ Old forts may attract you. In searching them out, you will find much diversity. The isolated, spartan Fort Fetterman in Wyoming, once on the western frontier, contrasts sharply with the elaborate structure of St. Augustine's Castillo de San Marcos in Florida.

▼ All the ordered beauty of Japanese gardens in the United States and Canada serenely await your contemplation. Exploring all the famous gardens of the South would take years. After that you could start on the famous gardens of the North.

▼ How about tracking down the largest trees of each species? They are located all over the country in nearly every state (check with local forestry offices for locations).

▼ Bodies of water are everywhere to explore and use for sport and recreation. Fish or swim in the biggest body of water in each state. Perhaps you would enjoy searching out the highest and largest waterfalls in the country. Some are easily accessible; reaching others presents a challenge. Do you know there are sizable waterfalls in Minnesota, Michigan, and Wisconsin, for example?

▼ Discover the fascination of exploring a river from its headwaters to its mouth. Pick a major river, such as the Mississippi or the Missouri, or a lesser one, such as the Red, the White, the Blue, or even the Mattaponi, which provides three avenues of exploration from its headwaters: the Matta, the Po, and the Ni.

▼ You could make it your aim to fish in every state. Try for trout in the Battenkill in Vermont, coho salmon in Lake Michigan, rockfish in the Chesapeake Bay, and steelhead in the Nehalem River in Oregon.

▼ Play all the challenging golf courses across the country.

▼ In your RV you can follow the route of the Intracoastal Waterway and watch the commercial traffic and pleasure boats making their way from the Virginia Capes, around Florida, and on to Brownsville, Texas.

People travel to faraway places to watch, in fascination, the kind of people they ignore at home.
DAGOBERT D. RUNES

▼ ▼ ▼ ▼ ▼ ▼ ▼ ▼ ▼ ▼ ▼ ▼

Great mother of big apples it is a pretty World!
KENNETH PATCHEN

▼ ▼ ▼ ▼ ▼ ▼ ▼ ▼ ▼ ▼ ▼ ▼

This land is your land, this land is my land, From California to the New York island, From the redwood forest to the Gulf Stream waters, This land was made for you and me.

WOODY GUTHRIE

▼ If the Intracoastal Waterway piques an interest in canals, travel inland to take a look at the remains of the James River-Kanawa Canal—started, but never finished, and intended to connect the Atlantic Coast with the Ohio River. Preserved sections of old canals exist in many states. The Erie Canal, now called the New York State Barge Canal, is still in use, with a variety of recreational areas situated along its entire length.

▼ If the Erie Canal does not interest you, maybe eerie ghost towns will. Nearly every western state has its share.

▼ Board the many old railroad trains still chuffing their way along scenic routes. Ride a logging train in the mountains of West Virginia, travel to a pioneer village across the Nebraska prairie, roll through California's Napa Valley while dining in elegant surroundings and sipping the fruitful beverages the valley is famous for, or clatter across breathtakingly high, narrow trestles in the majestic mountains of Colorado.

▼ Are railroads too earthbound for your taste? Then take off, at least in your imagination, with the astronauts at Huntsville, Alabama; the Kennedy Space Center in Florida; and the Johnson Space Center in Houston, Texas. Come back to earth watching the space shuttles land at Edwards Air Force Base in California. Fly with the Wright Brothers at Kitty Hawk, North Carolina, and hop with Lindy across the Atlantic in the *Spirit of St. Louis* at the National Air and Space Museum in our nation's capital.

▼ Birdwatchers can use every day of fulltiming to add their life list. Your RV can take you to habitats of rare, elusive, and uncommon species. Is the ivory-billed woodpecker really extinct, or do a few still exist in the swamps of South Carolina? Maybe you'll be the one to find out.

▼ With regional wildflower books, you can identify flowers that grow in the most beautiful settings and in homely waste patches by the roadside. You may even develop an appreciation for the beauty of some weeds you once tried to eliminate from a lawn. You might try to find a different wildflower from each state.

▼ If geology is your hobby, visit the unusual geologic formations found in nearly every state. For instance, discover the section of western Kansas that resembles Monument Valley in Arizona.

▼ On a less-grand scale, but still in the same vein, rockhounds can pursue their hobby in more places than they could cover in a lifetime. You might include in your collection a specimen representative of each state.

▼ Delve into ancient history with trips to fossil beds that are found in several states and the many museums that focus on paleontology.

▼ Shell collectors have miles and miles of beaches to comb where beautiful specimens can be gathered.

▼ Your RV can effectively be used as a base camp for making an ascent to each state's highest point. Some points can be reached in a vehicle while others require mountain-climbing skills. Climbing would not have to be a requirement for adding high spots to your list, however. You can make the rules. Perhaps it would "count" if you merely looked at some of the high spots in the mountain states. The highest points in many states are unnamed and unmarked; tracking them down can take you to interesting, off-the-beaten-path locations. Would you readily recognize Florida's 345-foot-highest elevation for what it is, if you found it? You would if you were on an expedition with some of the 300 members of the High Pointers Club, a nationwide organization whose elevating purpose is to visit the highest point of each state.

▼ Select a favorite historical figure in whom you have an interest and visit the places connected with his or her life. This sort of in-depth exploration of, say, George Washington, Sakajawea, Robert E. Lee, Jim Bridger, George Armstrong Custer, or Chief Joseph can give you a new appreciation of the person and the times. Going to the birthplaces of all our presidents will keep you busy for quite a while.

▼ All sorts of museums await your visit. Pick a subject, any subject, and there will be a museum or, more likely, many museums, devoted to it.

In the United States there is more space where nobody is than where anybody is. This is what makes America what it is.

GERTRUDE STEIN

▼ ▼ ▼ ▼ ▼ ▼ ▼ ▼ ▼ ▼ ▼ ▼

Yosemite Valley, to me, is always a sunrise, a glitter of green and golden wonder in a vast edifice of stone and space.

ANSEL ADAMS

▼ ▼ ▼ ▼ ▼ ▼ ▼ ▼ ▼ ▼ ▼ ▼ ▼

▼ Check out all the state capitals. The capitol buildings are varied and interesting, and cities in which they are located offer much in the way of both architectural and historical exploration.

▼ An interesting undertaking would be to visit every single national park.

▼ As a fulltimer, you can attend all the dog, cat, and horse shows you wish. Follow the rodeo circuit if that is more to your liking.

▼ Your RV can be used to carry you back in time if you attend rendezvous of modern-day mountain men held at different times of the year in many locations.

▼ Refresh yourself spiritually and aesthetically at great churches and cathedrals throughout North America. Many rival those found in Europe.

▼ The mansions of the wealthy will give you an insight into another lifestyle. See what the very rich called "cottages" on Jekyll Island on the Georgia Coast or Newport, Rhode Island. Who has the better life—the millionaires with their vast estates or you roaming free as a fulltimer?

▼ A search for regional foods can be rewarding. Or conduct a search for the country's best hamburgers. Are hamburgers too ordinary? How about oysters? Chili? Barbecue? Bratwurst? Locally made chocolate ice cream?

▼ Visit vineyards, wineries, and wine festivals. Don't overlook the unique scuppernong wine in North Carolina as you go from the more famous wine-making areas in upper New York State to the Napa Valley in California. Sample some regional cheeses, too, as you go about your countrywide wine tasting.

▼ You could "collect" sunrises or sunsets. Preserve your memories of them on film, on canvas, or by writing your thoughts about each one in prose or poetry.

▼ If none of these ideas interest you, perhaps your own forebears might. Start tracking down your ancestors. The trail might lead you to places you never dreamed of. Compile your information and send it to other family members and the Library of Congress.

We could go on—and on—but we're sure you get the idea.

Being a fulltimer and having the time to explore a subject thoroughly may make you an expert on it and possibly allow you to make some extra money. You might write articles, or even a book, about your subject, or you could find yourself giving talks and presenting slide or video shows to groups of fellow RVers, RV clubs, and other organizations. Collections made as you travel might be of value to other collectors or perhaps even be the beginning of a business.

We have continued our fulltiming life as we were writing this book, exploring many new places and revisiting some of our old favorites.

A FULLTIMER'S YEAR

You may recall we were in Duluth in the fall of the year when we first began working on this book. After spending two weeks in the Duluth area we crossed the Upper Peninsula of Michigan, ablaze with autumn-colored trees, and made our way down the east side of the state. To reach Lockport, New York, a few miles east of Buffalo, we took a shortcut through Canada from Port Huron, Michigan. We had lunch in Hamilton, Ontario, and also purchased a bottle of shampoo. (On an earlier trip to Canada we ran out of our regular shampoo and purchased a different type that was not available, we found out later, in the States. We liked this shampoo better than the brand we had been using, and now make a point of purchasing some whenever we are in Canada.)

We arrived in Vermont in time to catch the fall foliage. Indian summer weather was with us as we made our way south through New York, New Jersey, and Pennsylvania to Virginia where we spent some time visiting with friends in various parts of the state.

Friends were with us for Thanksgiving in North Carolina, after which we took the coastal route to South Carolina. We were trying to make up our minds about whether to spend Christmas in Charleston, South Carolina, or Savannah or Augusta, Georgia. Charleston won out.

When the holidays were over we did visit Savannah, then Brunswick, Georgia. It was mid-January when we cut across the

Americans have always been eager for travel, that being how they got to the New World in the first place.

OTTO FRIEDRICH

The border means more than a customs house, a passport officer, a man with a gun. Over there everything is going to be different; life is never going to be the same again after your passport has been stamped.

GRAHAM GREENE

▼ ▼ ▼ ▼ ▼ ▼ ▼ ▼ ▼ ▼ ▼ ▼ ▼

lower third of Georgia before moving north towards Atlanta, and the first week in March before we left the state.

As we had followed fall to the south, we found we were now following the spring north. Traveling through Tennessee and Kentucky took up the remainder of March. On the first of April we found ourselves in Indiana and ended up staying in various places in the Hoosier State for nearly a month.

When we left Duluth in the fall, we knew we wanted to return. We figured this was as good a time as any to revisit it, so we headed north, up the western side of Michigan this time. We crossed into Canada at Sault Ste. Marie (we stocked up on our shampoo when we found a place there that had it on sale) so we could explore the north shore of Lake Superior on the way to Duluth.

By early June we assumed it was warm enough to venture to International Falls, Minnesota. From there we struck out to the west, across North Dakota to Montana. We spent nearly three months in many different locations in Wyoming and Montana. Next week we will cross Lolo Pass in the Bitterroot Mountains on our way to explore the southeastern section of Oregon—a place we have never been.

As in every year of our fulltiming lives, we have had a multitude of new experiences and made many new friends. In Vermont we became acquainted with a couple we later saw again in Georgia. We intend for our path to cross that of another couple we spent many happy hours with in Savannah. This turned out to be our year for aiding visitors from other countries. We have an invitation to visit the homes of two Englishmen we met in a small Wyoming town. Mark and David were tent camping and trying to visit as much of the West as they could before their money ran out. Neither had ever met anyone who lived exclusively in a trailer. They marveled at the accommodations of our fifth-wheel—Mark more so than David, however, who was under the weather after having had two wisdom teeth pulled by a local dentist. We offered him ice to ease the swelling, and pudding and ice cream—treats we knew he could eat without too much discomfort.

We were staying in a city park in a tiny town in Montana when two Canadian couples on motorcycles pulled in for the night. They were on their way to the annual bikers' rally held in Sturgis, South Dakota. The wheel bearing on one of the bikes needed to be replaced. The men had the bike raised up on some short pieces of firewood they found at their site. The bike was not sturdily or safely supported, so we supplied them with a couple of stabilizer jacks and a hydraulic jack to use.

Next day, in the same campground, a Canadian family arrived. The car with which they were towing their small trailer had a radiator problem. As soon as they got in, the man, Steve, set to work on the car (we found out later that in addition to being a graphic artist for a Winnipeg advertising agency, he was also a skilled mechanic). We lent him tools and drove him to parts stores; they were close enough to walk to, but that would have taken more time. Steve's three charming daughters had been promised a shopping expedition in the next large town and were eager to be on their way.

▼ ▼ ▼

This last year, as we always do during our travels, we sought out regional foods to sample. We had pancakes with real maple syrup in Vermont, country ham, biscuits, and peanut soup in Virginia, and Lebanon bologna in Pennsylvania, along with some other Pennsylvania Dutch delicacies. We found a pocket of the country in Minnesota, Wisconsin, and the Upper Peninsula of Michigan where ham-salad sandwiches were on the menu of many restaurants, then moved into North Dakota where home-made caramel rolls were a feature. They were good, but they can't begin to compare with the Danish pastries found in the New York City metropolitan area and adjacent New Jersey. Most roadside diners in these locations usually have a superlative selection of baked goods. We devoured melt-in-your-mouth Calabash seafood in northern South Carolina, and savored the Low Country cuisine in Charleston.

We seek out barbeque restaurants wherever we go. One of our favorites, which uses a tangy mustard-based sauce, is in Charleston, and another, with the distinctive North Carolina vinegary taste, is in Wilmington.

The journey, not the arrival, matters.

T. S. ELLIOT

▼ ▼ ▼ ▼ ▼ ▼ ▼ ▼ ▼ ▼ ▼ ▼

▼ ▼ ▼

That long [Canadian] frontier from the Atlantic to the Pacific Ocean, guarded only by neighborly respect and honorable obligations, is an example to every country and a pattern for the future of the world.

SIR WINSTON CHURCHILL

▼ ▼ ▼ ▼ ▼ ▼ ▼ ▼ ▼ ▼ ▼ ▼ ▼

Years ago, when we visited Canada, we tasted pea-meal bacon, uncured back bacon with a coating of cornmeal, for the first time. This, like shampoo, is something else we purchase when we visit Canada. When we were in International Falls we crossed over into Canada for the sole purpose of purchasing some. The Safeway market in Fort Frances had none but was expecting a shipment the next day. We went back the next afternoon and, since we knew we wouldn't be in Canada again for some time, purchased a supply that we could freeze (we ate the last of it about two weeks ago). The American customs agent was in the middle of asking the usual questions prior to crossing the border, when he looked at us as if we were up to no good and said, "Didn't you come through here yesterday?" Lest he think we were running some sort of contraband over the border, we explained about the pea-meal bacon. Stern and unsmiling he listened to our story, then waved us on, shaking his head and grinning, as if he didn't know whether to believe us or not.

▼ ▼ ▼

Although we enjoy eating in restaurants, we usually have Christmas dinner at home. In the unusually mild weather of Charleston at Christmas time last year, we had traditional fare: turkey with all the trimmings and homemade pumpkin pie. As always, we trimmed our RV-sized tree with ornaments we have collected in our travels: the red glass chili peppers from Santa Fe; the porcelain snowflake from Livingston, Montana; the Hopi bead from Sedona, Arizona; a dove carved from myrtlewood from Oregon; and a Moravian star from Winston-Salem, North Carolina, among others. The tree was draped with garlands of beads we caught as they were thrown from Mardi Gras floats in Mobile, Alabama. A spray of branches of evergreen plants indigenous to the area, topped with a big red bow, greeted guests as they arrived at our door.

We were entertained by wildlife throughout the year. Just outside Voyageurs National Park in Minnesota, a curious black bear decided to inspect our parked truck. He made a thorough circuit around the truck and pushed his nose against the window glass to get a better look at us inside. Kit foxes serenaded us in Wyoming, and unaware that we were watching, four coyotes gamboled and cavorted in the late afternoon sun in a hillside hollow in Montana before settling down to sleep. We were treated to the sight of a beaver industriously building a dam. Moose and elk have wandered into campgrounds where we were staying, and we have seen numerous foxes, antelopes, and a pika—a small animal related to the rabbit family that makes its home in talus slopes.

The beauty and magnificence of our country never fails to awe us: The haunting marshes of Glynn in Georgia immortalized in the poems of Sidney Lanier, and on the other side of the state, Providence Canyon with its deep reaches and sculpted formations in a spectrum of tones ranging from creamy white to deep vermillion; mysterious swamps throughout the South with their coffee-colored water overhung by tree branches shrouded in Spanish moss; large clusters of violets and bloodroots blooming in the Indiana woods in the spring; a riot of color in a Michigan orchard—the pink-tinged white of apple blossoms above a thick carpet of grape hyacinths and dandelions. From a plateau hundreds of feet above the Missouri River we, and a bevy of bluebirds who were flitting about in the trees nearby, could look down on Cow Island, where Chief Joseph and the band of Nez Percé Indians he was leading crossed when they were fleeing from the army. Later, from an even higher vantage point, we gazed into the forbidding depths of narrow, sheer-sided Clarks Fork Canyon at the slim ribbon of green water far below—another place that figured in the flight of the Nez Percés.

We were treated to the glories of nature: Wispy, undulating shimmers of the northern lights viewed from a North Dakota campground; the brilliant swath of the Milky Way—brighter than we had ever seen it before—from high in the mountains in a forest service campground. A hilltop campground in Montana afforded us views of spectacular sunsets every evening for the entire time we were there, and we were in the middle of a wonderous display of lightning over the Absaroka Mountains when a sudden summer squall developed. After another squall in Judith Gap, Montana, the lowering sun created a rainbow whose iridescent colors were set off against the slate-gray skies of the departing storm.

America is not like a blanket—one piece of unbroken cloth, the same color, the same texture, the same size. America is more like a quilt—many patches, many pieces, many colors, many sizes, all woven and held together by a common thread.

JESSE JACKSON

▼ ▼ ▼ ▼ ▼ ▼ ▼ ▼ ▼ ▼ ▼ ▼ ▼

*I shall be telling this
with a sigh
Somewhere ages and ages
hence:
Two roads diverged in a
wood, and I—
I took the one less
traveled by.
And that has made all
the difference.*

"THE ROAD NOT TAKEN"
ROBERT FROST

▼ ▼ ▼ ▼ ▼ ▼ ▼ ▼ ▼ ▼ ▼ ▼

Niagara Falls was the largest and mightiest of the waterfalls we saw this year, but it was not necessarily the most beautiful. Vying for that honor would be Minnesota's many-tiered Gooseberry Falls; Shell Falls in Wyoming's Big Horn Mountains; and Montana's Gallatin Range Palisade Falls, which tumbles in a shimmering veil from a dizzying height, and mossy, tree-shaded Grotto Falls, which roars over giant, blocky, step-like rocks.

We are now in a forest-service campground in the Big Hole Valley of Montana (operating our computers and printer with our inverter/solar panel system). The Big Hole Valley is considered to be one of the most beautiful in the country, and, as we drove through it this time from east to west, it was at its most magnificent. The broad valley through which the Big Hole River meanders is ringed with mountains. The high mountains to the north form the Continental Divide and had just received their first snowfall of the season. Their white peaks, the golden grasses of the late summer fields, the fresh green of the willows along the river, and the dark green of the pines on the hills against the brilliant blue of the sky were breathtaking.

This campground, deserted now except for us and one other RV, is one of our favorites. At night there is no sound except that of the wind and an occasional night bird. A creek runs nearby. Yesterday we hiked a trail to the ridge beyond the campground, and tomorrow we may do some exploring on some of the forest-service roads in the area.

It's wonderful to be able to see so many sights, visit so many places, do so many things, and meet so many nice people, all without ever leaving home. These are the things that are important to us; they provide us with a continual fresh outlook and keep us young in heart and mind. It is really what fulltiming is all about.

Although we have no idea where we will go or what we will do next year, we know that fulltiming will provide us with a host of rewarding, interesting, and fullfilling experiences.

If you want to be a fulltimer there should be no hesitation about joining all of us who are participating in this wonderful lifestyle. The only regret you might have is that you didn't do it sooner.

Index

▼ ▼ ▼ ▼ ▼ ▼ ▼ ▼

Page numbers appearing in **bold faced** type refer to illustrations in the text.